Captains Courageous

*Donny Mackenzie, Gunner Gregg
& the liberation of the Val Nure, 1944*

For Benedict and Gabrielle.

Acknowledgements
Both I and Gabrielle will always cherish fond memories of the time which we spent with Tresham and Joan Gregg at their home in Glassonby. I am also deeply indebted to the following: the late Mr Brian Mackenzie and his daughter Sue Mackenzie-Gray, who gave me access to Donny Mackenzie's pre-war photograph albums; Mr David Unwin, who conducted an initial interview with "Gunner" Gregg in 2006; Miss Suzanne Foster, Archivist at Winchester College, who gave me more help than I can easily repay; Signor Claudio Oltremonti of Piacenza, who supplied photographs and information relating to the resistance in the Val Nure; Signor Andrea Saba of the Milan *Istituto nazionale per la storia del movimento di liberazione in Italia,* who supplied further documents and images and put me in touch with Signor Oltremonti. Further invaluable help was provided by the staff and archivists of: Bedford School; the British Library; Christ Church, Oxford; the Highlanders Museum; the Imperial War Museum; the National Archives; Oxford University; and the Tank Museum. My thanks to all those who gave me permission to use material from their collections.

Copyright © 2014 Shaun Hullis.
All rights reserved.
No part of this book may be reproduced or transmitted in any form or by any means, electronic or mechanical, including photocopying, recording or any information storage and retrieval system without permission in writing from the author.
Copying or reproduction by the family of Tresham Dames Gregg or Archibald Donald Mackenzie for distribution within the family is expressly excluded from the above statement of copyright.

Introduction

This book began as a record of Donny Mackenzie's wartime career, but in the end it proved impossible to write that story without telling Tresham "Gunner" Gregg's as well: it was a privilege to know him.

I am conscious, however, that the end result is full of imperfections. Had a publisher been willing to take on this book, it would have been properly proof-read and edited (and thus considerably shorter and more elegant), and possess an index and bibliography – though all sources used have been cited in the notes. A publishing house would also have been able to provide decent maps: a great gap in this work is a map of the Nure Valley near Piacenza. I recommend reading the relevant chapters with Google Maps to hand.

Because this account is intended to be read by family and friends, and is being published on a non-profit basis, I have not sought permission of copyright holders either of written works or illustrations: if any copyright holders have any objections I would be very happy for them to contact me on *shaunhullis@mac.com* and to make changes accordingly.

Gunner's friends and relations will want to know what happened next, of course: a further volume is written and will in due course, I hope, take his fascinating story on through the rest of his military career. Anyone who cannot wait is more than welcome to e-mail me and to receive a full text.

Shaun Hullis

Prelude
PG29

The Italian prisoner-of-war camp PG29 Veano[1] was a converted seminary which stood on a slope overlooking the river Nure in Piacenza province. By late 1942, it housed some three hundred Allied personnel – mostly British, New Zealanders and South Africans – who had been captured in North Africa. A large contingent had arrived after the fall of Tobruk in June that year. One of them was a Scot, Captain 64178 Archibald Donald "Donny" Mackenzie. He was in his late twenties, though he looked younger. One of his fellow prisoners later described him as a big, solid man, clearly highly intelligent (he had read Classics at Oxford), but quiet, perhaps even taciturn and slightly dour. No doubt his capture was partly to blame for his quietness. Having spent several years on the staff in the Middle East, Donny had returned to his parent unit – 2nd Battalion, Queen's Own Cameron Highlanders – only a month before they had made a determined and heroic stand at Tobruk. When the Germans had made it clear that further resistance would result in annihilation, Donny and hundreds of others had slipped away into the desert night, but Donny had been captured within sight of Allied lines, and sent to Italy. Captivity irked him, and he longed to excape. But Italian camps were much harder to get out of than German ones, and so far Veano had proven – as its commandant boasted – almost escape-proof.

The prisoners were always excited by the arrival of new inmates, who could bring news from the outside world. However, the six who arrived late that year were in some ways a disappointment. They had come not from the desert, but from another camp, PG35 at Padula near Salerno, much further south. Their papers bore the Italian endorsement *pericoloso* – "troublemaker" – because they had been caught trying to escape. One of their number, indeed, was a serial escaper: since being captured near Tobruk late in 1941, he had made two unsuccessful attempts whilst still in Libya, and two more since landing in Italy. This was a man after Donny's own heart. He was Captain 85707 Tresham Dames "Gunner" Gregg, of 3rd Battalion, Royal Tank Regiment (3RTR). A veteran of three major battles – Calais, Greece and Sidi Rezegh – he had seen his regiment decimated in each one. He had been wounded twice, by mortar-fire and by aerial bombing, and had survived three evacuations – from France, Greece and Crete – in a motor torpedo-boat, a destroyer, and a rusting tramp-steamer. He was, by his own admission, lucky to be alive.

The two men would plot escape and fight side by side until death finally dissolved their partnership some two years later. By then, they had liberated the whole of the valley of the Nure from German and Fascist control and had become legendary figures still admired and celebrated by the Italians. This is their story.[2]

Chapter One
Gunner

Tresham Dames Gregg was born in Dublin on April 7th 1919. His is an unusual name, but one which has been handed down since 1751 through the males of the family. Gregg's own son is called Tresham, as is his grandson. That is not the only tradition in the family: Gregg's uncles were soldiers; Gregg himself had a distinguished military career; his son made his name in action in Dhofar and rose to the rank of Brigadier, with a CBE;[1] and his grandson won the MC with the Light Dragoons in Afghanistan in 2009.[2]

Whence came this odd name, Tresham Dames Gregg? Family tradition has it that the 'Tresham' part comes from the name of Sir Thomas Tresham, a prominent Northamptonshire landowner in Tudor times, despite his Catholicism. Sir Thomas Tresham died in September 1605, having fathered eleven children. But his son and heir, Sir Francis Tresham (1567-1605) soon afterwards became involved in the Gunpowder Plot, was arrested in November 1605, and died in the Tower of London on December 23rd – of natural causes. Although he had not been put on trial or found guilty of any offence, his head was sent to Northampton to be displayed with those of other traitors, and his body was thrown down a hole at Tower Hill. The Tresham estates, heavily in debt, passed to his younger brother, Lewis Tresham. Alas for family tradition, which maintains that Francis Tresham's daughter, Rose, had married into the Gregg family after seeing her father and brothers all hanged, drawn and quartered.

A Rose Tresham *did* marry into the Gregg family, but not until September 11th 1740, 135 years to the day after the death of Sir Thomas Tresham. She was the daughter not of the Gunpowder plotter or his father, but of a plain Thomas Tresham, of Cornmarket, Dublin. But from her marriage to Hugh Gregg onwards, sons of the family began to be christened

Below: *a simplified version of the Gregg family tree, taking the story down to "our" Tresham Gregg.*

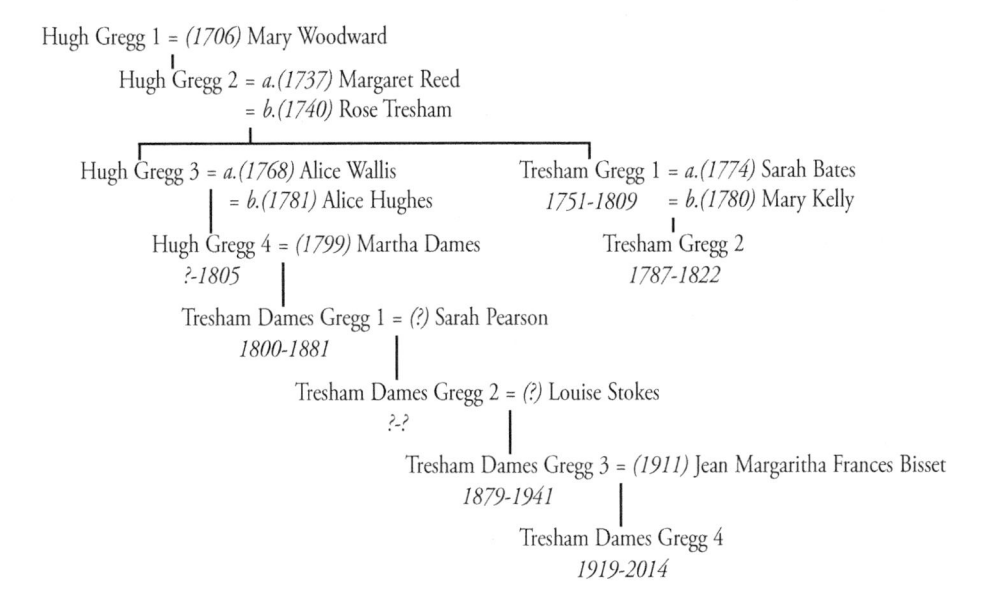

```
Hugh Gregg 1 = (1706) Mary Woodward
    |
    Hugh Gregg 2 = a.(1737) Margaret Reed
                 = b.(1740) Rose Tresham
    |
Hugh Gregg 3 = a.(1768) Alice Wallis        Tresham Gregg 1 = a.(1774) Sarah Bates
             = b.(1781) Alice Hughes        1751-1809       = b.(1780) Mary Kelly
    |                                                 |
Hugh Gregg 4 = (1799) Martha Dames                Tresham Gregg 2
?-1805       |                                     1787-1822
    |
    Tresham Dames Gregg 1 = (?) Sarah Pearson
    1800-1881             |
        Tresham Dames Gregg 2 = (?) Louise Stokes
        ?-?                   |
            Tresham Dames Gregg 3 = (1911) Jean Margaritha Frances Bisset
            1879-1941             |
                Tresham Dames Gregg 4
                1919-2014
```

Tresham. From a later marriage, the family also picked up the middle names Dames. The first Tresham Dames Gregg was born in 1800, and went on to be a prominent and fiery Protestant theologian in Dublin; his son was also called Tresham Dames Gregg; the third Tresham Dames Gregg was born in Dublin in 1879. The fourth child to bear the name was also born in Dublin, as we have seen, in 1919. Since then, two further generations have borne the name. The fifth Tresham Dames Gregg, son of our subject, was born in 1947; the sixth, his son, Tresham Dames Rowley Gregg, was born in 1983.[3]

* * *

Our Tresham Dames Gregg was known from a very young age as "Gunner". The family home, Sandymount, stood behind the Botanical Gardens in Dublin, and it was there that three prams were parked one day in the spring of 1919. There was a baby-boom as the soldiers returned from the wars, and Gregg's father (who had served in the Royal Artillery) and uncles (who had served in the Royal Army Medical Corps) had all fathered children in quick succession. Gregg's grandfather stood beside the prams and patted one:

> This must be the little gunner.

The name stuck. To avoid confusion – and because that is how his partisans in Italy later knew him – that is how we shall refer to him from now on.[4]

Gunner may have been born in Dublin, but within three months he was shipped off to South Africa, where his father and mother had met, married and lived until the outbreak of the First World War in 1914. Gunner's father, Tresham Dames Gregg (the third), had gone out to South Africa as an ADC to Lord Milner, who between the end of the Boer War and the foundation of the Union of South Africa in 1910 was High Commissioner for Southern Africa, Governor of Cape Colony, and colonial administrator of the Transvaal and the Orange Free State.

> Milner decided to have a pack of jackal hounds. The chief medical officer during the South African War, later General Sir Charles Burtchaell, recommended his nephew – my father – as an excellent man to run the hunt. My father was therefore made the Master and ran the hounds.[5]

Milner was accompanied by a coterie of able young men known as "Milner's Kindergarten"; one was John Buchan, the author and politician; Gregg would have rubbed shoulders with these men, of a similar age to him, on a daily basis.

It was here in South Africa that Gregg met his future wife. She was Jean Margaritha Frances Bisset, the only daughter of Walter Cargill Bisset, a director of the White Star Line; her mother, Emile Verpelat, was Swiss.[6] Emile had a twin brother – Emil – who would later help prove of great assistance to Gunner.

Jean Bisset had been born in Liverpool on December 17th 1898, and had trained as an artist in London at the St Martin's School of Art, which was of international repute.

> At that time, my mother's father was in Lourenco Marques [now Maputo, capital of Mozambique], where he and his brother's company were building the docks and the city. My mother used to go to Pretoria to hunt, and met my father. They were married in the British Consulate in Lourenco Marques, and my father left Pretoria and moved to Lourenco Marques. They spent their honeymoon in traditional covered wagons drawn by ten oxen in the Sabi Game Reserve, now part of the Kruger National Park.

Gregg became the British Consul-General in Lourenco Marques, but the marriage remained childless.

On the outbreak of the First World War, the couple returned to Dublin, where Gregg joined the Royal Dublin Fusiliers. He transferred to the Royal Horse Artillery, serving in 'N' Battery in France; his step-brothers Fredrick and George Shaw also served. After the war, Gregg returned to the family home in Dublin. There, on April 7th 1919, his son Tresham was born, the fourth Tresham Dames Gregg: Gunner.

> I was delivered by the Master of the Rotunda, the top maternity doctor in Ireland, at his nursing home, 40 Fitzwilliam Street, Dublin. He's always delivered the Greggs: my father, my grandfather...[7] So my mother had the best service. Not only that, but my Uncle Percy, P.H. Stokes, was a brewer with Guinnesses, and he used to send up a special keg each day. She hated it — she said it was awful — but they insisted that she drink the stuff. So I was breast-fed on a mixture of milk and Guinness.

* * *

On returning to Cape Town with his wife and three-month-old son, Gregg senior found himself a post there in the government's Statistical Directorate.

> When I was three months old, we got on a Union Castle ship. My father had got the job as head of the statistical department of the South African government, even though he had a Classics degree from Trinity. It sounds uninteresting, but in fact it was key, really, because if any of the ministers wanted to do something, it had to be vetted by the statistical people to see if it was necessary. So it was a plum job.

Gregg built a home for his family on a farm at Brackenfell, a few miles from the city centre. There the infant Tresham spent the first few years of his life.

> My only companion was a small black boy, Sammy, whose job it was to stop me being bitten by snakes.

However, within a few years the government moved its offices to Pretoria, and so the Greggs sold the farm and moved north.

> We had to move, because the South African government alternated between Cape Town and Pretoria — it was Dutch up there in Pretoria, and Cape Town was very English, and as they were always trying to have the balance. I moved up to Pretoria when I must have been about four.

In Pretoria Jean Gregg started work at the Botanical Gardens as a botanical artist. She also began to play tennis seriously; her husband was also a fine player, who won the Transvaal Tennis Championship.[8]

But all was not well. About two years later, Gregg senior resigned his position with the civil service and moved his family to Port Elizabeth.

> We lived in Pretoria until I was about six, and then my father got the job as editor of the *Cape Times*, which was published in Port Elizabeth. I was at Grey's College in Port Elizabeth; my granny stayed with us there once. But I lived there for no more than about a year or so, because my mother's marriage broke up.

Gregg was a compulsive gambler, and the strain had destroyed his marriage. Jean Gregg divorced him and took her son with her as she moved back to Cape Town in 1925. The third Tresham Dames Gregg lived until 1941, but he and his son had little contact in the intervening years.

Jean Gregg now had to support herself and young Tresham as best she could.

> My mother made her money by painting, and also took advantage of her general knowledge of languages. She worked for a very, very nice family of Jews, who imported and exported everything

there, and she did all their foreign correspondence and the like. Very well paid. And at the same time she was blossoming out in her tennis. She represented first of all Cape Province, and then South Africa.

Among many family photographs of which Gunner was proud was one which showed his mother playing tennis against Freda James, who went on to win the Wimbledon Doubles in 1935 and 1936.[9]

Gunner and his mother moved to the Cape Town suburb of Rondebosch, where they lived in a "lovely hotel", the Rookoop. Gunner became a pupil at Rossall, the junior department of a famous Cape Town boys school, "Bishops" – more properly known as the Diocesan School of the Diocese of Cape Town.

> Charlie Bull, who was a cousin of sorts of my mother, was the Deputy Head of Bishops. He'd been shell-shocked during the war, so he had a sort of stutter, but he was a very fine man, and he got me a place. I think that he probably got me special terms as well.

"Bishops" had been founded by Bishop Robert Gray in 1849 to educate young men of the colony on Anglican principles. After some rocky patches, the school reached an even keel just as Gunner arrived in the junior department, and has gone on to forge an outstanding reputation, having produced, for example, most of South Africa's Rhodes Scholars.

Gunner joined the senior school in 1927 and remained at Bishops until 1929. Bishops had an enviable sporting life, and while Gunner was there two fellow pupils – Tuppy Owen-Smith and Denys Morkel – played cricket for South Africa.[10] Jean Gregg knew Owen-Smith's family (his father worked for the Customs Service, and so she had contact with him through her work), and often played tennis against the young man, who went on to captain the England rugby team. Gunner, too, was an excellent athlete, who came to love the rugby which he learned at school.

> I come from a very athletic family on both sides: my uncle Freddie had won a medal in the Olympics, and captained the Gentlemen of Ireland at cricket. My great-uncle Percy was also an outstanding tennis player and for many years captained the Irish tennis team. He represented Ireland in three events – tennis, hockey and badminton – for three years.
>
> When I arrived at the junior school, Rossall, we had a cross-country run, which went right over to the Cape Flats – all shacks and slums now, I believe. I was already pretty fit, and I just stuck behind a fellow who looked like he would do well, and at the end I came in third. The Head of the junior school sent for me and congratulated me. But he did ask me to promise that I hadn't taken a short-cut, because it was astonishing that I'd come third in the school when I'd only just joined and was one of the youngest.
>
> It was there that I learned my rugby. I was in the first team at Rossall. I was a very fast runner and I played on the wing.
>
> Rather excitingly for us, Bishops had the perk of lining the touchline at Newlands Stadium, and whenever there was a big match we used to go and watch. So we saw the most fantastic games. I remember going and seeing the final deciding match of the 1928 New Zealand tour – All Blacks against Springboks. It was a fantastic match.

During his two years at Bishops, Gunner's mother met an electrical engineer called David Kinloch-Smith, who worked for the Eastern & Associated Telegraph Company (which became Cable & Wireless in April 1929) in their cable-laying ships. The two became engaged, and later married.

> My step-father David Kinloch-Smith and my mother met when he was in the *Mirror*, a cable-ship in Cape Town. They had quite a long courtship. When we came back from South Africa she may not have been officially engaged but they had every intention of getting married.

This should, perhaps, have resulted in a period of stability for the young Gunner, but it was not to be. In 1929, news reached Jean Gregg that her mother was very ill:

> We were there until I was about thirteen, by which time my Granny, who'd been living with us for some time in the Cape, was very ill with cancer in Switzerland. So we left South Africa late in 1929; my mother and I got on a boat and went to Switzerland *via* England.

Jean Gregg's mother, Emile, lived in Thun, some twenty miles south of Bern at the head of Lake Thun. However, when Jean and Gunner arrived, they found that the cancer was not as far advanced as had been feared, and the problem arose of how Gunner would be educated whilst his mother looked after his grandmother.

> I was sent for a few months to a little local school in Switzerland, which was German, being in the Bernese Oberland, but then they decided it was not good enough.

Jean Gregg chose instead to send Gunner to live with his aunt Mabel (his father's sister), who lived in Germany in Wiesbaden, near Mainz, with her husband, Billy Houston, an RAMC doctor. Wiesbaden was at the time the headquarters of the British forces which had been occupying the Rhineland of Germany since the end of the First World War. And so the Irish-South African boy now started school in Germany, attending the Gymnasium in Wiesbaden for some eight or nine months. As a result, his German became quite good (the Afrikaans which he had learned in South Africa gave him a head-start).

Soon afterwards, Gunner's grandmother died.[11] David Kinloch-Smith came to Bern, and took Jean off to Venice to be married. The Kinloch-Smiths honeymooned in Split – on the Adriatic coast of Croatia – before moving to Athens, where David had been put in charge of the Mediterranean cable-ships. But Gunner did not join them; his aunt Mabel and her husband had returned to England (the Allied occupation of the Rhineland ended in 1930), and Billy Houston had been posted to command the military hospital in Tidworth. Again, the problem of educating Gunner now arose:

> I went to an appalling, terrible prep school – Hillside, in Reigate. First time I'd had anything to do with England. I spent my holiday with Aunty Mabel and Uncle Billy in Tidworth... I wrote to my mother, saying that I refused to stay at Hillside, where there was much bullying – though not of me! I said to her that if she didn't arrange for me to leave, I was going to walk.
>
> The result was that I went off in the P&O boat SS *Ranpura*, which was taking hundreds of the children of the Raj to various parts of the empire. You've never seen such chaos. I don't think a lot of the children ever changed! It was the greatest fun.

But Gunner's life was never simple. Bound for Athens, he only stayed aboard the *Ranpura* as far as Gibraltar, where he was taken off the ship. Gunner's mother and step-father had unexpectedly been posted to Malta, and had cabled friends in Seville asking them to take care of Gunner until their move had been completed.[12]

> When I arrived at Gibraltar, an elderly couple came on board to take me to their home in Seville, as my parents were now moving to Malta and had left Athens. This couple had retired and they had a lovely old Moorish house in Seville: it was walled, and inside were all these citrus trees, fed by stone channels. I remember I used to pump the well up and then opened the thing and each tree was fed along the channels.
>
> I had three wonderful months in Seville before I was put on another P&O ship and went to Malta. For some reason it went *via* Marseilles. I was all alone, and I remember looking at the quayside and getting a bit bored. So I went down the gangway and I was wandering around the docks. And a horrible sort of greasy Frenchman came up and said "You want to see a blue film?" Of course, I didn't know what he was talking about!

Above: *a painting of the SS* Ranpura, *in which Gunner escaped English prep-school life (copyright holder unknown).*

In Malta, at last, Gunner was to have the chance to settle down.

> I lived for two-and-a-half years in Malta, just near Dragonara, and we have several very good Maltese friends. That most wonderful spell on Malta did more for my education than anything, thanks to Mr Robinson. He had once been the headmaster of an English public school, and he taught me much of what I know now. He lived in Strada Reale and the school was above a big chemist's shop, just opposite the opera house in Valetta. I used to go by bus from St Julian's, or by bus and ferry, every day. That two-and-a-half years was the basis of my education. I'd had none before that, really.
>
> In Malta they had a very, very strong Boy Scout movement, which I joined. I've taken Joan *[Gunner's wife]* three times to Malta, because it's home to me in many ways. She said: "You were in the Scouts. Would you show me the Scout hut?" So we walked along the promenade by Sliema, and there's a wonderful Fifteenth Century Spanish-built castle sticking out into the sea. "That's the Scout hut."
>
> We played team games, though no rugby. I did once play rugby for the Scouts or someone on the parade ground in the army barracks. I had no skin on my knees after that.
>
> Swimming, particularly water-polo, was the local sport. I didn't play water-polo, but I was in the water almost twenty-four hours a day – I was web-footed. I swam from the rocks by the house where we lived. I became a very powerful swimmer, and used to go right out to sea, beyond a buoy which was about half a mile out, and see the Gozo boats going past. Most of the vegetables were grown on Gozo, and these boats brought them to Grand Harbour on Malta itself.

Jean Kinloch-Smith, as she now was, painted a watercolour of Gunner sitting in his swimsuit on the rocks; he still has the painting hanging at home. She too threw herself into the life of the island:

> My mother was tennis champion of the Marsa. She was a great friend of the famous Mabel Strickland, who owned *The Times of Malta,* and was very popular with her when they had tennis parties.[13]

Chapter Two
Donny

Gunner's friend Donny Mackenzie had never met his father.

Captain Lynedoch Archibald "Archy" Mackenzie had been educated at Loretto School (like many of his relatives), and at Edinburgh University, where he studied Electrical Engineering.[1] Archy was a hockey-player of international standard, who played for his university, for Scotland as an inside forward for five years (1906-1910), and for Cheshire. On leaving university, he obtained a post as Assistant Superintendent at the Linotype & Machinery Works, at Broadheath, in Altrincham, Cheshire. It was whilst living there that he married Elizabeth Mary Dorothy "Dor" Yates.[2]

The Mackenzie family had a distinguished military background and a keen sense of their own history, which affected their naming of their children. Their ancestor, Baronet Douglas of Glenbervie, had served in Wellington's army and collaborated with his close friend Lord Lynedoch in founding 90th Perthshire Volunteers[3] –hence the traditional

Above: *Archy Mackenzie, Donny's father, pictured in Egypt in 1914-1915 before leaving for Gallipoli (Mackenzie collection).*

Mackenzie forename "Lynedoch".[4] The name "Archy" had a similar genesis: Donny Mackenzie's great-great-grandfather had been Major-General Sir Archibald Campbell of Ava, distinguished for his service in the Second Burma War. Donald was also a traditional Mackenzie name: our Donald Mackenzie is believed by the family to have been the twelfth generation of that name, and the total stood in 2008 at fourteen generations. Since Donny's grandfather was known within the family as "Don", his grandson became "Donny".

Archy Mackenzie had followed in his family's military tradition. Whilst at university, he had served for a few years with the Mounted Infantry section of the Queen's Rifle Volunteer Brigade, Royal Scots. When he moved to Cheshire, he obtained a commission in the Territorial Army, serving with 427 (1st East Lancashire) Field Company, Royal Engineers. This unit formed part of 42nd (East Lancashire) Division, the first Territorial division to head overseas on the outbreak of the First World War. The men were on summer camp when war broke out, and early in August 1914 were invited to volunteer for foreign service: the division began to embark at Southampton on September 9th. 42nd Division first served in Egypt, defending the Suez Canal, and then moved to Gallipoli.

There, on October 11th 1915, Archy Mackenzie was mortally wounded. He died on a hospital ship between Mudros and Malta on October 19th, aged thirty-one, and was buried at sea. He is commemorated on the Helles Memorial on the Gallipoli peninsula.

* * *

Archy's son, Donny, had been born in Altrincham on October 22nd 1914, six weeks after his father had left for war. His life had been changed for ever by the loss of his father; Dor never re-married, so that throughout Donny's childhood almost all male authority figures came from outside his family. Dor tried as hard as she could to bring her son up in a stable environment, and in those days it was considered that boarding school could provide just the routines and stability which a fatherless boy needed. Donny's childhood was as a result, except for the absence of a father, perhaps as stable and conventional as could be imagined – and certainly far less cosmopolitan than Gunner's.

Family memories of Donny start in the summer of 1921. Donny's cousin, Brian Douglas Mackenzie, was the only son of Mackenzie's paternal uncle and himself went on to distinguished war service in the Royal Engineers.[6] Brian's father Daniel was the nearest that Donny had to a father:

> My father, the baby of his family... was greatly influenced by his next elder brother Archy, Donny's father; so when Archy was killed my father felt himself *in loco parentis* to Donny.[7]

Dor was anxious that Donny should remember his Scottish heritage; from about 1925 she rented 'Rosefield', in St Cyrus, Kincardineshire, as a summer holiday home. She later bought the house, probably with money left to her on the death of Donny's grandfather "Don" in 1924. Donny was made the titular owner, and Dor settled there (though she did for some time have an address in Cheyne Court, Chelsea).

In 1925, there was a similar family gathering to that of 1921. The family stayed at Loch Feochan, near Oban, before decamping to Rosefield. In the summer of 1926, as Donny's own photograph album shows, the family stayed in Rhiconich in Sutherland (the photograph at right is from this holiday). Donny evidently owned a small camera, and over the years took photographs of his family, friends, animals (be they wild, domesticated or in London Zoo), the family car and caravan, school activities, and landscapes. In the albums which the family still possess, many pictures are labelled in neat white writing on a black background; Donny was clearly a meticulous and observant boy.

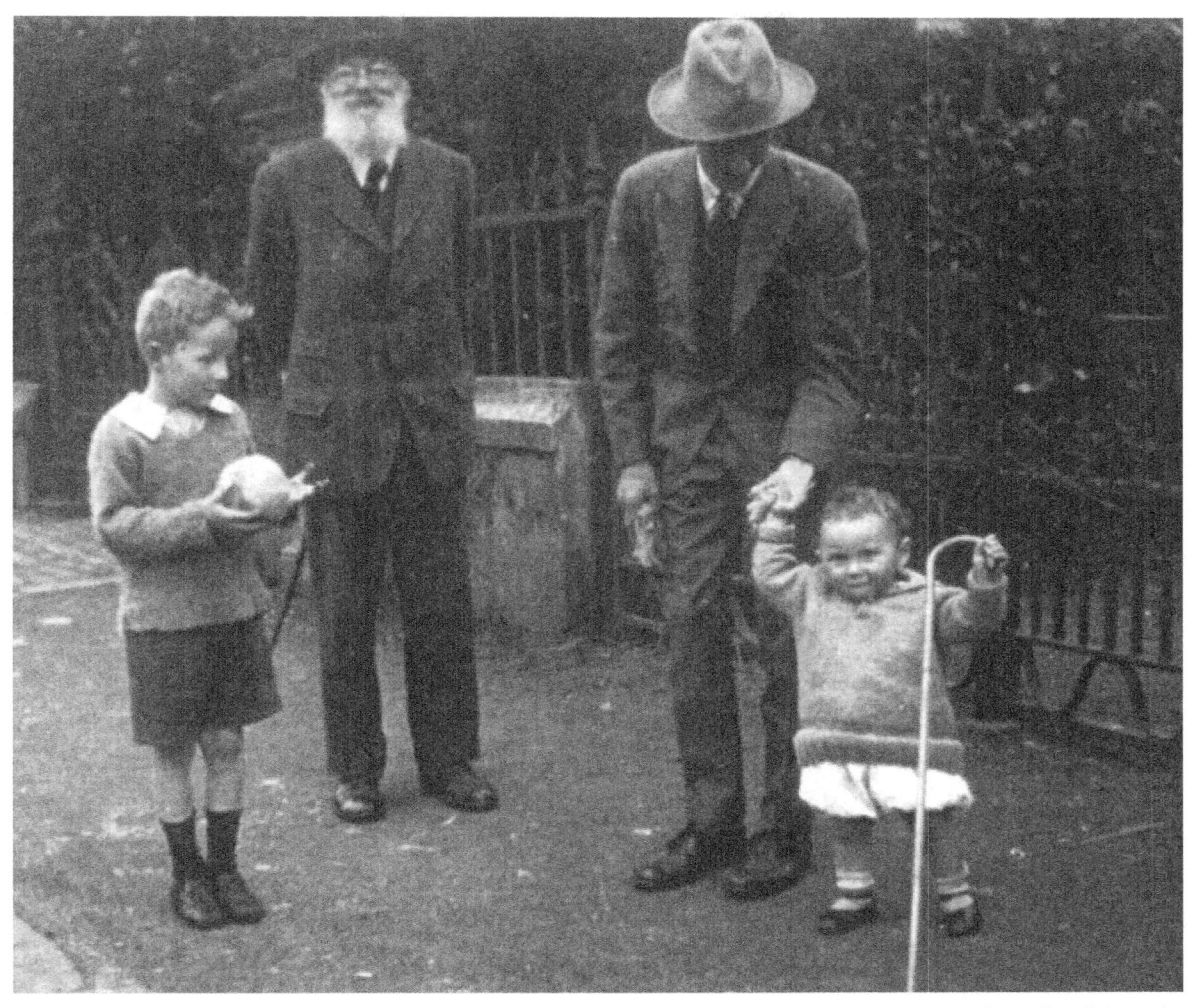

Above: *a Mackenzie family holiday in Aberfeldy in 1921, showing at left Donny (then aged six), his grandfather "Don", Donny's uncle Daniel, and Daniel's son Brian (Mackenzie collection).*

Donny was a boarder at the Reverend W.R. Mills' school, Highfield, at Liphook in Hampshire. Photographs taken by Donny and others show him playing rugby, representing the school at cricket, and enjoying family visits. In 1927 he seems to have travelled to France, since pictures show various details of Paris. The summer holiday of 1928 was again spent in Scotland. Donny seems to have enjoyed the outdoor life – his photographs often show him walking, fishing or shooting.

* * *

At the end of that summer, Donny moved on to public school, starting at Winchester College in September 1928.[8] Winchester College has operated on the same site for six hundred years, having been founded in 1382 by William of Wykeham, the Bishop of Winchester.[9] When Donny arrived, Winchester had some 450 boys and forty-seven teaching staff. The boys were divided between the scholars' house (College) and the ten 'Commoner' houses. The fees for Commoners in 1931 were £200 per annum.

Confusingly, each boarding house was known not only an official name (for example, Hawkins') but also by a letter ('A' to 'I', and 'K') and an official nick-name (Hawkins' being known as Chawker's). Donny was assigned to 'B' (Moberly's, commonly called Toye's). Membership of a house was denoted by the suffix *-ite:* thus Donny was now a Toye-ite.

Above: a typical photograph from Donny's childhood albums (Mackenzie collection).

This confusing nomenclature was just one of the many ways in which Winchester fostered a sense of belonging to a special and exclusive community. Like all public schools (but to a greater extent, perhaps, than any other), Winchester had its own arcane slang and peculiar rules of conduct, referred to as 'Notions'. For the first two or three weeks, each new pupil was allocated a pupil mentor – a *tégé* (pronounced "tee-jay") – whose responsibility it was to make sure that the new boy learned these 'Notions' in order to pass a test.

Winchester boys rose from their unheated dormitories – the windows were left open at night to promote good health – for cold baths before heading straight to lessons ('Morning Lines') at eight, returning to their houses for breakfast. Such a régime was not resented as much as we might expect; lives were harder then, and the boys who were to provide the ruling class of empire largely accepted that they needed toughening up. Certainly, several have commented that life at public school had prepared them well for years later spent in prisoner-of-war camps.

What boarding house a boy went into was far from a trivial matter, especially at Winchester. Until comparatively recent times, Winchester housemasters ('House Dons' in Winchester parlance) were lords of their own small realms, with reponsibility for almost all the administration, budgeting, and discipline of the boys in their charge. Different housemasters had different interests, priorities, and views on discipline. A weak housemaster might allow his senior boys to operate a reign of terror; a strong one might create his own. A housemaster's hobbies and interests defined what he expected of his boys. Donny's housemaster was to play an important part in his life, not only as a surrogate father during term-time but, according to some sources, almost becoming Donny's step-father. Horace Arthur Jackson, known at Winchester as "The Jacker", had been a pupil at the school himself, Head Boy in 1902, and had studied as an exhibitioner at Trinity College, Cambridge; he had joined the staff in 1908. The military author Patrick Delaforce, who was in Toye's later in the Thirties, describes Jackson as follows:

> A small, sturdy man, with an unmistakable squeaky voice, Jackson had a choleric visage, a stubby moustache, and wore either grey tweeds, brown tweeds, or occasionally suits. He was irascible, and carried a stout stick outside the house. He could be carelessly cruel. We always thought he was a dedicated misogynist. He had been badly gassed in the Great War.[10]

Jackson had joined the army in 1916, risen to the rank of Captain in the KRRC, been wounded twice and then taken prisoner in 1918 – which had probably saved his life, though it had left him, as one of his pupils of the time commented, with

> an abiding hatred of the Germans – but he did once tell us that we were shits if we bullied Peter Railing because of his German Jewish background.[11]

That did not stop Jackson from refusing to teach one German pupil who was placed in his form, as a contemporary recalled:

> We imported one of the first of Hitler's refugees, called Schlesinger, and he was stupidly put into the Jacker's form; he was out the next morning.[12]

In a debate at the school in 1934, Jackson spoke against a motion which expressed more sympathy for Germany than for France: he stated that Germany had been morally responsible for the First World War, had deserved her punishment at Versailles, and that her people remained deceitful and brutal. It seems likely that he spoke from the heart, as a story told by another Toyeite suggests:

> "If you could press a button and eliminate all Germans, surely you would not do it?" I heard him asked. "Certainly not. I'd stamp on it," was his typical response.[13]

It was rumoured among the pupils that Jackson concealed a rather alarming souvenir of his war service:

> Half his bottom had been blown off. He'd been blown up by a howitzer on the front line – this is what we always said – and his bottom was replaced with a ceramic one. He was known as "China Bottom."[14]

Jackson had taken over in Toye's in 1921 and remained housemaster for twenty-four years. Like so many staff of his era, he never married; most housemasters were in those days wedded to their jobs, and it is probably this which made him such an excellent record-keeper. But he seems to have become a close friend of the widowed Dor Mackenzie, as Brian Mackenzie recalled:

> Donny's housemaster (and later mine) at Winchester, Horace Jackson, used to visit Dor at Rosefield in holiday time, and a rumour went about that they would marry. I doubt if that was actually a serious possibility.[15]

Even if Dor did not seriously entertain the notion of marriage, Donny was a pupil on whose welfare Jackson would have kept an especially close eye.

Above: *Dor Mackenzie sitting with the Jacker whilst on holiday in Scotland: clearly a closer friendship than most schoolmasters enjoy with the parents of children in their charge (Mackenzie collection).*

As well as his other acomplishments and interests, Jackson was also a determined 'pot-hunter': at Winchester, inter-house sporting competitions are named after the trophy for which the pupils compete, and trophies are known as 'pots'. Under Jackson, Toye's had the reputation of being the top house for games and athletics, from bowls on the lawn (which Donny played with his friends) to the big three: cricket, soccer and Winchester College Football.

> The Jacker certainly had a house interested in games and the array of 'pots' won by the house was usually impressive. He was much interested in games of all sorts. To my mind we were rather proud of Toye's and all its pots, and looked up to the Jacker.[16]

The Jacker, however, did not get on with all his charges, as Delaforce remembered:

> The Jacker had his favourites. If the Jacker took against one he could delay one becoming a prefect, which he did with me. Just before I left, he said to me point-blank, "Patrick, you will never make an officer."[17]

As Delaforce went on to have a distinguished military career, he is right to say that Jackson was here "talking nonsense". But even the Jacker's least favourite pupils had fond or amusing memories of him:

> It was a very happy five years. He was a devout Christian and prepared me for confirmation. He also introduced me, indirectly, to Classical music, played for his pleasure: Dvorak's New World symphony was an example.[18]

> I remember that the Jacker used to to sleep on the floor of his study when correcting papers after dinner… When I got engaged to my wife, who is French, he wrote a charming letter in perfect French to my future mother-in-law telling her not to worry too much.[19]

Punishment in Toye's was typical of such establishments at the time: the prefects could beat fellow pupils, and routinely did, but the boys accepted it stoically. It seems, however, that the Jacker did not beat boys himself, despite his irascible nature and the stout stick:

> So far as punishment went, I think he ruled the house through his prefects, who could beat you – although I think they had to tell the Jacker.[20]

* * *

In contrast with modern practice, boys at Winchester were organized not according to their age and year of arrival at the school, but instead began in the form which seemed to the school best to reflect their standard on arrival, and were promoted ('removed') to the next form when their teachers felt that they were ready.

Donny was placed straight into an intermediate class – 'Middle Part 2' – on arrival, which suggests that he had impressed in his entry examinations.[21] There were twenty-three boys in the class, and when the averages were totted up at the half term stage, Donny had come third, as the Jacker recorded, with an enigmatic postscript:

> Good. Only beaten by two scholars; should do well all round. (His trouble about six times.)[22]

By the end of term in December 1928, Donny had maintained his position, and was selected for his 'remove' to MP1, Jackson's own form. The Jacker was always one for making predictions in his reports, but those which he made at the end of the first term for Donny were by his standards effusive:

> Good report; might get thro' me in a term. Obviously alert, but whether a scholar *[at university level]* we shall not know for a time. Should be head of the house some time, and should make this one of his ambitions.[23]

As the Jacker predicted, Donny sailed through MP1 in a term, garnering good reports on the way, showing good sense and industry; he once more earned his 'remove', this time to Senior Part 1. Despite suffering from bad colds, he proved useful in the house soccer team, and when the summer of 1929 came he did well at cricket. But once again there comes a cryptic remark amid the praise:

> Recurrence of his trouble...Very good practical brain, but ? scholar. Physical development come early; should not push too hard.[24]

The summer holidays that year were spent at Rosefield, as Brian Mackenzie recalled:

> [In the summer of 1929] we were all at Rosefield again (I was nine, Donny fourteen). We spent much time on the beach, playing golf and rounders – at which Donny half killed me by letting go of the bat, which hit me on the head (half asleep anyway!). The end of the holiday was quite traumatic – my sister got scarlet fever. What a to-do, with Donny going [back] to Winchester, I going for my first term at prep school in Kent, and my parents going back to India.[25]

Donny was fifteen in 1929, and Gunner ten. At such an age, had they met, five years would have seemed a huge gulf. By the time that they did meet – in 1942 – the age gap mattered not at all, especially after what they had by then gone through. But as Gunner left South Africa for Switzerland, and Donny began his second year at Winchester, the world in which they were growing up was changing in ways which would have a profound impact on their lives. Not least of these ways was that the third Geneva Convention was passed on

July 27th, which would have a material impact on their treatment in German and Italian captivity twelve years later.[26]

The Italians already had a Fascist government, which in 1929 took control of education. All school textbooks had to be authorized by the regime; all school teachers had to swear loyalty to Fascism; and in a devoutly Catholic country, children were to be taught to give the Fascist Party the same loyalty as they owed to God. But at the same time, the Lateran Treaty (signed by Pope Pius XI and Mussolini) made the Vatican City a sovereign state – a move which would later help hundreds of Allied prisoners of war.

But the most famous event of 1929 was, of course, the Wall Street Crash. Between October 24th and October 29th, more than thirty billion dollars – ten times the national budget – was wiped off the New York Stock Exchange. This had profound effects not only in America but also in Europe, and most dangerously in Germany, still under partial occupation by British and French forces, and crippled economically by the reparations forced on the country by the Treaty of Versailles; the level had finally been set in August 1929. Gunner, who lived in Wiesbaden at the time, remembered the bitterness which the Germans felt:

> The French had bled them white at Versailles. The French have a lot to pay for that, because it created tremendous bitterness, and it was really the spur on which Hitler got into power. He was going to restore the Saarland and he was going to have an army again and an air force, all of which had been forbidden at Versailles. The French insisted on reparations, so that while the Germans were trying to recover, the French were keeping them right down, so that they would never rise again. So, like all my German friends, I was very bitter against the French and what Versailles had done to their country.

The result of the Crash was the withdrawal of foreign investments from Germany, and by the end of 1929 there were three million unemployed. The Weimar government, relatively successful until then, was dealt a blow from which it never recovered, and the rise of Nazism was one consequence.

The insecurity of the times made a nonsense of the Kellogg-Briand Pact, which was just coming into effect. It had renounced war as an instrument of foreign policy, and was in tune with the anti-war sentiment visible in both Britain and Germany. 1929 saw the publication of *All Quiet on the Western Front* (by Erich Maria Remarque) and *Goodbye to All That* (by Robert Graves). *Goodbye to All That* displayed a jaundiced view of the trauma of the Western Front which, together with the pessimistic poetry of other authors, articulated the revulsion for war felt by many British people. The nation began to forget that it had won a stunning victory in 1918 and that the majority of British soldiers at the time had viewed Field-Marshal Haig not as a callous butcher but as a great war leader.

The Great Depression sparked by the Wall Street Crash hit Britain hard, and as unemployment rose it had been tempting to ask what the sacrifice of the First World War had been for. But disillusion with war could not prevent war, and despite all the rhetoric and heartfelt yearning for continued peace, human nature had not really changed.

* * *

Donny returned to Winchester in September 1929 ready for his fourth form in as many terms; he was now in Senior Part 2. But almost immediately he was struck down with appendicitis, which destroyed the first half of term entirely. When Donny was well enough to get back to academic work, the Jacker was concerned by his lack of physical fitness:

> Must work up his condition in the holidays (flabby at present); I take it he will be able to do everything normally.[27]

On his return in the New Year of 1930, Donny had fulfilled the Jacker's hopes for a full recovery, and his delighted housemaster recorded that Donny had come top of his form:

Capital recovery from last half... No sign of after-effects of operation; capital half.[28]

But Donny's academic progress now stalled, and he spent the next four terms in the same form. His housemaster noted in the summer of 1931 that Donny

generally has struck the typical unpleasant patch. Will come out of it and turn out well.[29]

In his summary of his March 1931 report, the Jacker mentioned that he and Dor had met and discussed Donny. Dor clearly considered that the Jacker was being unfair to her son. He noted that

I repeat I have no prejudice, and my plain speaking is well meant.[30]

Donny's teenage surliness does seem to have passed by Christmas:

Improving physically and getting out of unpleasing period of last summer. I now expect to see him come on all round.[31]

It was becoming clear that Donny was a solid performer academically, but no longer as impressive as he had at first seemed.

Very creditable, but not a scholar. Competent and sensible.[32]

In September 1931 Donny finally achieved his 'remove' into the top forms, entering the Junior Division of Sixth Book. He worked well all term, but showed more good sense than real scholarship, in his housemaster's opinion. By March 1932 the Jacker was looking ahead to Donny's prospects for Oxford or Cambridge:

Maintains his interest and good steady work; high second class at Varsity – just not a First... Should have a good last year.[33]

In September 1932 Donny embarked on his last year of school, in the Senior Division of Sixth Book. He was by now a school prefect (a "Co:Prae:" in Winchester jargon), but not quite good enough to be head of house.

* * *

Just as important as academic success, in the eyes of the Jacker, was sporting excellence, and Donny had also made his mark at Winchester in this respect. He first appeared in *The Wykehamist* in September 1930, when he was second in the Junior High Jump Purling: his last appearance was for coming fourth in the Senior Long Jump in March 1933, with a leap of over seventeen feet. But the main sports in which a Wykehamist was expected to participate were the three team games: soccer in January, cricket from May, and Winchester College Football from September.

One of the many unusual features of life at Winchester College was that the school had its own sport, played nowhere else: Winchester College Football ("Our Game").[34] For competition purposes houses competed against one another and also combined into two warring factions called "Commoners" and "OTH". Teams were either of fifteen or of six, and the big internal matches between Commoners and OTH were known as "Fifteens" or "Sixes". The rules of the game were (and remain) essentially incomprehensible, and seem even today to be in a constant state of flux. Pitches ("canvases") were flanked by nets and also by ropes supported at fixed intervals by posts, which were used in play; the grass pitches rapidly deteriorated into mud-baths laced with sharp-edged flints. Winchester Football combined elements of both rugby and soccer: for example, the ball was round, but there were scrums ("hots"). These hots remain a traditional feature of Wykehamist reunions wherever they may take place.

Donny played Winchester College Football very well, and in the 1931 season played for OTH XV. Match reports included statements such as

> Mackenzie made a fine rush down the ropes.[36]

The Jacker had hoped that Donny might make it into the élite OTH VI that term, at least as a reserve ('on dress'). But it was not to be, as he was just too slow for the fast-moving game. But Donny made it into OTH VI in November 1932. That term he again played for OTH XV against both the Cambridge and Oxford XVs. On October 29th 1932 he scored "from a *melée*" against College XV. Against Commoner XV, just over a week later, he scored again:

> Greenshields, Mackenzie and Bullock managed to get through a great amount of work, quite apart from winning the hots, in which they controlled the ball splendidly.[37]

He played soccer rather less well, though his housemaster commented that he was capable of

> useful soccer, as he can play in several places creditably.[38]

He represented his house in the inter-house Hawkins Cup from 1931 until he left in 1933. Against 'A' in 1932, he scored

> with a fine shot into the top corner of the net... Of the forwards, Mackenzie had one or two good runs down the wing.[39]

In 1932 he played soccer for the 3rd XI, scoring against the Old Wykehamist 3rd XI,

> with an excellent shot from the left wing.[40]

By 1933 he had progressed to the 2nd XI, though not on a regular basis, playing only once (against Charterhouse) as a forward. During his house team's progress to the final of Hawkins Cup that year, his play (as a forward) attracted several comments:

> Disney scored from an acute angle after Mackenzie had put the ball in the middle with a lucky plant... After some even midfield play, Mackenzie came in, picked up a pass from the right, and scored with a hard drive... A good centre from Mackenzie was then put in by Wrench... The last goal was scored by Disney, after Bird had fumbled Mackenzie's centre... 'B', however, continued to press, and could do everything but score, though all the forwards went near... Humphrey once saved well from a shot by Mackenzie... 'B' forced several corners, but could not score until Humphrey fumbled a centre from Mackenzie, and Wrench scored.[41]

Donny was not a distinguished cricketer, however, and his housemaster described his play as follows:

> Vigorous but rough; little defence; keeps [wicket] very fairly... Batting poor; keeping very fair.⁴²

It was as a wicket-keeper that Donny made it into his house team in the summer of 1932, batting at number ten. However, in the first round of Melhuish Cup in May, when 'B' (205 for six) thrashed 'K' (forty-four all out), Donny was the top scorer with eighty-seven, nearly double the combined efforts of the entire Beloe's XI.

In individual sports, Donny also merited the occasional mention. He played fives occasionally, and he boxed for the school;⁴³ he would later box for his battalion in the Middle East, and the family still possess a small silver cup which he won in Cairo.

* * *

Winchester, like most schools of its kind, operated an OTC (Officer Training Corps, re-named the Junior Training Corps during the Second World War), the predecessor of the modern Combined Cadet Force. The OTC of the Nineteen-Thirties had its roots in the Winchester College Rifle Volunteers, founded in 1860 as part of the nation-wide 'Volunteer Movement' which had begun in response to fears of war with France. Many schools had started uniformed units with the primary intention of learning how to shoot, competing for the prestigious inter-schools Ashburton Shield.⁴⁴ In 1908, as part of the Haldane reforms of the British Army, OTCs were formed in most schools and universities, with the aim of giving the officer class some military training, which would give them a head-start in the event of a major war. The 'Corps' was always voluntary, but most boys joined, and Donny was an active member: in December 1931 he came third equal in Recruit Cup, and by October 1932 had risen to head his house platoon (No.9), with the rank of Lance-Sergeant. The Jacker said that he was

> well up to standard as platoon commander.⁴⁵

Cadets in the OTC worked towards a test of elementary military proficiency called Certificate 'A', which consisted of a practical and a written examination. One contemporary remembered his Certificate 'A' test in the Thirties:

> It was dead simple. For my test, I was walked across Meads [the central playing field of Winchester College] by this officer who was testing me, and half-way across he said "Right. You're in charge of a Section, and you come under fire from a machine-gun, there. What're you going to do?" And I happened, for once, to react the way one should, and said: "Bren-gun here;⁴⁶ covering fire; right-

Above: *Donny's photographs of OTC Summer Camp at Tidworth in 1933 include this one of the Jacker inspecting a rifle (Mackenzie collection).*

handed; grenades." "Quite right, boy. You've passed!" That's the sort of thing Cert 'A' was. When you got it, it meant you started one notch up in your Officer Cadet training, wherever you went, whether you went on to Sandhurst to be a serious officer, or as a war-time joke.[47]

After passing Certificate 'A' – which Donny did in October 1932 – members of the Corps undertook courses in tactics, artillery, machine-guns, physical training, or surveying. Winchester had its own indoor shooting range, known as Cecil Range, which had been paid for by the mother of a Wykehamist killed in 1914; Rudyard Kipling had fired the first shot at the range's opening. Longer-range firing was conducted at the nearby ranges at Chilcomb. Donny proved to be a good shot, having been shooting since his youth. He also attended OTC camps such as the summer camp at Tidworth in 1933.

* * *

Donny was also an active debater, and from this we can perhaps gauge some of his political views and character. He spoke from the floor of the house in favour of closer ties within the British Empire, in support of the idea that the 1930s were much better than Victorian times, in support of the so-called 'blood' sports. He spoke against the introduction of Prohibition, increased investment in aeronautical research (as well as the practice of 'sky-writing'), greater restrictions on gambling, the granting of full Irish independence, a move to a four-day working week and four-hour working day, the contentions that Public School was not an adequate preparation for modern life and that the aristocracy had no future, and against the motion that if one wishes for peace, one should prepare for war.

Early in 1932, Donny spoke as first opposition against *the present widespread interest in the making and breaking of records is a useless and futile craze.*

> Mackenzie, against the motion, said that records stood for progress. We were continuing the enterprise shewn by our ancestors. Expense and loss of life were rewarded in many ways: by the advance of science (for the Schneider Cup, for example, was an excellent way of testing aeroplanes and engines for greater speeds); by the increase in trade (our small-car trade was flourishing, and nine nations now used Fairey aircraft); by service in linking up the world by rapid cross-continental flights; and by the help given to international relations, due to easier and quicker methods of travel, and so better familiarity with other countries. In athletics, outstanding runners always had an invisible rival in the form of the record; we improved our bodies physically, and this might help us to reach the state of perfect man. An interest in records was preferable to an interest in murders or society gossip. To vote for the motion was to betray all the brave men who had risked so much to win the records, and all that the records stood for. This speech had many good points, and was well delivered.[48]

The motion was defeated by twenty-five votes to eight.

On October 13th 1932 Donny spoke as second proposition in a debate on the motion that *This House endorses the Germans' claim for equality of status in armaments.* His opposite number in the debate was R.M.P. Carver, later Field Marshal Lord Carver, one of Britain's finest soldiers of the Twentieth Century: perhaps unsurprisingly, Carver won the debate.[49]

> Mackenzie said that the Allies, so far from fulfilling their promise to disarm, had now upon the average seventy per cent more armaments than in 1914. It is for Germany that security is required, since France is much more strongly armed; Germany wants not re-armament but a general disarmament, putting her upon an equal footing with other powers. Germany, along with the other great powers, signed the Briand-Kellogg Peace Pact, while in the last six years French military expenditure had increased by a hundred per cent. It is through the re-arming of France that she is again at loggerheads with Germany. The Great War was brought about by a race in armaments; another race in armaments will ensue unless the Allies disarm down to Germany's level. The Allies have been fourteen years without fulfilling their promises; why should Germany be held to hers? The need for French security is an illusion.[50]

What, then, was Donny like when he left school? Photographs only show what he looked like; for his character, we must turn again to his housemaster. The Jacker clearly saw Donny as a valuable member of the Winchester community:

> I'm very grateful to him for his good work for the house... Finished up well; good last month. Shall miss him personally; will be welcome [to visit]; hope he'll work at Oxford; not so simple as life at school.[51]

Perhaps the Jacker's most telling comment, however, is this one:

> Meets difficulty better than success.[52]

* * *

As Donny left Toye's, his cousin Brian arrived. They had seen a great deal of one another in holidays whilst Donny was at Winchester:

> My parents returned from India in 1931... and we lived at Glenalmond College, where my father was Bursar, so holiday contact with Donny at Glenalmond and Rosefield was quite frequent.[53]

Brian Mackenzie recalled that Donny came back to Winchester on occasion:

> His occasional visits from Oxford were delightful, as he always gave me a meal in the School Shop, as well as renewing friendship with Colin Pitman (also in Toyes).[54]

Not all Donny's friends were Wykehamists, according to his cousin:

> Donny had two particular friends in pre-War Scotland. Rex [surname unknown] was one frequently photographed... He went on to become a renowned expert on (I think) varieties of the mint plant family. The other was Barclay Pearson, who came from the Kincardine area; their friendship arose from social contacts. Barclay went into the Argyll and Sutherland Highlanders (going on to be a Brigadier DSO CBE), and Donny into the Camerons.[55]

Above: Donny Mackenzie in his final year at Winchester College, before going up to read Classics at Oxford (Mackenzie collection).

Chapter Three
Growing Up

Donny was five years Tresham's senior, and whilst Tresham was sunning himself and becoming tolerably amphibious in Malta, university beckoned for the Wykehamist. In October 1933 he went up to Christ Church, Oxford, where his grandfather, "Don", had studied. Donny was to read Literae Humaniores – Classics, then known as "Greats" – with a Kitchener Scholarship.[1]

It was an interesting time to be at Oxford. In February 1933, the Oxford Union debating society had stunned the world when it had voted overwhelmingly for the motion that *This House will in no circumstances fight for its King and Country*.[2] This was taken by many to sum up the attitude of the whole generation. The *Daily Express* thundered that

> there is no question but that the woozy-minded Communists, the practical jokers, and the sexual indeterminates of Oxford have scored a great success... Even the plea of immaturity, or the irresistible passion of the undergraduate for posing, cannot excuse such a contemptible and indecent action as the passing of that resolution.[3]

The Oxford Union received deliveries of 275 white feathers, one for each member who had voted for the motion. A week after the debate, Winston Churchill made a speech in which he condemned the vote as an

> abject, squalid, shameless avowal..., a very disquieting and very disgusting symptom. One could almost feel the curl of contempt upon the lips of the manhood of Germany, Italy and France when they read the message sent out by Oxford University in the name of Young England.[4]

And he was right. A year later, a Liberal MP stated that

> I remember very vividly, a few months after the famous pacifist resolution at the Oxford Union visiting Germany and having a talk with a prominent leader of the young Nazis. He was asking about this pacifist motion and I tried to explain it to him. There was an ugly gleam in his eye when he said: "The fact is that you English are soft."[5]

Patrick Leigh Fermor, walking through Germany early in 1934, found the Germans unable to comprehend the vote, and his feeble protestations that it was not meant seriously could not counter the impression that Britain had indeed 'gone soft'.

However, Oxford Union's unimportant motion did not represent a diminution of patriotism or of a willingness to defend freedom – when war broke out in 1939 nearly ninety per cent of Oxford students immediately volunteered for the armed forces – but a revulsion against jingoism and the attitude which said "my country right or wrong". When the Second World War came, Britain's young men fought for what they knew to be right. Whatever compromises had to be made in winning it, however flawed the victory and its aftermath, the Second World War was, for Britain, a just war. Both Donny and Gunner believed this – and Gunner, as we shall see, with better reason than most.

* * *

The world in which they were growing up was a volatile one. By the summer of Donny's first year at Oxford – 1934 – Britain was beginning to emerge from the Great Depression. Unemployment had reached a peak of 2,979,000 in January 1933, some twenty *per cent* of the working population; 1934 saw the first fall (to 16.75%) since 1929, and the National Government formed in 1931 claimed the credit. Local authorities had taken on the provision of free school meals and health services for the poor; an Unemployment Assistance Board was set up in 1934 to provide means-tested benefits for the long-term unemployed; the pound was devalued and the gold standard abandoned; a Special Areas Act increased government support for areas hardest hit by the depression (Scotland, South Wales, West Cumberland and Tyneside). The Chancellor of the Exchequer, Neville Chamberlain, seeing green shoots of recovery, reduced Income Tax to 22.5% and restored half of an earlier public sector pay-cut.

However, prescient Britons were looking at events in Germany with some disquiet, though their worries were not shared by many of those in government. In January 1934 the Nazis passed a law for the "prevention of hereditarily diseased offspring", and in March the police force was put under the command of a certain Heinrich Himmler; the last day of June saw the establishment of the first SS concentration camp at Oranienburg as the SA were purged in the infamous "Night of the Long Knives"; the Austrian Nazis assassinated their Chancellor, Dollfuss, during an attempted *coup* in late July; and in August Hitler became the German *Führer,* to whom the armed forces swore a personal oath of loyalty. A referendum a couple of weeks afterwards gave him a ninety *per cent* approval rating. The Fascists in Italy were still, however, somewhat more comic-book. In 1929 Italian schoolteachers had been forced to swear loyalty to the Fascist Party; in 1934, all were ordered to wear military or Fascist party uniforms.

Comic characters of a different sort were flourishing in 1934, which saw the publication of the first *Flash Gordon* comic strip; the first Donald Duck cartoon at the cinema; and Lionel Barrymore playing Scrooge in a Christmas Eve radio dramatization of Dickens' *A Christmas Carol.* Young men with a keen interest in soccer would have followed the FA Cup in April (Manchester City defeated Portsmouth 2-1 at Wembley) and the World Cup in June (Italy beat Czechoslovakia 2-1 in extra time); they also had opinions on the England debut of Stanley Matthews, and the MCC's controversial changes to the leg-before-wicket rules.

Those with literary interests might well have been reading newly-published novels such as F. Scott Fitzgerald's *Tender is the Night* or Robert Graves' *I, Claudius*; it was also a vintage year for readers of P.G. Wodehouse, with both *Thank You, Jeeves* and *Carry On, Jeeves* published. Cinema-goers enjoyed the new Frank Capra film *It Happened One Night,* starring Clark Gable and Claudette Colbert, the first motion picture to win all five of the most important Academy Awards. In New York, Cole Porter had written a new musical – *Anything Goes.*

In America, it seemed, anything did. 1934 catapulted the names of Bonnie Parker and Clyde Barrow to fame, when they killed two policemen before being shot themselves a month later by FBI agents; another gangster, John Dillinger – "Public Enemy No.1" – was killed in Chicago in July. The British had altogether more orthodox heroes for their young men, such as the pilots of the de Havilland DH88 Comet racer which won the MacRobertson Trophy Air Race by covering the eleven thousand miles from RAF Mildenhall to Melbourne race-course in seventy-one hours.

* * *

After his idyllic years in Malta, Gunner was ready for the final lap of his schooling, which began in September 1935, just before Donny entered his final year at Christ Church.

> When David was posted to Zanzibar, I was sent to join the Sixth Form at Bedford School to be educationally 'finished off'. I was placed in Crescent House. My mother stayed for some time settling me in at Bedford, and then went off to join David and I was left alone in Britain. I used to stay with my Aunt Mabel and Uncle Billy in their white bungalow in Tidworth.
>
> Bedford did me very well, especially on the games and sports side. My athletics went well, and I trialled at White City for England Schools. I went straight into the First XV rugby.

The Bedford School magazine, the *Ousel*, describes Gunner's play in 1937 as follows:

> Left wing. Had plenty of dash and a good turn of speed, but was rather clumsy and required a lot of room in which to move. A much improved tackler.

Gunner formed several close friendships at Bedford, one of which was to survive the war and to be a source of enduring happiness to him and his family:

> While I was at Bedford I took my School Certificate; I matriculated. I was very happy there, and had many good friends among the boys and the masters. Thanks to Malta, I had gone straight into the swimming team, alongside my best friend, Bernard Feilden. As Sir Bernard Feilden he became probably the most famous architectural consultant in the world. He saved York Minster from falling down, also the spire at Norwich, and St Paul's. He was later my son Tresham's very good and generous godfather – and his memorial service in Norwich Cathedral was a full house.[6]
>
> Bernard and I were very close to Barton, the art master, because we were interested in the subject and went painting together. I also got on well with the two German teachers, Stockton and Carling. This was possibly because they both knew that I had German school-friends whom I often saw in

Below: *Gunner pictured with the other members of the Bedford School First XV rugby in 1936 (photograph courtesy of Bedford School).*

> England and Germany. Naturally, they were both very interested in what was going on in Germany, and I showed them both the *Hitler Jugund* song-book, which was an eye-opener.

Gunner was a young man of many and varied accomplishments: his final entry in the *Ousel* shows that in addition to the successes mentioned above, he had become a Full Monitor, had won the school tennis doubles, hundred yards and hurdles, and had represented the school at athletics. However, the most unusual skill which he picked up whilst at Bedford would later prove useful in unexpected fashion: bee-keeping.

> Our next-door neighbour in Bedford was a doctor, who became a great friend even though I was only a boy. He had two or three hives of bees; it was his hobby, and he loved his bees. He encouraged me to come over and help him; he gave me a hood and I helped lift out the frames; he showed me how to cut the cappings off and put them in the extractor. He taught me everything he knew. I was bitten with the bug, but I didn't have the money to buy a WBC hive or a commercial hive, so I decided to make my own. He gave me a swarm, and I ended up with two hives of bees. I used to make a little money out of it: 10d for a pound pot of honey, a shilling for a section of honeycomb. The other source of income was that if you put the old combs behind a sheet of glass and left it in the sun, it ran off, leaving you the wax, which you could sell off to people for furniture polish or candles.
>
> When the doctor died, I was very touched to find that he'd left me his library of bee-keeping books. I treasured them, and still have some of them.

Looking back on his education, Gunner thought that despite its unconventional and disjointed nature it had actually done wonders for him:

> At a very young age I knew more of the ways of the world than the average British youth. I had lived all over the world and experienced several education systems: thirteen years in South Africa at school at Gray's College in Port Elizabeth and Bishop's in Cape Town; a Swiss tutor in Thun for three months; Wiesbaden Gymnasium for six months; Hillside in Reigate for a term – the low point; a coach *cum* tutor *cum* schoolmaster in Valetta for over two years; Bedford School. An excellent education. I also think that the education I got at home from my parents taught me most. My step-father was an electrical engineer who had seen much of the world; my mother spoke six languages and was a very good watercolour artist – she would have been excellent on *University Challenge* or *Brain of Britain*. Both of them had lived all over the world.
>
> I think that I was very mature for a young man, and my interests were correspondingly mature for my age. I was very cosmopolitan. I nearly became an artist, but my mother, quite rightly, said I was not nearly good enough.

Instead, Gunner was to become a soldier.

* * *

Gunner and Donny were finishing their educations against a background of the rise of Fascism in Italy, Germany, Romania and Spain, as well as attempts by the Communists to portray themselves as the leaders of the world's response to that Fascism. In Britain, both ideologies had adherents: in the General Election of 1935, a Communist Party MP was elected, whilst Sir Oswald Mosley's British Union of Fascists were attempting to emulate Mussolini's Blackshirts and Hitler's Brownshirts. Mosley, of course, was a Wykehamist, though not one of whom the school is proud. Many rebellious schoolboys of the Nineteen-Thirties tended towards Communism: one of them was Wykehamist Frank Thompson, whose communist convictions led him during the war which followed to volunteer for SOE and to be parachuted into Bulgaria, where he was shot by Bulgarian government forces in 1944. Part of the attraction of the British Communist party in the Nineteen-Thirties was that it vehemently opposed the policy of appeasement espoused by the Conservative Party of the day.

With hindsight, the march to war seems inevitable, and the provocations by Hitler and Mussolini insufferable. Italian imperial ambitions in eastern Africa took the form of an invasion of Abyssinia in October 1935. One of the reporters who covered the war alongside Evelyn Waugh and Bill Deedes was Wykehamist George Steer, later to break the news of the bombing of Guernica. The League of Nations imposed trade sanctions on Italy, though not including the vital commodities of oil and coal – neither Germany nor the United States were members in any case. In November, the British Foreign Secretary, Sir Samuel Hoare, met his French counterpart and agreed to cede most of Abyssinia to Italy in the hope of wooing Mussolini away from Hitler, but when word leaked out Hoare was forced to resign. The League of Nations stood by impotent and discredited..

In March 1936 Hitler defied the Versailles Treaty, which had ended the First World War, and sent German troops into the Rhineland. His advisors had been against it, expecting stern French reaction – but reaction came there none. Both the British Conservative Prime Minister, Stanley Baldwin, and the Labour Party admitted that Britain lacked the will or the resources to do anything. Although the United States considered boycotting the Berlin Olympic Games of August 1936, only one nation in fact did so – Spain. But Spain's decision to hold games of its own in Barcelona was overtaken by events.

July saw the outbreak of civil war in Spain, as right wing and Fascist elements combined against the Republican government and its working-class, Socialist and Communist supporters. The war became a litmus test of one's political leanings, with the idealistic youth of Europe flocking to support the Republicans, who were backed by the Soviet Union – whilst the governments of Italy and Germany armed and abetted the Nationalists. New weapons and tactics were tested in Spain which would shape the future of warfare. And Donny was not un-touched by the war: one of his contemporaries at Winchester, Prince Alonso Maria Christino Justo of Orleans Y Bourbon, was killed flying for Franco's air force in November 1936.[7]

* * *

Donny emerged from Oxford with a Second Class BA degree in the summer of 1936, and it would seem from one of his photograph albums that he visited Italy at around this time. He would return, under entirely different circumstances, some years later – and would never leave.

Donny had served with the Oxford University OTC whilst at Christ Church, choosing to join the Royal Artillery battery which the unit then had. He used the OTC as a route into the regular army. At Winchester, he had passed his Certificate 'A', and at Oxford he followed this with Certificate 'B' – which entitled its holder to a commission in the Special Reserve or Territorial Army without attending the Royal Military College at Sandhurst. He passed his Certificate 'B' in November 1934, and was commissioned into the Territorials on St Valentine's Day 1935, whilst still at Oxford.[8] His commission was not in any specific regiment – he was a Second Lieutenant on the General List – but over the next couple of years he enjoyed attachments to the Cameron Highlanders, training with 2nd Battalion at Aldershot. On leaving university, he converted his Territorial commission into a Regular Army commission with the Cameron Highlanders (gazetted August 29th 1936, with seniority from January 31st 1935).[9] He was posted straight to 1st Battalion at Catterick, where he was immediately put in charge of the battalion rugby team.[10]

But in January 1937 Donny received orders to join 2nd Camerons in Egypt.[11] He embarked aboard HMT *Dilwara* at Southampton on January 6th, and it only took eleven

Above: *Donny enjoying a cigarette break whilst shooting in Scotland towards the end of his time at Oxford (Mackenzie collection).*

days to travel the length of the Mediterranean to Port Said. It is not clear what he did for the next couple of months, since records state that he joined his battalion in Cairo in April 1937, being assigned to 'B' Company. His photographs of the period show fellow officers in sangars in the desert during their training over the next few months.

It must have been hard for Donny's mother Dor to watch her son head off for the Middle East as his father had done in 1914. She and her family would see very little of him, perhaps one short leave before the outbreak of war in 1939. Christopher ("Kit") Yates, Donny's godson, remembered him only vaguely:

None of us really knew Donny well; we were young, and often away at school. He was older than us, and was rarely in St Cyrus when we were there. I can't remember either his mother or our parents talking very much about him during our stay at 'Rosefield'.[12]

* * *

Gunner had joined the OTC at Bedford for his two years there, which provided him with the basics of military training – he reached the rank of Lance Corporal. As testimony to the quality of his education, unconventional though it had been, Gunner passed into Sandhurst with distinction when he finished at Bedford in the summer of 1937. Until the outbreak of war, RMC Sandhurst operated like an exclusive boarding school: the parents of its students – 'Gentlemen Cadets' – paid the army to turn their sons into officers. Tuition fees, boarding fees, books, equipment and uniforms had all to be paid for; there was an entrance examination, with a published order of merit and scholarships and bursaries for the academically gifted or sons of officers.

> I passed in third, I think it was, in the Sandhurst exam. There was also a set of interviews, which were critical. They were held in Burlington House. I had my interview with a lot of admirals and generals and people. One naval officer said to me: "I notice that you've put bee-keeping as your interest. What does that involve?" When I told the story, it went down very well. In the end I got two scholarships – which were very useful, because in those days you paid to go.

Gunner continued to thrive during his time at the RMC. His prowess at rugby had attracted immediate attention, and he was taken into the First XV a year earlier than would normally have been the case.

> I'd already made my name as a rugby player – my main value was that I was an extremely fast runner. If I was out on the wing and they could get the ball to me, not many people could catch me.
>
> I was the only Junior who played in the First XV and had two rugby seasons. It was bloody hell, because the Juniors were chased up and down hill – they'd knock you over for something or other every ten minutes – and I had to do First XV training on top. Not only that, but my friends were high-up Under Officers, so I was in rather a strange position. The next year I was Captain of Rugby, but by then I was a Senior. While I was Captain, I was approached by both Harlequins and Bath to join them; they both had a policy of keeping their eyes open for young talent coming through. I eventually chose Bath – mind you, I was tempted by Harlequins. I liked the tie.

Both Gunner's son and grandson would later follow in his footsteps at Sandhurst:

> My son Tresham was also Senior Under Officer and Captain of Rugby. And the names of the teams are in the gymnasium, and poor Rowley, when he was there, looked up and saw "T.D. Gregg, Captain... T.D. Gregg, Captain", and said he was letting the family down!

Gunner's family – all outstanding sportsmen themselves – were proud of his prowess.

> My granny's brother, my great-uncle Percy Stokes, was a brewer with Guinnesses; somewhat strangely, he was the same age as my father despite being his uncle. He was an outstanding athlete and had a fantastic row of cups. He used to come and visit me, because he hadn't got a wife and my parents were overseas. He used to come and watch me captain the Sandhurst rugby team, and I used to take him to the FGS, as it was called, for tea. He was bloody rich, but a terrific skinflint. Normally I had no money at all – five shillings for a week or something. They had these almond biscuits, macaroons, and he always used to have those and leave me to pay at the end.
>
> The big match of the year was always the Commandant's Match, between the Sandhurst XV and a Commandant's XV of elderly internationals, some of the best players in England in their time. They treated it as a jolly, and luckily they usually ran out of puff by the last quarter of an hour, when they began to feel their age, which was our only hope really. Anyway, I captained us to victory – I scored the winning try, I think.

The next morning, Uncle Percy gave me a cheque for £400. That was a lot of money in those days. I went up to London, to the Euston Road where they had all these new car showrooms, and I bought a Riley Sprite. It was a two-seater sports car, the basis of the ERA racing-car. It cost me about £210, at a time when most of my fellow Officer Cadets had £10 cars. So everyone thought I was rich.

Gunner was not only a superb rugby player, but had other talents as well:

I became Junior Under-Officer, Captain of Rugby, and Captain of Athletics; I had a blue for both of those. I represented Sandhurst at tennis as well. In athletics I fooled around with a lot of events – shot putt, discus, and so on, and I wasn't a bad high-jumper: I cleared five foot eight, which was good in those days. So I was often a reserve for those events. But hurdling and sprinting were my strengths. In sprinting, I was one of only three people in the country who had broken evens – that is, broken ten seconds for one hundred yards. So I was one of the fastest sprinters in England. I was also good at the 220 yards, though I was also occasionally bullied into doing the 440, which was far too long for me.

One of our compulsory subjects was Equitation – there were hundreds of horses, and in those days the subject was as important as drill. But I didn't enjoy it, and the Athletics officer didn't like me riding at all. It taught you all the wrong things if you wanted to be an athlete. For hurdling, you need loose leg muscles, but for riding we were taught to grip with our legs.

I even trained with the Olympic hurdle squad, and I reckon that the war put paid to my chances of taking part in the Olympics. The Olympic hurdlers had come to Sandhurst to train, and I and the chap who was next best after me trained with them. I could hold my own against them – in fact, I've got photos in my album showing me leading against Donald Finlay, the RAF hurdler.[13] Lord Burghley was there as well; very long legs but a short body.[14] So I was in pretty tough company.

Gunner's swimming remained very strong.

I was probably the best swimmer there – not that there was much, but I did any that was going. One day, when I was still a Junior, the Adjutant sent for me and told me that he'd been approached by the Secretary of the English Swimming Association, who wanted me to take part in a very important match against the Dolphin Club, which to some extent would be used as a trial. The Dolphins were then the top swimming club in England. I protested that I wasn't in training because I was spending all my time training with the rugby team. So I told him "I'm not going." He replied: "I've told them you are."

I went up to London and was told to do two events: a one-length sprint, which was no problem, even though I was matched against one of the best swimmers in England, a chap called Martyn French-Williams who'd represented Britain in the 1936 Olympics. The second event was a three-length swim – and that nearly killed me. I was out of training, and didn't have my breathing rhythm, so spent most of the race with my lungs full of water. When I got to the end I was so knackered that I couldn't climb out by myself; they lifted me out. I can remember still how I staggered along the wall to the changing-room, vomited copiously into a urinal, and slowly got dressed. I certainly didn't take any more interest in that day's swimming. I got a taxi, went to the station, caught the Camberley train – and woke up in Exeter.

I ended up catching the milk train back very early in the morning and walked all the way from the station. When I looked at the programme for the day I saw that it was Equitation. What the swimming hadn't finished, the riding saw to – it bloody nearly killed me that day.

I was later called on to represent the Army in a race at Catterick, and I did better because I was in training by then.

One further accomplishment which Gunner picked up at Sandhurst would be very useful in the years to come:

Several of us decided to learn how to dance. Elmhurst School for Dance were there in Camberley; my future wife Joan was later a student there. We took lessons from the Elmhurst students. I must admit that I just do the same step and just count to a different number depending on the dance: three for a waltz and four for a quick-step. I took a cousin of mine to the June Ball – a lovely girl, Sheila Houston.

It is fashionable to deride the training which British officers received before the war, and to accuse them of a lack of professionalism. Gunner disagreed:

> I loved my time at Sandhurst, and did very well there. I passed out at the end of the winter term 1938, and was commissioned in January 1939. I think that the Sandhurst training before the war was first class, and excellent preparation for war. It certainly produced young officers who refused to give in like the French, refused to be beaten, and won the war.
>
> I believe that our training methods were better than those of the Germans. Their main problem, in my view, was that their great General Staff was too remote from the regimental officer. Once on the German General Staff you stayed there. The British army had staff officers who, after a tour of duty on the staff, always returned for a tour at regimental level. They were therefore far better informed about the problems of officers who were doing the real fighting.

Donny provides a good example of exactly what Gunner describes; he did a good deal of staff-work in the early part of the war, only to return to duty as a front-line infantry officer and serve gallantly in the front line. He had not remained with 'B' Company of 2nd Camerons for long. On October 22nd 1937 he was officially posted to a temporary "Special Appointment" as a "Class HH" staff officer in HQ British Troops in Egypt (HQ BTE).[15] this "Special Appointment" was as an Assistant Cipher Officer, responsible for encoding and de-coding signals. It was a vital role and would become even more important in war-time, making Donny a precious asset to the staff. His promotion to full Lieutenant came quickly, since his commission had been back-dated to January 1935.[16] His personnel file also states that he passed his Colloquial Arabic Test at Abbassia on June 22nd-23rd 1938.

2nd Camerons confidently expected Donny to return – the 'B' Company notes of January 1938 said that he had "temporarily left us for the staff"[17] – but he had in fact left the battalion almost permanently. Apart from one brief period in 1940, he would not rejoin his comrades in 2nd Camerons until May 25th 1942.

* * *

Whilst Gunner worked his way towards his commission and Donny was learning the ways of the staff in Egypt, the world was stepping closer to the brink of war. In 1937 Neville Chamberlain had taken over as Prime Minister, pursuing a dual policy of appeasement and re-armament; Britain needed time to prepare itself if it was to take a stand against the Fascists. Indeed, until the failure of the Munich Agreement, Chamberlain's policy was for the most part a popular one, since at its simplest it was the pursuit of peace. Even Winston Churchill appreciated that Chamberlain was sincere in his desire to avoid war:

> Whatever else history may or may not say about these terrible, tremendous years, we can be sure that Neville Chamberlain acted with perfect sincerity according to his lights and strove to the utmost of his capacity and authority, which were powerful, to save the world from the awful, devastating struggle in which we are now engaged.[18]

Many, too, believed that the Germans had been hard done-by in the Versailles Treaty and that some, at least, of Hitler's demands were reasonable. Even the Labour Party, which opposed Fascism, feared war and supported Chamberlain; indeed, when the Prime Minister set out for Munich in September 1938 the whole House of Commons cheered him to the rafters. But the Munich Crisis finally made it clear to all – including Chamberlain – that war with Germany was inevitable. Britain braced itself for a conflict for which it was not yet ready. But at Munich Britain and France abandoned Czechoslovakia to the wolves, and Europe stepped back from the brink. Despite this apparent success for diplomacy, however, Donny and Gunner were in no doubt that they would soon be called upon to lead men into battle.

Gunner appreciated the dangers posed by the Nazis far better than most of his peers. Without a home in Britain, he spent most of his holidays from Bedford and Sandhurst – between 1935 and 1938 – in Germany with his childhood friends.

> As I had no home in England to go to – my parents being in Zanzibar – I often helped run the Sandhurst visit of our affiliated London boys' club. Otherwise I went to stay with friends in Germany.

Few officers in the British army could claim to have marched with the Hitler Youth – but Gunner did.

> Was I conscious of the Nazis? Good God, yes. I'd made all these friends at school in Germany, and then went and stayed with them in holidays. And they came and stayed with me in Britain. It was important to me. Even when I was a cadet at Sandhurst I used to spend my holidays with German school-friends who lived in Köln and Bonn. And so I got to know the Nazi party.

Gunner's friend in Bonn was called Klaus Beckers. Gunner used to take a collapsible wood-and-canvas canoe (faltboat, German *faltboot*) when he went to stay with him, enabling the young men to paddle along the Rhine, Mosel and other waterways.

> Klaus Beckers' family ran Beckers *Konditorei* [confectioners and patisserie] which was on the *Münsterplatz* in Bonn – a wonderful restaurant – and I used to come over with my *faltboot* and I'd get off at the station near the *Münsterplatz*, and I'd walk across, and I'd have all these *Kuche mit Schlagsahne* [cakes with whipped cream]; they were beautifully done. When they'd done their housework, all the Hausfraus'd collect there. The Beckers were all very proud of the fact that all their furniture was Chippendale – reproduction Chippendale, but it was a very up-market place.

Klaus also stayed with Gunner in England, and by the end of the Nineteen-Thirties had a job marketing wood-carvings from the Black Forest. During the war he joined the German signals corps as an officer.

Gunner's other great German friend was Helmut Kremers, whose father was a *gauleiter* in the Nazi headquarters in Bonn.

> He visited me at Bedford, and I took him to the school. He was very impressed with the English public school and said he would send his son there when he got married. He was with me when I ran at the English Schools Athletics Championships at White City.
>
> His family lived in a lovely house in Bonn, where I stayed about three times. Although he was a friend of mine he had certain traits which I did not like. He could easily become a bully to those physically weaker than himself, and believed – like most Germans then – that might was right. He dominated his brother and sister, even to the extent of using physical force, but they seemed to think that this was his right. He never tried to bully me, though; he knew that I was stronger than he was.
>
> His father seemed to enjoy having long and serious conversations with me, though I was not much more than a boy. The theme was usually the same. Hitler considered "England" – by which he meant the United Kingdom – to be an Aryan country, and thus it was only natural that we should be allies of Germany and not France. Herr Kremers said to me several times that Hitler considered that the combination of the English navy and the German army could rule the world, and that Hitler found it remarkable how England could hold and rule the vast Indian empire with the minute forces stationed there.
>
> I was always surprised how little Herr Kremers knew of the real world. He always used the term "English colonies", and I had to explain that the British Commonwealth was made up of independent, self-governing states. For the first time I heard it suggested that western Australia should become part of the German Third Reich and be settled with a million Germans – he seemed to think that the British government had the authority to impose this scenario on the Australians.
>
> Herr Kremers often stated that I was typical of the best Aryan type: I was strong and athletic and very blond with blue eyes. He wanted to know what training I went through at Sandhurst to qualify for a commission.

When war broke out, Helmut's father wangled him a commission in an anti-aircraft artillery regiment, probably in the expectation that this would be a relatively safe billet and most likely to be stationed in Germany itself. But he and Gunner never met again.

> After the war I lost touch with him. When I visited their house, it was occupied by a foreign diplomat's family attached to the German government.

Having in earlier years lived with the British army of occupation, and sensed the frustration and resentment of the German people at their treatment after Versailles, Gunner was conscious that the Nazis had struck a chord with the German people:

> At that time, the Nazis were doing the most impressive things – they were building the *autobahns*, for example. And the big thing Hitler did was the unemployment. It had been astronomically high. He cured that. The Nazis started up the *Arbeitsdienst*, who they used for building the motorways. I remember sitting on a bank watching my friends helping do the motorway between Bonn and Cologne.

But his friends were not taken in. Klaus Beckers, in particular, was a devout Roman Catholic, and had deep misgivings about what the Nazis had planned for his faith.

> I remember that on one occasion – when I was at Sandhurst – I was staying with Klaus Beckers in Bonn. I remember arriving at the *Konditorei*, which was my home there, and Klaus said "Come with me. I've got to show you something." We went up to his room, and he'd made a sort of closet inside his wardrobe – I thought he was going to bring out a bomb or something, but all he brought out was cuttings from Nazi papers. You see, he was convinced that Hitler was determined to destroy the Catholic church, because he'd destroyed anything that was a rival to the Nazi party, everything else, unions and God knows what. Klaus said: "You read them. It's obvious he wants to destroy the church." Now, such was his fear of the Gestapo that he even kept his theories from his family. He didn't even show his family this mass of cuttings, which gives you some idea of the hold the Nazis had on the normal person.

There were other disturbing features of life in Nazi Germany which worried Gunner:

> I can remember, for instance, in Bonn one day, they had a huge bonfire at Bonn university – and they were burning Jewish books. I loved the poems of Heinrich Heine –
>
> *Mein Kind, wir waren Kinder,*
> *Zwei Kinder, klein und froh;*
> *Wir krochen ins Hühnerhäuschen,*
> *Versteckten uns unter das Stroh.*
>
> *Wir krähten wie die Hähne,*
> *Und kamen Leute vorbei -*
> *Kikerekii! sie glaubten,*
> *Es wäre Hahnengeschrei.*[19]
>
> I'd learned them, I liked them. So I was horrified. Heine's books were being burned because he was a Jew.

It was all but compulsory to enrol in the Hitler Youth, and so even Klaus had to swallow his misgivings and show public allegiance to the regime. This gave Gunner first-hand experience of the Nazi youth movement.

> Naturally, both Klaus and Helmut were in the *Hitler Jugund*. I went on many trips with them, climbing the Siebengebirge and the like.[20] We'd march up there singing songs, and we'd go to a *café*, which we'd take over – and there I was with them.

It was with his friends in the Hitler Youth that Gunner even came within spitting distance of Goebbels and Adolf Hitler.

> Once, with one of their *Hitler Jugund* groups, I went to a Nazi rally at Bad Godesberg, just up-river from Bonn, an immense rally. Everyone turned up; there were thousands there. I went with them, and was sitting with my own friends in the *Hitler Jugund* – I was no further than from here to that brick wall [about twenty feet] to the dais.
>
> First of all we had Goebbels, who gave them a rousing speech to build them up, and then he stood down and Hitler got on to the dais. He talked for an hour, and his speech was fantastic – I mean you couldn't help listening to it and getting involved in it. He told the rally how he was going to "correct" and change all the unfair and cruel punishments which the Allies had imposed on the German people after the First World War. He then talked about what he was going to do about the *Untermensch*, by which he meant mainly the Jews, Gypsies, and all the Slavs in eastern Europe. What he wasn't going to do the *Untermensch* was nobody's business. I had little doubt that he had every intention of doing what he said he would do, that he would arm Germany and start another war. I then and there realized that the bloody man was mad.

* * *

However, although most people knew that war had merely been postponed by the Munich Agreement, not averted, there were still those who did not want to believe it. When he returned from Munich at the start of October 1938, Chamberlain was cheered by delighted crowds as he stood on the balcony of Buckingham Palace, and received forty thousand letters of congratulation. The press, too, were generally favourable to the Munich agreement. There were of course dissenting voices amongst politicians, among them that of Winston Churchill, who issued this warning in a press statement a week before Munich:

> The partition of Czechoslovakia under pressure from England and France amounts to the complete surrender of the western democracies to the Nazi threat of force. Such a collapse will bring peace or security neither to England nor to France.[21]

* * *

In March 1939 the Munich agreement was exposed for the worthless scrap of paper which it was. That month, German troops occupied Prague, and Czechoslovakia ceased to exist. Chamberlain immediately began preparations for war, and made improvements to civil defence. Italy, too, was beginning to make territorial demands in Europe: on March 25th she demanded that the Albanians surrender their country, and invaded on April 7th when King Zog refused. Events had now gained an unstoppable momentum; on August 23rd 1939 the last obstacle to Hitler's ambitions in eastern Europe was removed when Germany signed a non-aggression pact with the Soviet Union, an act of betrayal by the Soviets which dismayed the Communists of Europe. The treaty divided up Poland and the Baltic states, and it was clear that Poland was next on Hitler's list. In March, however, Chamberlain had promised to help Poland if she were threatened – and this time Britain was prepared to go to war. Prepared to do so, but far from ready.

* * *

From Sandhurst, Gunner had decided to join the Royal Tank Regiment, then one of the newest in the British army. During the First World War the British had invented tanks and pioneered their use in battle, and two prescient officers (Basil Liddell-Hart and J.F.C. Fuller) had articulated the lessons which could be learned for future warfare.

Unfortunately, these lessons were learned rather better in Germany than they were in Britain. The British had appreciated, however, that the days of horsed cavalry were over. The Royal Tank Corps had been formed in 1917 to use the new weapons; in 1928, the first of the traditional cavalry regiments began to mechanize. In 1939 the cavalry and RTC were brought together under one umbrella as the Royal Armoured Corps, the RTC being re-named the Royal Tank Regiment to avoid confusion. There were eight regular battalions of the RTR by the outbreak of the Second World War.

Gunner's reasons for picking the RTR were principally because it seemed the cutting edge of military technology at the time.

> Signing up to a regiment was a formality. But you had to get someone who expressed an interest in you. My Uncle Billy said that I should go to the Royal Tank Regiment, which was very popular: it was modern, it had vehicles. You didn't want to spend your time playing polo with some cavalry regiment. So it was very well subscribed for quality. Uncle Billy knew various people in the Regiment; I interviewed with the Colonel of the Regiment while I was at Sandhurst.

Gunner's commission was dated January 16th 1939, and was to run from January 26th 1939. From Sandhurst, he went to join the RTR at the RAC Centre at Bovington, near Wareham in Dorset. It is still the home of the RTR, and later in his career Gunner would actually command Bovington. But for now he was that most humble of beings, a newly-commissioned Second Lieutenant. His training at Sandhurst had been general; it was now to become much more technical and specific.

> You then went down to Bovington and Lulworth. You did gunnery at Lulworth, and you did your D&M [driving and maintenance] and signals at Bovington. At the school there they trained all the armour: the gunner SP regiments, the engineers, and the RAC. You had to do that so that when you went to your regiment you knew as much about that as your soldiers did. And it was a long course – nowadays they expect you to do your training in your regiment, and it's a bugger's muddle.

Whilst on his course at Bovington, Gunner was invited to play rugby for Bath, becoming by far the youngest member of Bath's first XV:

> During my young officer's course down at Bovington I accepted Bath's offer. I'd been a winger, but the Bath coach decided that he wanted more pressure in the centre, so he moved me to right centre. I was fast, and I was big – six-one and thirteen-and-a-half stone. That sounds very little now, but in those days that was big for a three-quarter. I tackled very hard, especially if I was allowed to get up speed. I made a speciality of getting my shoulder into their stomach; they'd lie still for a bit after one of those. The effect was that if they got the ball after that they'd pass it quickly.
>
> Bovington was near enough to Bath, and the doctor in Lulworth also played for them – he played for Scotland as well. He and I took it in turns to drive over every Saturday; we'd set off very early and drive the ninety miles or so. I used my Sprite.

Gunner's long journeys in the Riley to and from Bath, and to athletics tournaments, were not the most comfortable:

> It was very definitely a sports car. It got round corners quickly, but it had no springs at all. So you really felt it. I used to arrive at athletics matches already exhausted. So I went into Bournemouth to one of these big second-hand places where they had lots of doctors' cars and traded it in for a lovely hand-made Mulliner-bodied Lanchester. It was solid aluminium – must have cost a fortune brand-new. It had a pre-selector gearbox, air-cushioned seats with real leather covers, and meant that I was now travelling in complete luxury – it had a Daimler engine and just purred along. I'd drive down to Portsmouth for a match against the Navy and get there absolutely fresh. The only pity was that I was so in demand for sport that I didn't have time to use it to impress the girls. I was very naieve and young in those days.

I had that car right until war came, when I left it with a farmer in Bedfordshire, who put it up on bricks. It was there at the end of the war, and I sold it for about £700 – so I'd made a tidy profit on Uncle Percy's gift.

Many of the matches were in Wales.

When we got to Bath we often then got straight on a train and went to south Wales, which was where most of our fixtures were – though some were in the Midlands or London.

Whenever you played in Wales, you knew perfectly well that you weren't playing fifteen men; you were playing sixteen, because the referee was on their side too. After one match fairly early on we went to the pub which they used as their club house. They had three internationals playing for them and I was very impressed, being so young, and a bit overawed and subdued. I was talking to one of them and remember thinking that I should do something, so I quietly asked him if I could buy him a drink. The whole bloody room went still. Then every single one of them had his glass on the bar putting his order in – and there I was saddled with the whole bally lot.

Playing rugby, of course, is not without its risks, and Gunner did not come out of his Bath matches entirely unscathed. In a game against Leicester in April 1939, he injured his scaphoid bone, on the thumb side of his right wrist.

I tackled someone and fell on the thing. There was an awful sound and a lot of pain, but I carried on playing – which was foolish of me because I hurt it again several times more. After the match I didn't even change; I got straight in my car and drove back to Bovington. I was feeling bloody. I got as far as Blandford, just outside, but then thought I was going to pass out, so I pulled in to the verge. I was nursing it and looked up to find two policemen.

"Would you mind stepping out for a moment, please?" They were obviously going to see whether I'd been drinking.

"I'm not drunk, Constable, I've been playing rugby for Bath against Leicester and I think I've broken my wrist. I'm an officer from Bovington and I was driving myself back to camp."

They were wonderful. They told me not to drive on to Bovington, but to stay in Blandford for the night. They made me follow them and escorted me to a pub – I wish I could remember its name – where the landlord and his wife took me in. They couldn't do enough for me; pyjamas, hot bath, hot-water-bottle, comfy bed, bloody great slug of whisky or brandy. It turned out that the landlord had been RSM at Bovington. They didn't even charge me.

The next day I went into the little base hospital at Bovington, where they treated my wrist and put it in plaster. I was in there for a week to stop me from using the wrist. Matron said to me:

"That bed you're in now – Lawrence of Arabia died in it."

Gunner's ambition, of course, was to play for his country, which despite his peregrinations he considered to be Ireland. In 1939 his chance seemed to have come.

Like all countries, Ireland were on the lookout for young talent. They didn't contact me direct, but through the Secretary, who told me that they'd been in touch and wanted me to come for a trial. I was tickled pink. So over I went to Dublin. It was nice: I went to see the house I was born in, and the family home at Sandbanks down by the coast. I had my trial at Lansdowne Road; there were about five of us. We had a sprint, which I won – they were impressed by my speed. Then they gave us dummies to tackle and made sure that we could tackle properly. We then had a game, I forget who against, moving us around a bit. I wanted to be centre but they put me on the wing and made sure the ball got out there. So they gave me a trial cap – but then war came, and I never got the chance again. I blame Hitler for that.

Chapter Four
Phoney War

Gunner had not completed his training when the war which he had long expected finally broke out on September 3rd 1939.

> Bernard Feilden and I were staying in a water-mill on the River Dove owned by Barton, the art master at Bedford. Before I had gone on leave I had been made to state where I could be contacted in the event of war. One morning a local village policeman came across the field to tell me that I had to return at once to Bovington. Bernard asked me what that meant. I told him that we would be at war tomorrow. Bernard asked me what he should do, and I told him that I would drive him in to Bedford and that he should at once enlist in the local Yeomanry regiment of the TA – otherwise he would be kept for many months, even years, before being called up. This he did, and was later sent to India for his officer training, after which he was commissioned into the Bengal Sappers and Miners.[1]

Instead of finishing his course at Bovington, Gunner was posted almost immediately to his new unit: 3rd Battalion, Royal Tank Regiment, referred to as 3RTR or "Third Tanks".

> My course was just finishing. I'd known that I was going to Third Tanks – that had been decided by RHQ, the Colonel of the Regiment – and I'd visited them previously. When war was declared, all our Reservists came to Bovington, and I had to take all the Third Tanks ones in buses to Warminster, where the Regiment were.

Gunner joined his battalion at Warminster on September 25th. 3RTR, based at Swinton Barracks, were equipped with a bewildering variety of equipment, reflecting Britain's unpreparedness for war. For the first two years of war, British tank units were often issued with a mixture of three different models of 'cruiser' tank (models A9, A10, and A13), and light tanks (the Mark VIb) for scouting.[2] This complicated the supply chain and meant that different parts of the unit moved at different speeds from the others. In September 1939, 3RTR had no fewer than five types of tank in use: A9s, A10s, A13s, Mark VIs, and the antiquated Vickers Medium, of which the battalion had five. As the newest and most inexperienced officer, Gunner found himself in charge of these obsolete behemoths, far from the white heat of technology for which he had joined:

Below: *at left, a Vickers Medium of the sort still in service with 3RTR in 1939; at right, an A9 – clearly a more modern design, but nevertheless flawed (copyright holders unknown).*

Above: *at left, an A10 cruiser tank (in this case, a Close Support version armed with a howitzer); at right, an A13 with the 2-pounder main gun standard at the time (copyright holders unknown).*

> I was given a troop of Medium Tanks. They'd been designed right at the end of the First World War. Though they had a turret and hull-gunners as well, they were very thinly armoured. I'm glad we didn't have to fight in them.

Although the other types of tank were more modern, they were far from satisfactory. In 1936 the British had decided to design two forms of tank: the 'infantry' tank (which would provide fire-support for infantry in attack) and the 'cruiser' tank, which would operate like cavalry, by-passing enemy lines at speed and wreaking havoc on their lines of communication. It was a flawed philosophy and it created flawed tank designs. Gunner remembered the disadvantages under which he and his comrades had to labour:

> We were given A9s, A10s and A13s, which were cruiser tanks. All three had 2-pounder guns, which was better than being in a light tank. The A9s also had small hull-turrets with Vickers machine-guns. The A10 was the same but without the turrets and with more armour. The A9s and A10s were the most useless clapped-out lot of things with narrow tracks that kept breaking. Despite the name "cruiser tanks", the A9s and A10s had no speed at all – they were pathetic. I'd never heard of them until we were issued with them.
> The A13s had the Christie suspension system, which made them very very fast, but piss-all armour – little better than a light tank, fourteen millimetres mostly. At least the turret armour was angled *[which deflected enemy fire better]*. We were three in the turret and one in the driver's seat.

When Gunner arrived at Warminster with the reservists, he soon found himself on the move:

> On November 2nd they sent us to Hitchin, to be nearer to the coast.

The battalion thus spent the icy winter of 1939 to 1940 in Hertfordshire.

* * *

Western Europe had not yet experienced *Blitzkrieg*, and there was a sense of unreality about the whole period, the "Phoney War", so brilliantly satirized by Evelyn Waugh in his novel *Put Out More Flags*. The British Expeditionary Force (BEF) which had been sent to France, just as it had in 1914, was by now in position along the Belgian frontier. But the war continued quietly, with little obvious impact on life in mainland Britain. There were German raiders at sea; German U-boats scored some striking successes, including the torpedoing of the battleship HMS *Royal Oak* in Scapa Flow itself; and German aircraft continued to make isolated raids in the north of the country. However, the main threat which was developing was that of technologically-advanced magnetic mines sown in

British home waters. On November 21st one severely damaged the new cruiser, HMS *Belfast,* and on December 4th the equally modern battleship *Nelson* suffered the same fate. Indeed, it was only at sea that the war seemed to be prosecuted with any vigour, and on December 13th the British cruisers *Exeter* and *Ajax* and the New Zealand cruiser *Achilles* intercepted the German pocket-battleship *Admiral Graf Spee* off the River Plate in South America, crippling the enemy vessel and forcing its captain to scuttle his warship four days later.

The winter of 1939 to 1940 was bitterly cold, the coldest since 1894, a temperature of -18°C being recorded in Buxton in January 1940; both the Thames and Southampton Docks froze over. In France, the BEF shivered in its inadequate accommodation and winter clothing, but faced little danger from the enemy. Some indication of the quietness of the western front can be gauged from the fact that the first British infantryman to be killed in action in the Second World War died on December 9th, three months into the conflict. In fact, between September and December 1939, 4130 people had died in road accidents in Great Britain, whilst the entire British armed forces had lost only 2511 dead.

Despite the bitter cold, food rationing began in earnest in January 1940, when ration books were first issued: the weekly allowance for each person was four ounces of bacon or ham, four ounces of butter, and twelve ounces of sugar. Meat rationing began in March: each person was allowed 1s 10d worth of meat a week.

The harsh winter led to a shortage of coal, which in turn led to the cancellation of many passenger train services. An IRA bombing campaign that winter had caused explosions at Euston Station and in Oxford Street, which had done more damage in London than anything which the Germans had yet achieved.

* * *

In Hitchin, on December 11th 1939, Lieutenant-Colonel R.C. "Reggie" Keller took command of 3RTR. He would lead it into battle a few months later – but at the time, nothing could have looked more unlikely. The most taxing task which could be devised for his unit was a tactical exercise whilst *en route* to their new billets, at Fordingbridge in Hampshire. The move was scheduled for January 26th-27th, and Gunner was was one of those ordered to umpire the training which was to be conducted during the journey. There was an umpires' conference at the Pea Hen Hotel in St Albans, at 1400 on January 25th. The next day, 3RTR hit the road.

3RTR remembered Fordingbridge with affection for years afterwards. Each squadron of around 150 men was allocated its own complex of buildings in which to live and to park its vehicles. 'A' Squadron (commanded by Major R.H.O. "Simbo" Simpson) were billeted on the Greyhound Hotel; 'B' Squadron (under Major W.R. "Bill" Reeves) were billeted at 'Woodlands' in Sandleheath; 'C' Squadron (led by Major F.V. Lyons) were at 'Bowood' on the Boweswood Road. HQ Squadron occupied the Riverside Hotel, and were commanded by Gunner's friend Captain Toby Everett. As for the tanks themselves, these were conveniently parked outside the 'Load of Hay' pub on Station Road.[3]

The Medium Tanks were withdrawn, lamented by no one, and Gunner was posted to command a troop of light tanks:

> The tanks of the 'light' troops were the Light Tank VIb, which only had machine-guns. I was always 'A' Squadron, and I was always, at this period, right up to the desert, a troop leader in 4 Troop.

Above: a Light Tank VIb of the sort in which Gunner went to war in the early summer of 1940 (copyright holder unknown).

Gunner had other reasons to be fond of Fordingbridge. When the battalion had moved to the town, Keller had sent Gunner to search the area for some land suitable for use as a troop or squadron training area. Gunner spotted an area on the edge of the New Forest:

> On the map there seemed to be a big house with a large area of wild land at Blissford Pool. It belonged to a Mr Scott, who was an ex-headmaster, and the brother of the famous architect Giles Gilbert Scott, the designer of Liverpool Cathedral and Ampleforth Abbey. There was also a son – and a very pretty daughter, Pamela. I fell in love and took her out a lot – I knew she had another boyfriend in 3rd Hussars, but I had an advantage as I still had my car.

Pamela Scott was not only pretty but also talented. She was a student at the Royal College of Art's sculpture department, which was evacuated to Ambleside in 1940.

> She was a very good sculptor, and also a good horsewoman; she had her own horse with the Russian name "Andrushka."

Their relationship endured to the extent that Gunner wrote to her from Greece and the Middle East, and received letters from Pamela whilst he was a prisoner of war.

> She became a friend of my mother and helped her to send me the odd parcel. I'm sure that I loved her and would probably have asked her to marry me eventually. But in the end she married a pig-farmer from Romsey.

* * *

Meanwhile, Donny had spent a warmer winter in the Middle East, still serving with the staff at HQ British Troops in Egypt. He had returned home on leave in the summer of 1939, the last time that he saw his mother. His maternal cousins – Gervase, Tim and Christopher Yates, and their sister Myfanwy – remember meeting him when they returned from Ceylon just before the start of the war. But after Donny returned to the Middle East, he never saw his family again.

On December 1st 1939, he was transferred from his role as an Assistant Cipher Officer to become a General Staff Officer, Grade III (GSO3), a Captain's post – to which acting rank he was therefore promoted.

The war was then far away, but was not destined to remain so. On March 18th 1940, Mussolini and Hitler would meet in the Brenner Pass, where Mussolini would commit the still-neutral Italy to joining in the war on Germany's side at an as-yet unspecified "decisive hour". When this moment came and Italy finally entered the war, the Middle East would be the main arena in which the British would meet her, since Mussolini had previously carved out a small empire in Libya and east Africa. The British commander who would take on and trounce the Italians was General Sir Archibald Percival Wavell KCB, CMG, MC, perhaps the most distinguished Wykehamist of the Twentieth Century.[4]

On March 9th 1940 Wavell and other Wykehamists in Cairo assembled for a reunion dinner. Donny recorded the event in a letter to the school magazine:

> An Old Wykehamist Dinner was held at the Turf Club, Cairo, on Saturday, March 9th. Sir Frank Watson, KCMG, OBE, was in the Chair. The following were present:
>
> | | | |
> |---|---|---|
> | Sir Frank Watson, KCMG, OBE | F | 1892-97 |
> | General Sir Archibald Wavell, KCB, CMG, MC | Coll. | 1896-1900 |
> | A.E. Mills | I | 1898-1903 |
> | E.F.W. Besly | Coll. | 1905-10 |
> | Lieut.-Col. L. Monier-Williams | G | 1908-12 |
> | Lieut.-Col. I.D. Erskine | F | 1911-16 |
> | Major P.C.H. Grant | F | 1914-18 |
> | Major W.M. Leggatt | C | 1914-18 |
> | M.R. Wright | A | 1915-20 |
> | Captain C.D. Packard | E | 1917-20 |
> | Captain P.T.G. Lynden-Bell | A | 1919-23 |
> | R.V. Low | I | 1920-25 |
> | Captain J.T. Harington | D | 1923-27 |
> | Captain A.P.W. Hope | I | 1924-28 |
> | Captain H.A. Lascelles | A | 1925-30 |
> | Captain C.A.H.M. Noble | E | 1925-30 |
> | Captain D.C.B. Boyd | G | 1926-31 |
> | Pilot Officer N.M.H. Knowles | G | 1926-31 |
> | Captain W.G. Lowther | I | 1926-31 |
> | Hon. R.G.H. Phillimore | E | 1926-31 |
> | Captain G.W. White | H | 1926-31 |
> | Lieutenant R.E. Macdonnell | F | 1928-33 |
> | Captain A. D. Mackenzie | B | 1928-33 |
> | Pilot Officer W.N. Monteith | I | 1929-34 |
> | Lieutenant H.R. Woods | I | 1929-34 |
> | Lieutenant T.A. Bird | E | 1932-36 |
>
> Captain A.E.G. Haig (A, 1925-1930) was prevented from attending by illness.
>
> General Sir Archibald Wavell proposed the toast of the School which was drunk with acclamation. After a few words from Mr. Besly, hots were formed, but it was difficult to say who were victorious. Mr. A.E. Mills then produced a Commoner song book, and a most successful evening closed with the singing of "Drink, Puppy, Drink" and "Mr. John Blunt."[5]

By the time that he wrote this letter, Donny was attending the newly-opened Middle East Staff School in Haifa, which had been opened to provide staff training for officers unable to return to the Staff College in Camberley. Donny was part of the very first intake ("No.1 War Course") and began his staff training on March 18th. With him was another Wykehamist who had attended the dinner earlier that month, Major William Leggatt; it is testament to Donny's ability that he was on a course alongside this regular officer of over twenty years' service[6] – indeed, on relinquishing his appointment as GSO3 at HQ BTE, Donny had reverted to his lowly substantive rank of Lieutenant. Another student on the course was Captain David Belchem, who would serve alongside Donny in Greece the following year.[7]

The course lasted until June 29th, with fifteen weeks of lectures and practical exercises in all the tasks which a staff officer might be called upon to carry out. As well as producing copious amounts of practice paperwork, in May the students enjoyed visits to the Arab Legion's fort at Mafrak, the Allenby Bridge, Jerusalem, and Tel Aviv. They carried out a river-crossing exercise and a night operations exercise, inspected the Lysander army co-operation aircraft of 6 Squadron RAF, and watched a Royal Engineers demonstration at Kishon. On May 29th 1940 they flew to Heliopolis in Egypt in aged Valentia transports, before watching a demonstration by 'I' tanks – the famous 'Matildas' – and infantry at Gebel Kashab and an artillery demonstration at Gebel el Urfa. After a day's holiday in Cairo, they returned to Haifa by train on June 2nd.

On graduation, Donny returned to "regimental duty", in his case a brief stint with 2nd Camerons at Mena Camp near Cairo; he arrived on July 7th. On May 22nd, he had been appointed a Temporary Captain, probably in recognition of his merits whilst on the staff. He was considered too valuable to leave with his battalion, it seems: he departed for further staff duties on August 28th, being posted to HQ Mersa Matruh Area on September 1st as a GSO3. Over the next two years he would serve in Libya, Greece and Cyprus.

* * *

Below: *Donny Mackenzie, a picture probably taken in Palestine in 1940. His photograph albums from his time in Egypt are frustratingly thinly labelled, making it difficult to identify locations or those people whom he photographed (Mackenzie collection).*

Neither the British nor the French had any conception of the storm which was about to break. Indeed, on April 4th Neville Chamberlain announced in a speech that Hitler had "missed the bus" militarily, and could not now hope to win. By now, the Royal Air Force had dropped sixty-five million leaflets over Germany, a waste of aircraft, paper and, more importantly, trained aircrew. Meanwhile, on exercise in England on April 7th, Gunner celebrated his twenty-first birthday by cracking open a bottle of Lanson champagne as he sheltered from the snow under his tank. His family still possess the cork (below).

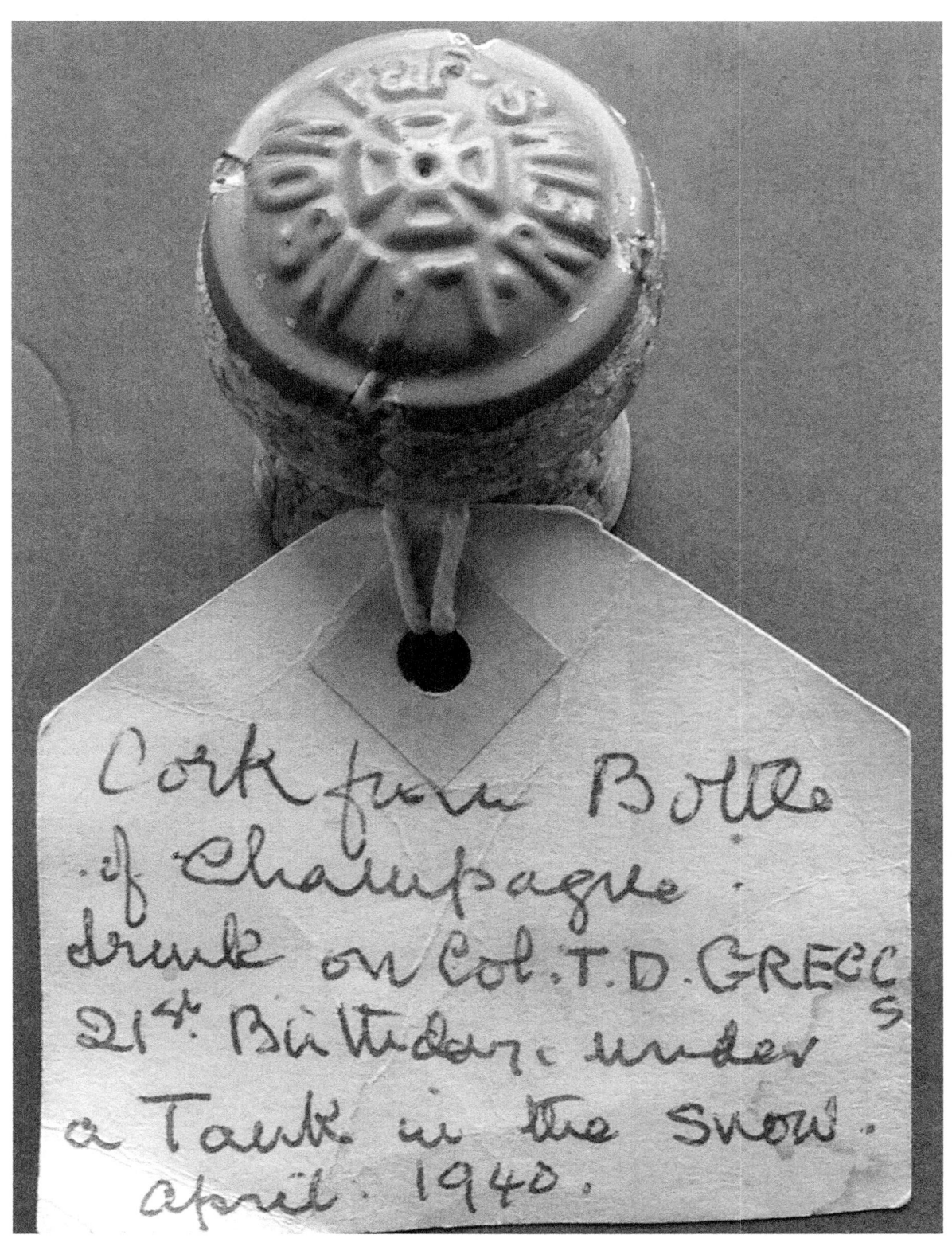

But the war was about to become a great deal more serious. On April 9th German forces invaded Norway, installing the Norwegian Fascist Vidkun Quisling as their puppet in place of King Haakon. At the same time, they invaded Denmark, thus securing their grip on the Baltic. Fierce naval battles took place in Norwegian waters between British and German vessels over the following week, and on April 14th British troops landed to support the Norwegian defenders. The British enjoyed initial success, and for a while it seemed that the German invasion might not only be halted but even driven back.

But by the beginning of May the evacuation of British troops had begun, a pattern to become familiar across the globe in the years to follow. Dunkirk, Greece, Crete, Malaya, Singapore, Burma – two years of humiliating retreat and bungling, interspersed with many a false dawn of victory. Flushed with his success in Norway, at the beginning of May Hitler authorized an attack on Belgium, Holland and France. His intention was to feint into Belgium, which he knew would draw the BEF forward into that country; he would then launch an armoured strike through the Ardennes, avoiding France's vaunted Maginot Line, and thrust for the Channel coast, splitting the British and French forces apart.

On May 7th, Neville Chamberlain faced angry opponents in the House of Commons, dissatisfied with his conduct of the war and in particular the Norwegian debacle. In a two-day debate, Admiral Sir Roger Keyes, the MP for Portsmouth North, poured scorn on the conduct of the campaign. The MP Leo Amery concluded his speech with Cromwell's famous words to the Long Parliament:

> You have sat here too long for any good you are doing. Depart, I say, and let us have done with you. In the name of God, go.

Chamberlain narrowly survived the vote, but then came the shattering news of the German invasion of Belgium, Holland and France on May 10th. Chamberlain resigned, and advised the King to let Winston Churchill try to form a government. In his resignation wireless broadcast, Chamberlain announced that

> the hour has now come when we are to be put to the test, as the innocent people of Holland, Belgium, and France are being tested already. And you, and I, must rally behind our new leader, and with our united strength, and with unshakable courage, fight and work until this wild beast, which has sprung out of his lair upon us, has been finally disarmed and overthrown.

On Monday May 13th Churchill made his first appearance in the House of Commons as Prime Minister in a new coalition government. Already the French were being out-fought and great gaps being torn in their lines; Churchill, at least, appreciated the seriousness of the situation, and declared that

> I have nothing to offer but blood, toil, tears and sweat.

The following day, the War Office announced the formation of the Local Defence Volunteers (better known as the Home Guard), to be made up of males between the ages of seventeen and sixty-five. Back in Winchester, Donny's old housemaster, the Jacker, bitter from his experiences of the British retreat before the German 1918 spring offensive, was full of "gloomy comment."

The Dutch surrendered on May 15th, after sixty bombers had flattened the centre of Rotterdam in an attempt to persuade them to capitulate more quickly. The French were in disarray, the inhabitants of Paris fleeing south in their thousands, and their premier telephoned Churchill that day to announce that "We are beaten; we have lost the battle."

German forces entered Brussels on May 17th, as the BEF pulled back from its advanced line in Belgium, now in terrible peril of being outflanked. The German attack into France had quickly forced a giant wedge between the BEF in northern France and Belgium and French forces to the south. By May 21st German troops had reached the Channel coast at the mouth of the Somme, and the BEF was in imminent danger of annihilation. German plans were in train to occupy Calais, Boulogne and Dunkirk, cutting the retreating British forces off from rescue. The German 1st Panzer Division was ordered to make for Dunkirk; 2nd Panzer Division was committed to the attack on Boulogne, which was defended by 20 Guards Brigade. Boulogne fell on May 25th, though its defenders had been successfully evacuated by sea. 10th Panzer Division headed for Calais.

Looking at a map, it was clear that Calais was a vital position if the western flank of the Dunkirk perimeter was not to be rolled up. At Gravelines, a programme of flooding was being undertaken which might stop the German tanks if given time enough to spread – but if that were to be possible, then Calais would have to distract the Germans for as long as possible. But the only troops which the British government had immediately to hand for the defence of Calais were the three infantry battalions of 30 Infantry Brigade, commanded by Brigadier Claude Nicholson:[8] the brigade had been formed only on April 20th, for service in Norway. In support of 30 Brigade, the government decided to send Gunner and his comrades in 3RTR.

Above: *Gunner and two fellow 3RTR officers just days before they went to France, laughing and smiling in the garden of their billet in Fordingbridge. Of the three men, only one would return from Calais (Gregg collection).*

Seated in the chair in Captain Toby Everett; standing is Lieutenant Hugo Ironside. Of the two, Gunner stated:

Captain Toby Everett was a Regular officer a few years older than myself, and was in command of HQ Squadron.[1] His father was I think Governor of Exeter Prison. Hugo Ironside was another Regular, just senior to me. Field Marshal Lord Ironside was a distant relation of his. Hugo was the battalion Intelligence Officer; among his duties was keeping, with the Adjutant, the 3RTR war diary.[2] He became a very good friend, and his parents were very good friends of my mother; they used to make up parcels together when we were prisoners-of-war.[3]

Toby and Hugo Ironside were both captured. Hugo ended up in Colditz – after the war he did very well and ended up as a Brigadier. But after Calais I never saw Toby again.

Chapter Five
Calais

Even by May 1940, Gunner's battalion was still not ready for combat. One third of its strength had been posted away in April to form a new unit, and had been replaced by personnel straight from training. Teams formed during peacetime now had to incorporate newcomers: relationships had to be forged, weaknesses and strengths assessed, tank crews welded together. But 3RTR seemed to have plenty of time to restore itself to high efficiency: earmarked as part of 1st Armoured Division, it was to work up in Normandy at the Pacy-sur-Eure training-grounds.

Despite the shocking news of the German invasion of France on May 10th, 3RTR continued to make preparations to travel to Normandy. On May 19th, the battalion sent its tanks down to Southampton for loading on to the *City of Christchurch*.[4] Staff officers clung to peace-time procedures, demanding that the vehicles be fully stripped down before embarkation, as Trooper Bill Jordan ('B' Squadron) recalled:

> All petrol had to be drained from them into two-gallon cans; all .303 machine-guns were removed from their mountings and covered in mineral jelly and placed in their boxes.[5]

The tanks were loaded first, as they were the heaviest: 3RTR had twenty-one Light Tanks Mark VIb and twenty-seven cruiser tanks of the three models. Above them were stowed support vehicles – trucks and scout-cars. The petrol was stacked on deck in seven thousand flimsy cans.[6] At this stage 3RTR were expecting to embark their personnel for Normandy on May 23rd – but it would not be until June 16th 1944 that 3RTR would reach Normandy, under very different circumstances.

The immediate crisis in France had now expanded to include them. At the War Office, on May 21st, General Morris[7] summoned Major "Bob" Foote, an RTR officer on his staff,[8] and asked him which unit of 1st Armoured Division was most imminently bound for France. Foote – whose career intersected several times with that of both Gunner and Donny, as we shall see – replied that 3RTR were at readiness to move. He received orders to divert them to Calais, as he later recalled:

> It had been decided to send a tank unit as quickly as possible to Calais to reinforce the Rifle Brigade in case Calais was threatened by the German advance. I was to motor down that night to Dover and tell Colonel Keller of the change of plans. I realized that the unit would not have any maps of the area, so I went round to the map depot and got a bundle of maps to give him at Dover. In the meantime, two movements had been arranged for the trains and ship to be diverted, and I set off by car to drive through the night to Dover.[9]

* * *

3RTR's carefree times at Fordingbridge ended on the evening of May 21st. Orders reached Battalion HQ that 3RTR were to depart at 2200 that same night. It was impossible to comply. Keller was enjoying a farewell dinner with his wife in Bournemouth. A telephone call at 2000 brought him rushing back to Fordingbridge, but his men were scattered across the local area bidding farewell to friends and family. Pubs were cleared, and emergency recall notices were flashed on to the screens of the Salisbury cinemas.

> We were told at a moment's notice that we were going to France or Belgium. Toby, Hugo and I were together when we were told that we had to take a train to catch the ferry at Dover the next day. It all happened in a great hurry.

By little short of a miracle, the train taking 3RTR to war moved off at midnight, only ten men and one officer short. Gunner and Ironside had just had time to tell their loved ones that they were leaving:

> Hugo's *fiancée* came down to see him off; my mother, who was in England then, came to see us off. I remember her there at the little station in Fordingbridge, waving us goodbye. We went by train to Dover, and got off onto the ferry-boat without our tanks.

As Keller arrived in Dover at 0500, he was met on the station platform by

> a Junior Staff Officer from the War Office, Major Foote... with a bundle of maps and a letter addressed to the Senior British Commander Calais, who could not be ascertained.[10]

Foote had no clear orders for Keller, except to make contact with the HQ of the BEF – then believed to be in Hazebrouck – and ask what they would like him to do. Such vague instructions hardly inspired confidence, and it is not surprising that Keller vented his frustration on Foote:

> [Keller] was very angry and wanted to know what the hell was happening and where his tanks were. I explained the situation and gave him the last intelligence reports I had received before leaving London. I told him that his tanks would arrive in Calais that morning. He pointed out that all his tank guns were in mineral jelly and it would take at least a day to clean and zero them.[11]

Foote informed Keller that the nearest German tanks were at St Pol, fifty miles south of Calais. Like much of the information reaching London at the time, this was some twenty-four to forty-eight hours behind events; the War Office's intelligence was completely out of date and their assessment of German strength and movements hopelessly inaccurate. German tanks were in fact preparing to attack Boulogne, only twenty miles south-west of Calais, and were also advancing on St Omer, some twenty-five miles south-east of Calais What Keller needed more than anything else was time; but the essence of German strategy was to give the enemy no time to plan or even to think.

Meanwhile, the three infantry battalions of 30 Brigade were also *en route* for Calais: the regular 1st Rifle Brigade (1RB) and 2nd King's Royal Rifle Corps (2KRRC), and the Territorial 1st Queen Victoria's Rifles (1QVR). Like 3RTR, they were rushed, and staff officers hampered their attempts to embark what they needed for the mobile warfare in which they had been trained. Gris Davies-Scourfield – of 'B' Company, 2KRRC – had been at Winchester (in Toye's with Donny) and plays an important part in Gunner's narrative of Calais.[12] As a prisoner-of-war, he would go on to be one of the greatest thorns in the side of the Germans, and would end up in Colditz with Ironside. Davies-Scourfield recalled the frustrations of May 22nd:

> In Southampton staff officers relieved us of all maps, and stuck labels on the vehicles. We moved on and halted under some trees close to the High Street. Here more staff officers ordered us to dismount and remove all personal kit, which would then be driven to the docks for loading on to ships... I spent the

rest of the day trying to get my [Bren-gun] carriers on the vehicle ship.[13] It was a lengthy and trying business, mainly because of the continual orders and counter-orders from the embarkation staff.[14]

He had an ominous conversation with one of these staff:

"I suppose you're pretty busy right now," I remarked chattily. "Plenty of people sailing and all that."
"Not many sailing," he replied, and, lowering his voice, added, "but there'll be plenty coming home. The regiment's going the wrong way, if you ask me."[15]

* * *

The officers and men of 3RTR arrived in Dover at 0700 on May 22nd, immediately boarded the Southern Railways vessel *Maid of Orleans*,[16] and set sail at 1100. Once at sea, the men received their orders, as Sergeant Bill Close later remembered:

Our tanks will be delivered there, and you will prepare them for action immediately. Light enemy forces have broken through somewhere to the north. We will find them and deal with them.[17]

There was thick mist as the ship arrived at Calais and tied up alongside the *Gare Maritime* at 1315. The battalion had no idea where its tanks were. As the men disembarked, personnel on the quayside were anxious to board; all non-essential troops were being evacuated. The British units in the Calais area were mostly air-defence troops; there was no artillery and no anti-tank guns. The town was reeling from German air attack, as Major Bill Reeves (OC 'B' Squadron) later recalled:

I tried to reconcile the peacetime Calais with that it looked like now. The glass from the windows of the Customs House and restaurants was strewn all over the quayside and railway platforms. Black smoke was belching forth from most of the quayside buildings and warehouses, and the whole area was pretty-well pock-marked with bomb-craters.[18]

Foote had given Keller a letter for the senior British officer in Calais, but it took Keller an hour to find him – he turned out to be a Colonel Holland, who was in touch by telephone and radio with London.[19] He was tired – Calais had been bombed on the previous two nights – but welcoming, and ordered Keller to unload at once and wait for instructions from GHQ. Luckily, *City of Christchurch* had just arrived, and the process of unloading 3RTR's tanks, ammunition and petrol could begin. Keller could only bemoan the appalling way in which the loading had been conducted:

It was found that the tank ship was loaded as follows: on deck, seven thousand gallons of tinned petrol; under hatches, all the transport; and, at the bottom of the ship, the tanks. This meant that the tanks would not be available in any numbers until about midday the following day. A truly disastrous state of affairs.[20]

As Keller gave the necessary orders, at around 1600, a senior officer from GHQ appeared: Lieutenant-General Sir Douglas Brownrigg, Adjutant-General of the BEF.[21] Like Holland, he was tired; out of his depth (he retired on July 1st), he was being evacuated from Calais, but paused long enough to give Keller definite orders. Keller was to move his tanks towards Boulogne and make contact with 20 Guards Brigade there. What Brownrigg and Keller did not know was that as they spoke, 2nd *Panzer* Division was launching its assault on the Guards Brigade, and 1st *Panzer* Division was moving towards Calais. Keller's orders were already obsolete.

It took all night to unload the *City of Christchurch*. Whenever the air-raid siren sounded, the French dock workers ran for shelter. At 2100 they and the ship's crew went on strike, and Major Mahoney (Second-in-Command of 3RTR) had to place the sailors under armed arrest. Power to the dockyard cranes was cut at 2100: when unloading resumed at 0130 on May 23rd, it had to be carried out using the ship's own derricks.

The battalion assembled piecemeal at Ramceau Farm, one mile south of Coquelles, on the Boulogne road, some two miles south-west of Calais. Their tanks were far from ready for combat. All the machine-guns had to be de-greased and fitted back into their mountings – but vital pieces were missing. Many of the radios lacked parts and would not work. There were no high-explosive shells for the howitzers on the close-support tanks – only smoke. The machine-gun ammunition was loose, and needed to be fitted into belts before firing. 3RTR were going to have a busy night.

Gunner long recalled the frustrations of finding his tanks so ill-prepared for battle:

> The Light Tanks had an ordinary .303 machine-gun, virtually no armour, and no radios. I mean, how can you operate a tank without a radio? You depend on it; it's your life-blood. But there were no radios. Everything was covered in grease; all our machine-guns were boxed. We moved off and went into a little wood just south-west of Calais, and we spent a chaotic night stinking of petrol, wiping the gunge free, putting the guns in, seeing that they'd fire, and so on – trying to make our tanks and machine-guns usable.

One of his comrades, Second Lieutenant Quentin Carpendale, also remembered that night's surreal quality:

> I remember the crews sitting on the sands thumbing rounds of ammunition into belts, and thinking this was the most extraordinary way to go to war.[22]

* * *

Meanwhile, Keller's orders had changed. As night had fallen on May 22nd, a second staff officer (a Major Bailey) had arrived from BEF Headquarters. His orders flatly contradicted Brownrigg's instructions to help the Guards at Boulogne. Instead of heading south-west, 3RTR were to move south-east towards St Omer, to prevent the Germans from crossing the Aa Canal. At 0100 Keller sent out a patrol of light tanks to find out what was happening in St Omer. The tanks were from 'A' Squadron, as their commander, Major "Simbo" Simpson, later reported:

> This [patrol] consisted of Second Lieutenant Mundy with No.2 Troop. I also detailed a patrol of three light tanks under Second Lieutenant Paul to report to the CO. These patrols moved off under orders of the CO, and I proceeded with all the remaining light tanks and scout cars that were off the ship to La Beussingue Farm. Second Lieutenant Mundy's patrol got through to St Omer and re-joined about 0400 hours 23rd May. Second Lieutenant Paul's troop re-joined just before that, and tanks gradually came out from Calais in driblets as they came off the ship.[23]

Mundy's patrol found St Omer deserted and in flames.

At 0300 a radio message from Brownrigg confirmed Keller's earlier orders to make for Boulogne. Faced with such contradictory instructions, Keller had to decide for himself what he should do. He sent another patrol to St Omer to re-assess the position there, as Simpson explains:

> About 0800 hours I received orders to send a light tank troop to escort Major Bailey (GHQ) to St Omer, where he believed GHQ to be. I ordered Second Lieutenant Eastman, with No.3 Troop (consisting of three light tanks) to do this. About half an hour after they moved off, I received a wireless

message from Second Lieutenant Eastman to say they didn't know where Major Bailey had got to, and asked me what to do. I told him, if he could not find Major Bailey at once, to proceed on to St Omer and get in touch with GHQ, which I understood from Major Bailey was essential in order to report the situation. I informed my CO that I had done this. About half an hour after this, Major Bailey turned up, having taken the wrong road and been wounded.[24]

Only one tank from Eastman's troop made it back, the other two being knocked out by stiff German opposition. The wounded Bailey nevertheless insisted that Keller take 3RTR south to St Omer. When reports reached Keller that German tanks were now advancing eastwards, south of Calais, he decided to try to break through them to St Omer. Such a move was pointless, but he had no way of knowing that.

* * *

At 1415 on May 23rd, 3RTR advanced into battle, not knowing that the rest of the BEF was in retreat. Five of the battalion's forty-eight tanks were still on the docks at Calais. 'B' Squadron led the way south from Coquelles, 'C' Squadron and Battalion HQ behind them, and 'A' Squadron at the rear. Because of the chaos at Calais docks, the squadrons had become mixed up. Squadron commanders had assembled whatever vehicles came off the ship and taken them off to prepare for battle – indeed, tank crews had been allocated almost at random, as a member of 'C' Squadron later explained:

> When we were assigned to tanks in Calais, my tank commander was Lieutenant "Ginger" Moir [another good friend of Gunner]... But it was a piecemeal operation. We were stood along the dock-side, the tanks came off the ship, and it was a case of "Gunner? You. Driver? You. Commander? You." I think it was a matter of luck whether you became a cruiser or a light tank crew.[25]

'A' Squadron went into battle with nine tanks in three troops composed of vehicles and men from all three squadrons. Gunner's three tanks – No.4 Troop – were at the front, and Gunner was in the leading tank.

> We drove off on the St Omer road. It was all hand-signals – advance, and all the rest of it – but no radio. My No.4 Troop was point troop. The road was crowded with disorganized groups of French and Belgian troops, mostly without their arms. We passed thousands of refugees, Belgians and Dutch, all sorts of people, all a rabble who'd thrown away their arms, not in uniform.
> I was on a crossroads, looking forwards, and a company of Pioneers, labour troops, most of whom were pretty old soldiers, came in dressed properly, with their arms; they were singing, they were marching in step, and of course they stopped there and gave me a terrific cheer. And they asked "What are you doing? We've had orders to go to Boulogne. And we were told we had to march." I was so proud of them, I really was, because they were the only people that had stayed as a proper unit. They just took it as natural.

3RTR had only gone about two miles, through St Tricat, when they encountered the enemy south of the village of Hames-Boucres. Assault Group Kruger of 1st *Panzer* Division were crossing 3RTR's front from west to east, but owing to heavy rain they had halted in the shelter of some woods.

'B' Squadron were the first to bump the enemy. The squadron had three light tanks, three cruiser tanks, and Squadron HQ (two A9s fitted with close-support howitzers). They were at first unsure what they had found, reporting to Keller that there were French or German vehicles halted on the road ahead of them. The Germans reacted first, rushing to unlimber anti-tank guns and opening fire. According to Carpendale, he was so close to the enemy when the fighting began that a German officer fired his pistol at him.

Keller immediately ordered 'A' Squadron to swing into action on the western flank, as Simpson recalled:

> When I was roughly about St Tricat, I heard 'B' Squadron reporting enemy armoured cars and light tanks. I then realized we must have run into a fairly large column. I was called to come on and get my tanks into action. I went on and got into action on the road running south-west from Hames Boucres.[26]

As Gunner's tanks accelerated towards the enemy, Gunner came under enemy fire for the first time:

> When I went round a corner of a barn we suddenly came under fire. Two holes appeared in the wall just above me. We had speaking-tubes in those things, not an intercom. "Driver, reverse!" I screamed. I didn't have to tell him twice. We pulled back and took up fire positions on each side of the barn, and we were being fired at by tank guns, 50mm at least. All we could see of the Germans was gun-flashes from a wood. We returned the fire.

The German *Panzer* III carried a 50mm gun, which was bigger than anything carried by any British tank of the day. Had Gunner been driving a cruiser tank, he would at least have had a 2-pounder gun capable of destroying a German tank; but his Mark VIb had nothing heavier than machine-guns. The cruiser tanks of 'B' Squadron were nearby, however:

> Barry O'Sullivan, second Captain in 'B' Squadron, had only just arrived back in England from commanding a Company of armoured cars on the North-West Frontier. He'd joined us at Fordingbridge, but been left behind when we boarded the train for Dover. He caught us up just before we sailed. As we were going along, he'd taken up a position in a cruiser tank about three hundred yards to my left.[27]

O'Sullivan was in a close-support version of the A9, which was fitted with a howitzer for which he had no ammunition except smoke-shells; the two hull machine-guns would not fit back into their mountings when the tank was being got ready for action the night before (though they had been jury-rigged to fire anyway). None of his radios were working. O'Sullivan described what happened when they encountered the Germans that morning:

> I saw a large mechanized force advancing up the main Calais road. The German tanks halted on the road in position behind trees. We were deployed on the fields advancing towards them. The enemy had superior fire-power over our three or four cruisers. We concentrated our machine-guns on the enemy lorries.[28]

The action lasted some thirty-five minutes, during the course of which Gunner's light tanks helped to knock out the German lorries and block the road. But the weight of German fire began to tell, and Gunner's vehicles were forced to retire. Meanwhile, O'Sullivan's cruisers knocked out two German medium tanks and two light tanks before his own vehicle was crippled, as Gunner saw:

> Most of the fire which would have come against me continued against Barry's tank, which unfortunately was hit and immobilized – I heard and saw it. His crew were all killed, and he was badly wounded, but he kept loading and firing back, which was an incredibly brave thing to do.

O'Sullivan described his role more modestly:

> My A9 was hit by a 2-pounder shell which smashed its off-side suspension and track. We swung broadside to the enemy, and crawled down a bank into a well-camouflaged hull-down position. The suspension was damaged beyond repair, and the tank settled into the marshy ground.[29]

O'Sullivan left his two unwounded crewmen firing their machine-gun whilst he went to find Keller, who informed him that he was sending in more tanks. O'Sullivan returned to his A9 to provide covering fire for the attack.

> Two light tanks and a cruiser subsequently appeared, but were all knocked out within a few minutes – though not before the cruiser had knocked out a further enemy cruiser tank... The Germans were using both anti-tank guns and the guns of the tanks... For ten minutes after seeing the Colonel we continued to engage the enemy before the off-side front-turret machine-gun was put out of action by two hits, the gunner Brown being wounded. I was at this moment on top of the tank engaged in getting out the third machine-gun which, owing to the angle at which the tank was stuck, could not be brought to bear on the enemy otherwise.
>
> For a further five minutes I fired this machine-gun from the top of the tank, till German troops who had infiltrated through the woods on either side of us opened fire with anti-tank guns at six hundred yards range. I therefore dismounted this machine-gun from the top of the tank and found a gap in the fence some fifteen yards away from the tank from which to deal with this threat. Whilst engaged in this and in getting ammunition boxes out, with four members of the crew of six, Galbraith and Price were firing the machine-gun co-axially mounted with the mortar [howitzer]...
>
> The two light tanks with me were both by now knocked out and appeared deserted, and the A13 cruiser was on fire... There was no sign of the battalion reappearing, and I judged by the shelling that they had met heavy opposition... Twenty minutes had now elapsed since I had seen Colonel Keller when two shells hit the tank in quick succession, putting both the smoke mortar and the machine-gun mounted with it out of action, and killing two of the crew manning them.[30]
>
> We now had only the machine-gun on the bank... We continued to engage the enemy for a further ten to twelve minutes and silenced the fire of one anti-tank gun in the wood.[31]

O'Sullivan now decided to extricate his surviving crew-members, but did not make it back to 3RTR. Instead, he linked up with searchlight troops at the crossroads at Les Attaques. When the Germans arrived, O'Sullivan was captured after some more fierce fighting. He took the opportunity to spread disinformation which may have delayed the German advance on Calais:

> As soon as the Germans found that he was a Tank Corps officer, they were much interested and could barely hide their excitement. It was soon clear to him that he was the first tank officer they had captured. They were particularly anxious to know two things: details of a large and powerful tank which they had heard we had kept very secret; and whether the whole of 1st Armoured Division had been landed at Calais. O'Sullivan obliged on both points. He told them the whole of the Armoured Division was at Calais, and that the new monster tank had been issued to it; he himself was not familiar with it in detail as he had but recently returned from India.[32]

For the time being, however, Gunner and his comrades had no idea what had happened to O'Sullivan.

> We found out years later that he'd been taken prisoner, but escaped from a prison hospital in Poland. He managed to travel across Poland, Germany and France to Spain, and, through Gibraltar, returned to England, where he had lunch with the King to tell him his story – as he did with Churchill.

In fact, O'Sullivan's story had been even more dramatic: returning from Gibraltar in May 1942, he was aboard HMS *Wild Swan* when it was sunk by German bombers; he spent two days in an open boat before being rescued. It is no wonder that those who de-briefed him on his return to England described him as depressed and nervous.

* * *

The German forces around Calais had already been surprised by the strength of the opposition which they had encountered on May 23rd: 3RTR's advance had seriously threatened 1st *Panzer* Division's flanks, and the stand made by the searchlight troops at Les Attaques had probably delayed the enemy by around five hours.

Meanwhile, unknown to Keller, 30 Infantry Brigade was arriving in Calais, under Brigadier Nicholson. The orders given to Nicholson at Dover were as unclear and out-of-date as Keller's:

> Some German tanks, with artillery, were moving in the direction of Boulogne from the east. The general situation was obscure... 30th Infantry Brigade would land either at Calais or Dunkirk and would then be used, probably with 3rd Royal Tank Regiment, to act offensively against the German columns. 229 Anti-Tank Battery RA would join the Brigade at Calais.[33]

Later, Nicholson was told to relieve Boulogne as quickly as possible. Nicholson ordered 1RB and 2KRRC to move into the Calais dunes to assemble; both were then to advance to cover the Calais-Boulogne road. 1QVR were already ashore and involved in skirmishing with the Germans.

The final elements of 30 Brigade reached Calais on the afternoon of May 23rd. With them were the eight 2-pounder anti-tank guns of 229 Battery.[34] Disembarkation began in earnest at around 1700, and as the infantrymen unloaded their vehicles and equipment, they began to find out more about the position in which they found themselves, as Davies-Scourfield remembered:

> Some administrative personnel from Third Tanks also appeared, and one of them, Douggie Moir, who had been at Sandhurst with me, suddenly greeted me with "So you're in this party too." He told me that a big tank battle was in progress south of the town, and he was desperately trying to get up supplies of petrol.[35]

Nicholson set out to acquaint himself with the area and the local circumstances. It soon became clear that any offensive mission was unfeasible. He decided instead to hold Calais as best he could, using the line of the Nineteenth Century ramparts and moats which surrounded it. 2KRRC would hold the western perimeter, from Bastion 11 to Bastion 8. 1RB would hold the east and north-east, from Bastion 1 to Bastion 4. 1QVR and other units slotted in on the north (between Bastions 11 and 12) and south-east (between Bastions 8 and 4). A fall-back line was provided by canals which surrounded the Old Town. The line of the ramparts was too long for the units available – some eight miles – and without artillery Nicholson's men were at a huge disadvantage. To bolster his defence, Nicholson badly needed the tanks of 3RTR. He set out to find them.[36]

*　*　*

3RTR were still in contact with 1st *Panzer* Division and trying to extricate themselves from the *melée* which had followed their attempt to break through to St Omer. Keller attempted to control the battle from his tank, but not all his subordinates were on the radio net, and so they were unable to hear his shouts of

> Why aren't you firing at the bastards?[37]

This was far from correct radio voice procedure.

3RTR was down to a total of only eighteen tanks – they had been forced to abandon several light tanks and cruisers disabled on the field of battle – and Keller and his men now had to try to break contact and retire to Point 63, just south of Coquelles. They were not even aware that they were under Nicholson's command. When Nicholson tried to contact Keller at around 1630 that day, he was given short shrift, as Keller noted:

> OC 'B' Echelon on air *re* a Brigadier Nicholson unknown to Commander 3RTR. Thought to be fresh GHQ orders. Replied middle of battle. What does he want? Put on air. Nicholson refused to talk, asked for map reference. Given and stated would come to see commander.[38]

Keller's actual words are alleged to have been:

> Get off the air. I'm trying to fight a bloody battle.

Nicholson finally met up with Keller at 2000, and informed him that 3RTR was under his command and required for the defence of Calais. Keller passed on the message through his squadron commanders, as Gunner recalled:

> "We've got orders to go back." So we turned round and drove back to Calais.

Even now, however, higher command had not grasped Nicholson's position, ordering him to escort a convoy to Dunkirk carrying 350,000 sets of rations for the BEF there: Keller was to provide tanks to accompany the convoy. Nicholson met Keller again at 2300 at the Pont St Pierre to discuss the convoy mission and other patrols. However, it was now far too late for major offensive action, as proven by a patrol from 'B' Squadron which set out towards Gravelines that night. The patrol consisted of three light tanks and one A13, commanded by Major Bill Reeves. They managed by stealth and luck to pass right through the positions of 1st *Panzer* Division astride the Gravelines road (the Germans were exhausted by their lightning advance across France), and reached Gravelines at around 0200, but the patrol was then cut off and had to fight a fierce little action later in the morning, knocking out five German tanks and two armoured troop-carriers.

30 Brigade's position as Friday 24th May began was unclear, but unenviable. At Boulogne, some of 20 Guards Brigade were already in the process of evacuation, and at 0300 Nicholson was informed that, in principle, the same had been decided for 30 Brigade. The soundness of such a decision seemed to be underlined by the failure of the convoy to Dunkirk, which left between 0400 and 0500, led by Major Lyons and five tanks of 'C' Squadron, but was forced to return by 1100. Keller passed on Nicholson's assessment of the position to his own officers:

> Calais is surrounded. Heavy bombing is expected tonight and a powerful attack will probably be put in in the morning.

Nicholson was correct. By now Calais was indeed surrounded, and the Germans were poised to attack from the west. Fortunately for the British, their main opponents were now 10th *Panzer* Division. At full strength, this unit had two hundred tanks, but after its long advance it was down to half strength, and the troops were exhausted. Its commander was also concerned by Allied air attack, which had plagued his advance, but ordered 90th *Panzer* Regiment to advance on Calais from the west, supported by artillery and the infantry of 86th Rifle Regiment. Meanwhile, 69th Rifle Regiment would attack from Guines, south-west of Calais.

3RTR and 30 Brigade would spend that day fighting for their lives. On their courage and slender resources would hang the fate of hundreds of thousands of men – and, perhaps, the outcome of the whole war.

* * *

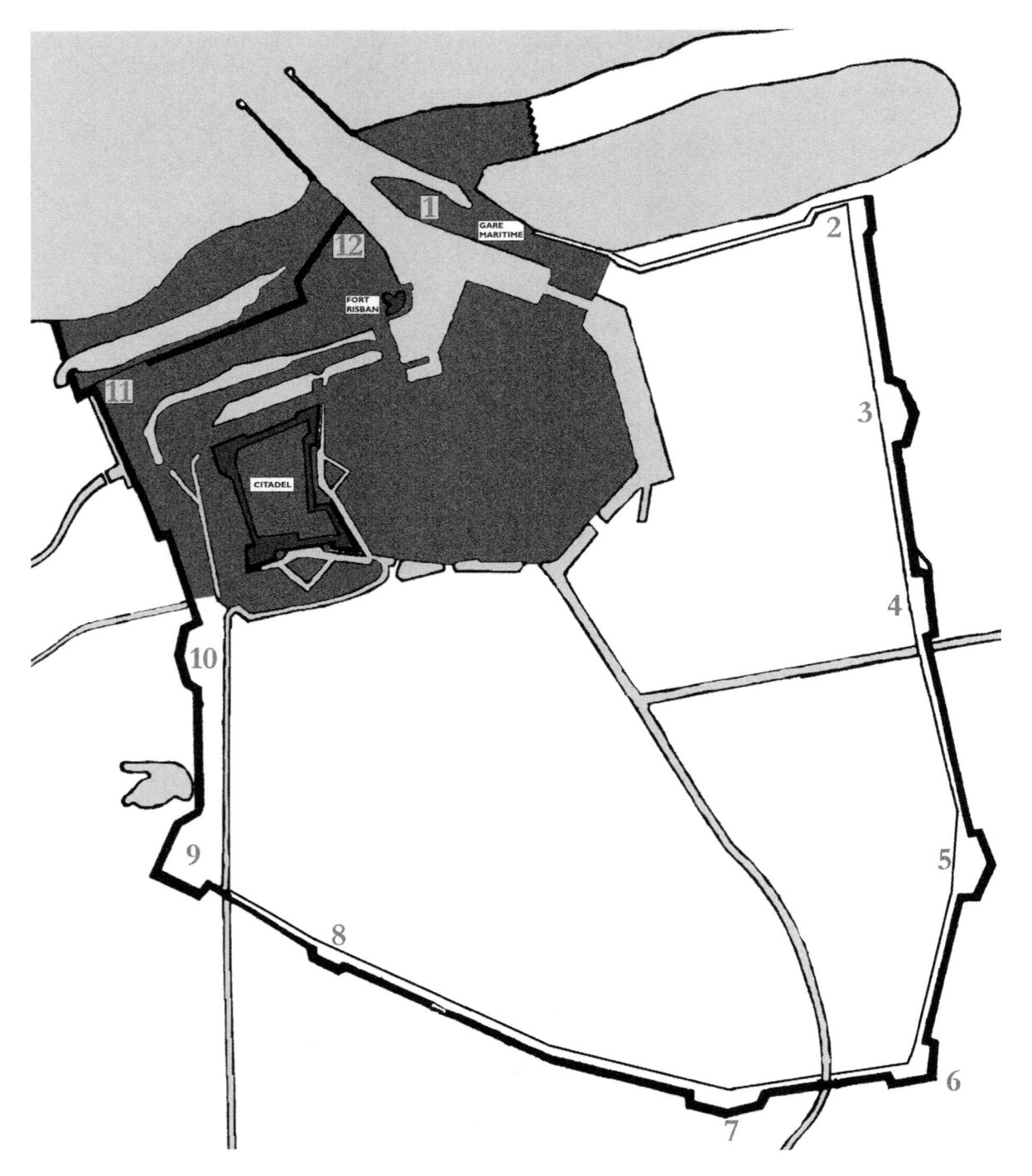

Above: a sketch-map showing the canals and old ramparts surrounding Calais. The bastions are labelled 1-12 and mark the original outer perimeter held by the defenders; Gunner was at Bastion 9. The dark shading represents the rough area of the inner perimeter to which the defenders retreated after the first day's fighting (author, after Cooksey).

Whilst the rest of 3RTR prepared for their re-supply escort task, however, Gunner and his troop of light tanks had been allocated a vital defensive mission in support of 2KRRC on the western side of the town.

> The Adjutant, and Hugo who was Intelligence Officer, came and said: "You're going to be detached. Second 60th[39] desperately want tank support, and you're to take your troop to the Boulogne gate and assist the infantry there." I was to join up with Second Lieutenant Davies-Scourfield's platoon of 'B' Company, Second 60th, and with him defend the entrance to the city. We were also given a portee 2-pounder anti-tank gun in charge of a Sergeant of 229 Anti-Tank Battery RA.

Davies-Scourfield had already had a busy morning, as his battalion had sent out several patrols in Bren-gun carriers, which had suffered casualties. He had taken one man down to the docks to 3RTR's medical post, and there had met one of Gunner's friends:

> Near the docks I found a familiar face under a Tank Corps beret; Toby Everett's. He had been my first Senior Under-Officer at Sandhurst, and we exchanged friendly greetings.
> The docks themselves, when I got there, were in a real mess: there had been more shelling, or possibly bombing; debris lay everywhere, and several buildings were blazing fiercely. It was all rather dramatic and exciting.[40]

When Davies-Scourfield returned to 'B' Company on the western perimeter, he was told to take up position on one of the old ramparts of the town, known as Bastion 9, just south of where the Boulogne road entered the town. He had a mixture of men from 6 and 7 platoons of 'B' Company, with his own Scout Platoon with Bren-gun carriers in reserve. He considered his position an excellent one:

> It lay immediately on the left of the main road to the village of Coquelles, and beyond it to Boulogne, and overlooked all approaches from that direction... It had concrete blocks along it at intervals, with plenty of cover from scrubby bushes, as well as from the blocks themselves... Digging was fairly easy, and if we had had some mines and wire, some artillery to provide defensive fire, and a weapon with some chance of destroying a German medium tank, then the Redoubt could have become a formidable strong-point... This promised to be a beautiful day – weather-wise, at least – and as we set about improving our positions, my spirits rose... There was a sublime confidence that we were about to give the Germans, coming along the road towards us, a very bloody nose.[41]

As Davies-Scourfield and his men dug in, refugees and stragglers flooded in. The defenders noted with disgust that whilst the exhausted British anti-aircraft gunners and searchlight troops immediately offered to help, French troops simply kept moving. Some French troops at Calais fought to the last, but not at Bastion 9.

Shells began to fall randomly around the defences, doing no damage but forcing the defenders to stay in cover. A patrol of Davies-Scourfield's Scout Platoon returned in tatters, having bumped into strong opposition outside the town and having lost two out of three Bren-gun carriers and eight casualties. Gradually the German pressure increased, until at 1100 German infantry burst from the woods in front of 'D' Company to the south. They were driven off, but then began to infiltrate more cautiously towards the British positions. Around noon, German tanks appeared, as Davies-Scourfield recalled:

> I watched fascinated, and I am sure the eyes of us all were on them, while what seemed to be a squadron of medium tanks slowly deployed into two long lines. Through my field-glasses they certainly looked powerful and full of menace... I wondered how we would stop them if they just kept rolling forward, which was probably what they intended to do.[42]

Just as Davies-Scourfield began to worry, Gunner arrived with his three light tanks and the 2-pounder anti-tank gun, the most effective weapon which the British had against German armour. The arrival of the tanks was a tonic to the tired infantrymen – as was Gunner's manner, which made an evident impact on Davies-Scourfield:

> [The tanks were] under the command of Second Lieutenant Gregg. In later years he was to become something of an RTR character and be known as "Gunner" Gregg, but now he was a real morale-booster, bursting with enthusiasm and spoiling for a fight.[43]

Gunner immediately saw that Bastion 9 was a superb position for his vehicles:

The Boulogne gate was through a high *bund* – a rampart – which marked where the city walls had been. A wonderful fire position. You could see beautifully from up there, and furthermore you could change your position under cover. Only a matter of a few yards, but then you'd pop up somewhere else. We were hull-down, and very effective.

Davies-Scourfield conferred with Gunner about how best to counter the German tanks:

I asked whether the Redoubt would be of any use as an obstacle to the tanks and whether our Boys anti-tank rifles would be effective, at least at close range.[44] I well remember his reply:

"None whatever," he said. "They'll laugh at this bank, and your Boys rifles wouldn't blow a track off at point-blank range. Our only hope is to bluff them; make them think we have a big force here. By Jove, what a sight if they come at us." And he went off to position his tanks, as happy as a king.[45]

Gunner takes up the story:

My Troop Sergeant's tank and Troop Corporal's tank I placed well to the right of the road; my tank was to the left, not far from Davis-Scourfield's HQ. Our anti-tank 2-pounder gun the RA Sergeant placed on the road. I thought he had an excellent field of fire, but was rather exposed. I remember I thought "That's a silly bloody place to be", but of course I didn't comment.

The Germans attacked soon afterwards with aircraft, infantry and tanks. It was the start of a hellish afternoon.

We were not long in position when we were heavily attacked by dive-bombers, which did us no damage. The enemy attacked us with at least two light tanks and half-tracks, with field-gun support and the like. The attack was stopped when two or three of their armoured vehicles were set on fire. My troop, the 2-pounder gun-crew, and Davies-Scourfield's Boys anti-tank rifle... all tried, good-naturedly, to claim credit for our success... All my tanks were firing at what we could see. I had a pretty good and successful action there. I mean, we certainly destroyed two light tanks... By this time two large oil storage tanks were on fire, and the smoke could be seen from England.

Davies-Scourfield recalled that

Gregg's tanks darted here and there, using their mobility to good effect. Our resistance must have impressed the enemy – the noise was certainly terrific – and he made no attempt to advance further. We were hitting the tanks hard with our Boys rifles and the machine-guns of our own tanks, but the penetrating power of the armour-piercing bullets was limited.[46]

However, the defenders' success could not last for ever; outnumbered and out-gunned, it was only a matter of time before their slender resources were stretched to breaking-point. Gunner always recalled his frustration with the French troops who refused to help. Elsewhere in Calais, French soldiers put up fierce resistance to the Germans, and showed spirit which put many of their countrymen to shame. But at the Boulogne gate, the only Frenchmen were cowering under cover:

The Corporal of an infantry section then told me that the air-raid shelter in the *bund* was full of French soldiers with heavy machine-guns. This made me furious, and I went into the shelter and told an elderly French Lieutenant with a white moustache – obviously a reserve officer – to come out and help us to fight the Bosche. He said: "I have not had my orders." But when I put my hand on my revolver-holster, he brought his guns out and placed them at the base of the *bund* and fired them into the air.

The Germans were impressed by the strength of the resistance at Bastion 9, as the war diary of 10th *Panzer* Division makes clear:

Enemy resistance from scarcely perceptible positions was... so strong that it was only possible to achieve slight local success.[47]

In the margin of his copy of Davies-Scourfield's memoirs, Gunner scribbled:

> Praise from the enemy. Looks like we did some good.

They did indeed. But it could not last.

> Unfortunately the anti-tank gun was hit by three shells, and all the crew were killed. We went and pulled the bodies back, but they were all dead. That was my first experience of handling dead bodies. The gun was shattered. So we were left without that, left without any weapon which could defeat German tank armour, though their light tank was fairly vulnerable to small-arms fire. But I was no use with just my machine-guns, even though we did have armour-piercing bullets. We could lay down a huge volume of fire, but that was one of my problems – I ran out of ammunition fairly quickly. And by this time we were virtually running out of petrol.
> I got out of the tank to see Davies-Scourfield, and said "You haven't got any spare petrol, have you?"
> "No. I've got a Bren-gun carrier, but none spare."
> "Well, are you in touch on the Regimental net? Because if you are, would you get back on the Regimental net and get a message sent to RHQ of 3RTR saying I am desperate for replenishment. I want petrol and ammunition desperately."
> He replied, "We're on the net, but I can't get through."

Gunner had been in France since the evening of May 22nd, and it was now the afternoon of May 24th. He had been at war for less than forty-eight hours – and now disaster struck:

> The noise from the French machine-guns had seemed to stir up the Germans. I was walking back, more or less in despair, to my tank, when we came under quite heavy mortar-fire. They must have got an observer up a chimney somewhere, because it seemed that they could see where the tank was. One mortar-bomb fell between me and the tank. The sprocket was damaged – I'd have required squadron fitters to come and put it right – and I was really quite badly wounded. In the right arm, with most of the *flak* mainly down the right-hand side – and, funnily enough, my left ankle was broken, swollen up to twice its normal size. I still have the shrapnel marks. It all hurt.

It was the first time that Gunner was to be blown up during the course of the war, but not the last. The severity and widespread nature of his wounds was readily apparent:

> Davies-Scourfield tore off my overalls and put four First Field Dressings over my battledress where I seemed to be bleeding the most. He said "Look, my Bren-carrier's going back to the dock area. There's bound to be something there." I got my crew, because my tank was useless and we couldn't do anything, and we destroyed what we could.
> The driver took us back to the docks, to the very dock where we'd landed. But we couldn't find anyone – no medical unit or anything. By now I couldn't move, really. I decided to send a man off to find our battalion medical centre. It had to be somewhere, run by the very good doctor we had, "Doc" MacMillan, our MO. He was a wonderful man, and went right through the war, pretty well, with Third Tanks; he was by far the longest serving and senior member of the battalion.

By now, the docks at Calais were a chaos of wounded men, shirkers, and leaderless units which had made their way to the harbour in the hope of evacuation. Over everything hung a pall of black smoke from burning vehicles, buildings and fuel stores. Even in his wounded state, Gunner was still alert, and it did not take him long to appreciate that his chances of finding medical treatment were slim. But now the guardian angel which was to carry him through the war put in its first appearance.

> I was just about to send my driver on a search when suddenly an MTB came into the docks. A very over-dressed senior Naval officer with a loud-hailer shouted: "Is there an officer present?" There was only us there. I yelled back "Yes, I'm an officer." He replied "I have orders for you to come back with me to Dover." Apparently Admiral Ramsay – responsible for the evacuation – wanted to cross-

Above: this German photograph shows a wrecked 2-pounder at Calais after the battle; it may even be the one which fought at Bastion 9 (Bundesarchiv Bild 1011-383-0337-28).

> question an officer. So I was carried on board by two sailors, and my crew came too. A first-aid trained sailor put yet more dressings on me. We had some cocoa, hot cocoa – we were awfully hungry.

This MTB formed just one part of the heroic efforts being made by the Royal Navy to support the troops ashore: by the morning of May 24th, of all the destroyers in Dover Command, only two remained undamaged.[48]

Somehow, amid the chaos of battle, Gunner had managed to pick up a present for his girlfriend Pamela:

> From Calais I brought her back a French sailor's hat and shirt. I also bought her some amber beads.

Thus, by the veriest fluke, Gunner had escaped from Calais, where most of the remaining defenders would either be killed or captured. The majority spent the next five years of their lives in German prisoner-of-war camps. At Boulogne, the defenders had been evacuated by the Royal Navy on the night of May 23rd – but the same was not to happen at Calais.

By 2000 on May 24th, the Germans were within a few hundred yards of the western ramparts. It had long become clear to Nicholson that the positions there could not be held for another day, and he now ordered a staged withdrawal to an inner perimeter line along the canals surrounding Calais Nord.

* * *

Twenty miles away – less than an hour's journey by sea – Gunner was being treated as a very important person.

> When we arrived at the docks in Dover there was a staff car there, and I was put in the back. I left a lot of blood on the seat. We went up into Dover Castle, straight into the Operations Room, and there

was Admiral Ramsay, who was of course directing the withdrawal from Dunkirk. He interviewed me for an hour, and I did my best to answer, but I only knew my area. I gave him all the information I could, and told him places where I knew our men were and the enemy wasn't, or where the enemy was and we weren't. Then he said "Thank you for all those targets you've given me. I'm sending a destroyer to shell them. Would you like to go with them?" I said that of course I would go as a liaison officer or something. He said "You'd better see a doctor first." A doctor was summoned; I was put on a table in the next-door room; and he just took one or two pieces off, turned to the Admiral, and said "He's going nowhere but hospital."

Thus Gunner's part in the battle for Calais had come to an end. But the information which he had provided did enable Ramsay to bombard German targets on shore on May 25th. HMS *Wolfhound*, on its way to deliver more ammunition for the garrison, engaged shore targets west of Calais. HMS *Greyhound* bombarded the Calais suburb of St Pierre, though she was damaged by air attack and a German shore battery. The results of the British naval fire are unknown, though it had little chance of materially affecting the outcome.

* * *

Gunner was now in the hands of the medical system, which was about to be swamped by the huge numbers of wounded being evacuated from Dunkirk. He was taken from Dover to Horton Emergency Hospital, near Epsom.

> I was put on a stretcher, went in an ambulance to the station, and was put on a hospital train. I didn't even know we *had* any hospital trains. And then we were taken to a lunatic asylum near Epsom, which had been taken over. They were virtually moving in still, and all the casualties from Dunkirk and everywhere were coming in, but I got very good treatment. I went straight into the operating theatre where they cut my clothes off me, because they were all caked solid with dried blood. Everything was dressed, and they cleaned me up very well indeed. I must have been in theatre two or three hours, and when I came out I was a mass of bandages. They also pumped a lot of blood into me, but the worst, the most painful of the lot, was that I was put on my stomach, and this huge syringe was stuck in my arse as an anti-tetanus shot. That was more painful than the wound, I think.
> Then the Matron said to me,
> "Now we're going to start the real serious treatment."
> "What's that?"
> "A cup of good, hot, strong, sweet tea."
> When it appeared, I looked in the mug.
> "Matron, what sort of tea is this? It's bright purple."
> "Oh, I'm sorry about that. We've just taken over a hospital for lunatics, and we're a bit disorganized — some one's just put the permanganate of potash crystals into the tea-leaves."

* * *

At the *Gare Maritime* in Calais, shortly after midnight on May 24th, Nicholson had received a visit from Vice-Admiral Sir James Somerville. When Somerville had returned to England that same night he reported that

> Nicholson is tired but in no way windy. His two chief anxieties are mortar ammunition and the need for artillery... [He] felt confident that given more guns, which were urgently needed, he could hold on for a time.

At 0430 on May 25th Nicholson transferred his headquarters to the north-east bastion of the Citadel, where the English had made their last stand in 1558 before the final loss of Calais to the French.

At 1100 on May 25th a German armoured car under a flag of truce approached 2KRRC on the new inner perimeter. The German commander had been told by his superiors not to take unnecessary losses, and he had sent the Mayor of Calais to ask Nicholson for 30 Brigade's surrender. Signals Lieutenant Austin Evitts was a witness of their meeting:

> A surprise visitor was brought to the citadel. He was a civilian and blind-folded. The visitor, I was told, was the Mayor of Calais, and he had come with a message from the German commander. It was in the courtyard of the quadrangle where the Brigadier received him, and the message was an ultimatum. If he had not surrendered within twenty-four hours, the Germans had said Calais would be bombed and shelled and razed to the ground, and the Mayor was making a special plea, he said, to save the town from further destruction and loss of life.
>
> "Surrender?" said the Brigadier in a decidedly brusque manner. "No, I shall not surrender. Tell the Germans that if they want Calais they will have to fight for it."[49]

When news of Nicholson's refusal reached the Germans, a storm of shell-fire was unleashed on the Citadel; machine-gun and mortar fire and aerial attacks lashed the British positions around the bridges and canals of the Old Town. At 1415, as this bombardment raged, Evitts' signallers in the Citadel copied down a message from Antony Eden, the Secretary of State for War:

> Defence of Calais to utmost is of vital importance to our country and BEF and as showing our continued cooperation with France. The eyes of the whole Empire are upon the defence of Calais, and His Majesty's government is confident that you and your gallant regiments will perform an exploit worthy of the British name.[50]

It was Nicholson's first indication that 30 Brigade would not be evacuated. He sent copies to all his battalion commanders. About an hour afterwards, there was a lull and the Germans again sent a messenger to Nicholson to request his surrender. Nicholson this time wrote down his reply.

Below: *the* Gare Maritime *after the battle (Bundesarchiv Bild 1011-383-0337-21A).*

The answer is no, as it is the British Army's duty to fight as well as it is the Germans'.[51]

The German barrage resumed. By now, the Citadel appeared surrounded by flames, and the shelling intensified at 1830. All along the perimeter German pressure was forcing the defenders back. At 1930 the shelling stopped again, but this time it was the signal for the advance of German tanks, against which the British had little defence. Still the troops fought back with everything they had. As darkness fell on May 25th, the British battalions were down to around two hundred effectives apiece. Luckily, the Germans halted their attack at 2145, since it was too dark to use armour safely. The British retired overnight to their final defensive positions, 1RB sending the following message to England since it was cut off from Nicholson:

> Citadel a shambles. Brigadier's fate unknown. Rifle Brigade casualties unknown. Being heavily shelled and flanked but attempting counter-attack. Am attempting contact with 60th fighting in the town. Are you sending ships? Quay intact in spite of very severe bombardment.[52]

Nicholson had spent almost the whole day visiting his troops in the front line. At 2100 Churchill had dictated the following additional signal to the besieged commander:

> Every hour you continue to exist is of the greatest help to the BEF. Government has therefore decided that you must continue to fight. Have greatest possible admiration for your splendid stand. Evacuation will not (repeat not) take place, and craft required for above purpose are to return to Dover.[53]

The German attack recommenced at 0500 on May 26th with a tremendous bombardment from the artillery of a whole army corps. At 0700 the shelling increased, and at 0930 waves of dive-bombers pounded the Old Town and Citadel. An infantry assault began at 0915, though fighting was still raging around the bridges at 1015. The Germans were taken aback by the continued ferocity of the British resistance, as the commander of 10th *Schutzen* Brigade recalled:

> The enemy had recovered; he fought to exist or not exist. Some storm troops broke into the Citadel, but were forced back by a British counter-attack almost to their starting positions. At the southern edge of the town, nearly all enemy machine-guns were operating again, blocking the crossing of the canal. Brave and stout-hearted officers, NCOs and men who tried to cross were gunned down. The same situation was evident on the right flank in the town. The flank battalion advanced, but despite heavy fighting only gained ground slowly. On the left flank, II Battalion... was pinned to the ground by defending fire from Bastion II. In the command post, the mood was rather subdued, though the Brigadier and artillery commander remained optimistic... Soon it became clear that casualties were low, but even so the failure of the attack had lowered morale... A new, concentrated artillery bombardment was ordered, to be followed by a repeat attack.[54]

But by 1530 the remaining defenders on the shrunken perimeter were at the end of their endurance, short of food and ammunition, with numerous casualties, and utterly exhausted. Their cramped and makeshift positions were over-run one by one, and 1RB were told 'every man for himself' at around 1600.

In the Citadel and Fort Risban, the final blow fell at 1630. By 1500 the Citadel had been surrounded by tanks, and half an hour later infantry had broken in. Nicholson and his headquarters troops were marched off towards the Theatre, though he and Colonel Holland were then separated from the others, as Holland later recalled:

> On the way, a German officer who passed us said to Brigadier Nicholson in French: *"Vous avez battu très courageusement."* The same sentiments were repeated at the German RHQ. Here, also, a German officer expressed surprise that we had no artillery.[55]

The gallantry with which 30 Brigade and 3RTR held the town for four days had won time for their hard-pressed comrades of the BEF to be evacuated from Dunkirk and the neighbouring beaches. On June 4th Churchill made the following Parliamentary statement:

> The Rifle Brigade, the 60th Rifles and the Queen Victoria's Rifles, with a battalion of British tanks and one thousand Frenchmen – in all about four thousand strong – defended Calais to the last. The British Brigadier was given an hour to surrender. He spurned the offer, and four days of intense street fighting passed before silence reigned over Calais, which marked the end of a memorable resistance. Only thirty unwounded survivors were brought off by the Royal Navy, and we do not know the fate of their comrades. Their sacrifice was not however, in vain. At least two armoured divisions, which otherwise would have been turned against the British Expeditionary Force, had to be sent to overcome them. They have added another page to the glories of the Light Division and the time gained enabled the Gravelines Walnlieu to be flooded and to be held by French troops; and thus it was that the port of Dunkirk was kept open.[56]

Churchill later wrote that

> Calais was the crux. Many other causes might have prevented the deliverance of Dunkirk, but it is certain that the three days gained by the defence of Calais enabled the Gravelines water-line to be held, and that without this, even in spite of Hitler's vacillations and Runstedt's orders, all would have been cut off and lost... I did Calais myself. I personally gave the order to stand and fight it out to the end. I agreed to the evacuation of Boulogne with reluctance, and I think now that I ought to have ordered them to fight it out there too. But the order to Calais meant certain death or capture for almost the entire garrison. It was the only time during the war that I couldn't eat. I was very nearly sick at dinner. But together with the Gravelines line, which was steadily flooding, it gave us two vital days.[57]

* * *

But the cost had been heavy. In the Middle East, Donny scanned the papers for news of his contemporaries at school and university, and soon the roll of casualties from Calais revealed the scale of the losses from Winchester alone – the rifle regiments were headquartered in Winchester and had traditional ties with the College. In 1RB, the commanding officer, Lieutenant-Colonel Chandos Hoskyns, and 2nd Lieutenant Edward Bird had been mortally wounded;[58] Lieutenant Anthony Gerard Hugh Bampfylde, 2nd Lieutenant Richard Wood, and Lieutenant Frederic Athony Vivian Parker had all been captured, though Parker would be repatriated in 1943.[59] From 2KRRC, the second-in-command, Major Oswald Segar-Owen had been killed;[60] 2nd Lieutenant A. Michael Sinclair had been captured, only to be killed in 1944 trying to escape from Colditz Castle.[61] Davies-Scourfield had been wounded in the head and left for dead; he was also captured and sent to Colditz (though he went on the run at one point for ten months). In 1QVR, 2nd Lieutenant Richard Raikes had been killed in action.[62] And, of course, Brigadier Nicholson himself had been captured, and would die in a German prisoner-of-war camp in 1943.

Gunner, too, had lost comrades. His Squadron Second-in-Command, Barry O'Sullivan, had been captured; so too had his friends Toby Everett, Hugo Ironside, and Douggie Moir.[63] Ironside later told the story of his own capture. When the order 'every man for himself' had been given, he had assembled a group of soldiers and headed along the beach towards Dunkirk. The next morning, however, they had bumped into a German patrol and been captured. As dawn broke, Ironside stood with the German officer, who, like so many in such stories, spoke perfect English owing to his Oxford education.

"I wonder when you will see those again," said the German, gesturing towards the White Cliffs of Dover, visible on the horizon.

"I suppose you'll be heading that way soon," Ironside replied.

Above: a 3RTR A9 CS (Close Support) tank abandoned on the streets of Calais, May 27th 1940. Its howitzer looks lethal but only smoke-shells had been brought across the Channel for it (Bundesarchiv Bild 146-1971-042-10).

"Oh, no," the German answered. "Russia next."

Locked in a cellar to sleep, Ironside was awoken by a drunken German who emptied his machine-pistol into the room, fortunately missing everyone. The Germans had made little provision for the huge numbers of prisoners, and those taken in France later recalled with bitterness the hunger and misery of their two-week march to Germany.

Ironside, like Moir, Sinclair and Davies-Scourfield, finished up in Colditz, where at the end of the war he was one of those building the famous glider in the castle's attic.

* * *

Belgium surrendered on May 28th, but when the evacuation at Dunkirk ended on the night of June 3rd, 338,000 men (including around 120,000 French and Belgians) had been taken off. Of over eight hundred vessels involved, some 240 had been destroyed; the RAF had lost over a hundred aircraft in defending them. The British Expeditionary Force had left behind it 2,472 guns, 84,427 vehicles (including all 3RTR's tanks), and 660,000 tons of ammunition and stores. Nevertheless, on June 4th, in the House of Commons, Churchill made perhaps his most famous speech:

> Even though large tracts of Europe and many old and famous states have fallen, or may fall, into the grip of the Gestapo and all the odious apparatus of Nazi rule, we shall not flag or fail. We shall go on to the end; we shall fight in France; we shall fight on the seas and oceans; we shall fight with growing confidence and growing strength in the air; we shall defend our island, whatever the cost may be; we shall fight on the beaches; we shall fight on the landing grounds; we shall fight in the fields and in the streets; we shall fight in the hills; we shall never surrender. And even if, which I do not for a moment believe, this island or a large part of it were subjugated and starving, then our Empire beyond the seas, armed and guarded by the British Fleet, would carry on the struggle, until, in God's good time, the New World, with all its power and might, steps forth to the rescue and the liberation of the old.

The whole atmosphere in the country had changed. The shocking collapse of France since the German offensive had begun on May 10th had changed the entire tenor of Britain's approach to the war. Italy now jumped on the bandwagon, declaring war on June 10th. Britain now stood alone and seemingly defenceless; the parlous nature of her defences was obvious to all.[64]

* * *

Gunner could do nothing to help: he was still in hospital in Epsom:

> I was there for perhaps a month. They were taking shrapnel out of me all the time. There was nothing really serious; apart from my ankle, I hadn't broken anything. My veins were all right, my nerves, I could do things, my limbs worked.

Apart from the swollen ankle which he endured to his dying day day, Calais was to provide one last memento for Gunner, however. It was not until after those captured in May 1940 returned home at the end of the war that the full story of the battle could be told, and it became clear that several of the defenders should belatedly be recognized for their bravery. Gunner was one of them:

> War Office, 20th September 1945.
> The King has been graciously pleased to approve that the following be Mentioned in recognition of gallant and distinguished services in the Defence of Calais in May 1940:
> R.T.R.   Major N.E.B.C. Mahony (14020).
>   2/Lt. R.H.C. Eastman (73367).
>   2/Lt. T.D. Gregg (85707).
>   7883945 Sgt. A. Laidlaw.
>   7883962 Cpl. R. Archer (killed in action).[65]

Chapter Six

Greece

Gunner recovered well from his wounds, and when discharged from hospital in June 1940 spent three weeks convalescing:

> They sent me to Rogue's Roost on Dartmoor. It was lovely; very remote, and I suspect much used by smugglers in its time. They made their own clotted cream. My mother was allowed to stay at the farm too. She and David had been living in a house called Queen's Yarn in South Petherton in Somerset,[1] near Yeovil, but by then she was living near Colchester: David had been posted there with the job of re-doing all the cables to the Pacific and Singapore.

Meanwhile, 3RTR was licking its wounds. The battalion had been shattered at Calais, and when Churchill had come to visit the men in their tents near Corby that summer they had given him the faintest possible cheer. They had been moved repeatedly, given new equipment only to lose it again, and fed many orders which were just as quickly countermanded.

Gunner was once again posted to command 4 Troop in 'A' Squadron.

> When I'd been fattened up on clotted cream I re-joined the Regiment. Everything had to be built up from scratch: we'd lost about fifty *per cent* at Calais, and the CO – without his Adjutant, without his Intelligence Officer – had that awful job.[2] Some, like myself, had been wounded or got back normally, and we got a lot of new people in, especially from the Westminster Dragoons – many of them were barristers. Some excellent ones from there were given commissions on the spot. Tom Eeley came to us from the Westminster Dragoons; a first-class man and officer, who became a good friend.[3]

Another of the new officers was called Bob Crisp.[4]

> I was sent down to the station to meet Bob, as he and I were South African. I welcomed him there and brought him back to the Regiment. He went to 'C' Squadron. The week before we left England, Bob married the sister of Diana Napier, the famous South African actress. Diana visited the Regiment several times before we left England.

Another new officer with South African connexions was Tony Viney, who came straight to the battalion from 102 OCTU.[5]

> Tony Viney's father was chairman of the Stock Exchange in Johannesburg. Tony was killed a year or two later at the Mareth Line in Tunisia – unfortunately one of many. Why do the best always go first?

Despite invasion fears, 3RTR were not destined to remain in Britain for long.

> My first job was to take fifteen tank drivers to Glasgow to help the dockers to load our tanks on to the *Clan Lamont*. I and my party then went to Liverpool where we joined a Union Castle ship, on which 3RTR started a luxurious trip round Africa to join up with our tanks at Suez.

The vessel on which Gunner sailed – together with the rest of 3RTR, 5RTR, and HQ 3 Armoured Brigade – was RMMV *Stirling Castle*.[6] She sailed as part of Convoy WS4 – the 'WS' allegedly stood for "Winston's Special" – tasked with the reinforcement of Egypt by way

Above: an A13 of 3RTR in England in August 1940, before embarking for the Middle East (IWM H3663).

of the Cape of Good Hope, a longer but safer route than the Mediterranean now that Italy was in the war and France out of it.

WS4 formed up on November 2nd 1940.[7] Typically, no sooner had 3RTR sailed than Keller was informed that his orders had changed: 3RTR would disembark at Gibraltar and be rushed by cruiser through the Mediterranean to Alexandria, where tank crews were urgently needed. Like so many of Keller's orders, these were soon cancelled, and 3RTR continued their cruise.

The first stop was at Freetown on November 14th. Troops were not allowed ashore, because of the fear of disease, but convoys normally called there to replenish their fresh water supplies. The convoy sailed again on November 17th, and passed Cape Town on its way to Durban, where it was again to re-fuel and replenish. Gunner was most disappointed not to have stopped at his childhood home:

> I was longing to go to Bishops to see Charlie Bull and Rayer Burt – I had a lot of friends there, you see. Rayer had been at school with me at Bishop's – his father was Lord Mayor of Cape Town – and he and I had built elaborate tree-houses in Rondebosch.

But Durban more than made up for the disappointment. Most troops shipping out to India or the Middle East remembered Durban fondly: servicemen passing through the city were entitled to free use of public transport, reduced entry to the cinemas, and free concerts in City Hall. There was also the famous "Lady in White", Perla Siedle Gibson, who sang patriotic songs through a megaphone from Durban's North Pier to welcome troop-ships as they arrived and left.[8] Gunner, however, had even better reason to remember 3RTR's stay (December 3rd to 5th 1940):

Above: RMMV Stirling Castle, *pictured in 1946 (copyright holder unknown).*

At Cape Town Tony Viney had got on the phone to his father and said "We want a lot of girls waiting in Durban." And my God they all came down, and did they give us a party. We were there about three or four days, and they were *wonderful* to us. God, was it fun. Not only that, but they kept it up. We kept on getting parcels from there when we were in the desert and Greece.

Bob Crisp contacted the *Mercury* newspaper in Durban, for which he'd been a sports writer, and the *Mercury* also staged a great party for us in the King Edward Hotel – one of the best parties I've ever been to. It lasted three days.

Indeed, some people had far too good a time, and missed the boat:

When our ship sailed out of the entrance to Durban harbour the famous Lady in White sang us a farewell song from the jetty. But hardly surprisingly the Brigade Major, a Major, two Captains and Bob Crisp as well missed the boat – a launch had to bring them out half-way into the ocean.

3RTR reached Suez on December 22nd 1940. On Christmas Eve 1940, Gunner and his comrades settled into the unlovely camp at Amariya to begin the process of desert acclimatization. There they spent their second Christmas of the war, before collecting their vehicles. Before leaving England, 3RTR had re-equipped with A13s, at the time the most reliable tanks in the inventory. The regiment still had some unreliable A9s and A10s as well, as was then standard practice, but for the most part it had tanks in which it had confidence. The omens for 1941 seemed auspicious.

* * *

The Desert War was one area which in 1940 had gone well for the British. Britain had intervened in Egypt in 1882 to secure access to the Suez Canal, and had declared the country independent in 1922 whilst retaining the right to base troops there. The Italians controlled Libya to the west and parts of East Africa to the south-east: Mussolini hoped to link the two and to sever Britain's lifeline to India and the oil-fields of Arabia and Iraq. On September 9th 1940 Italian forces in overwhelming strength crossed the Egyptian border with Libya, marked by a fence which everyone simply called "The Wire". The Italians quickly captured Sollum, the Halfaya Pass and Sidi Barrani, but on September 16th simply stopped, eighty miles short of the main British defences at Mersa Matruh. There the Italians sat. 3RTR had been dispatched to form part of Britain's response to this invasion.

Wavell's counter-attack, Operation Compass, began on December 9th, and was intended as a limited offensive, but the Italians proved so lacking in fight that by December 10th 20,000 had surrendered, and Sidi Barrani was re-captured on December 11th. Although the battle-hardened 4th Indian Division – including 2nd Camerons, Donny's parent battalion – was then sent to East Africa, 6th Australian Division proved more than capable of harrying the Italians back into Libya, capturing the ports of Bardia and Tobruk and driving hard on Benghazi. By February 1941 the Italians were in headlong retreat, and 7th Armoured Division was ordered to cut them off at Beda Fomm, south of Benghazi. At the Battle of Beda Fomm on February 6th, the Italian army in Cyrenaica was defeated and captured. 130,000 Italian soldiers and all their equipment had been captured. The Foreign Secretary, Anthony Eden, joked:

> Never has so much been surrendered by so many to so few.

The British advance halted at El Agheila, however, and the opportunity to drive the Italians from North Africa was lost. This was not Wavell's fault – events elsewhere were to distract the British at the crucial moment.

* * *

Fighting in the desert was a specialized skill, which units coming into the theatre had to learn quickly. As 1941 began, 3RTR began the process of learning how to work in this strange new environment. They had begun to practise their navigation even whilst still at sea – appropriately enough, since navigation in featureless desert has much in common with navigation on the oceans. Gunner remembered their training:

> We were trying to acclimatize very quickly, learn to move, learn to space ourselves out; we very quickly had to learn how to leaguer, how to park at night and dig a trench underneath your tank, how to replenish. We didn't really have anyone to teach us.

Shortly after the battalion's arrival in Egypt, Gunner was promoted to full Lieutenant, which increased his pay but made no great difference to his responsibilities.[9]

On January 7th the battalion received orders for the Sudan, but these were cancelled two days later, and instead, on January 11th 'A' and 'B' squadrons were ordered to the Western Desert, though this move took a long time to materialize. Before it did, on January 25th, 3RTR received bad news:

> They took away twenty-eight of our A13s, gave them to 5RTR, and in return we received twenty-eight of the ghastly A9s and A10s.

'A' Squadron left for a position known as "Charing Cross" on February 4th and arrived the following day.

> We went straight onto flats and went up to Mersa Matruh, and when we'd off-loaded all the tanks, we went along the Siwa road. The funny thing was that the next morning they'd had the first rain in nearly twenty years and it was just as if we were in the middle of a lake, because the desert was absolutely flooded. A terrific rainstorm and hail – we weren't expecting that.

Nor were they expecting what happened next.

> We were then aimed at Tripoli; that was the plan. We were half-way across the desert when suddenly we were told to halt. We were told to turn round and drive back to Alexandria. We couldn't think what the bloody hell was happening. So we went back to Alexandria, where there were a whole lot of men waiting who painted our yellow tanks bottle green.

One piece of army graffiti current at the time was

> Never in the field of human conflict have so many been buggered about by so few.

3RTR had been "buggered about" more than most: having just become used to the desert, and poised to take part in Wavell's great offensive which swept the British through Cyrenaica and beyond, putting them within sight of ending the war in North Africa, the battalion instead found itself *en route* for Greece.

* * *

Greece had tried to remain neutral when war broke out, but Mussolini had ended all that. He had become envious of Hitler's successes, and was fed up with being treated as an inferior, always the last to know Hitler's intentions. And so he decided to pick a fight with what he saw as an easy opponent. On August 15th 1940 the Greek cruiser *Elli* had been torpedoed by an Italian submarine, and on October 28th the Italians presented the Greek President, Metaxas, with an ultimatum which gave him three hours to agree to the stationing of Italian soldiers on Greek soil. Metaxas refused – Greece still celebrates October 28th as "*Ochi* Day" ("No Day"). The Italians had already invaded from Albania anyway. To their surprise, they were halted in their tracks by the determined though woefully-equipped Greek army. By November 8th the Greeks had taken five thousand Italians prisoner; within another week, the Italians had been driven back into Albania. When, after a bitter winter in the mountains, the Italians counter-attacked on March 9th 1941, they were again beaten off with heavy losses. Gunner was always full of praise for the Greek troops of 1941:

> The Greeks were wonderful and brave. Although all their transport was bullocks and things like that, their army was knocking hell out of the Italians. I really admired the Greeks for that. Hitler had to save Mussolini's face, because Mussolini had planned to take Greece and things had turned out the other way round – the Greeks had almost taken Albania.

Britain's involvement in the Greek campaign had begun in November 1940, since Britain was bound by treaty to guarantee Greek independence. British troops had taken over the security of the island of Crete, freeing Greek troops for the Albanian front, and RAF aircraft had been sent to provide air support for Greek forces. In January, the Greek government asked the British for nine divisions of troops, but Britain could promise only one, an offer which the Greeks rejected as it would simply make them a target for German aggression without giving them the strength to resist it. Unknown to them, Hitler had already decided to invade in any case.

Churchill hoped to forge an anti-Fascist alliance of Yugoslavia, Greece and Turkey, and his representatives met the Greek government in Athens on February 22nd 1941. The offer of an Allied expeditionary force for Greece was again made, and this time accepted. That it would soon be needed was suggested when German troops moved into friendly Bulgaria on March 1st, and Bulgarian forces massed on the northern Greek border.

March 2nd saw the first British and Commonwealth troops move to Greece as part of Operation Lustre. By April 24th there were more than sixty thousand of them there: 6th Australian Division, 2nd New Zealand Division, and the British 1 Armoured Brigade. Collectively they were known as 'W' Force, after their commander Lieutenant-General Sir Henry Maitland "Jumbo" Wilson. And one of Wilson's headquarters staff officers was Donny Mackenzie.

The headquarters of 'W' Force began to assemble in Athens on March 8th 1941: Donny was one of two GSO3s assigned as permanent staff to General Wilson.[10] At 1000 on March 12th he left Athens with Brigadier Galloway (also on Wilson's staff) to conduct a reconnaissance in the north, visiting Larissa, Veria, and Katerini. They returned from to Athens on the evening of March 15th, by which time various Commonwealth units had reached Greece and were entraining for the northern border. Among them were Gunner and his comrades in 3RTR.

* * *

On February 10th, 3RTR had been ordered back to Quassassin to join 1 Armoured Brigade, which was preparing for service in Greece. On March 5th its tanks had begun moving to Alexandria for loading, and on March 8th 'A' Squadron had embarked its tanks and crews, as Gunner recalled:

> The tanks were put on *Clan Macaulay* and *Singalese Prince* and we boarded the cruiser HMS *Bonaventure*. She was sunk off Crete three weeks later.[11]

The convoy had sailed on March 10th and reached the Piraeus on March 11th, the day before Donny had set out for his reconnaissance northwards.

> We shot across and unloaded in Piraeus, and went off to a place called Glyphada into the woods. We had about a week there, unloading the tanks, getting them ready, and so on.

The weather was poor, with frequent rain and snow. 3RTR were glad to receive orders to head for the frontier, for an area known as the "Florina Gap" and on March 16th 'A' Squadron moved to the station to entrain for the north. They loaded their tanks on to what Gunner describes as "a very old train". They would take two days to reach the frontier, and the journey was far from pleasant, as Sergeant Jock Watt recalled in his memoirs:

> The train had no accommodation for the tank crews who, throughout the long journey from Athens, had to survive the snow and freezing conditions wrapped up on the backs of the tanks...The train-load of tanks arrived on 'flats' which were just the width of the tracks and looked as if they were about to fall apart. Unloading was precarious, but apart from tearing a few planks from the decking there was no serious mishap.[12]

The battalion reached Amyntaion at 0530 on March 18th, and after unloading moved to a ridge two miles south of the town, where in the snow and rain 3RTR dug in and camouflaged itself:

> We parked along the hedgerows of a field, the only area available, and camouflaged against the possibility of spotter-planes. It was essential to hide our presence, but it was an added obstacle and hindered our frantic efforts to get these old A10s battle-worthy.[13]

Gunner's 4 Troop had been one of those inexplicably re-equipped with three A10s before leaving for Greece. He and his comrades knew from bitter experience just how useless

Above: a typical scene in the mountains of Greece in the spring of 1941: British vehicles pass Greek troops and supplies (copyright holder unknown).

their 'new' tanks were. Instead of the A13s which would have enabled them to meet German tanks on a level of equality, they had been sent off to Greece with clapped-out and unreliable vehicles. It still makes Gunner angry.

> They were the same old A10s, the same bloody old things. What was worse, everyone, even Anthony Eden himself, had told us "I know the tracks are useless, but new ones'll be waiting for you in Suez." The first thing we'd asked when we got to Suez was "Where are the tank-tracks?" No tracks. Then they said "Oh, you'll find them in Piraeus." We never saw them. That ruined us completely. To go round a corner, especially in the mountainous part where we were, you had to really just go at nought miles an hour, and get round it slowly. If you did it at any speed, you lost your track. It just broke and laid out flat. That was a disaster.

Watt explains just how much of a disaster:

> Soon it became apparent that someone had neglected to inform the Quartermaster in Egypt that we had exchanged our nice new A13s for these clapped-out A10s. All spares supplied to us were for the A13s. What a bloody shambles.[14]

The Germans did not defeat 3RTR in Greece: the A10s did. 'A' Squadron's notes on the Greek campaign make for shocking reading. Of the sixteen tanks lost, eleven were listed as "broken track"; three as "steering clutch"; one as "engine"; and one as "engine and steering clutch". Not a single loss was attributed to enemy action. But all this heartbreak lay in the future.

The bulk of Greek troops were concentrated in Albania, on the north-western frontier of the country, and in the defensive fortifications of the Metaxas Line along the Bulgarian frontier to the north-east. The central, northern, frontier was protected by friendly Yugoslavia. The British knew from bitter experience that German troops would be unlikely to respect Yugoslavia's borders and that therefore the whole northern border was vulnerable. General Wilson favoured holding the line of the Aliakhmon river, which would provide a strong defensive position and enable Commonwealth and Greek forces to be concentrated; however, this would necessitate abandoning the city of Thessaloniki in the north-west, and the Greeks refused. Wilson's forces were therefore deployed facing roughly north-west, the northern end of their line anchored on Florina and the southern end on the sea near Katerini, where Donny had finished his reconnaissance. 1 Armoured Brigade – including 3RTR – held the northern end, covering the Monastir Gap, a natural invasion route which could bring German forces down through Yugoslavia, through Florina and south into the plains of Thessaly in central Greece.

* * *

The personnel lived under canvas despite the cold and wet. Watt recalled how 'A' Squadron's tank crews coped with the wintry conditions:

> Here on the hillside it was cold and damp, so a bivouac was erected on one side of the tank to contain the warmth and keep out the rain and mosquitoes. It was constructed quickly and simply: the tank-sheet was attached to the mud-guard, dropped down to ground level, along the ground for about six feet, and back up to the mud-guard. It was dry and reasonably comfy with four of us keeping each other warm.[15]

The tanks had reached the frontier in good time, and were not going to be pitched into battle immediately as they had been at Calais. Gunner described their mission:

> We had about a month there, which we spent recceing. We were to the west of Mount Olympus, right on the edge of Yugoslavia, watching the Monastir Gap. It was the only way they could come. Anyway, we did our reconnaissance, slept on our tanks. We were all ready, just waiting. It was a wonderful country for defence, and we'd worked out exactly where we were going to be when they came. We had everything ready for them. Our 2-pounders could do quite a bit of damage.

The battalion war diary also noted the opportunities which 3RTR took to prepare their defence:

> During the whole period there, extensive recces were made by all squadrons of all area north of Veve Pass (or Monastir Gap) up to the Jugo-Slav frontier. Tank country was noted, and all routes, paths, villages explored… Inhabitants very friendly… Country very hilly.[16]

Gunner remembered that not all the villages were as friendly as the war diary suggests:

> If you came to a village and the locals were all sour-faced bastards, they were Bulgarians. Then you'd come to a Greek village and you'd have eggs and gifts and so on.

The war diary is, however, right about one thing:

> Very suitable country for A10s if complete reliance could be placed on tracks, which were old and needed replacement badly.[17]

The war diary was being compiled by the battalion's intelligence officer, an old friend of Gunner from their days together at Sandhurst: Hugh Munday.

A very brave, nice, kind, friendly Regular officer. His father was a rural vicar in a Devonshire village, and I had met him when I was at Rogue's Roost. Hugh was not all that bright, though, and while we spent that month before the Germans attacked recceing the area we were going to fight over, Hugh spent his time with the CO, and in the evening he had to write up all the CO's comments and reports. He usually had to ask Tom Eeley how to spell many of the words. One evening I remember him saying that he had written the word "daytour" (instead of detour) and that the Colonel had told him off for getting it wrong.

* * *

As was standard British army practice, 3RTR's tanks had distinctive markings to distinguish individual vehicles. A tank's identification numbers were applied in 3RTR's regimental green, and surrounded by a symbol of the same colour to denote the squadron: a triangle for 'A' Squadron; a squre for 'B' Squadron; a circle for 'C' Squadron; and a diamond for HQ Squadron. Pennants on the wireless aerials also served to identify command tanks.

In many British armoured regiments, it was customary to name tanks, and to paint these names on the vehicles. Sometimes these all began with the same letter – so all the tanks in 'C' Squadron might start with a 'C'. However, 3RTR seems to have allowed individual choice, as Gunner recalls some tanks being named after girlfriends: his own was nick-named *Swiftsure,* after one of Lord Nelson's ships at Trafalgar.[18] He would use the same name on a post-war tank as a squadron commander in 6RTR. The A10 which he used in Greece lived up to the name which Gunner gave it; it managed to keep working and to stay ahead of the advancing enemy until Gunner himself was put out of action.

* * *

"Jumbo" Wilson had decided that Athens was too far to the rear to make an effective headquarters, and by March 18th had sent an officer north to find a suitable site for an advanced base. It was decided that "Advanced HQ" was to be established at the village of Chaoichani – now known as Tsaritsani – near Elasson at the foot of Mount Olympos, about twenty miles south-west of Katerini. New Zealand engineers were ordered to dig underground shelters for the staff, and by March 27th the position was ready for occupation. The war diary of HQ British Troops in Greece records Donny's move there:

Athens, March 27th, 0815
Brigadier General Staff, Major Belchem, Captain Mackenzie and 'G' Office left for Chaoichani; Captain Street remains Athens.[19]

* * *

Meanwhile, 3RTR continued to prepare for battle. On March 23rd 'A' Squadron moved from Amyntaion to Ptolemais, an area with which it became usefully familiar, since it would later be fighting over it. But, as usual, 3RTR suffered from constant order and counter-order: 'A' Squadron went to all the trouble of loading its tanks on to trains on April 4th for a move by rail, only to be told to unload them again and drive back to Amyntaion. There it took up positions at Sotiras, just south-west of Amyntaion, guarding the southern approaches to the Vevi pass and the road which led south from Florina to Kozani.

* * *

Wilson took over the reins of command at Tsaritsani on April 5th. The following day, all hell broke loose. As the morning wore on, it became clear at Advanced HQ that Wilson's predictions as to the likely course of events had come true. The Germans were using a route through southern Yugoslavia to outflank the Metaxas Line and to cut off the Greek Second Army and Thessaloniki. By the late afternoon, Advanced HQ was reporting streams of refugees heading south. Commonwealth forces, however, had not yet been engaged.

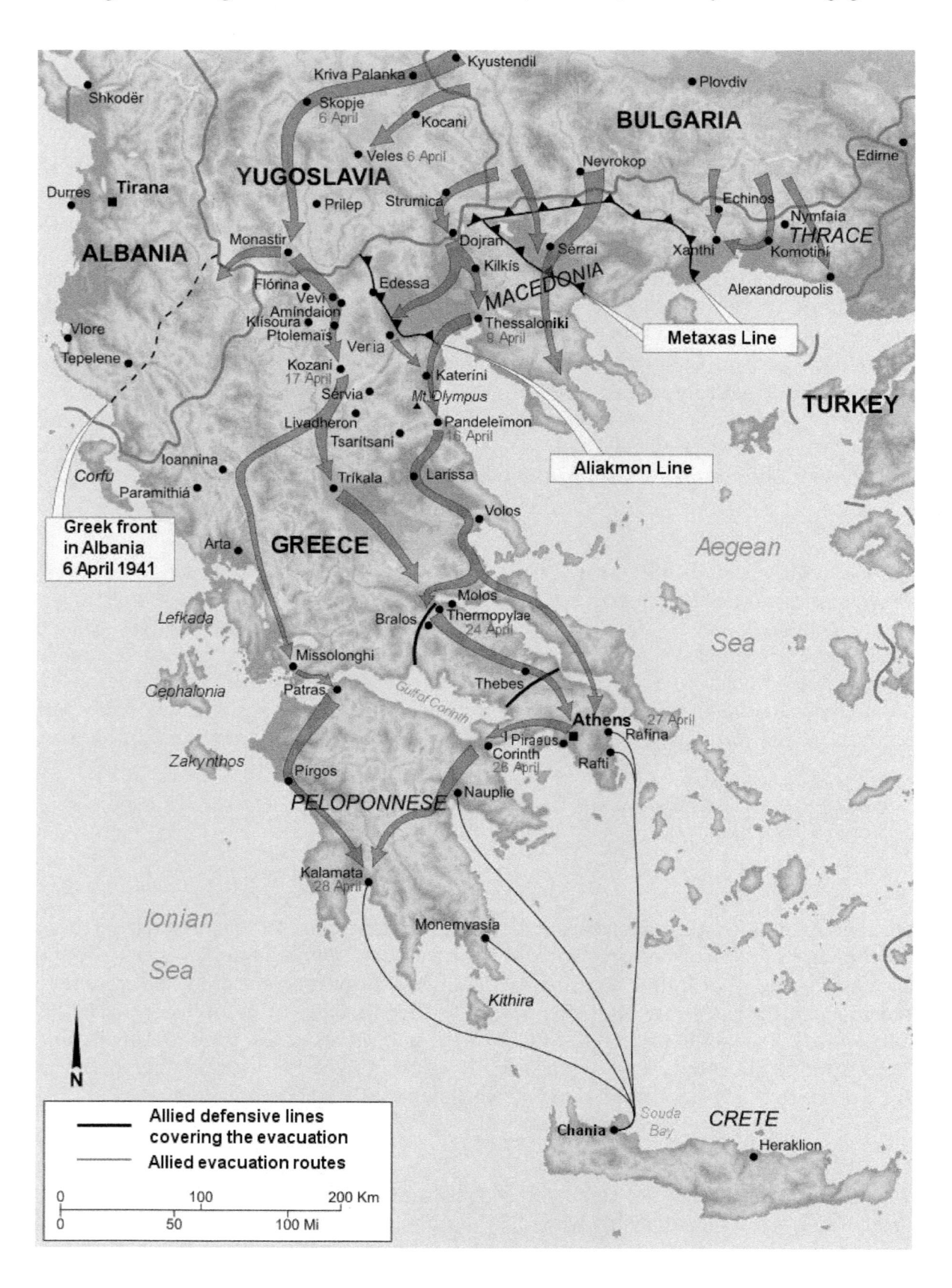

The first that Gunner knew about the German invasion was the following day, April 7th – a special day for him in several ways:

> Our wait ended on April 7th, my twenty-second birthday, when the Germans attacked, using a lot of spies. Greece and Germany hadn't technically been at war so their embassy was still operating and noting down everything. The Germans had sent a lot of spies ahead to find out where we were. We had several Military Police with us, and they were shooting people left, right and centre. We asked them "Who are you shooting?" and they said "Oh, he's a spy."
>
> When the Germans appeared, the first thing we suffered was bombing. I've never had such bombing. Calais was bad; but, my God, Greece! They'd diverted all the bombers that they were going to use to go for Russia, and we got the full blast of them. We were bombed to buggery. Stukas used to come, and then you used to have Heinkel 111s cruising along, which just kept the pot boiling.

Within three days of the start of the offensive, the bulk of the Greek army had been eliminated. The Germans then pushed through the Monastir Gap and towards Florina, hoping to turn Wilson's northern flank. At Advanced HQ, Donny helped to push out orders which instructed 1 Armoured Brigade to retire southwards, blowing bridges as it went. Wilson was under no illusions as to the likely fate of his forces if they held their exposed positions in the north.

Donny and his fellow staff officers desperately tried to assimilate a deluge of information – much of it contradictory and out of date – which flooded in concerning German advances, Greek intentions, and Commonwealth units trying to redeploy in bad weather and difficult terrain. On April 9th, for example, Donny spoke by telephone to Lieutenant-Colonel Peter Smith-Dorrien, one of the British Military Liaison team attached to Greek Military Headquarters.[20] He also recorded the results of the RAF's reconnaissance missions that day, which were telephoned to him that evening:[21]

> *1600 hours*
> No activity seen Axiopolis; railway and two road bridges destroyed. Road bridge Gephyra intact. Much MT movement towards Edessa. Sindos road and railway bridges destroyed. Two fires still burning Salonika.
>
> *1830 hours*
> Bomber and recce aircraft turned back owing to bad weather. Considerable MT movement seen between river Axios and Yannitsa.

The following day, Smith-Dorrien's superior, Colonel Guy Salisbury-Jones, informed Wilson that the Greek commander-in-chief, Lieutenant-General Papagos, intended to retreat to a line running from Olympus to Servia. Donny handled calls to the RAF and to his counterpart in Athens as Wilson tried to co-ordinate the reeling Allied reponse to the German onslaught.[22] By now, German forces had reached the Vevi pass, where the Australian defenders awaited them, backed by tanks from 1 Armoured Brigade.

Wilson decided that he needed to meet Papagos, and at 2200 set out for Pharsala, accompanied by Donny. The conference took place in the small hours of April 11th:

> *0045*
> General Wilson met General Papagos at Pharsala and discussed withdrawal to Olympus-Aliakhmon position. Colonel Vimblis and Colonel Salisbury-Jones and Captain Mackenzie were present.[23]

The meeting broke up at 0200: it is likely that as the most junior of those present, Donny was responsible for the minutes. Since Papagos had on previous occasions gone back on his word after making agreements at such meetings, minutes were vitally important. In

Donny's minutes, several of Wilson's statements are given in inverted commas, so as to leave no doubt as to what Wilson had actually said:

> General Wilson said: "It was only a matter of days before the Germans could put in a heavy attack in the Amyntaion area. He would probably try tomorrow. He had himself been at Perdika that afternoon and met General Carassos, General Mackay, and Brigadier Charrington... General Carassos had stated it would take him three or four nights to withdraw his troops from this position and General Wilson had instructed him to start doing so at once... The main object was to achieve the withdrawal unmolested..." General Wilson explained the necessity for this withdrawal, due to the fact that the Amyntaion position had been hurriedly organized, and a break-through there would cut off all troops to the east of the Kozani-Elasson road.
>
> General Papagos asked how long General Wilson thought he could hold this new position. General Wilson replied: "It was impossible to say, as it depended on the scale of the attack, but the position was very strong, though troops – particularly on the Greek front – were very thin on the ground..."[24]

The line of defence to which Wilson was retreating was the Aliakhmon river, his original preference. Papagos said that he hoped that with reinforcements which he was sending from the Albanian front, the Aliakhmon line might hold for ten or twelve days.

> The main problem was to stop the enemy breaking the line quickly. General Wilson again said that as far as that went he was satisfied about the Olympus and the Servia part, but again emphasized his thinness on the ground in front of Grevena... It was only a matter of time before the whole Albanian front would have to be swung back...
>
> General Wilson concluded with two words of warning:
>
> The Yugoslav troops should be kept well away from the Greeks, as their morale was very bad.
>
> Many refugees had crossed the frontier from Yugoslavia into Greece. The security police aught [sic] to check up on them as soon as possible, as they probably included enemy agents.[25]

* * *

Later that day, in torrential rain, the *Waffen* SS forced the Australian defenders at the Vevi pass to give way. 1 Armoured Brigade found itself unable to fall back as planned, but became involved in bitter fighting to prevent Wilson's line from being rolled up.

On April 12th 'A' Squadron moved back to Ptolemais, where it took up positions on the Proasteion Ridge one mile south of the town. The remainder of 3RTR was withdrawing in the face of determined German attacks; 'B' Squadron was down to six tanks, 'C' reduced to four. The war diary blamed "mainly track trouble." The weather cleared again, and that night there was a very heavy frost.

'A' Squadron dug in with the rest of 1 Armoured Brigade to await the enemy. By noon on April 13th they were ready for the Germans, who arrived at 1330. Gunner's memories of the ensuing battle were very clear:

> When the attack came, we in 'A' Squadron did rather well.
>
> There was one very good range of hills there, and it had a river running along in front of it. The road, such as it was, came over a bridge down at the bottom of the hills. Now, 'A' Squadron had our four troops. Mine was on the extreme right, then there was No.1, under a chap called Denis Bartlett, who'd been a reporter. And then we had two more troops and SHQ on the other side of the road. I really could see more than anyone else from the position. We saw the normal enemy motor-cyclists and armoured cars and armoured half-tracks and the like, and they all went up to the bridge. I didn't open fire until they'd all collected round looking at their maps and this blown-up bridge. Then when there were enough people we let them have it, both No.1 Troop and No.4 Troop – we really shot them to pieces. They all disappeared pretty sharpish.
>
> Then we got these Storch planes coming over to have a look and see what it was holding them up. I think they then had us pretty well spotted, because we were then bombed a bit more. That was

our main battle. There's no doubt about it, we were winning hands down; they weren't going to get through us.

But although the position was holding well, the enemy troops of 33 *Panzer* Regiment were trying to find a way round its flanks. 'A' Squadron's war diary describes what happened:

> At approximately 1330 hrs enemy forces were observed approaching Ptolemais along the road to the south, and by 1400 hrs the advanced elements had reached the town. Attempts were then made by reconnaissance motor-cycles and armoured cars to penetrate along the road running south through 'A' Squadron's position, but these were checked by a small bridge which had been blown up some eight hundred yards north of the ridge, and No.1 Troop, who were covering the road itself, dealt successfully with an armoured motor-cycle combination and a light tank.[26]
>
> The enemy then commenced to shell our position and aircraft flew low over the ridge and machine-gunned it. The shelling continued throughout the afternoon.
>
> Enemy AFVs were seen to be taking the track from Ptolemais to Ardessa, which lay left and well forward of the squadron's line, and some which turned to attempt a flanking movement at this point were seen to become bogged [down], but were out of range.
>
> Others continued to the foot of the hills which ran at right-angles to the squadron's positions on the left flank, and a steady stream continued throughout the afternoon to trickle down this flank, well out of range, via the village of Asvestopetra, which lay at the foot of the mountains.
>
> No.2 Troop, less one tank, was ordered by Brigade to give support to the 4th Hussars who were defending this flank.[27]

4th Hussars were equipped only with Light Tanks VIb, whose heaviest weapon was a .5-inch Vickers machine-gun. In any contest with German armour, they needed the support either of anti-tank guns or cruiser tanks with their 2-pounders.

> Owing to the nature of the ground it was not possible to approach within two thousand yards, at which range fire was opened on a large formation of enemy medium tanks; three were knocked out. The enemy tanks got round to the rear of our left flank, where they were engaged by No.3 Troop, who had been in reserve up to now, and three enemy tanks were destroyed.[28]

Gunner's Squadron Commander was again, as at Calais, Major Simpson:

> Simbo Simpson was in my opinion a bloody useless Squadron Leader, but funnily enough he became a very good commanding officer – he later commanded Second Tanks.

Whatever his abilities, Simpson now found himself in an impossible position. There were by now, he estimated, forty enemy *Panzer* IIIs on his right flank, and although he had the assistance of the anti-tank 2-pounders of the Northumberland Hussars and a 25-pounder of 2RHA firing over open sights, it was time for him and his men to leave.

> As it seemed possible that the enemy would get astride the road, thus cutting off our force, Brigade HQ ordered a withdrawal at approximately 1930 hrs. No.4 Troop moved from its position on the right flank to support No.3 Troop on the left. The squadron withdrew, after the 4th Hussars, in the order Squadron HQ–2–3–1–4, smoke being used to cover the withdrawal, and got away without any casualties owing to enemy action.[29]

Brigade HQ estimated that twenty enemy tanks had been destroyed, and described the fighting as being

> like a Crystal Palace fireworks display.[30]

'A' Squadron had left only one tank behind, crippled by a track-breakage. Simpson would later be awarded the DSO for his conduct of the action.

Above: German Panzer IIIs of the type faced by Gunner and 3RTR at Ptolemais. Pictured in Greece on April 16th, these Germans have acquired a British or Commonwealth prisoner (Bundesarchiv Bild 146-1994-009-17).

'W' Force was now in full retreat. Wilson decided to make a stand on the Aliakhmon line and then pull back south-east to the famous pass at Thermopylae. There he could again stand and delay the German onslaught, buying time for what he by now understood was inevitable evacuation. The Aliakhmon line, anchored on Mount Olympus at its seaward end, held for three days. Gunner remains proud of how the tanks of 1 Armoured Brigade held their ground.

> On the right were the Australians and New Zealanders, covering the main routes. Quite honestly, it was obvious the Germans weren't going to make their main thrust through us, because we could hold them – and they must have realized that. So the Allied line was absolutely firm on the left, thanks to us. On the right, unfortunately, the Germans broke through, and the Anzacs were being forced back. As a result, we had to leave our good positions and withdraw so we didn't get out-flanked.

On April 13th Donny telephoned Lieutenant-Colonel Elliott of the ANZAC staff to try to clarify their situation. There was no good news.

* * *

'A' Squadron's withdrawal on the night of April 13th was a difficult one: they had to break contact with the enemy and drive through the night to find the rest of their battalion. Watt remembered it well:

> Throughout the night our little convoy crawled slowly south. There was no choice; the roads were choked with traffic. Broken-down vehicles littered the roadside; many were tipped over the side in an attempt to keep the traffic flowing. They may even have crashed on to another road further down the hill, but no one seemed to care in this atmosphere of self-preservation... It was a night of near panic.[31]

Gunner and 'A' Squadron reached a ridge a mile south of the Aliakhmon at 0630 on April 14th, five tanks short of complement. A composite squadron was now formed using all that was left of the battalion: nine tanks from 'A' Squadron, two from 'C' Squadron, and two from RHQ. They waited on the river line all day, but were heavily dive-bombed, and at 2359 moved to a ridge just south of Grevena, from which they retreated on April 15th. Gunner described the battalion's progress:

> It became a fighting retreat. There was more bombing, and we had a few targets – mainly their reconnaissance vehicles to begin with – and the railway bridges and everything were being blown up. That was our main worry, being left on the wrong side of a river. We had to keep going, all the way through the mountains, through Elasson, through Larissa.

Gunner's 4 Troop still had its full complement of three A10s, but with tanks breaking down constantly this was too good to last. When Bob Crisp's tank broke down at the river Venetikos on April 16th, he asked Simpson if he could take over one of 'A' Squadron's vehicles, and Gunner handed over one of his remaining three tanks to Crisp; it was the vehicle crewed by Watt.

* * *

The retreat also sucked in Wilson's Advanced HQ at Tsaritsani, now becoming dangerously exposed. News reached them of 3RTR's action at Ptolemais late on the evening of April 14th, by which time orders had already been issued for a move the following day. Donny and the staff joined the stream of Allied personnel and vehicles heading south.

Not far behind them, the sorry remnants of 3RTR kept moving, losing tanks to mechanical failure along the way and setting them on fire after removing their machine-guns. These they retained to fire at the enemy aircraft which constantly harassed the

Below: *an A10 of 3RTR abandoned during the retreat: it has clearly thrown a track* (Bundesarchiv Bild 1011-161-0317-26).

column. They passed through Kalambaka, where they found a NAAFI store from which they obtained sweets and tinned fruit, and continued towards Trikkala. There they acquired fuel and even some rum. On April 17th Gunner and his comrades again engaged enemy reconnaissance elements, as Trooper Fred Dale of 3 Troop, 'A' Squadron, remembered:

> We only had five tanks left...We were lined up overlooking a valley...When the Germans came we did what we had to do. I took the first three motor-bikes with machine-gun sidecars, and three troop-carriers full of infantry. The other four tanks did the rest. After all our ammunition was finished, the valley was truly blocked.[32]

On the remainder pressed through Larissa. As vehicles broke down or were damaged by air attack, the men were told to make their way to Athens as best they could; many attached themselves to New Zealand or Australian units which were acting as a rearguard. Gunner finally came to grief as the pale shade of his battalion passed the last Allied defensive line.

> At Thermopylae, the final line we could hold, my sole remaining tank bought it, and that was the end of my fighting. We had gone up on a hill where we could get a good view, and the vehicle threw a track. So I was stuck there in a fire position, though I'd no ammunition for the main gun as I'd been firing the 2-pounder at enemy tanks all the way. But we had to do what we could to support the infantry.
> First there came a Stuka attack; when they'd gone off, we said "Good, we've got a bit of peace. Forty minutes at least." I was standing on the back behind the turret, on the engine-deck, seeing what I could see. But then there was this bloody Heinkel 111 which was dropping bombs at random along the road, keeping the pot boiling. I didn't hear it coming. The bomb came in at an angle and blew up under the track, under the tank, and obviously the tracks and everything went. But the main thing was it blew the tank upwards. I don't know how far it went up in the air; it seemed a lot.

An A10 tank weighed fourteen tons.

> The tank came down on to one side. I was thrown off onto a wall, a dry-stone wall, and I landed half-left, on my lower back and mainly on my pelvis. I was in absolute agony – God, it was painful. Of course, my unit couldn't give me any treatment – there was no medical set-up left at all.

The injured Gunner now found himself in the care of the New Zealanders.

> Luckily there was a very nice New Zealand infantry company there, and they took me in and fed me, and the local doctor looked at it. They saved my life. In the end they took me back all the way as far as Argos in the back of one of their lorries. I think we went through the outskirts of Athens, and then across the Corinth Canal. My crew came with me, and all the way we carried our BESAs[33] and ammunition which we'd removed from our tank. When we'd abandoned our last tank at Thermopylae we'd thrown any secret or useful stuff over a cliff.

* * *

By now the evacuation of all Commonwealth forces from Greece was about to commence. Donny and the rest of Wilson's staff had the unenviable task of attempting to co-ordinate the retreat to the evacuation beaches specified by the Royal Navy. As early as April 20th, they were trying to persuade the Navy to assist Commonwealth troops who, it was feared, were cut off in the north.

High Grade Cipher

To: PIGO
From: UMBO   O 208   April 20th

Further to O 206 of 20/4(.) Naval patrol also requested Keramidi-Skiathos to locate elements of 21 NZ Battalion and 2/2 Australian Battalion known to be making for coast east of Volos.

Time of origin 1715

Immediate.   A.D. Mackenzie (Captain) for Brigadier General Staff[34]

As it came to the army's rescue again, the Navy would come under concerted attack from every aircraft that the Germans could muster, opposed by a handful of RAF Hurricanes. Behind the retreating troops the Germans continued to pour men and *materiel* into the country, but hard intelligence was difficult to obtain. Donny and his colleagues did their best to distribute news to those who needed it:

> To: UNBA
> From: UMBO O 214 April 21st
> Air recce results 20/April. Road Kalabaka-Trikkala 50 MT. Trikkala-Larissa 5 MT moving east. Elasson-Larissa no movement seen. Larissa-Pharsala 100 MT moving south. No movement seen other roads Larissa. Time of recce not known. *Time of origin 0940*
> Immediate. A.D. Mackenzie (Captain)
>
> To: ANZAC Corps 82 Base Sub-Area
> From: HQ BTG O 687 April 23rd
> Air recce reports 1000 hours. No movement seen on roads or coasts Euboea. No movement seen coasts and roads north of Euboea. No unusual numbers small craft seen. *Time of origin 1145*
> Immediate. A.D. Mackenzie (Captain), authority GSO1
>
> To: ANZAC Corps repeated 82 Base Sub-Area
> From: HQ BTG O 689 April 23rd
> From Greek General Staff. 200 Germans landed OREOI Y85 1130 hours 23 April. *Time of origin 1320*
> Most Immediate A.D. Mackenzie (Captain), authority GOC[35]

By April 25th, with the evacuation – Operation Demon – in full swing, there was nothing left for Wilson and his staff to do. They had reached the small coastal village of Mili, across the bay from the port of Nauplion, one of the main points of evacuation. There they awaited their own transport.

* * *

The scattered personnel of 3RTR were also making their way out of the country by any means they could find. Gunner must have passed the Corinth Canal on Friday April 25th, for that was the day that German parachutists landed there and cut off the remaining Allied troops north of the Isthmus.

> At the Corinth Canal I saw my first parachutists come down. From there we went to Argos, and we formed a sort of perimeter. I saw a Sunderland flying-boat going off [April 26th] with Jumbo Wilson.

Also aboard the Sunderland, it seems, was Donny Mackenzie, though other elements of HQ BTG were evacuated by sea. Gunner had to wait for a ship to take him off.

> The boats came in and during the night we got on board a destroyer. I needed a lot of help to walk; I was virtually carried. As the sun came up [April 27th] the convoy of boats was really bombed; I mean, our guns must have been red-hot. They'd run out of ammunition by the time we got to Suda Bay.

Although Gunner thought that his rescuing destroyer was HMS *Diamond*, he must have made the voyage in either HMS *Hotspur* or HMS *Isis*, which picked up twelve officers and 180 men of 3RTR from Nauplion on the night of April 26th-27th. Other personnel from Gunner's battalion were picked up from Monevasia or Kalamata. Once again the Royal Navy was suffering heavy losses in its support of the army; as the ships from the Nauplion area made their run across the Crete on April 27th the troopship *Slamat* and destroyers HMS *Diamond* and HMS *Wryneck* were sunk with heavy casualties.[36]

But 3RTR had also lost heavily. The Second-in-Command, "Shufti" Carey, had been captured along with Dennis Bartlett, two other officers and one hundred other ranks; they were concentrated in a camp near Corinth before being marched to Salonika on a daily ration of potato soup and three ounces of bread. Carey was a great loss to the battalion.

> The best officer in the Regiment was Major Basil Carey, who was known as "Shufti" – Arabic for "Look" – owing to his only having one eye. He would have been a wonderful CO, far better than Keller.

Gunner had now fought twice against overwhelming odds: both times his battalion had been shattered, and both times he had been wounded and evacuated by sea. As at Calais, he had been lucky to escape with his life.

* * *

The survivors of 3RTR were now at Suda Bay on Crete, and it was obvious that the Germans intended to make this their next conquest. Gunner recalled that the enemy aircraft which had plagued them in Greece now swarmed in the skies over Crete.

> We were met there with bombing: the Germans were already building up for their parachute drop. We'd collected about a quarter of the Regiment, and tried to concentrate them in one place. I could just about walk by this stage, though it was painful and I shouldn't have done it – on the whole I was mainly carried. We went up into an olive grove just inland from Suda and took up defensive positions, and we mounted our BESAs in trees as anti-aircraft defences. There were only a few tanks on Crete – only light tanks. So we really missed the serious fighting, because of an order that all tank crews must be got back to Egypt, where they were desperately needed.

If only there had been more tanks on Crete: the German parachutists had no weapons capable of knocking them out, and a few troops of cruisers or infantry tanks might have tipped the balance. However, two Matildas at Maleme would be mis-handled and later counter-attacks therefore lacked offensive punch. With no tanks to man, the personnel of 3RTR – now under the command of Major Bill Reeves DSO – were surplus to requirements.

On May 9th, convoy AS30 (code-named Pollux) assembled in Suda Bay to evacuate non-essential personnel to Alexandria.[37] Gunner and Donny were both allocated places on this convoy. Donny was to travel on the *Rodi*, which was to load at 1530 and was to carry wounded troops, New Zealanders, British consular staff, seven women and six children – a total of 654 passengers. Among them appear to have been the author Lawrence Durrell, his wife, and their infant daughter Penelope, as well as Wykehamist Major "Toby" Low DSO, later Lord Aldington.[38]

At 1700, the men of 3RTR boarded the SS *Popi* (also referred to as the *Popi Vernicos* because it was owned by the Vernicos shipping line), a decrepit Greek tramp steamer which could have given even an A10 lessons in mechanical unreliability.[39] According to the naval operations order, the 3RTR party numbered seventeen officers and 188 other ranks, all that remained of the battalion. With them were fourteen RAF personnel and, unexpectedly, a group of German prisoners-of-war – mostly airmen downed over Crete – who had been intended for another vessel:

> Suda area will arrange that the twenty-one POW embarking in SS *City of Canterbury* are handed over to 16 Heavy AA Battery, who will be responsible for their custody until they hand them over to the appointed authority in Egypt.[40]

For some reason, the prisoners were instead entrusted to 3RTR, and because Gunner could speak German he found himself responsible for them.

Above: the Popi Vernicos *in better days, when thirty years younger and operating in British waters as the SS* Cairnisla *(copyright holder unknown).*

> They put us on this fifty-year-old Sunderland-built tramp-steamer, the *Popi Vernicos*. When we got on the boat, even though I was wounded and in considerable pain, I was given a present of twenty-one prisoners.

But this was not his only problem. As the *Popi Vernicos* sailed that afternoon, it rapidly became clear that she could not keep up with the rest of the convoy. Trooper Jim Caswell ('B' Squadron) and Jock Watt both remembered the conditions on board the "Pop-Eye", as the vessel was christened:

> The ship had not been at sea for twenty-seven years, had no food aboard, and was unable to exceed four knots speed, lagging behind the convoy bound for Alexandria. The daily ration was a tin of bully between two, a packet of biscuits, plus a pint of water for all purposes.[41]

> We loaded our gear, all the food that could be begged, borrowed or stolen, strapped the machine-guns to the rigging, and sailed round the west end of Crete before turning east towards Egypt... Our living quarters were the deck, and we slept rolled up in a blanket with some equipment for a pillow. Food was very scarce and limited to half a tin of bully and a few biscuits each day – not a gourmet's delight, but a good solid constipating diet. The first couple of days were a bit nerve-racking, expecting planes to appear any minute.[42]

Gunner used to recall another problem with the boat; its boilers were coal-fired, and there was not enough coal to get the *Popi Vernicos* to Alexandria.

> We were running on coal-dust and wooden fittings, riddling the cinders to get little bits of coal. Not a piece of wood remained on the boat.

Fred Dale, one of Gunner's comrades in 'A' Squadron, also remembered the fuel shortage:

> Our officer Lieutenant Upcott-Gill took over the boat. When the coal ran out we all had to take a spell in sieving the coal-dust. We looked like black minstrels, and after that we started to burn all the wood we could find: doors, the wheelhouse, everything.[43]

The voyage was not without other incident, as Gunner recalled:

At one point a submarine came up beside us. It must have been one of ours. But eventually we docked.

Major Reeves explained that even this was not without its difficulties:

Our junior officer managed to read the charts on the bridge and so steer towards Alexandria. When the destroyer HMS *Grimsby* signalled to us to stop, no one knew how to stop the ship.[44]

Captain George Witheridge was the unfortunate who had to read the *Grimsby*'s signal "Stop or we will sink you" and flash a reply by torch: "Have stopped." The destroyer escorted the decrepit steamer into Alexandria, where the 3RTR party were welcomed by the sirens and hooters of all the ships in port. It was May 13th 1941. The battalion had been at war for less than a year, and in that time had been shattered twice and evacuated by sea three times.

Gunner had to dispose of his German prisoners before he could rejoin the battalion:

I was sort of priority, because I had to hand our prisoners over to the Military Police. That was great, because they did everything for me: they took me to the Cecil Hotel, and then arranged a Military Police vehicle to take me to Heliopolis, where we were concentrating what remained of the Regiment. From there I was sent off to the Cairo hospital.

* * *

Back on Crete, the defenders fought a vicious battle against German parachute troops, who landed on May 20th. This ended in the loss of the island, but only because of the fall of Maleme airfield; elsewhere the defenders more than held their own. Gunner's own views on the battle were clear:

This was the first and last large scale use of parachutists by the Germans. They also tried a landing by sea, which the Navy dealt with. All the main airfields were on the north side of Crete, which is where the parachutists landed. They suffered heavy casualties and two of their drops were defeated: Heraklion and Khania – the only place they took was Maleme. It wasn't a big airfield, just a landing-strip. In my book the battle for Crete was a victory, not a defeat, for the Allied forces. After the casualties the Germans suffered, they never used parachutists again. It probably influenced them against trying an airborne attack on Cyprus or Syria.

Since the war I've been back several times to see the graves of two of my comrades in the Suda Cemetery. Every Cretan I've met has to tell the story of what went on; I've got a great admiration for them. There's a big German cemetery at Maleme now, with these red flowers they have in all the German cemeteries. When I went there was a book with all the names of the people who were buried, and some German had written: "German soldiers: the finest in the world." And I wrote under it: "Who won the war?" In German.

Chapter Seven
Crusader

The history of a battle, is not unlike the history of a ball. Some individuals may recollect all the little events of which the great result is the battle won or lost, but no individual can recollect the order in which, or the exact moment at which, they occurred, which makes all the difference as to their value or importance.
(The Duke of Wellington, letter to John Croker, dated August 8th 1815)

Records of what Donny Mackenzie did on his evacuation from Crete in May 1941 are hard to find. Regimental records are silent, and his personnel file has gaps. It may be that he returned to HQ Mersa Matruh Area for a while. However, his personnel file tells us that on August 18th 1941 he was posted to HQ British Troop, Cyprus, as Deputy Assistant Adjutant and Quartermaster-General (DAAQMG).

The fall of Greece had focused British attention on their weakness in the eastern Mediterranean. The Vichy French held Syria, and there were fears of a German invasion through Turkey, threatening not only Egypt but the oil pipeline from Persia and Iraq into Palestine and Jordan. Cyprus was considered a likely target for an airborne invasion, and a scratch defence force of Australians was assembled there in May 1941. The German losses in Crete, however, made the threat recede, but the British nevertheless remained concerned. On June 14th they began a deception operation, establishing a fake headquarters for an imaginary 7th Infantry Division. British troops arrived in August 1941, and it was probably as part of this movement that Donny came to the island. Later, the deception was extended with the creation on Cyprus of a fictitious XXV Corps, and Donny was administratively posted to that formation as part of the deception plan. On November 25th he was promoted to the acting rank of Major.

He was hospitalized on December 16th 1941 and was not discharged until the 31st, at which point he was granted a fortnight's sick leave. This was probably a bout of malaria, which Donny appears to have contracted earlier in Palestine. A recurrence of this disease was later to change the entire course of the last year of his life – and was to have profound implications also for Gunner.

* * *

After Greece, once again, 3RTR had required re-building. After a spell of local leave – during which the men blew their accumulated pay and evacuees' allowances on celebrating their good fortune – the remnants found themselves in the peculiar position of being a tankless tank battalion.

> We'd lost about fifty *per cent* of our personnel in Calais, and we lost about the same in Greece and Crete. We got reinforcements at Heliopolis, but no tanks.

It could have been worse: out in the deserts and hills of Libya, 3RTR's sister battalions were participating in the disastrous battles of June 1941 against newly-arrived German forces under Rommel. Instead, once the men of 3RTR were rested they were sent on courses.

Gunner, having at last received proper mdeical care, had spent most of June 1941 recuperating from the severe injuries to his back and pelvis.

> I had wonderful treatment in the Cairo Military Hospital. I don't think that they put me in plaster, though my pelvis was in pretty poor shape. About fifty years after the war a doctor looked at it and said: "My God, what's happened to your pelvis? There's a ridge right across it." He followed the line of it all the way from side to side. I think that it had been fractured but hadn't actually come apart.
>
> When I went back to Heliopolis, I spent most of my time swimming up and down the Heliopolis Club pool to try to speed my recovery. They'd done all sorts of things to my back, and before they discharged me said that one of the best things I could do for it was swimming. Well, the Club Secretary saw me and asked if I played water-polo. I told him that I'd never played in my life, though I'd watched it a lot in Malta as a boy.
>
> "We need a centre-forward for an important match against the Egyptian Army tomorrow."
>
> What he didn't mention was that the Egyptian Army team was one of the best in the world. They were officially soldiers but all they actually did was play water-polo. They were all as fat as anything – they didn't have to swim, they just floated naturally.
>
> I had a quick practice. When the referee threw the ball in, my job as centre-forward was to grab it and flick it back to our team, and then swim forwards to stand in front of the Egyptian goal. The rest of the team had to get the ball to me, so that I could slam it in past the keeper. It all worked quite well in the practice session.
>
> The match itself was somewhat different. Playing against the Egyptians was one of the most dangerous things I've ever done. As soon as I touched the water-polo ball, it was a free-for-all: they kicked, they punched, they smashed up from underneath – absolute bloody murder. So as soon as I got the ball I made sure that I got rid of it sharpish. By the end I was bruised all over. How I had any balls left I don't know.

By July 12th Gunner was sufficiently recovered to go on a course at the RAC Base Depot at Quassassin. By the time that he returned to 3RTR on July 24th, he was an Acting Captain. His duties that summer included attachments to two other units: 8th Hussars – to whom he taught desert navigation – and before them, the Polish forces.[1]

> As 3RTR didn't have any tanks to fight or train with it made sense to use us to pass on our experience to other units. General Kopański was training the Polish Brigade, made up of exiles who had streamed across Europe after the German and Russian invasions of 1939. A lot of them were officers – they had more officers sometimes than other ranks.
>
> There was a little Major who looked like Mussolini and was called Shermuski – though I called him Benito. He and I had the job of producing a handbook, a glossary of British Army military terms, to be given to every Polish soldier. I had a copy of the British Military glossary, and I'd explain in German to Shermuski what it was. He then chose a Polish equivalent. We ended up with an English-Polish military dictionary. Thousands were published.
>
> I had a great time with the Poles out at El Amariya near Alexandria, where we were in tents. We had a guest night for the General, in a huge room with glass-topped tables all the way round. We could have been in a shop; there was food everywhere. Pickled herrings, the works. They were all helping themselves. I thought that this was the main meal. I was introduced to everyone, and everyone I met suggested a toast in vodka. When we greeted one another in the morning or whatever we used to say *"Czołem!"* and that's what we used as the toast. I'm not normally a drinker and I was stuffing myself with food, and frankly I was getting a bit full. Suddenly the doors opened and a couple of people started blowing bloody trumpets – which was the call to dinner. In we went and sat down for an ordinary guest-night dinner. The drinking went on, and for the only time in my life I was so drunk that I had to be put to bed. in my tent. When I woke up in the morning I felt like death.
>
> I wasn't with the Poles for very long, because as soon as the first new tanks arrived the Regiment called me back sharpish.

3RTR's duties at Heliopolis were largely dull, but enlivened by an active social life in nearby Cairo.[2] Bob Crisp had happy memories of the summer of 1941:

Our leisure hours were spent pleasantly enough, sipping tall, cool John Collinses on the paved perimeter of the swimming pool of the Heliopolis Club, eyeing with indecent speculation the cosmopolitan bathing beauties of the region, their figures still trim in youth but burgeoning with discerning plumpness in promise of early seduction. Later, as we got to know our way around, we deserted the unrequited lovelies of Heliopolis and sipped our long, cool John Collinses around the swimming pool at Gezira, where the only difference was that there was more of everything, and it was not so unrequited...

Defence duties, training and re-equipping were the banal watchwords for our existence. We forgot them whenever we could at the sporting clubs, at Groppi's, on the roof of the Continental, in Shepheard's bar or Tommy's and, on more opulent evenings, at the huntin'-shootin'-fishin' inn out on the Mena Road, where we occasionally shared the same dance floor with King Farouk... It was all very pleasant, and I kept on telling myself that this was the way that American millionaires spent a lot of their millions.[3]

But the pace of life quickened early in August as the new equipment arrived with which 3RTR would return to the fray. This time, mechanical problems were not going to get in their way, as Gunner recalled.

The Americans weren't in the war yet, but they gave us their tanks, brand-new M3 Stuart light tanks – the Honeys. Everyone's heard the story of how they got their nick-name, but I heard it first said: we asked one of the Americans who came to show us the thing how reliable it was, and he replied, "Oh, gee, she's a honey." And the name stuck.

It was wonderfully reliable – such a contrast to our British tanks. It was incredibly fast; you could turn on a sixpence at sixty miles an hour, pretty well; and the only trouble was that they didn't know how to design a fighting turret. It was all manual; no power at all. The gunner controlled elevation with his shoulder, but to get traverse he had to bend to the other side of the turret and turn a big wheel. It was impossible – how can you do both? So as a fighting platform it was absolutely useless. I don't know how they did it, but our own mechanics of the LAD moved the traversing wheel to the gunner's position. So he could then do the two together.

Below: *Honeys of 8th Hussars advancing in training in Egypt, August 1941. The tanks' compactness is clear, as is its high profile. The pennants attached to the whip-aerials made the tanks even more visible (IWM E5062).*

With the Honey, the British crews felt much more confident. However, their tactics had not evolved to match those of their opponents. The Germans used tanks and anti-tank guns in close co-operation, the tanks luring the British on to devastating ambushes; the British still assumed that tanks fought tanks.

The first three Honeys reached 3RTR on August 12th, and were followed the next day by a new commanding officer, Lieutenant-Colonel A.A.H. "Bunny" Ewin.[4] A week later the battalion moved to a tented camp at Beni Yusef, which stood beside the Sweet Water Canal twenty-five miles from Cairo. Here the battalion joined 4 Armoured Brigade, and spent September training on the Honeys which arrived in batches throughout the month. By the end of September they were ready to begin practice shoots with their main armament. Soon enough they would use their guns for real; Gunner was about to go into battle with 3RTR for the third and final time.

* * *

The war in North Africa was one in which logistics played a vital role. Everything which an army required to fight – food, fuel, ammunition, water – had to be brought with it.[5] The further that an army advanced, the more strained became its supply arrangements. The two major ports on the North African shore were Tripoli, for the Italians and Germans, and Alexandria, for the British and their allied contingents. Between these major ports lay smaller ones – Benghazi, Tobruk, and Mersa Matruh – control of which constrained the whole conduct of the campaign.

The desert was a peculiar environment, where there were few civilians and little chance of living off the land; armies had to have motorized transport, and were thus dependent on their supply of petrol. The further from base they drove, the less and less fuel reached the front line – especially for the British, whose petrol still travelled in impractical flimsy four-gallon tins which split and leaked at the slightest provocation. Thus it was as though the British and German-Italian armies were on elastic: the British elastic seemed to reach full stretch westwards at Benghazi, and the Axis elastic looked as though it might just stretch eastwards as far as Alexandria.

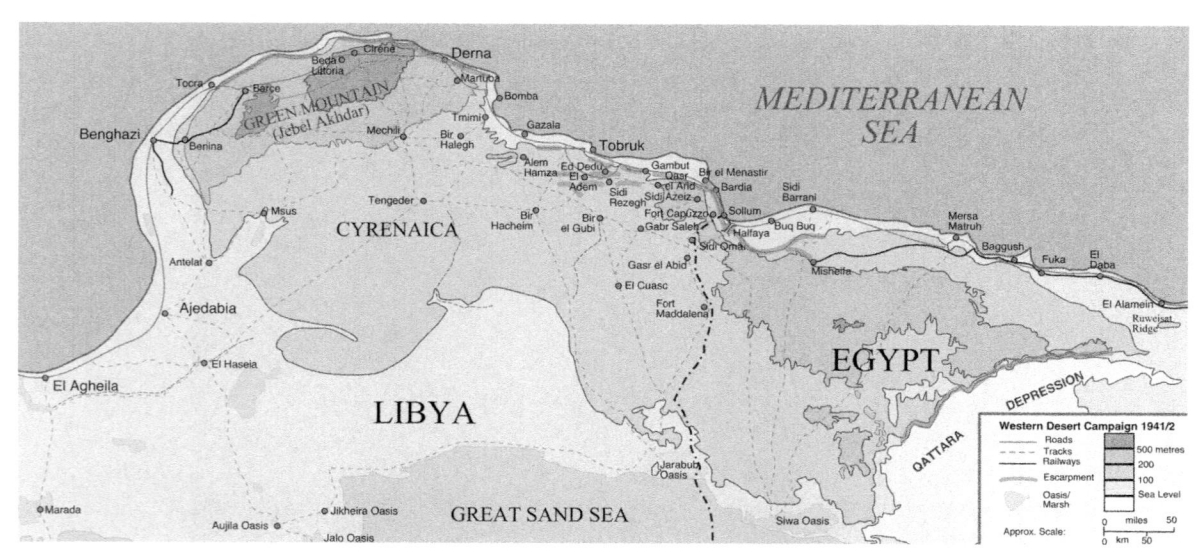

Since 1940, the war had flowed this way and that through the Western Desert of Egypt and the area of Libya known as Cyrenaica. First, in September 1940, the Italians had moved east from Libya into Egypt; then between December 1940 and February 1941 the British had driven them back into Libya and past Benghazi; then the Germans had arrived and forced the British back to the Egyptian border in March and April 1941. But the British had managed to fortify the port of Tobruk and to hold it against everything which the Axis forces could throw against it in terms of air-power and ground assault. Gunner was in no doubt that the relief of Tobruk was an absolute priority:

> The next big thing was the relief of Tobruk, which we were holding to stop Rommel from using it, and were having to supply from the sea. The defenders were almost all Australians, who were doing very well.

The Royal Navy ran tremendous risks maintaining the supply-line to Tobruk, whilst seventy-five miles to the east British land forces planned their counter-offensives. These aimed to raise the siege and to drive Rommel's troops back to Benghazi and then, it was hoped, out of North Africa entirely. Operation Brevity in May 1941 had enjoyed limited success; Operation Battleaxe in June was a failure, and led to Wavell being relieved of command and being replaced by Auchinleck. British and Commonwealth forces in Egypt were now designated the Eighth Army, and prepared for a third – and, they hoped, decisive – attack into Libya: Operation Crusader.

* * *

The British offensive of November 1941 resulted in immensely complicated battles in which great heroism was displayed by both sides. When 3RTR advanced on November 18th the men would have been horrified to know that they would spend the next fortnight continuously in combat without a pause, covering over 1500 miles, very little of it in a straight line. Indeed, Gunner's part in the battle would not end until December 16th, during which his unit would have only two or three days out of contact with the enemy.

The desert over which this long and difficult fighting took place had a unique character, which is best explained by an officer who was there:

> It is unlikely that anyone who did not personally experience the desert in war will understand clearly the impressions of those who did. In the tales that will be told in the future will be many contradictions. Some people will dwell on the desert's hostility to all forms of life, and the discomforts it occasioned to those who had the temerity to try to support life in its sterile bosom. They will tell how myriads of flies, the most faithful camp followers in the history of warfare, plagued them throughout the day and sometimes clustered so thickly on their vehicles as to turn them from brown to black. They will describe the abominable *khamseen*, the hot wind from the burning deserts of the south, which spread a smothering blanket of fine sand over everything, choked the nostrils, infiltrated into ears and eyes, and, when mouths were opened to swear, got into them too.
>
> On the other hand, there will be others who will speak wistfully of sunsets, when coolness came upon the desert like a benediction after the heat of the day, and the sky was beautiful in pastel shades of heliotrope and pink; who will speak of long journeys through trackless wastes, accomplished by means of magnetic and sun compasses; who will affirm that there is a special joy in the desert in a beer or whisky and the light of a hurricane lamp at eventide.
>
> The contradictions will be understandable to those who realize that the desert has many moods and is very large. The northern desert of Africa is, in fact, bigger than India. The coastal strip... consists in Egypt of a coastal plain which is backed by an escarpment which runs parallel to it. From the top of the escarpment a plateau extends to the south. Up this barrier, at Sollum, the coastal road winds painfully; and a little to the south-east a secondary route – no more than a track – clambers to the top of Halfaya Pass.
>
> Westward through Cyrenaica the escarpment is for the most part close to the coast, and in the semi-circular bulge between Gazala and Benghazi it develops into the Akhdar Hills, green and pleasant, and colonized before the war by Italian smallholders. The Gebel, as this country was called in the Eighth Army, is one of the few green areas in Libya. Along the coastal strip there is, generally speaking,

just sufficient rainfall to support a thin, sporadic vegetation. In places the desert suddenly blossoms, and in spring small depressions may be carpeted with flowers. Such oases in the barren lands seem doubly beautiful by contrast with their surroundings. Here and there the Bedouin succeed in growing a thin crop of cereals. But in stark contrast to such glimpses of gentler country great tracts of sterile sand stretch away to far horizons under the staring sun, and fantastic mirages are the nearest thing to beauty which the traveller will find.

One piece of desert is very much like another, for the wilderness is full of repetitions. The newcomer, looking at a map produced in those early days, would sometimes say: "But why is all this space blank?" He would not yet have learned that the desert itself is sometimes blank for scores of miles. Landmarks were few. Rock cisterns, dug and cemented by the Romans, and usually flanked by twin mounds of excavated material, were invaluable guides to one's position. *Bir* (pronounced "Beer") was their Arabic name. Occasionally the map would show the tomb of some desert personage. Sometimes it was just four low walls, like a miniature village penfold, with white rags fluttering from it. Occasionally the humble grave of a desert commoner, just a few stones apparently pitched on to the face of the desert, would help an anxious navigator.

Tracks there were, and when these were marked by route posts they were invaluable. But often the criss-cross comings and goings of the vehicles of two armies had resulted in a maze of tracks to which it was safest to pay no attention.

Natural features, with a few notable exceptions, did not exist in any marked form, though experience taught the soldier to recognize slight rises and falls in the desert for what they were. "Return to this depression tonight," said an officer to the leader of a small patrol. "What depression?" was the reply. "The one we're in now," said the officer.[6]

At Calais, Gunner had fought in close farmland and in the suburbs of the port; in Greece, among the steep limestone hills; now, in Libya, he was to fight in a very different sort of terrain. And his rôle was different as well: Gunner was this time entrusted with the battalion's navigation.

* * *

One of the best analogies for desert fighting is that of the sea; there were no front lines, and few commanding features or fixed points. Armoured units manouevred through the featureless terrain like warships. For example, on November 24th, 3RTR would receive orders to join Brigade HQ, and would be told to navigate as follows:

Six miles on 117° and then six miles on 158°.[7]

Gunner explained how this worked in practice:

Navigation at night was actually easier and more accurate, because you could use the stars. You'd work out the bearing you wanted to drive on, and you'd then look at the stars. You've got to remember that the skies were almost always clear. You'd fix what star lay on your desired bearing, and work out how far it would move across the sky in half an hour. So you'd allow for that movement, set off, and check again after half an hour, make a new fix, and so on. You'd tell your driver: "Can you see that star straight ahead? Keep it in front of you until I tell you." It was so easy that on a night move you'd almost always arrive exactly bang on. The only problems came if you met a patch of rough going and had to swing off your course and come back on to it later.

Daytime navigation was much harder and actually a lot slower. Maps were useless, as in the desert there were very few or no features – rivers, roads, villages, towns, mountains, and the like. About the only features shown on maps were water wells and the graves of Islamic "saints" – *Sidi* whatever – and there weren't many of those. Every dip and hollow you drove into, your horizon disappeared. So you never had a landmark to drive upon, no fixed point or nice star to tell your driver to aim for. Navigation became almost the same as being at sea: we had to use dead-reckoning on compass bearings. You depended on your prismatic compass and the milometers of your vehicles. The prismatic compass was absolutely accurate and reliable, but to use it you had to take it as far away as you could from any bits of metal, such as your tank. So you couldn't use it whilst on the move. Every time you went through a dip and lost the horizon you had to re-set your bearings, which slowed you down.

To keep a steady course you also had the help of your sun-compass. It wasn't quite as accurate as the prismatic compass, just a paper dial, but meant that you could keep on driving and check your direction as you went along.

Gunner had been fortunate in that he had received some excellent training whilst en route to the Middle East before the Greek campaign:

For our navigation training we had been very lucky. Basil "Shufti" Carey had a lot of experience in the Middle East and was an absolute expert on desert map-reading and navigation. On our way out, on the ship, he had given every vehicle commander and all the young officers a wonderful course in desert navigation. He had a sun-compass on board, thank God, so we knew all about that.

Since returning from Greece, Gunner had been honing the navigational skills which he had learned from Carey (who had of course been captured in Greece).

I had done well on Basil Carey's course; I got really quite good at desert navigation. So when we got to the desert I was made Regimental Navigator, an important job but not on the establishment.

I helped train 8th Hussars, who were alongside 3RTR in 4 Armoured Brigade, and were stationed in a camp near Mena House, close to the pyramids. When I came out of hospital after Greece, my CO sent me to them to run a course on desert navigation, to pass on some of our navigational expertise. A chap called Richard Roffey was doing the job of Regimental Navigator for them, but I had to train him in his role.[8] I lived in their Officers' Mess rather than sleep at Heliopolis and drive over each day.

Mena House Camp was right on the edge of the desert, and they had a lot of excellent training areas right at hand. 8th Hussars were learning to drive their new tanks – Honeys, like ours. To fire the main guns, they didn't need to go to special ranges, they just fired them there in the desert. All the vehicle commanders and commanders of replenishment vehicles came to me – anyone who had to use a sun-compass – and I described to them the process of day and night navigation.

They were quite unlucky that autumn. They had quite a lot of training accidents, which was inevitable really when you think of all the things which could go wrong. We had one tragedy during a night navigation exercise: they'd been out into the desert, and were coming back to camp on a bearing, bang on, but forgot that there was a cliff in between, and went straight over it and were killed.

In the battle which followed, they had about one hundred *per cent* tank losses: I lost a lot of friends.

* * *

4 Armoured Brigade comprised 3RTR, 5RTR, and 8th Hussars, supported by the 25-pounder howitzers of 2nd Regiment, Royal Horse Artillery (2RHA) and the infantrymen of 2nd Battalion, Scots Guards.[9] In theory, each tank regiment co-operated with a battery of field guns and a company of infantrymen, but in practice this often broke down.

This is not the place to tell the full story of Operation Crusader, or even of 4 Armoured Brigade's part in it. To do so would be an impossibility in any case, as the Duke of Wellington observed. It is hard enough to tell even 3RTR's story. Gunner's view of the fighting was necessarily limited, and the potential for confusion was enormous:

When you were fighting you often had very little idea of the bigger picture. There were no front lines at all. The Germans were using large amounts of captured transport, and quite a few of them spoke English quite well. All very confusing. Whenever any tanks approached, you were never quite sure whether they were German or British; you never knew who it was you'd met until they opened fire – or not. In consequence there was always a possibility of being the target of "friendly fire".

What follows is as a result sketchy and incomplete.[10]

The plan for Crusader was that Commonwealth troops would drive across the Libyan frontier well to the south of the main German concentrations, and then hook northwards

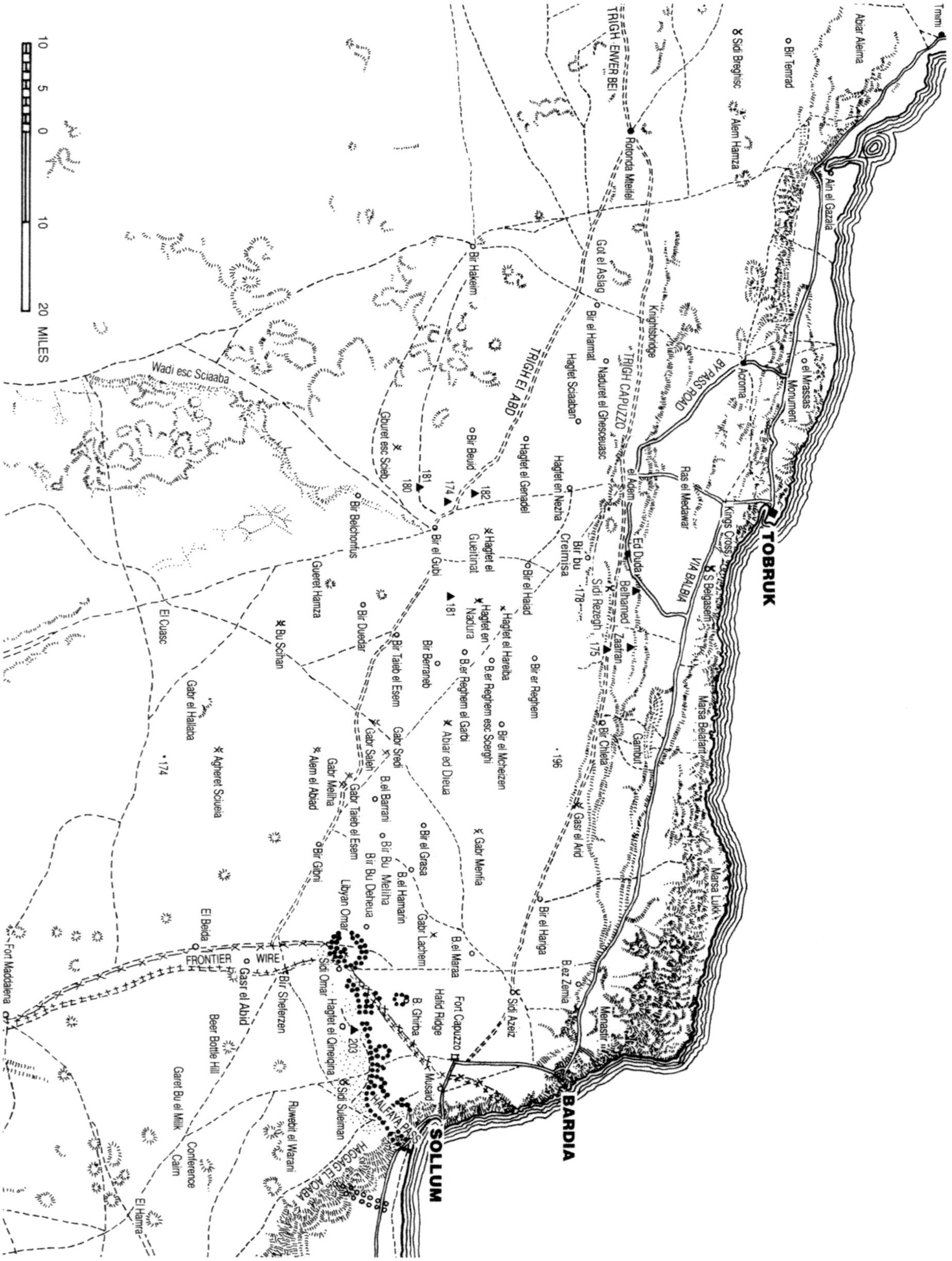
Tmimi
Abiar Aleima
Bir Temrad
Sidi Breghisc
Alem Hamza
TRIGH ENVER BEI
Rotonda Mteifel
Ain el Gazala
Got el Aslag
Knightsbridge
Bir Hakeim
Bir el Harmat
Naduret el Ghesceuasc
TRIGH CAPUZZO
BYPASS ROAD
Acroma
el Mrassas
Monument
Haglet Sciaaban
TRIGH EL ABD
Wadi esc Sciaaba
Bir Beuid
Haglet el Genadel
Haglet en Nezha
Ras el Medawar
Kings Cross
TOBRUK
Gburet esc Scieb
181
180
174
182
el Adem
Ed Duda
Bir bu Creimisa
VIA BALBIA
S. Belgasem
Bir Belchonfus
Bir el Gubi
Haglet el Gueitinat
Bir el Haiad
Sidi Rezegh
178
Belhamed
Zaafran
Gueret Hamza
El Cuasc
Bir Duedar
Haglet el Hareiba
Haglet en Nadura
Bu Scihan
Bir Taieb el Esem
Bir Berraneb
B.er Reghem el Garbi
B.er Reghem esc Scerghi
Bir er Reghem
175
Marsa Belafarit
Bir Chleta
Gambut
Gabr el Hallaba
196
Bir el Mcheizen
Abiar ed Dieua
Gabr Sredi
Gabr Saleh
Agheret Sciueia
174
Alem el Abiad
Gabr Meliha
Gabr Taieb el Esem
B.el Barrani
Gasr el Arid
Bir el Grasa
Bir Bu Meliha
Gabr Menfia
Bir Gibni
Bir Bu Deheua
B.el Hamarin
Marsa Luk
Libyan Omar
Gabr Lachem
Bir el Hariga
El Beida
FRONTIER
WIRE
Sidi Omar
Bir Sheferzen
Gasr el Abid
B.el Maraa
B.ez Zemla
Fort Maddalena
Haglet el Qineqina
B. Ghirba
Hafid Ridge
Fort Capuzzo
Sidi Azeiz
Menastir
Beer Bottle Hill
203
Musaid
BARDIA
Garet Bu el Milik
Sidi Suleiman
HALFAYA PASS
Ruweibit el Warani
SOLLUM
Conference Cairn
HAGGAG EL AQABA
El Hamra
10 5 0 10 20 MILES

across the German and Italian lines of communication. The enemy would then have to retire from the Egyptian border and, it was hoped, abandon the siege of Tobruk. They would have to attack the British armour if they were to open up their supply-lines again, and so the advantage of being on the defensive would, in theory, pass to the British.

* * *

3RTR advanced to "The Wire" with its tanks disguised as 3-ton trucks, having endured a torrential downpour and thunder-storm the previous night. The rain had the positive side-effect of preventing the large dust-clouds which usually marked the advance of armour. Gunner was no longer in command of 4 Troop (now run by a Lieutenant Owens), but serving with HQ Squadron:

> When the whole Regiment streamed on through The Wire, I was with the CO, because I was doing the navigation. The CO had to know where he was and had no time to work it out himself. Even when we weren't in action, he was on the move the whole time, always having to head off and see what was happening on the flank or whatever.
> He certainly couldn't navigate as well as fight his tactical battle. During a tank battle, an armoured regiment was using over sixty radio sets on several different nets, and when someone came up on the air he'd sometimes be cutting across the CO or other people. You had to train your people to spend the minimum of time on air: "Four. Wilco. Out." "Four-B; contact." "Four, report." People had to be very, very disciplined. If you started waffling on air you'd get all kinds of hell from your Squadron Commander or CO.
> Co-ordinating all that was a nightmare in itself, not to mention the fact that the CO had to command his own vehicle. As a tank commander, as well as being on the radio net, you had to be on the intercom, speaking to the crew, controlling the gun. Even though fighting wasn't going on all the time, it made it very difficult to establish exactly where everyone was.
> So the CO had a Regimental Navigator, who travelled with RHQ and whose sole job was to work out RHQ's exact position. He moved behind the CO's tank with a large black flag on his vehicle. So that's where I was for most of the time for the next few weeks, usually in a Honey – which once again I'd christened "Swiftsure". I was always busy with the navigation; I didn't fire my main gun at all when I was with RHQ – though I was fired at often enough. I couldn't spend my time firing; I had my map, compass and so on and had to keep plotting where we were. Tank commanders didn't tend to close down inside – we were always head and shoulders out of the turret hatch – but that was especially true for a navigator. You just couldn't do the job unless you could see your surroundings.
> Whenever RHQ stopped anywhere, I'd get down and go across to the CO and say "You're here, Sir." Often he'd say "Good God, I didn't realize we'd come as far as that."

4 Armoured Brigade crossed into Libya before dawn on November 18th. Gunner had gone ahead to see where his battalion would cross the frontier:

> As Regimental Navigator I had to see exactly the right spot. I was told to report to Uniacke, who was Brigade Major; he'd been Adjutant at the RTR Depot when I first joined. He led the party who were to cut The Wire which went from Fort Capuzzo right down to the sea.

After passing through The Wire and driving westwards, 3RTR turned north, drove for sixty miles without encountering the enemy, and stopped for the night at Point 185, a meaningless mark on the map.

Night always brought an end to movement or fighting in the desert: both sides used the hours of darkness to regroup and to resupply their vehicles. This was especially important for the fuel-thirsty Honeys. It was British policy to operate widely dispersed by day, so as to decrease the dangers posed by air attack, but to contract into a tight formation at night, called a "leaguer". This term was derived from the Afrikaans word *laager*, the wagon-circle

Above: British troops crossing "The Wire" at the start of Operation Crusader (IWM E6686).

which the trekking Boers had used when colonizing the African *veldt*. Watt describes 3RTR's typical night-time formation:

> Darkness was our only true hiding-place, but even that depended upon strict procedures being maintained. no radio transmission during approach to the selected area, and no lights or fires; even the glow of a cigarette can be seen with binoculars. A radio switched to transmit could be detected by direction-finding equipment, and your location pin-pointed to a few yards on the ground. To avoid discovery by patrols, the Regiment's leaguer occupied the smallest space possible; the three sides of a square were formed by the tank squadrons, each tank facing outwards, and the end closed by HQ Troop; the soft vehicles of the infantry, artillery and supply Echelons occupied the centre area.[11]

The Germans used a very different procedure, guiding their supply vehicles to their night-time positions by firing flares and tracer into the sky. Since neither side operated at night, this was probably no more dangerous than the British method, and at least had the advantage that scattered units could re-group under cover of darkness. The Germans also used the hours of darkness to recover disabled tanks from the battlefield and repair them, so that their losses were always lower than the British expected. It was not until later that the British adopted a policy of blowing up disabled German tanks to prevent their repair.

For the British tank crews, even the hours of darkness provided little scope for rest, as Gunner explained:

> When you stopped and went into leaguer, the replenishment vehicles would come round, and you'd say what you required in the way of ammunition and fuel and so on. The fuel was still in what we called "flimsies" – they were useless and never worked. A whole lorry would come up with a load of flimsies in the desert and there'd be nothing in them. So we tried to capture as many jerry-cans as we could and use those, which speeded up the process of re-fuelling a tank considerably. You might also have some repairs needed doing and so you'd call up one of the Squadron's fitters to do it. You and your crew acted as a team to get it all done. In a tank crew of three or four, it was just like being

in an aircraft – you were one team: you ate, lived, slept, fought, went to the lavatory as a crew. You slept beside your crew and took it in turns to do all the jobs; you didn't say "They're the crew, I'm an officer". You were very careful who you chose as your Driver, your Operator, your Loader. It was a very close arrangement. The infantry just don't have the same feeling. I would be humping in jerry-cans of fuel, my Operator would be pouring it into the petrol-tank, somebody else would be getting the shells into the racks.

As well as all this, the crews had to get hold of food and try to eat it despite the 'no fires' rule; sentries had to be posted and regularly relieved.

We lived on bully beef and biscuits – and sand with everything. As for keeping clean, we just stayed dirty; we only had enough water to make tea, so we didn't really shave and we certainly didn't wash.
It got very cold at night and we all had sleeping-bags, which we wrapped up and strapped on to the outside of the tank. We could sleep on the engine-decks or next to the tank, or even in the turret. Drivers often used to like sleeping in their driving-seats, which folded back. We slept well; we were usually very tired. But sometimes it was lovely to just lie there in the peace of the leaguer and stare up at the stars. We would do a spell on sentry duty as well, unless we had very good reason not to.

Officers got even less sleep than the crews, since they had to attend briefings and then to pass the orders on to their subordinates – and then attend fresh briefings and re-issue the orders when, as so often, higher command changed its mind.

For one or two nights, the lack of sleep was bearable – but 3RTR would remain in action for over three weeks. The cumulative effects of daily combat and nightly sleep-deprivation were debilitating.

In action, you weren't frightened – well, you *were* frightened, but that wasn't the main problem. The main problem was that after about three-quarters of an hour in action you were absolutely exhausted. You learned very quickly the art of cat-napping. You only had to stop for a couple of minutes; you learned to put your head down on the turret, shut your eyes, and go to sleep. Even if you only managed to sleep for three minutes or five minutes, it somehow completely refreshed you.

The sleeplessness was worse for Gunner: because he could be trusted to find his way around, he often spent his nights driving across the desert on various errands, adding to his own exhaustion. As a result, his memories of Crusader were a mixture of sharp pictures of incidents and hazy recollections of time and place.

My crewmen changed so often that I can't remember their names; I'm ashamed that I can't even remember who my Driver was, or my Troop Sergeant for that matter.

* * *

For 3RTR, November 19th began half an hour before dawn, when the battalion spread back out into day-time formation, the crews grabbing a quick breakfast and cup of tea if they could. The crews had making tea down to a swift drill.

Whenever we stopped, even if it was only for three minutes, there'd be a shout of "brew up" and we'd get out jerry-cans of water which we had boiling. We just clamped them on to the Honey's exhaust pipe, which kept them permanently boiling. Out came our dixies, tins of milk and sugar, and we could have a cup of tea in our hands in thirty seconds. If the order came to move on even five minutes later, we'd have had our cup of tea. It took no time at all.

The battalion pushed on, splitting up as squadrons were detached to support other units. The afternoon of November 19th saw the first major battle of the offensive as 4 Armoured Brigade, now sixty-five miles from where they had crossed The Wire, engaged 15th Panzer

Division at Gabr Taleb el Essem,[12] some twenty miles inside Libya along an important east-west route known as the Trigh El-Abd. The British tanks were out-gunned both by the enemy tanks and by their anti-tank guns, which were of 50mm and sometimes even 88mm calibre, compared to the 37mm main armament of the Honey. However, the Honeys were fast, and this enabled them to 'jink' as they advanced and retreated, making them hard targets which stopped only to return fire. Nevertheless, 8th Hussars suffered badly in this action.

* * *

On the morning of November 20th, battle resumed, the enemy being reinforced by 21st Panzer Division, but that night the Germans retreated westwards. 3RTR pursued, and on November 21st fierce fighting broke out again, this time at Gabr Saleh. The Germans then withdrew north towards Sidi Rezegh, where 7 Armoured Brigade had captured an airfield located on the escarpment some twenty-five miles south-east of Tobruk. Rommel was concerned by the British presence on the airfield and had ordered his armour to converge on Sidi Rezegh and crush the forces there.

Shortage of fuel meant that 3RTR lost contact with the enemy, though not before suffering several officer casualties, including Gunner's replacement as OC 4 Troop, who had been killed.[13] Once again, Gunner's luck had come to his rescue: had he not proven an able navigator, he might well have been in a front-line Honey that day instead.

Not all casualties had been inflicted by the enemy; Crisp noted one 3RTR tank which had clearly been destroyed by so-called "friendly fire". Such accidents were all too frequent – but the tank's commander, Captain Peter Williams MC, had been a close friend of Gunner.[14]

Below: *a disabled Honey (nick-named "Bellman") in the Libyan desert during Operation Crusader. Luckily perhaps for its crew, this Honey had not burned when knocked out (IWM E7044).*

> There were three of us from Bedford in 3RTR: Peter Page, Peter Williams and myself. Peter Williams was roughly my contemporary, just younger than me. His mother lived on De Parys Avenue in Bedford; she was a widow, as her husband had been killed right at the end of the First World War. Peter had joined the Royal Tanks largely because of Peter Page and myself. He'd been in 'C' Squadron and had done very well at Calais; he'd driven off towards the Gravelines canal and won an MC there. He was a bloody good young officer, and his death was a personal and devastating blow. That it was the result of our own fire was a tragic and sad end to Peter's promising fighting career.
>
> We buried our casualties where they fell. You stuck something in the ground with a tin hat on top to mark the grave, and recorded the details so that they could be picked up later, you hoped. If you were with your unit you at least had the Padre there to conduct the burial.
>
> One of the awful things when we had casualties was that either a friend of the chap, or the Padre, would write a letter to the next-of-kin. Our Padres were bloody good in the war. But I wrote to Peter's mother, because I knew her very well. It went off with the mail, and that was that. When I was next in Bedford, when I finally got back to England in 1945, I went to see her to commiserate and to tell her what had happened and roughly on the map where he'd been buried. I said that eventually his body would be collected up and moved to a war cemetery.

In fact, Peter Williams has no known grave; he and his crew still lie where they were hurriedly buried by their comrades.

> Mrs Williams thanked me for my letter, but what she said next was most disturbing. My letter had been the first news she had received that Peter was dead. She had not been officially told until a month or two later.

Despite all the action which 3RTR had seen in Calais and Greece, the officers who died that day were the first in the regiment to have been killed. The shock to the system was considerable, as Crisp recalled:

> That day... we shed our lightheartedness and eagerness. The sense of adventure had gone out of our lives, to be replaced by grimness and fear and a perpetual, mounting weariness of body and spirit.[15]

* * *

3RTR caught up with the Germans again on November 22nd, just in time to assist 7 Armoured Brigade against the full weight of 15th Panzer Division, 21st Panzer Division and 90th Light Division. Sidi Rezegh airfield was perched on a plateau sandwiched between two escarpments: that to the north fell away to an east-west track (the Trigh Capuzzo) and a second escarpment which marked the edge of the coastal plains. To the south of the airfield rose another escarpment which led up to the desert beyond. As 3RTR arrived, 21st Panzer Division was in the process of attacking the airfield from the west and north.

3RTR moved in on the airfield from due east at 1530, as the war diary records:

> Assisted in attack on aerodrome. Very confused. Two squadrons – 'B' and 'C' – went in, and Battalion HQ and 'A' Squadron were on left flank trying to contact 22 Armoured Brigade.[16]

The fighting at Sidi Rezegh was some of the most confused of the desert war, and the scene on the airfield as British and German tanks eddied across it in all directions was one which many participants have likened to a vision of hell. Bill Close, 'B' Squadron's Squadron Sergeant-Major, described it as follows:

> Sidi Rezegh was hidden by a low mushroom-cloud, from the base of which came thumps, booms, rumblings and streaks of lightning... [We] looked down on a scene which bewildered as much as it shocked... Motionless wrecks, some hundreds of yards apart; others in groups, facing in all directions. Some were black and silent; others smouldering and cracking; and a few blazing brightly, black smoke curling busily up into the dirty sky. Geysers of dirt shot up haphazardly among this flotsam.[17]

Above: Honeys advancing at speed. Those involved at Sidi Rezegh were too busy to take photographs, but 'C' Squadron's charge across the airfield must have looked something like this (IWM E5065).

Crisp had an exciting time that day – he records in *Brazen Chariots* that several senior officers later suspected him of "line-shooting". Gunner watched the fighting from the escarpment, from his post near Colonel Ewin's command tank, and is clear as to what went wrong.

> When 'C' Squadron went in across the airfield, their tanks had piddling little 37mm guns, 2-pounders, and the Germans had 50mm and 75mm guns on their tanks. And whenever you were fighting a tank battle, you'd suddenly find yourself facing a row of their anti-tank guns, which didn't have any armour but could out-range you. The German tanks stayed behind them, encouraging us to go and attack them – they'd even withdraw sometimes, drawing us on to their guns. It was a vicious system and it killed many of my friends. Whoever decided that we should attack – well, it was just murder. Before they got half-way across nine of them were burning, and the survivors limped back with holes all over them. Someone had sent 'C' Squadron into a death-or-glory charge, and what I saw of it really shook me. I realized that we were fighting against such awful bloody odds.

When Crisp tried to summon the rest of the battalion to join him on the airfield, Colonel Ewin was unable to help:

> From somewhere in the middle of the tank-manufactured dust-storm he said: "I don't know my arse from my elbow, let alone east from west..." I saw several tanks come out of the dust, and mill about blindly. Two of them fell into an anti-tank ditch... It was a hopeless shambles, and after a depressing few minutes I heard the CO order all tanks to rally on top of the escarpment.[18]

By the time that 3RTR received orders to disengage at 1715, the battalion was in a sorry state. The war diary was kept at Battalion HQ, which by now was a headquarters without a battalion:

> Withdrew in dusk. Only five tanks with Battalion HQ. Attempt to rally Battalion not too successful... 3RTR ordered to rally as many tanks as possible and to withdraw behind ridge to south.[19]

4 Armoured Brigade's headquarters was over-run that evening, with the loss of thirty-five Honeys amongst much other material. This is probably the occasion which Gunner recalled as follows:

> I had to go to Brigade HQ for some reason one night. It was only about four or five miles away, and as I approached there was a mass of flares going off, with green flares going up over Brigade HQ. The Brigadier, the bloody fool, was expecting replenishment vehicles and had announced over the wireless that he would put up green Very lights to guide them in. Well, they saw tanks coming in and so kept putting up flares, but when the tanks got close enough they opened fire – they were Germans. They hit a troop of 8th Hussars who were providing close protection for Brigade HQ. That was typical of the initiative which the Germans always showed; they were very much on their toes, and some Squadron Commander will have got a pat on the back for that.

But a far more important loss that day had been another of Gunner's friends, the second regimental comrade whom he known since Bedford: Major Peter Page, one of 3RTR's Squadron Commanders.

> Peter had been older than me and Peter Williams, quite senior in fact, and his father was the main coal-merchant in Bedford. They lived in a lovely house in De Parys Avenue. Peter had served with First Tanks in the desert and then gone across to Brigade Headquarters. Then when we were in Cairo he'd suddenly turned up as a Liaison Officer or something. Then he'd got his squadron. So I'd lost two school-friends in two days.[20]

* * *

The next morning, November 23rd, was a Sunday. In Germany, this Sunday is referred to as *Totensonntag* – "Sunday of the Dead" – and that is how the members of Germany's *Afrika Korps* remembered the day, one of death and destruction for the Commonwealth forces pitted against them.

At 0530 the remains of 3RTR moved off on a bearing of 210°, through 5 South African Brigade and on towards Hagfet el Garbia, five or so miles south of Sidi Rezegh. German armour appeared, however, and there was a sharp exchange of fire:

> *1130*
> Enemy driven off. Much jubilation. Our total force now ten tanks; only eight "runners", and ammunition and petrol very low. Filled up partially with Grade III petrol [the Honeys, having aero-engines, usually ran on high-octane fuel]. Kept constant watch during rest of morning and early afternoon.[21]

But now things began to look black. 5 South African Brigade and 22 Armoured Brigade were over-run by the Germans – and at 1600 on November 23rd a hundred enemy tanks approached 3RTR's positions from the south-west:

> 3RTR engaged until ammunition ran out. Little heavy fire from enemy. We withdrew east and contacted New Zealand Brigade, where we spent the night... south of Carmuset En-Nbeidat.[22]

* * *

3RTR was now in sorry shape: 'A' Squadron and 'B' Squadron had both vanished, and what was left was effectively just Battalion HQ and some of 'C' Squadron. These sad remnants – a mere six Honeys, topped up with some high-octane fuel that morning – headed off on their compass-bearings ("six miles on 117° and then six miles on 158°") to join the screen protecting Brigade HQ – hardly an aggressive role, though one suited to a battalion which was still less than a squadron strong. They contacted Brigade at another random spot in the middle of nowhere, labelled Bir el Haleizen on the map. Moving east, they crossed the route by which they had approached Sidi Rezegh from the south on November 21st – 3RTR was literally driving around in circles. By now the tank crews were in shock and exhausted. Crisp hauntingly describes the chaos and the discomfort of their existence:

> From that moment on I can truthfully say that none of us had more than the vaguest idea where we were from day to day and hour to hour, or what was happening either to our own forces or the enemy's... One morning we would be south-west of Sidi Rezegh; the next afternoon we would be well east of the point at which we had spent the first night after crossing The Wire... There was no such thing as advance and retreat. We roared off to areas of threat or engagement depending on the urgency of the information. We chased mirages and were chased by mirages. Every few hours a landmark or a name would punch our memories with an elusive familiarity... We went without sleep, without food, without washing or change of clothes, without conversation beyond the clipped talk of wireless procedure and orders.[23]

At 1530 on November 24th 3RTR received orders to join 5RTR in an attack on an enemy column passing four miles away. But nothing was found. The war diary describes the chaotic events of the afternoon: even for a battalion long used to order and counter-order, the desert war plunged new depths of confusion.

> *1550*
> Ordered to return to Brigade where an attack by tanks was expected from north-west or west.
> *1600-1615*
> A certain amount of confusion. Battalion ordered to about-turn once more and attack a column which was moving south-east.
> *1615-1715*
> Column chased about twenty-miles. Lieutenant Maegraith knocked out German Mark III tank at fifty yards range; also got a field-gun. Enemy abandoned a certain amount of transport on the line of march.
> *1715*
> Running short of petrol and dusk approaching when a second, larger, enemy column with tanks was seen crossing the tail of the original column. We engaged the tanks with assistance of 5RTR. While at point-blank range CO's tank crashed with link tank and broke a sprocket-ring. Tanks got out and withdrew. 4 Armoured Brigade ordered rally one mile to rear.
> *1800*
> 4 Armoured Brigade marched approximately four miles and formed close leaguer at 452365 south of Gabr Farhat. 'B' Echelon replenished us; Lieutenant Johnson in charge, who brought news of 'A' and 'C' squadrons. Watch on every tank all night.[24]

The war diary's reference to 'A' and 'C' squadrons being missing contradict's Crisp's account, since Crisp was with Battalion HQ and he was in 'C'; in *Brazen Chariots,* he states that 'A' and 'B' were the missing ones.

* * *

The following day – November 25th – 3RTR and 5RTR contacted a column of some seventy enemy tanks which had been attacking the South Africans near Bir Taleb el Essem, to the south, back where the battalion had been on the 21st. The British tanks took up hull-down positions and, supported by fire from 2RHA, enjoyed an excellent shoot against an Italian column as it refuelled.

Meanwhile, 3RTR's supply vehicles – 'B' Echelon – had lost touch with Battalion HQ. The battalion's supply lorries were supposed to make the journey to and from 62 Field

Above: Italian M13-40 tanks of the sort engaged by 3RTR on November 25th, December 1st and December 7th 1941. Italian tanks were of inferior design to those of the Germans, and never as well handled (copyright holder unknown).

Maintenance Centre (FMC) at Fort Maddalena every day, catching up with the battalion at night to carry out the vital replenishment of water, fuel and ammunition. Gunner was with 'B' Echelon at the time – his skill as a navigator was vital to these supply vehicles in their attempts to keep up the supply of fuel and other essentials to the fighting squadrons.

Gunner could not be everywhere at once. On the night of November 25th, 'B' Echelon's supply column ran into trouble, sparked by navigational problems, as Crisp recorded.

> Our own replenishment column had failed to arrive... It had set off from base with the rest of the Brigade transport on its routine night run to the camp area. In the darkness it had gone off its bearing, and had become completely detached from the other echelons. In the leading vehicle, the officer in command had wisely decided not to risk his hunches and to stay where he was for the night, since the whole area was full of German columns swarming towards the frontier in the tracks of the panzer regiments. At first light he lined his truck on a bearing that he hoped would take him to the Brigade outpost, formed the convoy nose-to-tail behind him, and set off into the gathering light. All round him he could see other vehicle convoys... There was no way of telling friend from enemy... Three armoured cars came up alongside the column out of the half light, and moved parallel with it about a hundred yards on the flank... Then one of the armoured cars moved forward across the front of the convoy... slap in the path of the leading truck.[25]

The armoured cars were German; and 3RTR's supply column had gone "into the bag". Neither the battalion nor the remainder of 'B' Echelon back at the FMC would know for certain what had happened for some time.

* * *

The main body of 3RTR spent November 26th performing some much-needed maintenance on their vehicles and themselves. For the first time since crossing The Wire there was time for them to remove clothes and have a wash, and to shave with hot water. The relief of feeling even minimally clean, and of putting on some clean clothes, was psychologically refreshing as well.

The missing 'A' Squadron had turned up after some interesting adventures, and it was possible to assess the losses and damage of the past few hectic days. Rommel had surprised everyone by pushing east towards the Egyptian frontier, leaving the field around Sidi Rezegh to the Allies. But now, short on supplies, and with their supply-lines threatened by the British tanks in their rear, the Germans were recoiling westwards back towards Sidi Rezegh. Rommel's famous "dash for The Wire" was over.

As 4 Armoured Brigade assembled around Bir Berraneb, 3RTR crossed its own tracks once more to join them, around fifteen miles south of Sidi Rezegh. Twelve fresh Honeys came up from the rear that afternoon, and by the end of the day 3RTR had two under-strength squadrons: 'A' with nine tanks, and 'C' with ten. Battalion HQ had only three Honeys. A full-strength battalion should have had fifty-two tanks.

Not only had tanks arrived, but also the Officers' Mess truck, in which there was a crate of beer. It did not last long.

* * *

By the morning of November 27th, Operation Crusader was a total shambles. It was unclear whether the Germans planned to recapture Sidi Rezegh and close the corridor which had been opened to Tobruk, or whether Rommel was in full retreat westwards. 7 Armoured Brigade had been sent back to Egypt, too shattered to fight; 22 Armoured Brigade, by salvaging derelict tanks from the battlefield, had brought its strength up to forty-two vehicles (when it should have had nearly 170); and by comparison, 4 Armoured Brigade was in remarkably good shape with a tank strength of seventy-seven. Three tank brigades had been reduced to the numbers usually fielded by two battalions. The desert was littered with the wrecks of abandoned tanks, some burned out, others abandoned and crewless but otherwise reparable. Gunner recalls one occasion where he found some tanks which had become separated from their unit:

> It was early in the morning and we saw three A15s stationary; when we came up to them, all the crews were lying in their sleeping bags next to the tanks. But they weren't asleep – they'd been machine-gunned. So some raiding party must have come, found them sleeping without a guard, not in a leaguer or anything, killed them and just disappeared. That shook me. We had to bury them there.

That afternoon 3RTR moved rapidly north-east to assist 22 Armoured Brigade, which was about to attack a vast enemy column, said to consist of two thousand vehicles, including fifty tanks, moving west along the Trigh Capuzzo. 4 Armoured Brigade fell upon the Germans near Bir el Chleta, ten miles east of Sidi Rezegh. The attack proved a disaster for 3RTR.

> First attack put in with serious loss. Nine tanks shot up in action and another damaged. Wounded and missing: all crews of [tanks of Lieutenant Stuart and Corporal Hardy] missing except driver of Lieutenant Stuart's tank. Subsequently reported that Lieutenant Stuart and Lieutenant Hickson had been killed.[26]

That evening, 4 Armoured Brigade concentrated again at Bir Berraneb, leaving the Germans in control of the battlefield and free to move along the Trigh Capuzzo.

Fierce fighting continued along the Trigh Capuzzo on November 28th, as the British tried to prevent two main bodies of Germans from linking up with one another. By now, the garrison of Tobruk had made contact with the New Zealand Division which formed part of the relief force, but the Germans were pressing hard at Sidi Rezegh. Once again, 3RTR regrouped at Bir Berraneb that evening.

* * *

Back at 62 FMC, 'B' Echelon were chafing at the bit, eager to get forward to supply their comrades. However, they were told that they were not to move forwards. On the 28th, Gunner had been sent to try to persuade Headquarters to allow them to go:

> Sent Captain Gregg to Advanced HQ 7th Armoured Division; he came back with orders for Echelon to remain at 62 FMC.[27]

The battalion was desperate for supplies that night, as Crisp recalled:

> The 'B' Echelon party with our petrol, rations and ammunition failed to arrive during the night, and we had barely enough fuel to disperse at first light... A patrol was sent out to find the replenishment party, and we lay around in open formation, glad of the chance to make a quick brew in spite of the shortage of petrol.[28]

3RTR was in poor shape: half of 'A' Squadron had vanished again, leaving a total of fourteen Honeys. Without fuel, these were useless, and if the Germans had stumbled upon them the battalion would surely have been annihilated.

However, during the night 'B' Echelon had finally obtained permission to send forwards a replenishment column, which reached the regiment at 0815 on November 29th. What little there was of the battalion was now a going concern once more.

Word came at noon that the Germans were assembling on Sidi Rezegh airfield "to attack our friends in the north" – the New Zealanders – and 4 Armoured Brigade listened to the sound of heavy firing before moving to help. As they did so, however, 5RTR was engaged by fifty enemy tanks approaching from the west, and shortly afterwards fifty more German tanks approached from the east. There was, in the words of the battalion war diary,

> considerable confusion and shelling from both sides.[29]

However, a mass tank battle failed to develop, and that night the battalion leaguered peacefully eight miles south of Sidi Rezegh airfield – back, once again, at Bir Berraneb.

* * *

> To be Regimental Navigator under these conditions was almost impossible. The difficulty was for the CO to know where his replenishment vehicles and reinforcement tanks were, and for them to know where we were. Almost every move depended on our ability to navigate, so the CO was always asking me, as one of the few who had any idea of our position or where the other units were (or thought that they were).

That night Gunner set out to collect replacement tanks from Brigade HQ:

> We'd lost rather a lot of tanks, especially in 'C' Squadron, but seven replacements and a few replenishment vehicles had arrived at Brigade HQ. The CO desperately wanted new tanks, because we had quite a lot of crewmen who'd lost their vehicles. We could have sent the crews back, but the CO decided that I should go back and collect the tanks, get the RASC drivers to bring them up, and distribute them where we were.

I only had a vague idea of where to find Brigade HQ; all I had was a grid reference. I estimated that I would have to travel about ten miles before I reached them. Luckily, the night was clear and it was possible to navigate on a star, and by good luck I ended up at the right place. I gave up a short prayer of thanks to the officer who had given me the right grid reference.

When I got to the command vehicle, I couldn't find a duty officer; the duty wireless operator told me "I think he's in that bivvy over there." The occupant turned out to be an elderly man, who was writing by the light of a torch, whom I thought was the G3, so I asked him where our replacement tanks were. He replied "I don't know. Ask my ADC." He was an Australian general who'd been attached to get some front-line experience. And boy, was he getting it.

The duty officer told me where the tanks were and so I went over to where they were parked. All the drivers from the tank delivery unit were asleep, so I got them up, told them who I was, and told them that we were going to drive off in line astern to Third Tanks where the vehicles would be allocated to squadrons. As they were getting ready to move, I went up to one tank to ask him a question – and he answered in German, which rather shook me. I asked him if he was German and he replied *"Ja. Ich bin Deutsch."* I couldn't believe he was a bloody German.

"What are you doing here? Shouldn't you be on the other side?"

He told me that he'd escaped from Germany before the war – he'd been brought up in Dresden – and then joined up to fight the Germans. I should think he was probably Jewish.

I made the tanks close up one behind the other and told the drivers that we were going to go very slowly, though the ground was perfectly clear and there was nothing dangerous along the way.

"Stick close to the red tail-light in front of you. I don't want any headlights. And follow me."

When we arrived, they had everything ready for us. The Adjutant met me and told me to get the tanks into the leaguer, where they'd be met by people from each squadron and allocated where we needed them. I went and had a bit of kip while I could.

Thanks to Gunner, seven replacement tanks had reached the battalion early on November 30th, bringing 3RTR up to a total of twenty – still only a third of its notional strength.

That morning 4 Armoured Brigade moved up towards a feature designated Point 175, east of Sidi Rezegh, with 3RTR guarding the west flank. At 0900 thirty Italian tanks were encountered to the east; 5RTR and 8th Hussars "bagged nineteen" as 3RTR watched with interest. At 1300 twelve more enemy tanks appeared moving across the battalion's front, but before 3RTR could engage them three columns of enemy vehicles were spotted on the western flank, and the battalion had to sit tight rather than launch an attack. For the next three hours they listened to the thunder of artillery on the airfield at Sidi Rezegh, before pulling back four miles southward for another night at Bir Berraneb. As darkness fell, five further replacement tanks reached the battalion.

'B' Echelon, meanwhile, had not enjoyed the most peaceful of days. At 0900 they had been dive-bombed, without suffering any casualties. A more serious raid came in at 1230, which destroyed a truck and damaged four more. A third raid, at 1630, damaged two more lorries. Crisp later commented that during Operation Crusader air attack seemed concentrated more on the supply vehicles than on the tanks. Perhaps the German pilots realized that by destroying the Allied supply trains they could cripple more tanks than by direct attack. Jock Watt certainly felt sorry for the men of the supply train; he felt it preferable to be in a tank, behind armour-plate, no matter how inadequate, than to be in a truck full of petrol without the slightest protection.

* * *

The fighting had been going on now for nearly a fortnight without let-up. 4 Armoured Brigade's orders for December 1st were to move at top speed to the airfield at Sidi Rezegh to cover the retreat of the New Zealanders, who were being attacked by German tanks from both the north and south. The inconclusive skirmishing of the previous few days, and the nightly withdrawal of the British armour, had alowed the Germans and Italians to concentrate their forces against Sidi Rezegh. Some of the New Zealanders had been surrounded; they had little ammunition left and had been given permission to withdraw.

4 Armoured Brigade moved off at 0630 on December 1st with 3RTR on the right, aiming to drive to Belhamed and across the airfield, splitting the German attack in two. The history of 4 Armoured Brigade explains what happened:

> At 0800 hrs we advanced into a situation resembling in almost every detail the charge of the Light Brigade at Balaclava. We reached Belhamed, rallied and protected a brigade of the New Zealand Division which had been partially overrun and held off all counter-attacks, until the New Zealanders had withdrawn to the east and re-organised.[30]

Put like that, it all sounds rather neat. 3RTR's war diary paints a more complex picture:

> *0730 to 1230*
> Considerable confusion north of aerodrome (below escarpment). 8th Hussars had withdrawn and 3RTR and 5RTR were very heavily shelled from all sides. New Zealanders withdrawing (apparently east). Reported that 4 Armoured Brigade was surrounded, but rallied successfully three miles south of aerodrome block-house.
> *1300*
> Replenished.
> *1345*
> 3RTR moved to take up position of observation on west and north-west of 4 Armoured Brigade.
> *1430*
> Moved to watch north and north-east fronts. Certain amount of shelling on both sides, and apparent sniping by enemy. No enemy tanks seen, but parties of MET and guns were shelled.
> *1645*
> 'C' Squadron considering engaging some lorried infantry to north-east and 'A' Squadron taking on some six M13 (Italian) tanks to north. Three of these later proved to be derelict.
> *1730*
> Withdrew to Bir Berraneb 443274 to leaguer.
> *2130*
> Three more tanks and crews joined [bringing the battalion's strength up to twenty-eight].[31]

The defenders of Tobruk often commented that the Germans appeared to bomb them on a strict time-table. 'B' Echelon had good grounds to confirm this, since on December 1st, as the day before, they were dive-bombed at 0900, 1230 and 1630. Four lorries went up in flames during the second air-raid.

* * *

Tobruk had once again been cut off; to its east, the Axis garrisons of Halfaya and Bardia were similarly besieged. The mobile forces of both sides, exhausted by the ebb and flow of battle, skirmished over the next few days, but there was no attempt by either side to deal a crushing blow. Indeed, the Italian and German forces were by now at the end of their resources, and although they had driven the Allies from Sidi Rezegh they were unable to exploit their victory – indeed, one could argue that in winning the battle and squandering their last strength, they had lost the campaign. As they began to retire westwards towards Benghazi, the Germans and Italians left screens of rearguard forces to slow down the British advance.

The British plan now required 4 Armoured Brigade to engage the enemy north of Bir el Gubi, ten miles to the west of Bir Berraneb – the furthest west that 3RTR had yet

Above: a Honey undergoing repairs and maintenance somewhere in the Libyan desert on December 10th 1941. The crew's essential brew-kit can be seen in the foreground (IWM E7008).

penetrated into Libya. The battalion was to assist the infantry of 4th Indian Division in attacks on a line running from Bir el Gubi north to El Adem.

* * *

For almost all of December 2nd and 3rd, 3RTR rested at Bir Berraneb, and by dint of improvization and borrowing a squadron of tanks from 8th Hussars managed to bring their strength up to forty Honeys. Colonel Ewin also reorganized his officers: he and the OC 'A' Squadron, Major R.N. Wilson, had fallen out, and so Wilson was posted to command 'B' Echelon. 'C' Squadron was taken over by Major George "Withers" Witheridge, who had been a Sergeant-Major in the pre-war army.

On December 4th 3RTR engaged the enemy for the first time in several days:

> Attacked enemy column moving north. Quite a lot of damage done. One M13 bagged. Heavy anti-tank fire... Patrols to north being fired on by anti-tank guns from area of some burnt-out vehicles. Applied small dose of HE... Casualties for the day: six tanks. Captain Caldwell (4th Hussars) and Trooper Ashton 'B' Squadron killed.[32]

It was clear that the enemy had left plenty of anti-tank guns to screen his front line, a very effective means of preventing the advance of armoured forces. Out-ranged by the German 88mm and 50mm anti-tank weapons, the first that British tank crews often knew of the enemy's presence was when their tanks began to "brew up". This was no pursuit of a fleeing enemy, but a slow game of Russian roulette.

On the morning of December 5th, 3RTR were surprised to find themselves moving back east to Bir Berraneb, though it meant that they missed an armoured counter-attack by the Germans at Bir el Gubi. It is hard to decide who would have come off worst if the tanks of the two armies had collided that day; Rommel revealed to the Italians that evening that he only had forty functioning tanks in the whole *Afrika Korps.* They had no choice now but to abandon Cyrenaica and re-occupy the line south of Benghazi from which they had advanced in March.

* * *

As December 6th dawned, 4 Armoured Brigade set out to drive ten or so miles on a bearing of 280°, orders which would take them back towards Bir el Gubi. By the end of the day, 3RTR was operating thirty-seven tanks, and had not made contact with significant numbers of the enemy. It looked as though the character of the battle might be beginning to change.

December 7th 1941 was, of course, "a date which will live in infamy" according to President Roosevelt. The attack on Pearl Harbor was to be followed by Allied collapse in Malaya, Burma and the Dutch East Indies. But in the desert of Libya, no one knew anything of the day's significance.

A battle developed east of Bir el Gubi, in which 3RTR first took on anti-tank guns and Italian M13s, before forty German tanks appeared at 0830. Supported by the 25-pounders of 2RHA, 3RTR committed all its tanks to the action. The German tanks and anti-tank guns were screening large numbers of soft-skin vehicles, and seemed happy to remain inactive as long as the British did not get too close. As the day wore on the Germans began to drive away to the west; they had held on as long as they could, but now had no choice but to head westwards or be cut off and surrounded. 3RTR leaguered for the night and at first light on December 8th drove south-west to Bir Belchonfus before advancing westwards in the wake of the retreating enemy forces.

On December 9th – "some doubts as to position, but finally landed in Bir Hatiet Genadel area"[33] – 3RTR took its first German prisoners, when nine of the enemy fell into the battalion's hands. As the British advanced and the Germans pulled back there was some confusion: at 1115 the battalion found German columns on its left and right, and a German anti-tank gun position to its front, probably along the wadi which lies near Bir Hatiet Genadel, which would have made an ideal defensive position. The war diary records the action that day:

1200
Still in same position, trying to get order out of the confusion. Apparently both columns enemy. A certain amount of shelling of our position...
1430
A troop of 'A' Squadron approached very close to a battery of enemy field guns and scattered the crews with Browning fire, but on attempting to get the guns came under intense anti-tank gun-fire and was forced to withdraw. HQ 3RTR apparently proving attractive target for enemy OP – had to move about a bit.
1700
Engaged by twenty enemy tanks from hull-down position, assisted by a battery of anti-tank guns.

> More tanks reported on right... Our very hot fire kept off enemy and may have inflicted considerable casualties.
> *1800*
> Moved to leaguer only three miles away. It took five hours.[34]

On December 10th 3RTR advanced westwards about ten miles to another random spot on the map, Point 161. There the battalion enjoyed its first full day of rest since crossing the Libyan frontier on November 18th. The only event of the day was when an RAF Boston bomber was shot down over 'B' Echelon, the sole survivor being its bomb-aimer. Seven new Honeys arrived, enough that three squadrons of twelve tanks could be formed.

Similar calm prevailed on December 11th and 12th; there was even an issue of fresh bread and fresh meat on the second day. But December 11th had another profound significance which escaped the notice of the combatants in the desert: that day, Germany and Italy had declared war on the United States of America, and the benevolent neutrality which had hitherto aided the British war effort was to be replaced by active participation.

* * *

December 13th saw the battalion move off fifteen miles on a bearing of 256° to take up battle positions facing westwards near Bir al Hakim, though the war diary recorded that

> fifty enemy tanks reported ahead of us previously had turned out to be camels.[35]

4 Armoured Brigade were now ordered to take part in a wide outflanking movement, which was intended to cut off the enemy to the north. They first moved south (bearing 193° for twenty-one miles, putting them at Bir Zeidem) on December 14th, before preparing to advance north-west towards Bir Halegh el Eleba (modern Bir Halq al Ilbah, forty miles south of Derna). The following morning they drove thirty-five miles due westwards and then, at 1030, swung northwards on to a compass bearing of 006°, heading for the coast. The outflanking move had begun.

By 1500 on the afternoon of December 15th, 3RTR had covered another thirty-two miles and reached Bir Halegh el Eleba, thirty miles to the rear of the enemy front-line troops now counter-attacking 4th Indian Division. There it took up battle positions as the northern face of a square formation of armoured regiments; 5RTR were the east face, the Royal Gloucestershire Hussars the west.[36] The south of the box was formed by an infantry battalion. 4 Armoured Brigade had staked its claim, and it remained to be seen whether the Germans and Italians to the east would attack. Crisp noted that the British, whilst confident, were short of fuel after the long advance:

> All the Honeys were very short of petrol. None of them had enough in their fuel tanks to see them through a battle if one developed in the morning. The replenishment on the march had emptied all but one or two of the accompanying petrol lorries... Gatehouse decided to move the whole Brigade back some miles to the south at first light to connect up with 'B' Echelon, which was following on in the night.[37]

All around, German and Italian columns were streaming west as quickly as they could, trying to steer their way through the British front-line forces. As the Germans wriggled free and the British tried to cut them off, the usual intermingling and confusion took hold. It was this confusion which was to bring Gunner into closer contact with the Germans than he would have wished.

On December 16th, as 4 Armoured Brigade pulled back slightly, 'C' Squadron of 3RTR was sent north to contact the enemy – which it did. In the ensuing action, Crisp was badly wounded and his friend Harry Maegraith killed.[38] 3RTR found itself under fire from both front and rear, and had a lot of trouble spotting the enemy.

When a replenishment column reached the battalion's forward positions the following morning, it reported Gunner missing.

> 1210
> Rations arrived, and Lieutenant Tomlin reported that he had Captain T.D. Gregg's replenishment vehicles with him, but Captain Gregg had apparently got lost the day before.[39]

On December 18th, the war diary recorded:

> BTO reported disappearance of Captain T.D. Gregg on night of 16th.[40]

What had in fact happened was as follows. Gunner had been with Battalion HQ on December 16th when a retreating enemy column was reported in the area.

> Reports came that the Germans were withdrawing. My CO sent me a short distance forwards to confirm the reports. I drove out in an 8-cwt truck and quickly came in view of the enemy driving west.

Gunner had run into one of the many German columns retreating across the desert towards Benghazi. He took cover and kept a careful watch on the enemy, hoping that they would pass without seeing him.

> I got into a nice small hollow behind a mound, and I saw them all streaming back, nose to tail. They weren't frightened of our fighters or bombers or anything. I could report back how many 88s I saw, how many Mark IVs, Mark IIIs. And that worked extremely well, because it meant that they knew what there was. They had quite a few of these eight-wheeled armoured cars, which were a very frightening thing in the desert, because they had a high-velocity 75mm gun and the cross-desert performance of a tracked vehicle. I didn't want them to see me and think that there was an enemy there and send one of those bloody things to beat us up.
> My driver said to me "There's one of our 3-tonners stopped about a quarter of a mile away." And I said "What's it doing?" I'd taken my belt and holster off and put it on my seat, and I'd been leaning against the radiator observing the enemy through my binos. I looked at this vehicle with my binos, and it had the red "Shitehawk" sign as we called it, which meant 4th Indian Division.[41] There was a chap in khaki in the front. I said "It's one of ours. For God's sake bring him in behind us to get him out of sight. He's going to draw attention." Anyway, they signalled to him, but he still stayed there. I was cross because the lorry was not doing as I wished.
> Meanwhile, I was busy doing my job, reporting back by radio to the CO what I could see, and how fast they were going, what they had. In the end this truck came towards us and pulled up beside me. And out jumped a whole lot of bloody Germans with sub-machine guns and covered us.

Gunner had no opportunity to flee or to fight. He could only surrender:

> One of the most unhappy days of my life. It came out of the blue as a total surprise. I was not expecting it. I was so shocked that my nose started bleeding.

As the shock of capture hit him, Gunner experienced one of those coincidences which would sound ludicrous in a novel, but which occur so frequently in real life.

> They had a young Lieutenant in there, who took my gun-belt – which was on the seat – and spoke to me in English. I answered him in German, and he asked me:
> "Where did you learn your German?"
> I replied, "Well, I was at school in Germany for a bit."

"Were you really? Whereabouts?"
"Wiesbaden."
"I don't believe it. I come from Wiesbaden. Where did you live?"
"Alexanderstrasse, Drei."
He burst out laughing. "Good God," he said. "I lived in the next street."

It turned out he'd worked in a bank in Wiesbaden – and not only that, but his brother had been to my school. He was a wonderful chap. I and my driver spent the night in the German divisional HQ, and the Lieutenant even got us some Officers' Mess food and shared it with me and my driver. I wish I could remember his name.

* * *

The emotional turmoil of capture was one of the most effective restraints upon a new prisoner's ability to escape. One of Gunner's friends in captivity later described his own reactions when he was captured in the desert:

> Now... I realized fully the enormity of what had happened. If I could have killed myself I would have done it. For a free man to be suddenly a prisoner is terrible. It must resemble castration. It seemed to me that everything was lost. A blinding hate for our curious and kindly guards filled me one instant, and next instant I felt like a small boy who arrives at a new and fearsome school, and wants to cry every time anyone addresses a word to him, especially a kind word.[42]

Gunner was to become a thorn in the side of his captors, a determined escaper who never missed an opportunity to slip out of the enemy's clutches. And despite the shock of capture, and the remarkably civilized beginning to his captivity, he at once began to look around for opportunities to escape. In those days, there was nothing in the way of formal escape and evasion training, but Gunner instinctively knew one of the fundamentals of escape: that the earlier one made one's break, the more likely success was. Once in the enemy's rear areas, where the processing and security of prisoners was well-organized, a prisoner stood less chance of getting away, and also cut a more conspicuous figure. Gunner began trying immediately.

> In the morning we had a very early start to go back to their lines. I got into the back of this Lieutenant's truck, the 4th Indian Division truck, and in it was the CO of the Buffs, who had been overrun.[43] Also there was his Adjutant, Simon Dendy, whom I knew. All the German rations and petrol were in the back with us. We had two Germans sitting on the tailboard, with their Schmeissers, and so I said:
> "Simon, give me a bit of cover. I'm going to do something with their rations."
> So he went near to the Germans and kept them busy. In the rations they had packets or tins of sugar, and I opened all the jerry-cans of petrol and I poured about four pounds of sugar into them. All I wanted was for them to fill up somewhere in the middle of the desert. We'd stop, and our our people could then come and scoop us up. But it didn't come off, unfortunately. Before they'd put the new petrol in, I'd been handed over to the Italians.

Chapter Eight
"Pericoloso"

Allied troops captured in North Africa were sent not to Germany but to prisoner of war camps in Italy. Transit arrangements were appalling; the Italians proved disorganized and brutal captors, and holding camps were often squalid in the extreme. However, it was not just filth with which prisoners had to contend. British submarines and aircraft operating from Malta, unable to tell whether Axis vessels were carrying prisoners of war, made transportation onwards to Italy a hazardous affair.

Once safely in Italy, however, the prisoners found that their lot was much worse, in almost every respect, than if they had been in a German camp. Italian captivity was harder to escape from – perhaps why it has not caught the public interest as much as have the German camps – and much more uncomfortable. One former prisoner of war wrote that:

> It may surprise many people that prisoners who experienced captivity under both Germans and Italians were unanimous in their preference for captivity in Germany. In Italy, a prisoner of war was always exposed to the pettiness, meanness, dishonesty, excitability or self-dramatisation, of individuals, and in a country where the general standards of hygiene and medical attention are so much below that of other civilized countries, the prisoner, with the best will in the world, gets a raw deal.
>
> True, the German scale of rations was much below that agreed under the Geneva Convention, but it was enough to support life and it always arrived, scrupulously measured to the last gram; in Italy rations, at whatever scale, were always uncertain. A prisoner prefers to know where he stands.
>
> The Germans too, were always at great pains to impress on their service prisoners their honesty in small matters, and it was a common belief in prisoner of war camps that cigarette parcels that failed to arrive were more likely lost on our own than on German railways. In Italy pilfering was the rule; in Germany it was the exception.[1]

An inmate of PG29 at Veano, where both Donny and Gunner found themselves later, was Australian Major Gordon Lett, who shared the common view of Italians and their camps:

> Our experiences in various prison camps had taught us something about our Italian hosts, and our opinions of the country and its people were, consequently, though understandably, far from flattering.[2]

Like Donny and Gunner, Lett would have good cause to revise such opinions in the years to come.

* * *

Before the arrival of the Germans in the desert, there had not been that many British prisoners-of-war from North Africa, and the Italians had been able to cope with the numbers which came their way. Prisoners were concentrated in a transit camp at Sidi Hussein, outside Benghazi. But the fierce and confused fighting of November and December 1941 – even though it resulted in a British victory – sent a flood of British, Australian, Indian, South African and New Zealand prisoners back to swamp the Italian administrative system. This was partly because of German efficiency; they had a policy of sending prisoners-of-war to the rear as quickly as possible. The result was two-fold: first, it made life as a prisoner-of-war uncomfortable and in many cases demeaning; secondly, it provided opportunities for the determined escaper. Gunner had failed to escape from the Germans; he now had the chance to try his luck with the Italians.

By December 5th 1941 the camp at Sidi Hussein held some six thousand prisoners, far more than it had been designed to cope with. They were forced to sleep under groundsheets or on the concrete floors of vehicle sheds, seven hundred to a shed. There were only a few taps, for which long queues formed. The latrines were simply trenches, which rapidly filled. The resulting flies spread dysentery among the unwashed and unshaven inmates, whose daily rations consisted of half a pound of bread, some macaroni soup and a little tinned meat. Soon enough prisoners began to faint through lack of nourishment.

As the Allies approached Benghazi later that month, the Italians began to evacuate their prisoners. By the time that Gunner arrived at Sidi Hussein, around December 20th, it held only fifteen hundred, though it remained filthy.

> The Italians took us to a small transit camp at Benghazi. Not a very nice place. But by this time, everyone was trying to evacuate the place, because the British were advancing.

On December 21st the inmates were marched down to the docks.

> We were formed up in threes or fours, columns, to march off, and there was a sentry every ten yards or so. We were going through the outskirts of Benghazi, towards the docks, where we were to be put on a German freighter which would take us to Tripoli – we'd learned that.

Gunner now saw his chance.

> I made my first escape attempt. I wanted to get into the rubble of the port or into the desert, waiting for my side to come along. I was on the outside – well, I moved to the outside – and when we were turning a corner, there was what had been a shop on the corner. Everything looted inside, of course. And as we went round, soon as I got out of sight of all the chaps on guard, I turned in and went and hid behind the wall. When the coast was clear, I was looking around for the exit to get to the roof or back into the rubble. But there was no bloody door. So all I had was the opening onto the street, which was a very busy street. I wondered, what do I do? I just hope no one comes and I can hide out till it's dark. For about six hours I hid in that shop.
> After a bit two little Italian soldiers, with their funny rifles and their knitting-needle bayonets, came in – they were obviously looking for loot. So I spoke to them in German, *"Kameraden"* and all this bloody nonsense, and I started to pee on the wall, to try and pretend that I'd come in there for a pee. They looked at me rather suspiciously, but then they pushed off. I thought, thank God for that. But when I looked out, they'd stopped about fifty yards up the road and were looking at the shop and jabbering away. Well, I couldn't go on peeing any longer. So I waited for a moment for people to be around, and nipped out and started walking very hurriedly in the opposite direction.
> But when I looked round these two Italians were running after me, their bayonets fixed. When they caught up with me they said *"Prigioniero di guerra Inglese?"* Of course, I said *"Nein, nein. Deutsche. Amico Italiani."* All this nonsense. But they weren't fooled. I said *"Auf wiedersehen. Arrivederci."* And I started to walk off. But one of them started poking his bayonet in the middle of the back of my tunic, so I stopped. Quite obviously they knew what I was. So I was marched down to the docks and put on a destroyer and we shot across to Tripoli.

Gunner was not the only prisoner who had ducked off from the column marching down to the docks. Several were luckier than he was; one New Zealander hid under a pile of cement sacks, and three others hid in a ruined hotel for three days. Allied forces entered Benghazi on Christmas Eve.

Gunner and the other prisoners from Sidi Hussein arrived in Tripoli on December 23rd, and were immediately packed into goods-wagons for a train journey inland. The engine had broken down and they spent that night in the sidings. On Christmas Eve, the train took them some of the way to their destination; the last nine miles they walked.

> At Tripoli we boarded a train which took us to the bottom of the escarpment, at the top of which was a sort of *Beau Geste* fort, called Garian. They'd collected quite a few of our prisoners there, and a lot of our people were wounded. When we got there there was no food. We were there for a few days. I spent Christmas 1941 there.

According to some sources, Christmas Day was marked by an issue of cigarettes, extra rations and a tot of brandy – but Gunner had no memory of such a bonanza.

> We were formed up again, and we had to walk down this zig-zag road down the escarpment to the train. The train took us to the docks in Tripoli, where there was a collier, which had obviously unloaded its coal. We were pushed down into the coal bunkers in the bowels of the ship; a lot of our people were wounded; half our people had dysentery. The smell in there was appalling. It was a pretty dreary 'Black Hole of Calcutta'. Lavatory arrangements didn't exist. From the bunkers they had two ladders nailed to the side, and two lavatories on the deck. The ladders could not cope so you can imagine the state of the hold, and the smell.
>
> Our captors had given us a tin of Italian bully-beef and two *biscotti* – very thick Italian army biscuits – between two of us. This had to last us until we got to Italy.
>
> We all thought we were going to be sunk by the submarines from Malta so we were very pleased when we arrived at Palermo. I don't know why we went into Palermo, as we weren't there very long. Then we shot across to Naples, where we berthed outside two Italian tramp-steamers, across which we had to make our way to the docks.
>
> They formed us up, and I remember that they were baking in the kitchens, from which there was this marvellous smell of baking bread. All the smokers were desperate for a cigarette, which they hadn't had for some time. These greasy bloody Italians in the cook-house smoked nasty cigarettes, and when they threw away the stub-ends I saw a Guards officer actually pick one up and put it in his pocket. That shows you the state which compulsive smokers get into. I've never smoked in my life, and that sight confirmed me in that all the more.
>
> We were put in trucks on a siding on the wharf of the docks. There was a tenement just beside us, and up above on a tiny little balcony were two little girls and a little boy. They were having a wonderful game; the little boy was standing there trying to pee on us. He had to aim off, of course. He had the encouragement of all the prisoners, and every time he scored a hit he got a terrific cheer.

* * *

On arrival in Naples, the prisoners were finally given a hot shower and their clothes de-loused. From there, most were sent by train to a transit camp at Capua: PG66. This camp was one about which no ex-prisoner had a good word to say, and which was to be the subject of war crimes investigations after the war (several men were shot whilst trying to escape from PG66). Although it could be quite pleasant in summer, in winter it was muddy and windswept. Worst of all, however, was the lack of food. Italian rations for officer prisoners amounted to only 780 calories a day.[3] Gunner always recalled the misery of January 1942:

> The Capua transit camp had no Red Cross parcels, which was one big worry. We were in stone-cold army sheds. For food, twice a day we had a bowl of soup with two or three brown-coloured bits of pasta in it. And that's all we had, except in the early morning they gave us some of the German *ersatz* coffee made of monkey-nuts or pine-nuts or acorns or something. That's when we were really starving and cold. You got to the state that if you were sitting on your bed and you stood up too quickly you got giddy. So it was pretty depressing, in that very cold winter.

* * *

The well-being of prisoners-of-war was the responsibility of the Red Cross organization, with each nation's prisoners being looked after by a "Protecting Power". Until its entry into the war in December 1941, the neutral United States had been the Protecting Power for Allied prisoners-of-war; that role was then taken over by the Swiss. Gunner had reached Italy at a moment of transition, therefore.

The lack of Red Cross parcels at Capua was a serious problem. Prisoners were entitled to these regular parcels to supplement the basic rations with which their captors were supposed to supply them; as we have seen, the Italian rations were a starvation diet, and without Red Cross parcels life in a prison-camp rapidly became insupportable. The parcels were usually sent out on the basis of one per man per week, and a typical British parcel might contain:

¼lb packet of tea	tin of cocoa powder	bar of milk or plain chocolate
tinned pudding	tin of meat roll	tin of processed cheese
tin of condensed milk	tin of dried eggs	tin of sardines or herrings
tin of jam/marmalade	tin of margarine	tin of sugar
tin of vegetables	tin of biscuits	bar of soap

Prisoners were almost always hungry, even when the parcels arrived. Apart from illicit trade with the guards, prisoners in permanent camps often had access to a canteen, where if they were lucky they might be able to purchase fruit and other foodstuffs – though these were usually expensive. All prisoners were issued five cigarettes a day by the Italians, which provided a useful exchange currency (especially for the non-smokers such as Gunner) – more cigarettes came through the Red Cross.

Below: a typical Red Cross food parcel and its contents.
Without these parcels, the rations provided to prisoners of war would have been wholly inadequate (copyright holder unknown).

Not only were the conditions in PG66 unpleasant, but Gunner was almost immediately to experience the worst treatment of his entire captivity. To a certain extent, he brought it upon himself, since his determination to break out of the camp had led him to make another audacious escape attempt.

> This place had a lot of barbed wire around it. I had a good look round, and next door there was a compound full of black South African drivers. They weren't soldiers. They'd been taken prisoner, but they weren't really guarded. They were used by the Italians for work parties, doing manual labour. We used to see them being formed up. I decided to get in there. The wire partition went just behind one of our huts, and there was a little sheltered area there, and I got in there and was able to pull the barbed wire up. I crept into the Negro compound. So I'd escaped out of one prison into another one.
>
> I quickly got in touch with some of the occupants and they took me to their boss man. I told him that I'd lived in South Africa for thirteen years and sang a bit of *Sarie Marais* to prove it.[4] I was accepted, and I told them that what I wanted to do was to get out, to walk to Naples, and to get into a neutral ship. I couldn't think of anything else. He thought this was a terrific idea, so he got a blanket and when they were forming up a work party I got in the middle between some rather big Kaffirs, as I'd been brought up calling them, and I put this blanket over me and pretended to be very cold. We went out through the gate, but I hadn't gone very far when suddenly the Italians began shouting something, and they came up to me and pulled the blanket off and found an escaped prisoner. I think my desert boots gave me away.

The effrontery of this attempt by a white British officer to walk out of a prison-camp posing as a black labourer enraged the Italian commandant, Captain Pasquale Dota, especially since it was standard policy for an Italian prison-camp commandant to be sacked if there was a successful escape from his camp. Given that command of such a camp was a safe billet, any threat to a commandant's position was taken personally.

> They put me into a most awful place, a corrugated iron shed, half concrete – it was a cell, a punishment cell. There was a concrete bed, with one threadbare blanket. It was bitterly cold; *bitterly* cold, especially at night. The food I had was negligible. I thought I was going to die, I was so bloody cold in there.
>
> I was then taken inside to be tried by the Commandant. The Senior British Officer was allowed to be present, and we had an interpreter. This silly little Commandant, a pompous little bugger, said "You have made an attempt to escape, and in consequence you will be denied all privileges."
>
> So I said: "What privileges are there?" I was determined to take the piss out of him.
>
> He didn't answer that, so then I asked "When are you going to move me out of this cell? I'm dying of hypothermia in there. I don't get enough food." I started playing the Geneva Convention card, which all prisoners do, winding the bugger up. I pointed out that there was no heating in the huts, and that on the food we were given we were starving. I told him we had none of the protection required by the Geneva Convention, and that I'd only tried to escape because I was starving and wanted food. He got more and more angry and was screaming at me by the end. Then he turned to the SBO and yelled "I am giving this officer a severe reprimand. All his documents will be stamped *pericoloso* [dangerous]."
>
> I also had to do thirty days *rigoroso* – solitary confinement in the punishment cell – which was the punishment you always got after an escape. I was marched out back into this freezing bloody tin hut.

At that time of year, and on rations only a third of those required for survival, a month in the punishment cell was tantamount to a death sentence. Gunner was imprisoned without heating or the means to keep himself warm, and on rations which did not enable his body to fight the cold. He believed that he would not survive his thirty-day sentence.

> I spent two or three more nights in there. I got worse and worse. I really felt desperate. I tried to get a message to the SBO when they brought food, but there appeared to be nothing he could do. I'd done a week in the tin hut. I was freezing and all I had to eat was a cup of *ersatz* coffee and twice a day a bowl of thin soup with about ten bits of grey pasta in it. I was in a very poor way, and I even thought I might die of hypothermia.

However, just as Gunner began to despair, a Swiss inspector arrived in PG66 to carry out the checks on inmate welfare expected of the Protecting Power. Once again, Gunner's luck had come to the rescue.

> The SBO said to the Swiss representative, "Would you ask the Commandant if you may have a look at the punishment cells?" The Commandant apparently agreed that he could come and interview me provided that there was an Italian interpreter present. But when the Swiss came in, we spoke German – which the interpreter did not speak. I said "I'm partly Swiss", which was a good start. "I have an *Onkel* Emil who lives in a house just near the bear-pit in Bern."[5]
> He said, "I know where that is. I come from Bern."
> "I'm desperate. I think I'll die of hypothermia in here. Or starvation. One or the other will get me."
> The Swiss was appalled at my conditions, and said that he would ask the Commandant to return me to the main camp. The effect of that was that he went to the Commandant and said that the cell wasn't fit for anyone to live in. The Commandant agreed to release me from the punishment cell, on condition that the Swiss did not mention in his report what he had seen. And so I was marched back into the camp.

Even better, Gregg had taken the opportunity to establish contact with his grandmother's twin brother in Thun, his great-uncle Emil:

> What the Commandant did not know was that I'd written a letter to my "Onkel" Emil, telling him that I badly needed warm clothing and high-energy food. This I had slipped to the Swiss.
> "Could you give this note to my uncle? I'm asking him to send me a parcel with something warm and some food."
> He said he would see that it was delivered, and that he would personally visit Emil and tell him everything. Shortly afterwards, I was moved to another camp at Padula. Imagine my delight when a most wonderful parcel arrived from Switzerland, which included everything that I could possibly want. Good old *Onkel* Emil.

* * *

Gunner probably moved into PG35, at Certosa di Padula, near Salerno south of Naples, with the first batch of officers to be transferred there on March 23rd 1942. PG35 was a converted monastery, built in 1306, and had been used as a prison-camp for Austrians during the First World War. The old high-ceilinged refectory now became the officers' mess; there were two acres of gardens and grass for playing fields. Certosa di Padula is now a tourist attraction – indeed, a World Heritage Site – not least because it has the largest cloister in the world and a spectacular white marble stair-case leading to its library. Gunner remembered Padula almost with fondness:

> After the horror of the transit camp at Capua and the punishment cell in a tin shed and the starvation diet, Padula was almost too good to be true.
> It was right down near the toe of Italy, in the warm climate of Calabria; it was a lovely camp, one of the most comfortable prisoner of war camps in Italy. It had been built by the Spaniards, who owned that part of the world for a long time, and it had been a Carthusian monastery. Over the entrance were carved cowled death's heads with "Abandon hope all ye who enter here", or words to that effect. [In fact, "renounce the world if you enter".] But it was a very comfortable place to be, a proper prisoner of war camp. They had food parcels, so we were well fed and retained our strength.

A Swiss representative of the Red Cross first visited Padula on April 14th, by which time there were already 383 officers in residence (with three NCOs and eighty-one men). The inspector described the camp as follows:

> The camp is located on a plateau about 1640 feet high, in a fine and healthy position... It is located in a Fifteenth Century monastery. The lodgings occupy a two-storied solid stone building with stone

Above: Certosa di Padula as it appears today. Gunner inhabited a monk's cell on the ground floor of the cloister, whilst the four sides of the upper floor were each one large dormitory.
The picture is taken from the town which overlooked the camp (author's collection).

staircases. The former cells of the monks, which are very spacious, are used as bedrooms. Three to four rooms, each with three or four beds, constitute a section with separate toilet-rooms provided with modern wash-basins and water-closets. Each section has its own garden where the prisoners can grow vegetables and flowers... A large courtyard and lawn is situated in the centre of the building. Here and in the wide open grounds outside the monastery walls the prisoners have ample space for exercise and can spend the day outdoors until the roll-call in the evening.[6]

A fellow inmate of PG35, who became Gunner's great friend, was George "Josh" Millar. Millar later wrote two superb books *(Horned Pigeon* and *Maquis)* about his wartime experiences.[7] He described the layout and atmosphere of the camp in detail:

Our vast inner court-yard was the last, and by far the biggest, of a series of court-yards. You entered it from the former working part of the monastery, through a great door..., now shut and guarded. Living on the other side of it, in a maze of court-yards, corridors, and old, high, stone-floored rooms, were the Italian officers and men who were responsible for keeping us alive and keeping us in.

If you turned right at the doorway you walked down a long blank wall. Behind this wall was the former refectory, now our dining-room, a heavily panelled, vulgarly religious place... Next to it was the kitchen, the monks' kitchen, with huge boilers and cooking equipment not less than two hundred years old...

Immediately above the monastery itself was perched the village of Padula, one of the richest in the whole valley. As we stood on roll-call we could look up to the balconies, the weathered grey walls, and the pinky-red pantiles of the terraced village...

Barbed wire and sentry-boxes in profusion circled the great, confused plan of the monastery, like a tight-fitting girdle, except immediately beyond the ceremonial staircase, where the wire perimeter swept out to leave for our day-time use a rough field amply large enough for football. Seven olive trees stood there; and it was altogether a most agreeable field with a fine view of the village and the hills to the south...

If I felt happier in the monastery than in other prisons, my happiness was shared by few of my comrades. Most of them looked at the place from the practical point of view, and decided that it was a hole. It was bitterly cold, both in the wings and in the dining-hall, where, as prisoners poured in from other transit camps, we were obliged to eat in two sittings. Soon there were nearly five hundred officers and sixty British batmen in the camp. The kitchens were quite inadequate to deal with such numbers. The latrines were inadequate. The water supply was inadequate. The food was inadequate...

> At intervals down the wings the Italians had installed box-shaped red tile stoves with asbestos pipe chimneys that rose straight for eight feet, then angled back and through the outer wall of the building. There was not enough wood to made a proper fire. But we could take turns of placing our hands on the stove...
>
> The Italian staff were not able to organize a reasonable system for roll-calls. It was a bleak and stormy month of April, with blustering winds, torrential rain. We spent much of the time standing shivering in greatcoats beneath the damp cloisters, waiting for our names to be called.[8]

The prisoners slept around the cloister: the more senior officers were in the former monks' rooms on the ground floor, whilst the junior officers were in four vast rooms on the first floor, each room making up one side of the cloister, as Gunner remembered well.

> The bottom floor was all divided into priests' cells. When I arrived at Padula, I was put in one of them, down with various friends – I think there were about five of us in there. There was one Chief Petty Officer who of course wasn't actually an officer, but they treated him as an officer; he'd been God knows how many years in submarines, and was known as "Chiefy", naturally. He was a wonderful chap. The second floor was enormous rooms which were full of beds; hundreds of them.

These large rooms originally slept sixty to ninety men, but Millar, who slept in a corner of one of them, was later able truthfully to tell his wife in a letter that he shared his bedroom with one hundred and thirty-two other men. Gunner, however, being slightly more senior, was lucky enough to sleep in a room down on the ground floor.

It was not only the surroundings and the supply of food parcels, however, which made Padula memorable. Millar organized a highly successful black-market operation which flooded the camp with illicit cheese, ham, eggs, poultry, and milk. Gunner also found that the guards were not above a little bartering.

> Being in a rural area there was a small but regular supply of certain local produce – including wine. We could also trade certain of the contents of our Red Cross parcels with the guards for eggs and the like.

It was whilst he was incarcerated at Padula that Gunner's pre-war hobby of bee-keeping became unexpectedly useful.

> There was all sorts of study going on the whole time: people were learning Mandarin Chinese and Russian, even learning how to be solicitors. London University sponsored a course on agriculture, and sent out the materials for those who were going to give the lectures. We had farmers, all kinds of experts, and it was a very popular course because it had to do with food, which was everyone's obsession. A notice went up saying that the university wanted us to include apiculture, and asked if anyone had any knowledge of bees. I owned up and so I suppose I became a lecturer in Apiculture for London University. They sent me all the bumf I needed, and all the time I was there I ran a course on bee-keeping. I had good audiences, because I was describing honey and honeycombs and so on.
>
> Years later, after the war, when I was walking about in London, people stopped me on various occasions to ask if I remembered teaching them bee-keeping in Padula.

But neither Gunner nor Millar were among those prisoners who were prepared to settle down and wait for liberation. Millar eventually made a "home run" from Germany, but for now the pair discussed how to get out of Padula.

> George Millar was an inveterate escaper: he was brilliant. He was a very determined man: before the war he'd been a reporter, and he told me that he once lay down in the road in front of the car carrying the Duke of Windsor and Mrs Simpson in order to get an interview. He and I were planning various escapes in the six months or so I was there. But in the end he was not on my escape attempt, because he was busy with other plans.

A tunnel had already been dug at Padula, down into the cellars, through which ten officers had escaped: all been recaptured. Millar and two other officers also tried simply to walk out of the main gate in disguise – but did not make it out of the building. For his third attempt at escape, Gunner decided to tunnel his way out, also through the cellars.

> We were fairly near the outer wall, and below us were cellars and things. We soon found our way into them by moving a "Stufa", as we called it – a stove; we managed to make a hole and get down. The cellar went right up to the monastery's outer wall. We chose a spot where we thought we could get through, and worked bloody hard to clear it away. We had to be very quiet, because of course there were sentries walking up and down outside. We had no problem disposing of the earth, but we had to make sure that the whole thing didn't fall down and expose the hole prematurely. We planned to leave just a thin layer of stone to conceal the exit.
>
> We were really very badly prepared, compared to my other escapes; when I was trying to escape later, I had all my times and routes planned exactly – I knew exactly what I was doing. But at Padula I don't think we even had forged papers, so we were going to have to do all our travelling at night. I was going to head for Malta; if we could get somewhere near the coast, I might steal a small boat. We really hadn't done the preparation which we should have done.
>
> One night we slowly broke through – and as soon as we could see outside there was a whole lot of Italians pointing machine-guns at us. I think they already knew about it. So thirty days' *rigoroso* again.

Millar, who also spent some time in *rigoroso* at Padula, described the punishment cell, which was much better than the tin shack at PG66:

> The cooler at Padula was then a double cell, formed of what had been a kind of reception office when the monastery was a money-making concern... One cell, which had a table and two chairs in it, looked through a heavily-barred window to the dark cloisters of a small cobbled court-yard. The inner cell had a window looking on to the entrance passage. It contained two beds. Since the electric light was good in the cells, and I had books and interesting company, I thoroughly enjoyed my time there.[9]

* * *

Gunner was now marked down by the Italians as being too troublesome to keep in an ordinary camp. Like the Germans, the Italians had established higher-security camps which were intended for troublesome inmates (the German camp, of course, was Colditz Castle, where several of Gunner's friends and comrades ended up).

> I'd already been reprimanded for my attempt to escape from Capua. They now decided I wasn't a welcome guest at Padula any more. We were sent to what they considered a punishment camp. The main punishment camp was Gavi [PG5], and that's where they'd sent George Millar after his failed escape attempt. The other one was Veano [PG29], which they considered escape-proof, and so that's where they put other people they wanted to keep: for instance, they had one or two Generals and Brigadiers. Six of us were moved up to Veano.

And there in PG29 Gunner met Donny.

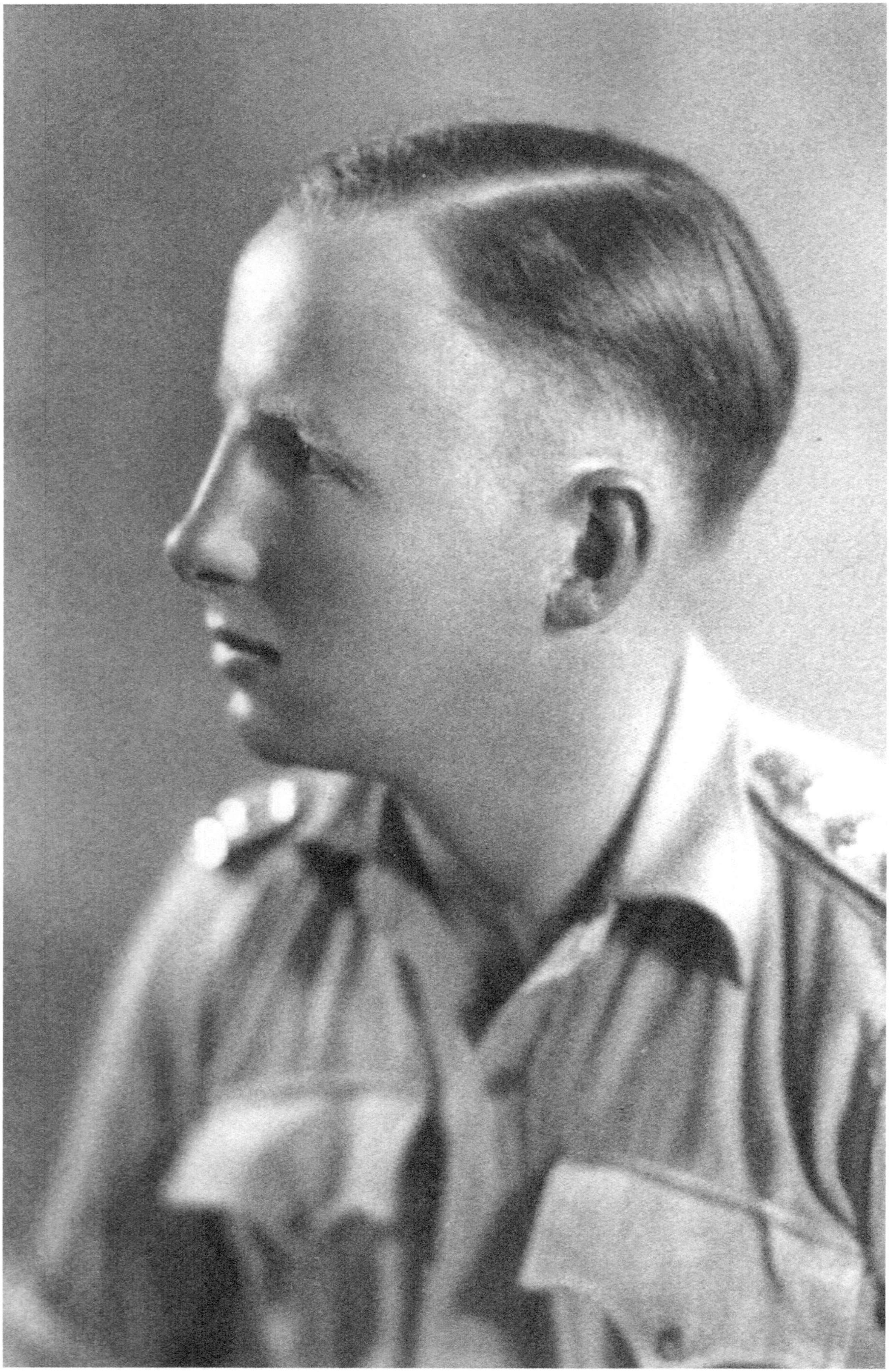

Chapter Nine
Tobruk

Although for Gunner personally Operation Crusader had been a disaster on several levels, the British had succeeded in sweeping Cyrenaica clear of Axis forces and driving them back to El Agheila. Tobruk had been relieved, and the Allies now controlled the port of Benghazi. But on January 21st 1942, after the shortest of pauses, Rommel's Afrika Korps counter-attacked. His opponents were weaker than in 1941: now that Japan had entered the war, Australia had recalled many of her troops; and the experienced 7th Armoured Division had been replaced by the novice 1st Armoured Division. Rommel rapidly forced the Allied troops into headlong retreat. Benghazi soon fell, giving the Germans and Italians a major port from which to supply their forces. Rommel consolidated his gains, and the front stabilized west of Tobruk, on the "Gazala Line". The Axis forces needed to capture Tobruk if they were to have a chance of attacking into Egypt; the Allies were determined to drive Rommel back away from the port and to force him to abandon Benghazi once again. By May 1942, both sides were preparing to attack.

The prospect of renewed fighting meant that units were anxious to gather any detached personnel in the rear to bring them up to strength. 2nd Camerons – part of 11 Indian Infantry Brigade, in 4th Indian Division – had seen some bitter fighting, and were running short of officers; at the end of April 1942 they requested Donny's return. All that they knew was that he was serving with HQ British Troops Cyprus. Their request was granted – in fact, Donny was already on his way, having relinquished his post as DAAQMG (and acting rank of Major) on April 1st and embarked on a ship for Haifa on May 14th. On May 15th he entrained for Egypt. After several years away from the battalion to which he belonged, Donny was to return to the front line.

It was probably the prospect of action which made Donny think about his future. He had a girl-friend, and he now proposed to her. *The Times* of May 6th 1942 included the announcement that he was to marry Sarah Diana Tomlinson, the eldest of four daughters of Sir Thomas and Lady Tomlinson, of Ellerhowe, Grange-over-Sands, Lancashire.[1] The Tomlinsons were related to the Mackenzies by marriage through Dor's side of the family, but it is not clear whether Donny and Sarah had met before the war, or in the Middle East; Donny's photograph albums of his life before the army contains many pictures of girls, all annotated but none called Sarah. However, the photograph album covering the years after 1936 contains five unlabelled photographs of a girl in Egypt, who may therefore be Sarah.

Having made this formal commitment, Donny returned to 2nd Camerons, relinquishing his temporary rank of Major and reverting to the rank of Captain. On May 25th 1942 he took over 'C' Company near the top of the Halfaya Pass on the Egyptian border. He would spend less than one month with his battalion.

* * *

Opposite: *Donny Mackenzie in the spring of 1942. He sent this photograph home to his mother, who passed on a copy in 1945 to Gunner as a keepsake: he kept it to his dying day (Gregg collection).*

As Donny made his way back to his unit, 2nd Camerons were on the Gazala Line at Ed Duda, south-east of Tobruk. One member of the battalion recalled this period:

> In May 1942 the temperature was about 110°F. 11 Infantry Brigade then moved into the desert, spread out like a convoy of ships at sea, but with swirling dust which covered everything and everyone until we halted at the Ed Duda ridge... It was a hard rocky area where it was impossible to dig in. I was sent with my section to give covering fire to the Indian sappers and miners who were laying a mine-field in front of our defensive positions... Lying in the open with no cover was the first time I'd experienced enemy shell-fire, which had our range. Then after a while the shelling stopped. During the night, while listening to the dull thuds of hammers striking the metal fence posts, I [wondered] how we could defend ourselves against those enemy tanks we could hear moving about in the dark. All we had was a rifle and fifty rounds each.
>
> During the next few days the sounds of battle could be heard approaching, together with increased air activity overhead.[2]

The Gazala line was coming under severe pressure from Rommel's forces, and General Auchinleck had decided that Tobruk, which had withstood a nine-month siege by the Germans in 1941, must be held again, to deny it to the enemy. However, Tobruk's defences had been allowed to deteriorate to a shocking extent. Of the original outer and inner lines of defences, only the outer was now serviceable, despite being far longer.

On June 5th 1942, 11 Indian Brigade received orders to support 2nd South African Division in manning the Tobruk defences. The majority of the garrison was on the west and south-west of the perimeter, the direction from which the Germans were expected to attack. 11 Indian Brigade was commanded by Brigadier Anderson, who had joined the army as a Private, risen through the ranks, and served as commanding officer of 2nd Camerons. The Brigade found itself in charge of a thirteen-mile stretch of the defences, 2nd Camerons alone being assigned a frontage of three miles. Anderson did his best with the limited resources at his disposal.

> The Camerons, with the Mahrattas and Ghurka battalions, had moved into Tobruk and occupied trenches and dug-outs previously held by Italians in earlier battles, and defended the south-eastern perimeter of the port behind an anti-tank ditch and mine-field of unknown quality.[3]

Anderson's report on operations amplifies the comments on the mine-field:

> Portions of the mine-fields were non-existent. Mines which had been removed and taken forward to the Gazala position had never been replaced. Records of lifted mine-fields were not available. It was estimated that 20,000 mines would be required to place the perimeter and inner mine-fields in a reasonable state of defence. Only 4000 were available; these were laid on the perimeter, giving more protection to infantry posts and anti-tank guns. The majority of the mines were of Egyptian pattern and had been laid a year previously, with the result that many were defective and, as was proved later, were no real obstacle to the enemy.[4]

2nd Camerons put three companies in the line, with no reserves since Donny's 'C' Company was temporarily elsewhere, as the Battalion's history states:

> The following mobile column was provided for operations with 7th Armoured Division in the area El Adem-Bir Hacheim-Bir El Gubi: 'C' Company in lorries; one section anti-tank platoon; one troop 25-pounders, 25th Field Regiment RA. This was known as "Salmon Column", and was commanded by Captain A.D. Mackenzie. A similar column, named "Trout", was provided by 2/5th Mahrattas.[5]
>
> These remained out for ten days, and were supplied by a special supply column, under Brigade arrangements. They were almost continually in action during this period and, according to reports, they carried out some magnificent work.[6]

One of Donny's men later recalled a tense moment for "Salmon" column:

> The column halted, spread out and took cover, as many dark moving shapes were seen on the skyline. We lay sweating it out in the sand dunes for a long time, expecting the enemy to attack, until the dark moving shapes were identified as camels.[7]

As the enemy drew nearer to Tobruk, Donny brought his men back within the perimeter:

> On the evening of the 16th, "Salmon" and "Trout" columns returned. This enabled the Battalion to have one company and one anti-tank section in reserve.[8]

The Germans cut the port off on June 18th, and 2nd Camerons immediately made contact with the enemy, sending out patrols towards El Adem. After a brief lull, the Axis attack commenced at around 0600 on June 20th with a furious bombardment from the air:

> We had completed the usual 'stand to' before dawn. Then with two of my section, I went to collect breakfast from the cooks situated in the sand dunes about two hundred yards away. On our return loaded down with containers of tea, porridge, etc., Tobruk was attacked... by over six hundred aircraft, including Stuka dive bombers. This continued throughout the day, together with a sustained bombardment from enemy artillery. Fortunately we had no casualties in our trench.[9]

> Never have I seen such a mountain of dust and smoke [as the one which] towered in the sky after those bombers had done their work. They came again and again, and I realized that from now on we should get this hourly, for their aerodrome was only ten miles off, and we were never going to see a British fighter.[10]

The Germans laid smoke in front of 2/5th Mahrattas and on the left front of 2nd Camerons, and at 0630 launched their ground attack. Their initial assault troops, the *Sonderverbund,* had been specially trained in attacking desert fortifications; they were followed by Panzer IIIs and IVs of 21st *Panzer* Division and motorized troops of 90th Light Division. The main point of attack was through the smoke-screen.

2nd Camerons drove off all the attacks on their left, despite the poor visibility. However, to the north-east, the forward companies of 2/5th Mahrattas were rapidly over-run:

> A concentrated bombing attack on the Indian regiments on our left flank gave the Germans and Italians a breakthrough into the area behind our battalion positions.[11]

At 0700, Anderson requested an immediate armoured counter-attack – but the first tanks, from 4RTR, did not arrive until 0930. Anderson bitterly recorded that

> had the divisional reserve arrived at least one hour earlier, the gap would in all probability been closed before the enemy tanks entered the perimeter.[12]

In front of the Mahrattas, German infantry lifted mines by hand to create a gap through which poured forty tanks. At 1000, Lieutenant-Colonel Lancaster of the Mahrattas reported that his HQ was about to be over-run by tanks and that he was destroying his radio set.

There was a lull between 1000 and 1100 as the Germans paused to check for mines and tanks of 7RTR moved up in support of 4RTR to counter-attack. The battle hung in the balance, and everything depended on the armour.

Many of 7RTR's officers were well known to Gunner from leave in Alexandria and Cairo. They were led by Lieutenant-Colonel "Bob" Foote, whom we last saw on the docks

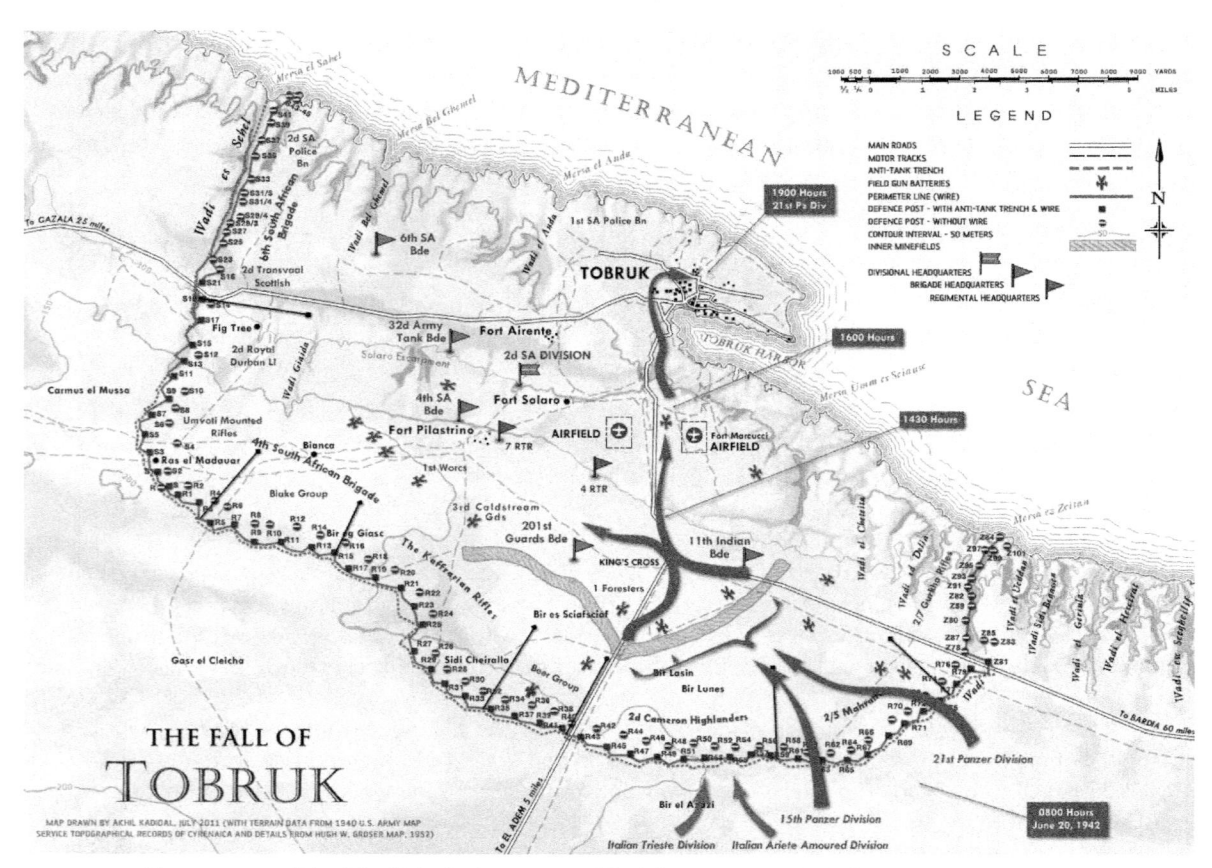

Above: a map of the fall of Tobruk; the postions of 2nd Camerons can clearly be seen at bottom centre (copyright holder unknown).

at Dover in 1940 and who will re-appear in this story later. Like Gunner, Foote was an old boy of Bedford School, and became a close friend.[13] Gunner later described him as

> my hero. Footie was a good and thoughtful man, the best and most modest officer I knew. He was one of the great soldiers of the war, despite being a tubby, smiling man who looked like Mr Pickwick or a kindly vicar. Nobody looking at him would have known that he was one of the bravest men in the army.

Foote was an inspired leader of men – despite his other nickname of "Fairy" – and had been in the thick of the fighting throughout June 1942. On June 5th, in fighting in an area known as 'The Cauldron', he had had two tanks shot out from under him, and, despite a wound in his neck, had continued to control his regiment.

> Whenever one of his tanks came under fire, Bob drove over to it in his scout-car and stood behind the tank commander.

A week later, on June 13th 1942, Foote had conducted a series of brilliant tank attacks near the 'Knightsbridge' position. 21st *Panzer* Division had advanced along Rigel Ridge, destroying twenty-five British tanks, over-running 2nd Battalion Scots Guards, and wiping out a South African anti-tank unit. Only Foote's counter-attack with 7RTR had enabled British forces to cling to their positions. For this gallant defence he would later be awarded the Victoria Cross.

If anyone could restore the defence at Tobruk, it was Foote.

* * *

Foote conducted a quick reconnaissance of the front line before reporting to Anderson:

> OC 7th 'I' tank battalion (Divisional Reserve), who had been forward on a recce, reported at Brigade HQ and gave the following information. 4th 'I' tank battalion, owing to the entry of enemy tanks, had not been able to clear the situation but had occupied a 'hull down' position with the majority of his tanks, where it was intended to hold the enemy tanks whilst the 25-pounders and anti-tank guns engaged them. At that moment the enemy advance had been checked and the situation appeared to be in hand.[14]

Anderson asked Foote to send tanks to take up positions behind 2nd Camerons, thus blocking the route westwards along the inside of the perimeter; Foote sent 'B' Squadron, keeping the rest of his battalion in reserve at a position known as King's Cross.

When the Germans resumed their advance at 1100, reinforced by another twenty tanks, they sliced through the British defences – though on their western flank, 2nd Camerons drove them off, disabling three tanks. 4RTR was down to six vehicles when it broke at around mid-day, and Anderson's telephone link with General Klopper was cut. Foote recalled 'B' Squadron to try to stem the German advance, but it fell into an ambush and was annihilated. By 1345, the Germans were within three hundred yards of Anderson's HQ; he ordered all documents to be burned and radios to be destroyed, and moved his personnel into cover in a nearby wadi. from now on, 11 Indian Brigade's units would have to fight without co-ordination.

Below: a Matilda II 'I' tank knocked out at Tobruk in June 1942; the damage to its thick frontal armour can easily be made out (copyright holder unknown).

At 1400, 2nd Camerons lost communications with Brigade HQ, and as German tanks broke through towards Tobruk harbour, Battalion HQ was 'shot up' for an hour or so, and moved into the forward company positions to avoid capture. By nightfall on June 20th, 2nd Camerons were cut off, and prepared their positions for all-round defence.

Klopper's headquarters had not appreciated the seriousness of the enemy breakthrough until around 1400, and had reacted slowly and indecisively. As the night passed, Klopper gave up hope, and tried to order a break-out by any troops who were able to escape – but there was much bickering amongst his subordinates, and nothing was done. Shortly after dawn on June 21st, Klopper surrendered, though most of his division had not even been in action. The Camerons' commanding officer, Lieutenant-Colonel Duncan, received the news at 1000 on June 21st, but only in the most informal of fashions: a Corporal in the neighbouring South African battalion stated that "De Beer was clearing out", that being the name of the battalion commander. Duncan sent an officer to De Beer to confirm this, but could not find him. The reports of a general capitulation seemed so unbelievable that the battalion continued to fight on.

2nd Camerons were by now under attack from the Italian *Trieste* and *Ariete* divisions, but the battalion held them off successfully throughout June 21st, a remarkable performance. Several sources testify to the ferocity of 2nd Camerons' defence:

> During the subsequent fighting, 'D' Company was over-run, but the remainder of the Battalion repulsed all attacks.[15]

> [The Italian *Ariete* armoured division] was preoccupied with mopping-up operations. It was now inside the perimeter and still engaged with the stubborn Camerons, who refused to accept the orders to surrender as genuine. Instead, they had formed all-round defensive positions in expectation of an attack from within the fortress. At 0800 *Ariete* sent three M14s forward from the direction of Tobruk to approach the Scots' hastily-organized positions. They were within a couple of hundred yards when a single, well concealed 6-pounder anti-tank gun knocked out all of them, and the infantry picked off their crews as they bailed out. The Italians subsequently lost another three M14s in the same way. A seventh M14 appeared with an officer in the open turret, who vainly searched for the concealed gun through binoculars until he was shot dead and his tank blown up. At 1300 *Ariete* reported that its armour was meeting 'strong enemy resistance', including anti-tank, machine-gun and mortar fire. It therefore called for concentric artillery fire on the enemy positions from both inside and outside the fortress.[16]

> A column of six Italian tanks approached along a track and halted about a hundred yards from our position. Sergeant J. Cameron DCM, MM, was firing grenades from a discharger cup when a shell from the leading tank exploded a few yards along the top our trench, wounding him with splinters to his chest. His wounds were attended to and I was pleased to see the destruction of this tank by one of our anti-tank guns dug in nearby.[17]

> A column of tanks which appeared in line-ahead over a rise from the north was engaged by Corporal C.S. Pickett's anti-tank gun. The gun remained silent until all were in view, then opened fire and knocked out six; two managed to get away, but men of 'B' Company finished these off with 'sticky bombs'. Corporal Pickett was awarded the DCM and his two gunners the MM...
> Throughout the day their positions were pelted with mortar and machine-gun fire, while field-guns sniped at any movement. The enemy meanwhile continued to use the El Adem road. Later in the afternoon a three-ton lorry attempted to pass within fifty yards of the Cameron positions. When this vehicle went up in flames, aircraft dive-bombed the Highlanders viciously. Dauntlessly they replied, and an Me 109 disappeared with smoke pouring from its engine and losing height. When night fell on 21st June they were still fighting and in good heart. They had not even sustained serious casualties.[18]

> Stuka dive bombers made continual attacks on our artillery a few yards away, but seemed unaffected by the machine-gun fire from our section as they pulled out of their dives flying low over our trench. The

Above: front-line defensive positions of the sort occupied by 2nd Camerons at Tobruk, though this photograph shows Australians on the perimeter there in August 1941 (IWM E4791).

> noise of the explosions and screaming flight of the bombs was deafening, which affected my hearing for several days afterwards.
>
> The bombing and shell-fire continued throughout the day, and by dusk we heard that our headquarters, commanded by a South African, General Klopper, had surrendered. We were still intact, and carried on although surrounded on all sides...We were the only unit still in action.[19]

2nd Camerons saw no reason to surrender. However, by the afternoon of June 21st, the 15th *Panzer* Division and all Rommel's heavy artillery were massing to destroy them.

> After dark, Germans approached a Cameron outpost. A spokesman hailed the sentry:
>
> "*Kamerad* English, you are safe now. The war for you is over." A reply was given in short bursts. Later in the evening a South African soldier crossed from the 'De Beer' Battalion to advise that a German officer had sent him to contact the commander of the resistance group. Captain Mackenzie sent for the German and conducted him to Lieutenant-Colonel Duncan. It was then learned that Tobruk had fallen that morning. The Germans [said] that we were the only troops fighting, and that General Klopper had ordered a general surrender (this was confirmed by the South Africans) and that if we continued we would be annihilated...
>
> Lieutenant-Colonel Duncan promised a reply by 0500 hours next morning. The Germans offered to postpone attack if the Camerons would undertake to parade on the El Adem road at that hour ready to march to the prison cages. Lieutenant-Colonel Duncan gave his assurance that he would be there, but he added that he expected very few of his battalion to be on parade at such an early hour.[20]

In fact, Duncan had other plans:

> Immediately afterwards steps were taken to destroy equipment: all officers were instructed to take out parties of men... These parties were recommended to go south-west, then to turn east when well south of El Adem... Only those considered unfit for the long trek did not attempt a break-out... When all weapons, stores, and documents had been destroyed, fifteen officers and approximately two hundred men disappeared into the night in an endeavour to reach safety in the east.[21]

Among the escapers was Donny. His companion Lieutenant A.B. Mitchell later recalled how they spent the small hours of June 22nd:

> At 0130 I found myself at Company HQ with Major James Marshall (the OC) and Captain Donald Mackenzie. We decided to make a break through the El Adem gap to the south, over the escarpment, and then due east. We hoped that, if all went well, we should join with our own troops on the Libyan border, where we hoped a stand would be made. The distance was some 120 miles, about six days' marching.[22]

* * *

When the remainder of the Camerons paraded in the morning to go into captivity, they did so with pride. Duncan had demanded the full honours of war:

> What was left of the battalion marched, not as a defeated unit, but under its CO and headed by its pipers.[23]

Duncan allegedly reprimanded the German officer who took his surrender on 22nd June, taking exception to his slovenly appearance. Witnesses who saw the Camerons march into captivity were profoundly moved:

> The might of the Axis at that moment seemed to be enormous... captivity yawned before us unknown, abysmal, inevitable.
> It was midday when we heard it. Faintly at first, and then louder it came, a rhythmic swinging sound, unexpected but unmistakable – the skirl of the pipes. We scrambled out of our shelters to look, and saw, swinging along bravely as though they were marching to a ceremonial parade, a tiny column of men, led by the pipes and a drum, with the Drum-Major striding ahead. Silence fell as they came, and the drum tapped the pace for a moment as the pipers gathered their breath. Then, as they wheeled in towards us, they broke into *"Pibroch o' Donuil Dhu"* with all the gay lilt of the Highlands and all the defiance and feeling a Scot can call out of his pipes. Smartly they marched to attention, and halted as if on parade. To the strains of their regimental march, the Camerons had come in to surrender.
> We looked at this show of defiance, and deep down within us something moved, a strange akin feeling of pride. A man wept. And bubbling up through our numbness a ragged faint cheer broke aloud. Here was something that called deeper than capture, deeper indeed than men's fate – the indomitable spirit of Britain, that scorned to be trailed in the dust.[24]

Even the Jerry sentries sprang to attention as the battalion neared the gates. There, the Camerons halted. Their Colonel reported to the Brigadier, saluted, and dismissed his men, who had held out for twenty-four hours after the surrender order had been issued.[25]

* * *

Donny, Marshall and Mitchell had set off into the desert night at around 0230 on June 22nd. Mitchell's account of their experiences was printed in the regimental history, and makes fascinating reading: no apology is made for quoting it at length here. Around them, the desert was full of evaders, but since the Germans were swarming in the same direction few made it to British lines.[26] In the end, only six members of 2nd Camerons successfully reached the El Alamein line: one officer took twenty-six days to make the journey. Donny and his companions did not have supplies to last that long:

> Our rations consisted of the following items: two one-pound tins of tomatoes; six tins "Bully"; one dozen packets of biscuits; one two-gallon tin of water (carried in a pack); six water-bottles, filled. We were each armed with a .38 pistol and had maps, compasses, and binoculars.[27]

The trio made for a gap in the defensive mine-fields in front of their battalion positions, picking up more escapers as they went:

> We reached the gap without incident, and after warily negotiating the mines on the road, found ourselves outside the Tobruk perimeter. In the darkness four others had joined us: Sergeant Fisher, who was Motor Transport Sergeant; Sergeant Wood; Private Nicol, a batman; and one other private whose name I cannot recall. As they had no maps or compasses, we let them come along with us. The first few miles were traversed slowly, as we could hear voices all around us.[28]

As daylight came, it proved necessary to take cover from the victorious enemy troops who now filled the desert:

> Daybreak found us still below the escarpment on the west of the Axis road, and only about a hundred yards from it. We made for a derelict three-tonner top, complete with cover, and decided to "lie up" there for the day. It was soon evident that we were in the centre of a hive of activity. Tanks and lorries rolled down the road towards Tobruk, and more could be seen all along the escarpment, while Ju52s poured in with German troops.
>
> Pooling our resources, our daily ration for the next six days consisted of ½ pint of water, one-seventh of a tin of "bully," and some biscuits. It was decided to make two meals of this: one before we started each night, and the other when we stopped to lie up in the morning. We could well imagine, from the first day of intense heat, that the water situation was going to be a serious problem.[29]

The party resumed its march that night:

> At 2100 it was dark enough to move, and anything that could rattle was muffled. We reached the top of the escarpment by 2300, where we had to pick our way through enemy tanks and lorries. We must have been seen, as one of the tanks put on its lights and started moving towards us. Fortunately, we were not in the beam, and we scuttled for a slit-trench close by. All seven of us squeezed in, and the tank came on to within twenty-five yards of us and turned away. We breathed again: we were safe; but made sure by breaking into a run until we had put about a mile between those tanks and ourselves. After a steady march at three miles an hour, stopping for ten minutes every two hours, we found ourselves about fifteen miles south and a little east of Tobruk.[30]

Donny's party now needed to lie up again for the day, partly because they were only too visible in the flat desert surroundings, but partly because it was too hot to march under the blazing summer sun.

> *June 23rd 1942*
> We were not so fortunate this morning, as we found no shelter from the sun, save a few gorse bushes. With an old ground-sheet, we rigged up a crude shelter. Although tired, we could only sleep for a few hours in the heat of the day, and by midday everyone was awake. We thought it safe enough to make a short recce in all directions to try to improve our position and, if possible, find some water. To our surprise, however, we found a large German leaguer only a mile away in a wadi and in our line of march. Further movement was out of the question. As we could see no end to this group to the south, we decided that night to skirt it to the north, which we did without incident.
>
> *June 24th 1942*
> We stopped beside some abandoned Italian vehicles from the 1940 push. They provided good shelter, but it was still frightfully hot, and thirst more than hunger was having its effect. Examination of the

Above: *an Italian M13-40 tank in position overlooking Tobruk harbour after the fall of the fortress in June 1942 (copyright holder unknown).*

vehicles found traces of water in one of the radiators. About three pints of very filthy water was drained from it. It tasted awful, but we drank it nevertheless. James Marshall and one of the privates had blistered feet, and some clean water had to be spared to clean the burst blisters. James was persuaded to dump some spare clothing he was carrying.

We started this evening at 2000 and plodded on, adding an extra hour in the morning after daybreak in order to reach the shelter of a crashed CR42 [an Italian biplane fighter]. We lay up as before. Nothing to report.

June 25th 1942
We were now on familiar territory. Our desert barrel-routes and the broad vehicle track, the Trig-el-Abd. We hoped to make "The Wire" on our next bound, but were not very hopeful of reaching our own troops there, as we had seen no sign of any action for two days and we were travelling only about five miles from the coast.

The water ration was getting smaller, and if we did not reach our troops in a couple of days, the position would become desperate. Our party were beginning to string out. Sergeant Wood and the private with sore feet were lagging, and the pace had, of necessity, to be slowed.

June 26th 1942
Morning found us on a clearly defined track about ten miles from "The Wire", and we again found shelter by an abandoned Italian Breda vehicle full of 60-pounder shells. This vehicle appeared to have been only recently abandoned, but hopes of making the thing go were soon shattered on examination. Sergeant Fisher made a splendid effort here.

We did find water, however. We drained about six pints from the radiator. We could hardly believe our good fortune, and as someone produced a little tea and sugar, we had a fire going in no time.[31]

After the disappointment of the lorry, the party now got a second chance to get hold of some transport:

It was my turn as look-out, and I scanned the desert while we waited for tea. There, to the north, about two miles away on the horizon, appeared a moving vehicle. I warned everyone, and the fire was put out. For hours we watched this vehicle move round us in a half-circle, always keeping just too far away to identify the two figures moving in the back. We did notice that it stopped each time it reached the barrels on the tracks, and deduced that it would, in all probability, eventually come along our track, as there were a couple of barrels only a hundred yards ahead of us. We had not long to wait, and we made our plans, having distinguished the Afrika Korps hats of the two Germans in the back.

The two privates were to act as decoys, and lie under our vehicle with their boots off, and to make movements to attract attention should they come past. We placed the two sergeants in the front, and James, Donald and I, who were armed, hid in the back.

Everything went according to plan. The German vehicle, an open 30-cwt., approached from the rear; the two Germans in the back spotted the men underneath and hammered on the canopy for their driver to stop. This was our cue. I jumped out and went for the driver, Donald covered his mate, and James, with the two Sergeants, covered the two Germans in the back. We must have looked pretty desperate, not having washed or shaved for more than a week. Those Germans were certainly scared. Donald and I disarmed them and kept them covered; Sergeant Fisher attended to the vehicle, whose engine was still running, and James organized the loading of our bits and pieces.

The Germans, who were all bearded, were sappers and were plotting our barrel-routes on to their maps. We destroyed their maps and left them sitting in the desert with the sordid remains of our water and rations. We had found that their vehicle had ample supplies of both. All this had taken only about five minutes, and we were soon heading due south after an adventure only to be imagined in a Wild West film.[32]

This audacious and well-executed ambush had totally transformed the party's fortunes. They now had transport, food and water; the only drawback was that they were now considerably more conspicuous. Donny and Mitchell took the precaution of disguising themselves as Germans.

We had spotted another vehicle at the same spot as the first, and had therefore no time to waste. We had relieved two of the Germans of their hats, which fitted Donald and me, and we took up our positions in the back of the vehicle as the Germans had, keeping the others low down, while James, went in the front with Fisher.

A rocky surface kept us down to a steady twenty-five miles an hour, and after twenty miles we took stock. We found food and water plentiful, most of it having been looted from the Tobruk NAAFI: tins of stew, potatoes, fruit, milk, etc. The petrol situation, however, was not so good; there was only sufficient in the tank to take us about ten miles more.

We turned again due east and luck was with us. Having gone only about five miles we found an abandoned German armoured car with a tank containing about twenty-seven gallons, and ten miles farther on we hit a British dump of petrol, and loaded as much as we could carry with safety. We knew then that we could not be far from the border, and when we found a dump of water, we decided to call it a day. That night we ate and drank until we felt ill, and having posted our look-out settled down to a well-earned night's sleep.[33]

The next day, Donny and his companions headed south-east until they hit "The Wire". However, they were far from being home and dry; Eighth Army had been pushed back beyond Mersa Matruh some two hundred miles into Egypt, and was attempting to stabilize the front line in the area of El Alamein, where a choke-point was formed by the Qattara Depression, which left only a forty-mile gap of desert next to the sea.

June 27th 1942
We now decided to move by day, keeping well away from the coast. We hit the wire soon after we started at 0700, and found a gap about five miles south of Fort Maddalena. We suspected mines, but kept our fingers crossed and tore through. Night found us on the Mersa Matruh to Siwa track. We were then mid-way between those two places, having found a kilo mark 75.

June 28th 1942
A decision had to be made here: whether to make for Siwa oasis, where we were sure that one of our fighter squadrons was still operating, or to continue due east and make direct for Alexandria. We decided on the latter.[34]

The run down to Siwa would have taken the party well out of the line of the German advance, and they would almost certainly have been safe. Psychologically, however, it was out of their way home. By driving eastwards towards Alexandria, they were approaching the bottle-neck between the Qattara Depression and the sea. The whole Afrika Korps was pouring into this forty-mile front, becoming more and more concentrated as they did so. With hindsight, it was the wrong decision, and may ultimately have cost Donny his life.

> Full of food and high spirits, we set off, and stopped again almost immediately. Donald had sighted a speck on the track moving south towards us. It proved to be two Italians on a motor-bike. Donald and I took up our positions wearing our German hats, and we moved on slowly towards them. They approached unsuspecting and stopped alongside. They were petrified when I dug a Luger pistol into the stomach of the driver. We questioned them in very poor Italian, and, as far as we could make out, our troops were making a stand in Matruh. They could tell us nothing of Rommel's panzers, whom they had not seen. They belonged to the *Bersaglieri* Regiment and were deserting. We took them with us, after destroying the bike.[35]

It had all gone so well. Donny and his comrades had managed to trek across hundreds of miles of desert, had acquired transport, weapons, food and water, had made it back to Egypt, and had now even taken two prisoners-of-war. Soon they even managed to add to their "bag".

> We had only been going for a couple of hours, and making good progress over a hard rocky surface, when suddenly, out of a wadi only half a mile ahead, came a German jeep driven by a German officer, followed about an equal distance in the rear and about four hundred yards to our right, by a British pick-up driven by a German soldier. We had no time to formulate a plan of action, and this is what happened.
>
> We approached the officer slowly (Donald and I were still wearing our *Afrika Korps* hats), and drove between the two vehicles, keeping the jeep on our left. I shall never forget the look of amazement on the face of that German officer as we pulled him out of his seat and threatened him of the consequences of uttering a syllable. His capture on the blind side of the other vehicle took only a matter of seconds, and when the pick-up closed in to investigate, its driver too was soon made our prisoner. The German officer, who spoke fairly good English, told us that we were wasting our time, because Rommel would be in Alexandria and Cairo in a few days. His confidence had soon returned, and with it the usual German arrogance.
>
> We destroyed his jeep and all the wireless installations contained in the pick-up and took the latter with us. The German officer was dumb to our questioning, but he was obviously a recce officer and his own troops could not be many miles away.[36]

It was clear that if German reconnaissance troops were in the area that Donny and his friends had reached the forward edge of the battle area. Ahead of them, in all probability, lay only friendly troops. The trick would be to out-run the German advance.

> Speed was therefore essential. We had now four prisoners and had to organize our loads. James and I [sat] in the front of the pick-up and two Italians, with one private to look after them, in the back. Sergeant Fisher and Donald [were] in [the] front of the 30-cwt., with Sergeant Wood and Private Nicol looking after the two Germans in the back.[37]

The little convoy set off eastwards once more. Divine providence had seen them this far; but now it deserted them. It may seem harsh to say so, but what happened next was caused by greed and pettiness, which undermined all the efforts which Donny and his fellow officers had made to get their party back to their own lines.

> All set for Alexandria, and approaching the area south of Garawla Wadi, but still on the escarpment. A shot rang out, and we stopped the pick-up, which was ahead. Shouting from the other vehicle made us go back to investigate. We found that Sergeant Wood and Nicol had been struggling for possession

> of a Luger pistol, when it accidentally went off, severely wounding Nicol in the thigh, breaking his leg near the hip.
>
> Everybody, including the Germans, lent a hand in making a crude splint, and making Nicol as comfortable as possible, with blankets we had taken from the Germans. Four shell-dressings which we had retained came in useful, but Nicol was in bad shape. Our plans to keep away from the coast had now to be dispensed with, as it was vital to get Nicol to a hospital without delay, if we were to save his life. We knew the country well, and made for Garawla Wadi to get off the escarpment and reach the coast road. We had lost two valuable hours attending to Nicol.[38]

Only a few miles from Allied lines, the increasing density of German forces finally put paid to the heroic efforts at evasion. Had Wood and Nicol not got into a dispute over the Luger pistol – one of the most desirable items of loot – it might all have ended happily. As it was, however, their run from Tobruk now came to a depressing end.

> After going about an hour, north and slightly east, we sighted a great column of yellow dust to the north and west about four miles away. *Panzers*, without a doubt. We went all out for the *wadi*. The bumping and swaying as we hurtled along must have been absolutely hell to poor Nicol in the back. Within sight of the familiar defences the Battalion had made in 1940 we were spotted, and within half an hour two German half-tracks mounting two-pounder guns were gaining on us rapidly. We had allowed the slower-moving 30-cwt. to go ahead, and the first of the German vehicles bore down on us. We stopped, and I turned round to find the muzzle of the gun only about a foot from my nose. The German officer in charge barked something in German, which I could not understand, but I had forgotten that I still looked like a German myself with my Afrika Korps hat. He waved us on. I made frantic signs to James to go on, and to remove his balmoral in doing so. Alas, it was too late. The German had spotted him, and he ordered, "Schottlander aus."
>
> We had treated our prisoners fairly well, and our captive German officer put in a good word for us. His "I told you so" was a bitter pill to swallow... Only an hour after our capture we were being shelled by our own 25-pounders. So near, but oh so far.[39]

Mitchell remained a captive until the war's end; Nicol recovered from his self-inflicted Luger wound and remained a prisoner of war; Wood and the other nameless Private seem to have done so as well.

But the other members of the escape party proved their determination to escape even at the cost of their lives. Sergeant Fisher was killed at Benghazi whilst trying to escape;[40] Major James Marshall died whilst escaping from Italy.[41]

Donny was the third who did not survive the war.

Above: PG29 Veano in pre-war days.
Below: the chapel at PG29 Veano in a pre-war photograph.
(Photographs courtesy of Signor Claudio Oltremonti of Piacenza.)

Chapter Ten

Veano

The first Swiss Red Cross report on PG29 at Veano was based on a visit made on June 4th 1942, a month after the camp had opened for business, initially with some 210 officer prisoners and 120 other ranks (many of them acting as servants, referred to as "orderlies").[1] The camp stood near Ponte dell'Olio, a small town at the point where the river Nure flowed northwards out of the mountains to the plain around the city of Piacenza. The Swiss inspector commented that

> the camp is situated in mountainous country, altitude 450 metres. The surroundings are beautiful.[2]

The buildings of the camp formed an H-shape, the central bar of the 'H' running from west to east and housing the prisoners' dining-room (referred to as the "refectory" or "mess"), a reading-room, a games room, a kitchen and the camp shop ("canteen"). The eastern upright of the 'H' was the main accommodation block for prisoners; its ground floor was taken up by the orderlies' kitchen and recreation hall, the sick-bay, the office of the Senior British Officer, a barber's shop, a food store, showers, and a guard-room. Both these sections of the camp were three storeys high, the two upper floors providing sleeping-quarters of the inmates. The western upright of the 'H' comprised a chapel (to the north) and the Italian camp administration (in the old abbot's quarters at the southern end).
As well as the buildings themselves, the Swiss report recorded that inmates had access to outside spaces:

> The prisoners have two courtyards thirty metres by eighty metres at their disposal, one of which has been turned into a sports ground and vegetable garden.[3]

The yard in which vegetables were grown was surrounded on three sides by a high brick wall. The vegetable plots were to be of vital importance to Gunner's attempts to escape, as we shall see. Major the Very Reverend "Bob" McDowall, a New Zealand army chaplain, grew tomatoes there, and in September 1942 he recorded in his diary that he had been able to give three crops to the camp kitchens.[4]

The other courtyard, on the south side of the complex, contained five chestnut trees and what little grass the climate and the constant tramp of feet allowed to survive. Major d'Arcy Mander – Gunner recalled that "we called him 'Hooky' Mander, because of his hook nose" – described this yard as follows:

> There was another smaller yard, more of a quadrangle, surrounded on three sides by the Italian Wing, the Refectory, and the south aspect of the New Wing. The front of this yard, which gave onto a pleasant garden, was wired in by a double wire fence constantly patrolled by Italian sentries. In this yard most of the business of the camp was conducted. The camp shop opened on to it. Those who wanted to read sat in the sun leaning up against the wall. The buying and selling of Red Cross items was conducted here, and if you wanted to bet on any mortal thing under the sun, Major Fieldhouse, a chartered accountant and the camp bookie, would lay you odds on it.[5]

On the southern-western side of this yard stood the Italian officers' quarters, which were accessed through a small secure gate, locked and bolted.

Another inmate of PG29 in its early days was the redoubtable Admiral Sir Walter "Tich" Cowan, whose career reads like something out of a novel.[6] When he was repatriated in March 1943, Cowan wrote a detailed description of the camp.

> On a clear day there is a lovely view of the Alps, seventy miles away... There are generally two [men] in a room, and everyone has a proper bed. There is a large mess room, just big enough for the numbers, and two or three other ante-rooms with tables, benches and chairs. The kitchen is a little small, but there is almost always enough food...
>
> The corridors are warmed with terracotta stoves burning wood, the supply of which is very limited. To each corridor there is a wash place, a row of about eight basins and one bath. Also there is another place with four rather primitive WCs and one urinal to each corridor. The water for these and for washing was never enough, especially in the summer, and in consequence [there was] almost always a smell of drains in the compound used for exercise and for sitting out in warm weather. This compound was thirteen times round to the mile.[7]

The Swiss reports on Veano stated that the electrics were inadequate, and that officers were entitled to only one hot shower a week; Cowan, however, felt that even this was somewhat optimistic:

> Washing in hot water was by means of shower-baths perhaps once a week, but no certainty ever of hot water.[8]

Indeed, by the time of the last Swiss report (dated September 1st 1943, less than ten days before the camp was abandoned), there had been no showers for three whole months, owing to water-shortages, and the only hot water available was used for shaving. Mander recalled the problems:

> Water was always in very short supply, particularly in summer. The well at the back of the camp was totally inadequate and a mule-drawn water-cart was pressed into service to supplement it... Washing water was carefully preserved, then used to wash down the floors; this in turn was saved, and the murky remains would be slopped in small quantities down the squat-type latrines – and thus we got by without disease or epidemic, although the results were somewhat odorous.[9]

Major Hugh Clifford thus found his camp duties less onerous than they might have been:

> I afterwards became officer i/c baths; it was less than a half year job. In the summer months I would just put up the notice "NO WATER: NO BATHS".[10]

The Swiss also reported that prisoners were allowed two walks outside a week, provided that they gave their word of honour not to attempt to escape during these. Cowan describes these walks and other forms of exercise:

> Exercise is by way of walks in droves of seventy, about four miles, taking about two hours altogether. These walks are rather at the caprice of the Italian officers, and I doubt if any single officer averaged more than two days a week like that through the months. Quite often it was too wet underfoot for the Italian guards, or their officers were on leave or had other duties. There is a back yard used by the British batmen for washing clothes, etc., and the officers could there play "volley-ball", a most valuable means of getting up a good sweat in a short time.[11]

Medical arrangements at PG29 were summarized by Cowan with typical humour:

> In the camp there were, when I left, three or four British army doctors, and in general charge an Italian army doctor who is also a fair amateur dentist... There is an Italian military hospital a few miles away

> where they send anyone who is at all seriously ill. It's not bad, but not so very clean or sanitary. The Italians are like that.[20]

Spiritual health was also well provided for: as a converted seminary, it possessed a fine Roman Catholic chapel, and Cowan recorded that there were three British army chaplains – two Anglican and one non-conformist.

* * *

The Senior British Officer in the camp, a key figure in setting the tone of life in captivity, was Colonel George Younghusband.[12] He was lucky in that the Italian Commandant – *Colonello* Cornaggio Medici Castiglioni – was co-operative and clearly a more pleasant figure than his counterpart at PG66, for example. Castiglioni had himself been a prisoner-of-war in the First World War, and whilst his experiences in Austrian captivity made him sympathetic to his Allied charges, they also helped him to understand how best to stop them from escaping. Mander thought him and Younghusband a good team:

> The *Commandante* was an elderly Italian cavalry officer and a gentleman. He tried to treat us as well as he was able, but the Senior British Officer and his staff must take the credit for the excellent way in which the camp was so smoothly and efficiently run.[13]

As a result, conditions in Veano were no worse than was to be expected, and a good deal better than in some other camps, as Mander later reflected:

> Although we did not appreciate it at the time, we were lucky to find ourselves in [PG29]...The rooms were clean, new and bare; iron bedsteads, mattresses, sheets and blankets were provided; there was even a cupboard for our non-existent clothes and belongings. The more senior officers (Brigadiers, Colonels and Lieutenant-Colonels) occupied the rather larger rooms over the refectory, and we Majors, Captains, and the like took up residence in the north wing.[14]

Under the efficient camp authorities, Red Cross parcels were regularly distributed and a camp shop begun. The prisoners were paid by the Italian authorities, the sum being deducted from their salary back in England. The Italian pay came in the form of paper money which was only valid within the camp, and the sums were recorded in a camp pay book; Gunner kept his.

The camp shop sold a variety of products which could be purchased with this otherwise worthless currency – according to the Swisss, the stock (in alphabetical order) included anchovies, benzine lighters, boracic talc, brilliantine, caramels, chocolate drops, cigar-cases, cigarette-holders, *Creme d'Istric,* cups, dried figs, fly-traps, fountain-pens, gramophone records, ink, jam, lavender, liquorice, marmalade, matches, Milk of Magnesia, mineral water, note-pads, paper, pencils (HB, coloured, propelling and styptic), pen-holders, pen-nibs, pickled capers, pickled onions, pickled vegetables, pipes, razors, razor-blades, shaving-cream, shoe-polish, stock-cubes, sun-glasses, tinned mushrooms, tinned pears, toothpaste, and, perhaps most importantly, wine – as Cowan mentions:

> On the average at this canteen, each of them could get about one and a half tumblers of drink a day – Marsala or Vermouth or that red wine – and there is no doubt it was of the maximum value in making glad the heart of man, as the Almighty put it into the world for.[15]

The real currency in the camp was cigarettes; a pair of socks cost fifty cigarettes, and a pair of gloves could be obtained for thirty. As a non-smoker, Gunner was spared the dilemma of whether to smoke or spend.

Above: the final entries in Gunner's Italian pay-book from Veano.

Letters from inmates of German and Italian camps were published in *The Prisoner of War*, a magazine produced to show families in England that their men-folk were being looked after under the protection of the Red Cross and the Swiss authorities. Obviously, published letters were meant to be reassuring, but there is no reason to think that those from Veano were not genuine:

Campo PG29
23.3.43
There is no need to say that we are all as usual very fit and in great form, and have the very comfortable feeling that all is going well and, though we may have to wait for a bit yet, all will soon be well and we will be together again. We get Red Cross parcels regularly once a week and the extraordinary part is that they get better each time. We get a slice of bacon nearly every Sunday and porridge one day a week.[16]

Campo PG29
21.6.43
I organized a party the other day of fathers who had children they had never seen; it was very successful and there was an attendance of fourteen. I got a photograph from each, stuck them into a sheet of stiff cardboard, numbered each one and ran a guessing competition to say who was the father of whom.[17]

Many prisoners tried hard to overcome the tedium of their existence, and to turn their incarceration to profit, as Cowan explained in his report:

Every sort of lecture went on every day, and to almost all of them everybody went. Then once a week after dinner there would be a very cleverly prepared digest of the week's news as gathered from the Italian papers, and another as gathered from the private letters of as many as were good enough to contribute itsems of general interest, and so very many did. News about fox-hunting, farming, racing, Parliament, well-known public men, high service appointments – every sort of varied facts... of interest to every sort of mentality. Such a lot of them in real life were not soldiers at all that it made the whole community a much larger reservoir of varied interests than most people would ever foresee.

Then there were debates now and then on many unexpected subjects: one initiated by an old Etonian to urge and prove that public schools should be done away with – tremendous interest and close argument. Another in defence of fox-hunting (by a Northumberland Blackett). Another urging that divorce should be made more difficult...

A number of them were writing books of one sort and another, and also were becoming really good picture-painters. One, George Fanshawe of the Bays, the polo-player, almost a second Lionel Edwards, and a very good lecturer on anything to do with horses...[18]

There was a most ample supply of every sort of books, and really good ones. I left behind, I should think, at least fifty.[19]

When Gunner arrived at Veano, he joined a circle of bridge players, and considered his love of the game one of the best gifts with which captivity provided him.

* * *

The prisoners' clandestine radio receiver was a vital boost to morale. The original was adapted from a five-valve film-projector provided by the Italians, which was safely locked away. The inmates picked the lock every night, substituted a realistic cardboard copy in case of a random spot-check, and temporarily converted the apparatus into a five-valve radio receiver to listen to the BBC.

The BBC news was passed on to the inmates by way of a lecture given by Brigadier Desmond Young, as a fellow prisoner recalled.

> Characters galore were in this camp. Not least was Desmond Young, who wrote the book on Rommel and many others. I think that Desmond was probably the most interesting man I have ever met. He had been editor of the *Times of India* when the war broke out… He was given the equivalent rank of either Brigadier or full Colonel and was in charge of all the war correspondents in the desert. Not being a base-*wallah* at heart (he had been in the Rifle Brigade once) he was up at the front and was captured… He gave lectures… Another thing he did was to organize the equivalent of a newspaper in the camp. How he did this was to give a weekly news lecture. He split the camp up in many ways. One group of Italian-speaking specialists would go through all the enemy papers which they let us have, and listen to the odd bulletin they broadcast to us. They had to allow for propaganda, of course. Another group would go through any letters from home with bots of interest in them, passed on by the recipients. Also, eventually, we got in touch with the BBC. This was the cleverest act perpetrated on the enemy. Two Majors, each brilliant in his own line, built a radio from scraps and bits of wire. One day, as we all sat in the large dining room, we were told during the next few days to pay no attention to the fact that the small bit of flexible cable from the ceiling to the ceiling light in each of our rooms would be shortened by three or four inches. Pay no attention to what is going on. Ask no questions. We did as we were told, and then Desmond Young got to his feet on the news night. We had always our own sentries posted, of course, and when all was safe, we were told that we were now able to be in touch with the BBC. Desmond's news talks then assumed even more importance.[21]

As well as the news, there were other publications. A magazine was produced at Christmas 1942, bearing the self-chosen motto of the prisoners at Veano: *Cave Leonem Sine Dente* – "Watch Out for the Toothless Lion." The official Italian interpreter was amused by this, as his name was Dente.

* * *

Despite the generally pleasant tenor of their incarceration, many prisoners were far from happy. To almost all prisoners of war, captivity was hateful. One of Gunner's friends in

Veano, Major Ian Bransom, wrote a poem entitled *Depression in Captivity*. Bransom would have been the first to admit that his poetry was amateurish (it was published under the title *Still Inferior Verse*), but it does convey how the claustrophobia and unchanging scenery and company sapped morale.

> The same two hundred faces,
>   Same drab wall and wire,
> The same small lawn,
>   Seven chestnuts we admire;
> The same words now
>   As they said yestermorn;
> Perhaps that's how
>   There are so many traces
> Of what will form
>   From captive suppressed races.
>
> The same to come
>   As we have had before,
> The breathless silence
>   As the wireless news comes o'er –
> The sickening suspense
>   Of the small defeat,
> The pulsing gladness
>   Of the Bosche retreat.
> Oh! futile sadness
>   Of a prisoner's madness.
>
> Just one mad effort now to make us free,
>   To hear again the music of our guns,
> And failing stay to watch the laggard second flee
>   That pass, 'ere peace and long-for freedom comes.

Cowan's report gave his reflections on captivity:

> One thing that astonished me was the way in which the days rather flew by, owing I think to there being no horizon, no term of weeks or months to live down and count the days of. The life is rather that of a cow in a field, but every day full of hope, and every now and then an abnormal wave of it.[22]

Captivity at Veano reminded Mander of boarding-school (he had been at Charterhouse):

> The food was awful and inadequate. The lack of privacy, the routine, the sameness of each week made it in some respects a little like a Dickensian boarding school. There we had been sent and there we stayed, like it or not... The geographical distance [between us and our homes] was no measure of our feeling of isolation from our families, our homes and our own people. We might as well have been on the South Pole without a boat.[23]

However, although they all hated being prisoners, that did not mean that everyone did anything about it. About a quarter of the inmates were dedicated escapers; most of the rest paid lip-service to the idea, and a tiny percentage were anti-escape, fearing reprisals from their captors and disliking the disruption which, as Cowan explained, escape attempts brought in their wake:

> After every attempted escape there would be a most rigorous search of everyone and everything, which would take many hours.[24]

Gunner, as we have seen, was a dedicated and enterprising escaper, not one of those who was prepared to sit the war out in captivity.

> I think the main reason why I tried to escape was because I felt ashamed that I had allowed myself to be captured. To make up for that and to retore my self-esteem and pride, I felt that I should do all that I could to escape. I also felt that I was wasting my life doing nothing. I did not like anyone telling me what I could or could not do.

He was not alone. Veano contained many other fine soldiers who were itching to escape. One was Lieutenant-Colonel "Bob" Foote, the former commanding officer of 7RTR, who had been captured at Tobruk at the same time as Donny, and would later be awarded the Victoria Cross when full details of his exploits in the desert became known. As the senior RTR officer in the camp, he had particular influence over the other members of his regiment, such as Gunner:

> In Veano I became very close to him. He impressed on all of us that it was our duty to escape – and with his encouragement, advice and support, several of us planned and executed a first-class escape.

There were several other 7RTR officers in Veano, many of whom Gunner had known in Egypt before their capture. Ian Bransom, for example, was a TA Royal Artillery officer who had been attached to 7RTR; before the war he had been a country solicitor.[25]

Above: *Gunner's hero, friend and colleague, the later Major-General Henry Robert Bowreman Foote VC, CB, DSO (1904-1993). It was only when Foote reached Switzerland in April 1944 that he learned of his Victoria Cross. This photograph was taken in 1960, after his retirement from the army (NPG x170562).*

Bransom dedicated his post-war collection of poetry to Gunner.[26]

> I liked and admired him very much. He was a dark Jew – sometimes we used to call him the "Black Bastard". He was one of the leading lights of our escape party.

Captain "Johnnie" MacLean had also been in 7RTR, and he and Bransom were particular friends of Donny and Gunner.

> Johnnie was a big, strong, disgustingly good-looking man – God's gift to women. I had known him in Egypt, and whenever we had leave in Alexandria or Cairo I had always kept very close to Johnnie – there was always a spare pretty girl left over from the many who flocked around him. In prison we became very close, and he was my digging partner on our tunnel.

Another 7RTR officer was Captain "Jock" McGinlay, who had been Foote's Intelligence Officer and could

> play the piano like an angel.

This musical talent was not irrelevant: McGinlay provided covering songs and accordion music to drown out the noise of escape attempts. Another inmate later commented that the Scottish reels which the prisoners learned during the winter of 1942 at least helped to keep them warm.

McGinlay was a brave man who had won an MC and bar (and had been recommended for a DSO late in 1941).[27] Like Gunner, he was immensely proud of Bob Foote:

> He taught me a great deal, and was to prove to be the most professional soldier I have ever met... Those of us who were with him when he earned [his Victoria Cross] feel one mile tall every time we think of it.[28]

McGinlay was Johnnie MacLean's room-mate, and made good money on him in the camp volleyball sweepstake:

> Johnnie, my friend, had recently arrived from hospital. Now what they did not know was that Johnnie, over 6'4" in height, was a magnificent athlete, good at all games. I bought him for a song, and with him in the team he played for the others did not have a chance. I won over £65 on him.[29]

There were, of course, nearly three hundred other inmates,[30] and not all of them were British. New Zealand, for example, was represented by Majors Orr, Kedgley and Evans. Gunner particularly admired "Hil" Evans, an artillery officer who had been captured at Sidi Azeiz in 1941:

> A a very good man: a small, tough New Zealander, he'd owned a dairy in Wellington before the war... He'd fought in Greece and Crete. He was a great chap, and just the type to have on your side when times are rough.

Another prisoner described Evans as a

> rabid escaper, prowling around like a caged wolf, examining every potential means, however fantastic, of getting out.[31]

Evans had by this time been involved in several PG29 escape attempts. In the first, he had aided another New Zealander, Brigadier George Clifton, who had got away from a first-storey window which the Italians had bricked up. Clifton had made it as far as Lake Como before being caught.[32] Those left behind had made careful note of the lessons which could be learned: Gunner, even though he arrived afterwards, nevertheless knew all about it.

> We studied it in detail when we were planning our own escape.

* * *

Gunner and the other five *pericolosi* – "boys who'd been misbehaving", as Gunner later put it – arrived at Veano late in 1942, and Gunner found himself a few beds away from Donny. Over the next two years, they became the best of friends and comrades-in-arms.

> I don't know why, but there was an affinity between us right from the beginning... He was bright, highly intelligent; a big, solid man, but very taciturn, a quiet type, a very dour chap – I mean, he was definitely a Scot, and he thought carefully before he did things.
>
> He was a very religious man, Donny. He surprised me one day and said that he really believed there was a Heaven and a Hell, and that people who sinned would go to Hell and people who were good and Christian would go to Heaven. Now, there are very very few people I've met in my life who genuinely believe that, and so I realized that here was a very sincere and good man. He worked and behaved according to those principles. If people came into the camp, and they'd been wounded and they had torn clothes, Donny would be the first person to go and give up whatever he had: if he had a spare pullover, or something, he'd give it to them.
>
> I admired him. He was a good man, to my mind, and if I was going to do anything I'd rather do it with someone like Donny than a lot of far more flamboyant people... We just fitted.

Although five years older than Gunner, Donny looked young for his age. They talked about the other camps which they had been in: Donny had come to Veano from another notorious transit camp, PG75 at Torre Tresca, near Bari. There is some hint in the sources that Donny had been involved in an escape attempt there, since the Swiss recorded that on June 17th 1943 he had written them

> a letter of protest against the charges made for damage to blankets at Camp 75.[33]

The most usual reason for damage to blankets was cutting them up to make civilian clothing for an escape.

Donny and Gunner also talked, as men will, about their homes and their careers; they laughed together, and shared Red Cross parcels. Donny spoke fondly of his *fiancée*, Sarah Tomlinson, and mentioned that he was a Wykehamist, though the two men had better things to discuss than their boarding-schools, so similar to what they were now enduring. Gunner had already served with Wykehamists, having defended a bastion at Calais with Davies-Scourfield and fought in Greece alongside Upcott-Gill. This latest one he found equally reliable a comrade.

Most importantly, however, the two men talked seriously about the possibility of escape. Indeed, it is probable that Donny had been drawn to befriend Gunner in the first place because he knew that he was such an active escaper.

* * *

The difficulty for the inmates who wanted to break out was that Italian security was actually quite good, as Mander explains:

> Behind the camp, our Italian guards were accommodated in a wired-in compound, and I may say they did the job of guarding us very efficiently... The Italians were very good at keeping prisoners or war captive – much better than the Germans. Campo 29 was very difficult to run away from.[34]

The commanders of Italian prison-camps were generally sacked if a prisoner made a successful escape, and so were very keen to ensure that such escapes did not happen. The Italian commandant at Veano had made strenuous efforts to keep his charges inside, and Gunner recalls that he boasted of his security:

> The Commandant at Veano said his camp was escape-proof, but we did not believe him. He shouldn't have said it – it was a challenge. He was tempting providence.

Brigadier Clifton had already proven that the Commandant's confidence was not quite justified. But it was very close to being true.

The Swiss reported that there were three roll-calls daily. Although these could be circumvented, they were held at irregular intervals simply to make it difficult for the prisoners to establish a working routine. Gunner explains how such an *apello* might be circumvented:

> If you wanted to 'fudge' a roll-call, the officers would parade in three rows with the biggest in front. Most Italians are fairly small, and they would have to go along the lines jumping up to see how many there were at the back. Two officers would then have to move up to fill gaps on their left, and they would be counted twice. This could be a bit of a tricky job. We often had to use the 'fudge' after an escape if we did not want the Italians to know someone was out, but only twice to hide the fact that diggers were underground.

At night, Mander reports, there was a curfew:

> The 'Last Post' was sounded at ten o'clock every night, and we all had to get out of the refectory and go to our cells, and the whole of the ground floor became the domain of the Italians for the night.[35]

Cowan details some of the measures taken to check that the prisoners were still where they should have been late at night:

> About three times in the night, every room would be visited by the guards; and also three times a day, at uncertain times, they would all be fallen in and mustered.[36]

The nocturnal bed-check had originally been conducted only once nightly, but Clifton's escape had led to a tightening of the régime.

There were almost as many guards at Veano as there were prisoners; and some of them were solely employed at sniffing out escape attempts, as Gunner recalled.

> There were about two hundred guards (I think at times it went up to three hundred) who lived in the barracks and provided the sentries. There were also soldiers who we called "ferrets". The "ferrets" went about in pairs and their job was to see we did not dig tunnels or escape, so they had to be watched very carefully while we were digging our tunnel. They also had surprise roll-calls to try and catch us out, if we were down a tunnel. So we had many problems which had to be solved if we were to keep a tunnel secret.

The camp and its walled courtyard were surrounded by barbed-wire fences. Clifton later wrote that the barbed wire at Veano was worse than elsewhere:

> Someone wrote in a POW autograph book, "Stone walls do not a prison make, nor iron bars a cage – but this barbed wire is a bloody nuisance." Our Italian Commandant, being an engineer, had great and justifiable faith in unlimited barbed wire. It wrapped our hostel round so thickly that only the rats could slip through; most of it was the high-tensile steel type which merely blunted the jaws of ordinary pliers and broke the hearts of would-be escapers…

> All Italian camps had two main deterrents, barbed wire and police; but we always felt both worked more efficiently at Veano than anywhere else, excepting always the "Hell Camp" at Gavi.[37]

Around the wire were sentry-posts manned around the clock, and equipped with machine-guns and searchlights. Gunner remembers this aspect of the security well – he studied it intently.

> The camp consisted of a large building, where all the beds were, and a very big exercise ground where we used to play volleyball and exercise and have our roll-calls. It was all surrounded by a very high walland then a barbed-wire fence which went all the way round. There were four main towers which had search-lights and machine-guns. There was a sentry path and sentry-boxes all the way round. Behind each sentry-box was a little slit-trench, one of which was very valuable to us later.

As usual in prison camps, to approach the barbed wire without permission was to court death: the guards had permission to open fire without warning and to shoot to kill. Indeed, in an unsuccessful escape attempt by four officers in September 1942, Lieutenant-Commander David "Frosty" Fraser was shot in the knee.[38] Mander recalls that another prisoner was also shot during an unsuccessful escape attempt:

> One chap had the idea of hiding under a refectory table and getting out, perhaps through the *Commandante*'s office or by some other means. Unfortunately, he was spotted by an Italian patrol, who opened fire on him with his hands already raised in surrender. He was wounded in the hand and the fusillade in the confined space awakened the entire camp and stirred up a veritable hornets' nest of activity.[39]

To make it even more difficult for the prisoners to exploit the hours of darkness, the camp was illuminated at night. This seriously inconvenienced Clifton when he was making his bid for freedom in February 1943:

> In addition to numerous perimeter lights giving almost continuous local illumination, there were strong floodlights controlled both by a master switch in the main-gate guard-room and also individually by a switch alongside the local sentry. Orders allowed the sentries to put the floods on whenever they felt inclined, and they did so with damnable irregularity, particularly if bored or jittered, often merely to register the fact that they had not fallen asleep.[40]

British prisoners were very good at undermining the loyalty and scruples of their captors, often using the contents of Red Cross parcels as a means of bribing guards to supply equipment or information for escapes. The Italians were alert to the possibility and guarded against it, as Mander explains:

> There was always a Fascist in the camp whose main function was to see that we were not treated any better than was absolutely necessary and to make sure that the guards didn't get too friendly with the guarded.[41]

This official, at Veano at least, proved less than effective, as we shall see. But the guard force was supplemented by members of the para-military police force, the *Carabinieri*, as Clifton explained:

> The Italian police, the *Reala Carabinieri* – known as Caribs for short – claim to be second only to the London Metropolitan Police. Judged on their uncanny ability to "smell out" escape plots and gear, they were most efficient, maintaining equally close supervision over the prisoners and the soldier-guards. The latter could be got at if expertly handled and heavily bribed in kind; the Caribs, in my experience, never were open to corruption.[42]

Other measures also existed to make life difficult for would-be escapers. The *Carabinieri* made routine checks in the evening of every window, door and bar. They also searched the prisoners' rooms and belongings for escape materials and signs of tunnelling. Mander recalled that they

> had a nasty habit of having a search when everyone was at dinner and not allowing anyone out of the dining room until it was over.[43]

Mander eventually decided that the Commandant was correct: Veano *was* almost impossible to escape from.

> Until one has been put inside a prison you do not appreciate how extremely difficult it is to get out... Almost every loophole was... closed tight... I could see no way out of the confounded place.[44]

Chapter Eleven
Vault

The first stage in any escape was gaining the approval of the Escape Committee, a panel of senior officers who had to consider whether the proposed method of breaking out was feasible. At Veano, the committee was run by Desmond Young, who, being very keen to explore any possible avenue of escape, gave a sympathetic hearing to every proposal.

Some schemes, however, did not stand up even to a kindly scrutiny. Mander's only suggestion as to how it might be done was rightly rejected:

> My plan was simple. Our exercise yard was bounded by a high brick wall on three sides. One could see the sentries on the outside from the upper-storey windows. I proposed that a large number of us (there were nearly two hundred of us) should push the wall over – with rhythmic shoving I reckoned it could be done in seconds, and those who wished to leave could scramble over the wire and dash into the vineyard, over the fields, into the woods, and away, while the rest could make suitable diversionary noises or even pick some grapes if they liked. The trouble was that one or more of the sentries might get hurt or even killed if the wall fell on them, and some of us would quite likely get shot, as the Italians were excitable and opened fire at the slightest chance – sometimes for no reason at all, as the holes in my trousers well testified.[1]

The Escape Committe also considered whether would-be escapers had a viable plan as to how to evade re-capture and make it to friendly territory. It was not enough simply to hope for a few days of freedom and the concomitant waste of Italian resources hunting down an escaper; this had to be balanced against probable reprisals against the prisoners who remained, as well as the possibility that other, worthier escape attempts would be compromised. These were stringent tests.

However, Gunner and his friends had taken account of this mass of complicated factors when planning their escape.

> We considered various plans, and eventually decided that we would have to dig a tunnel. But when we did a very very close reconnaissance inside the main building, we came to the conclusion that there was nowhere we could start a tunnel. It would have been found in no time at all. We realized that it was going to be extremely difficult to get out.

Although Veano had massive stone cellars of great antiquity, they were so solidly built that tunnelling from them seemed impossible, and were so obvious a starting-point that the *carabinieri* patrolled them incessantly.

If a tunnel could not be begun from inside the camp buildings, then the only alternative was to start it from the eastern yard, used by the prisoners for exercise, drying laundry, and growing vegetables. Boldly, Gunner's team decided to dig their way out from a vegetable patch. If they could get in and out of their tunnel unseen, they would be able to dig from a totally unexpected starting-point.

> We had a brilliant idea, on the "Wooden Horse" principle – though we'd never heard of that escape and came up with it independently. I think we were really inspired when we chose the most public spot to dig the shaft, right in the middle of the open exercise-ground. It could be seen from the

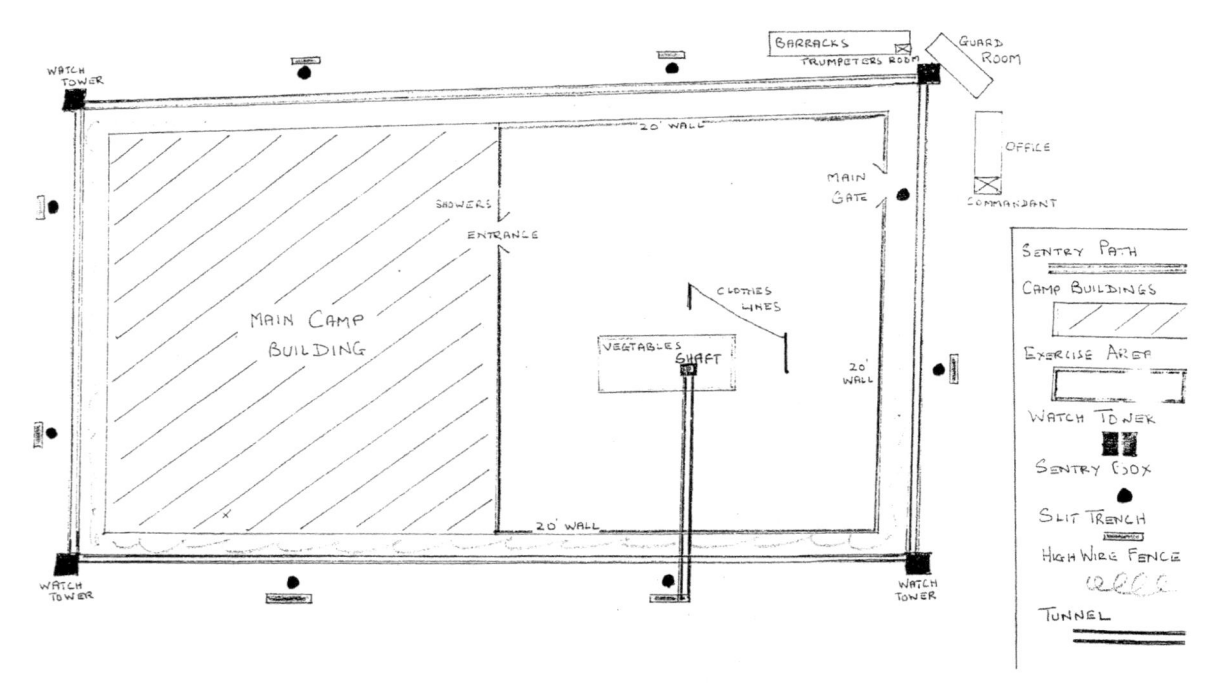

Above: *Gunner's sketch-map, drawn from memory fifty years later, shows the audacity of the planned tunnel and the complex measures which the Italians had put in place to prevent an escape (Gregg collection).*

> Commandant's office. Every Italian who went in and out of the camp went right past it. The Italians – and particularly the "ferrets" – can he excused from believing that no escapee in his right mind would choose such an unlikely, exposed place to dig the shaft of an escape tunnel. I think it was a brilliant escape, because, damn it all, that was the main thoroughfare of the camp, and our only concealment was clothes-lines. No one would have thought it possible.

The "Wooden Horse" to which Gunner refers was a famous break-out from a Nazi prison-camp in which three tunnellers dug from the open ground of the exercise area of their camp, concealing the tunnel's entrance with a vaulting-horse. But this escape did not take place until late in October 1943, months after the success of Gunner's tunnel.[2]

Young and the Escape Committee were impressed with Gunner and Donny's scheme, and approved it. Once the project had been approved, the Committee could provide a great deal of assistance for the potential escapers. Documents, maps, letters and anything else required for a successful escape were supplied by an expert forger, Major Pat Clayton, who had served with the Long Range Desert Group and had been instrumental in mapping the Western Desert in the Nineteen-Thirties.[3] Gunner admired Clayton enormously:

> It was wonderful to have such a talented man as Pat on our Escape Committee, which organized forged papers, letters and maps.

Clayton could make almost any document with even the most limited of materials. Mander knew him from desert days:

> The most useful and talented prisoner from the escaping fraternity's point of view was undoubtedly Major Clayton...As a cartographer, Major Clayton could print anything and make it look indistinguishable from the original. This talent was put to use to produce forged passes, papers, certificates, etc. He did the printing and, if the document was in German, I wrote in the particulars in German script. In addition to this most valuable gift, he could pick any lock in the camp with a piece of bent wire.[4]

German script could also be provided by the only Pole in the camp, Major Kazak.

Clayton's documents were so perfect that the Italians could not believe that they were hand-written:

> [He produced] "type-written" Italian *tèssere*, or passes, so indistinguishable from the real thing that the SBO had to go to the Italian commandant to save the life of the Italian orderly-room Sergeant, suspected of lending us the office type-writer. When the difference in the type-face was pointed out, the *carabinieri* almost tore the camp to pieces in search of our non-existent machine.[4a]

The British government by now operated a system for smuggling escape materials in to the camps by way of welfare parcels, from which Gunner and his fellow would-be escapers benefited:

> The Escape Committee used to get information, money, and the like sent to us by the people in England. You would have private parcels and uniforms sent to the camp; they would contain everything needed, including silk maps, compasses, Italian money – all the things we asked for.

However, the Committee did throw one spanner in the works: they refused to allow Donny to join the escape as a digger, even though Gunner and fellow tunneller Johnnie MacLean warmly backed his candidacy. The list of those who would be allowed to join the escape was limited to Gunner, Bransom, MacLean, Lieutenant-Colonel Thomas G. "Gerry" Gore RAOC, Major "Jimmy" Williamson – another RTR officer – and Hil Evans. Four of the escapers were thus RTR men:

> It was very much a regimental project: everyone in the camp referred to it as the "RTR Escape".

When asked why, if this was so, the "super-tough little New Zealander" Hil Evans had been brought on board, Gunner replied:

> *Because* he was a super-tough little New Zealander, and he wanted to get out.

Bob Foote, however, was not invited:

> He was probably thirty-two or something and we thought that he was too old. We were all incredibly young. I was twenty-three.

Gunner was never normally one to speak ill of anyone, but the stress and strain of digging the tunnel produced antagonisms which persisted seven decades later. Gore – who had been allocated a digging place in the project instead of Donny – was also involved in the administrative side of the tunnel. But this proved an error of judgement, and events were to show that this decision had been unfair on Donny.

> Gore was a great big tall chap. We diggers made a very big mistake when we were planning the break-out: we put Gore in charge of co-ordinating all the non-digging activities of the escape – look-outs, disposal of soil, decoys to lead the ferrets away from digging activities, bribing and later blackmailing the guards, and so on. But Gore was rotten all through. We should have had Donny, who'd have done the job far better. The price we had to pay for Gore helping behind the scenes was that he had to be given one of the places on the escape.

Williamson, too, proved less than satisfactory, though he had helped during Brigadier Clifton's escape by sleeping in Clifton's bed to cover his absence. Gunner, usually the politest of men, found Williamson a trial:

Below: an illustration from Bransom's book of poems about his time at Veano, showing details of the tunnel's entrance and how it was concealed (Gregg collection).

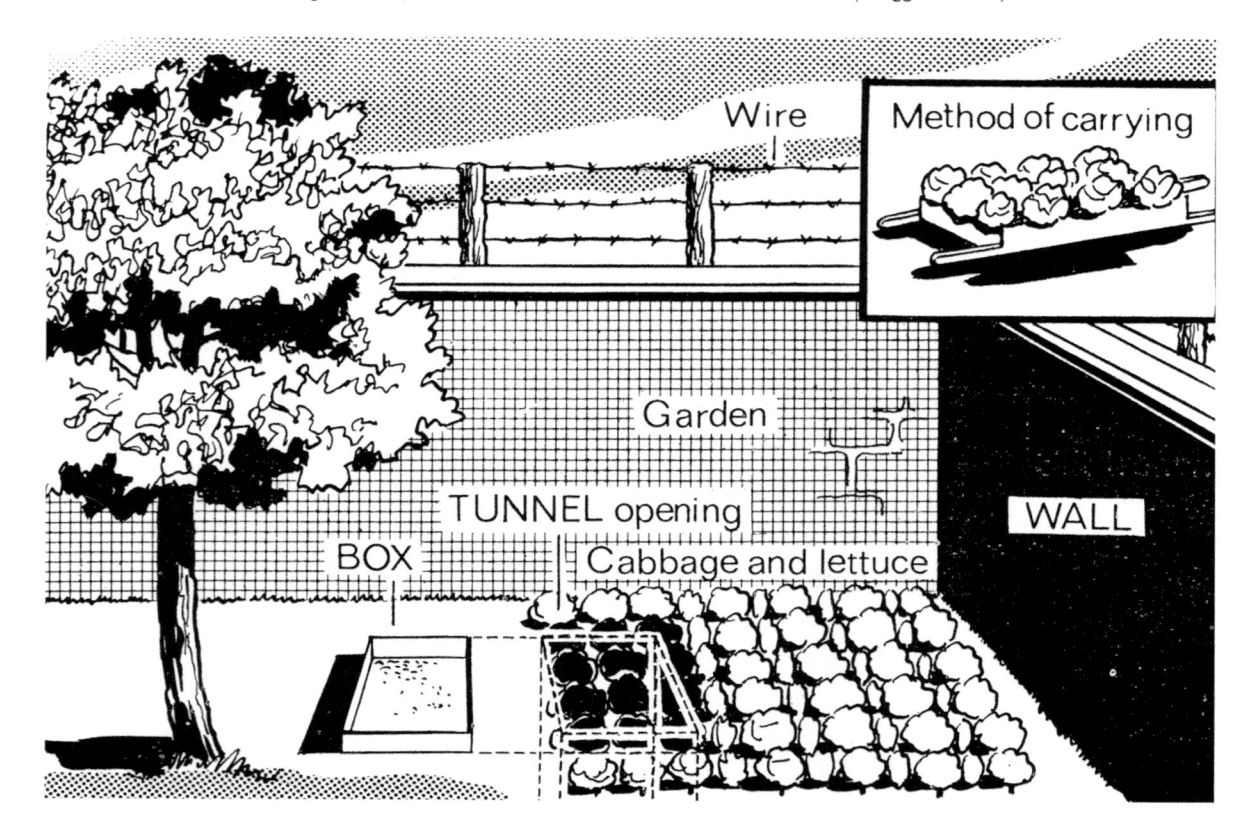

> Williamson was a disaster. He was in my regiment – not Third Tanks, but RTR; he may have been Seventh as well. We were foolish to let him in on the project. He was a defeatist, used to argue like hell, and generally disturbed the thing. In one of his poems, Ian Bransom describes the endless bickering – well, that would usually surround Williamson. He was only on the tunnel because he was in the Regiment.

The "RTR Escape" was audacious. As we have seen, the tunnel's entrance was in the centre of a large open square, which was surrounded by a twenty-foot wall. Whenever the tunnel was in operation, careful arrangements were made to screen the main gate through the wall from the vegetable patch where the tunnel began:

> We did this by hanging blankets or whatever over the clothes-lines in a strategic position, pretending to be drying them. This meant that the guards could not see the shaft entrance from the gate – nor could the guards walking past.

The mouth of the tunnel itself was formed with a packing-case.

> There was a certain amount of agriculture going on, and we took this up very seriously. We were lucky in that we had a tea-chest, which we very quickly let into the ground. Then that was covered up with rubbish and soil, and we started digging from that. We had a ladder going down, and we went down about sixteen feet.

Initially, only one digger could fit into the tunnel, but as it started to burrow horizontally two could fit in at once, and the diggers worked in regular pairs.

> I worked with Johnny MacLean – God's gift to women. We had a horizontal dig of over sixty feet., which we dug in about six months.

The amount of time and effort that these prisoners were prepared to devote to their escape is humbling. In August 1943, Bransom wrote a poem – *Veano Vault* – commemorating the work which he and his fellow escapers had put in. It gives the flavour of the task and mood of the diggers:

>Six hard-working months we had in all,
>   'Spite swarming jailers sneaking all around;
>Our careful watchers ready with a call
>   As down we went into the stony ground,
>   The pitch-black shaft, where reached no human sound.
>Then smoky lamp beneath the poplar roots.
>   Wet, shimmering walls and slimy, muddy boots,
>The agony of spells of gasping toil,
>The blackness with the ending of the oil.
>
>Full sixteen feet the shaft went down,
>   And sixty odd the onward drive did measure;
>Hard stone, soft clay, black and brown,
>   Springtime with flood to check our pleasure
>   And set us cursing at unwanted leisure;
>Pump improvised and tin-built air-line,
>   Ants burying spoil, like secret treasure;
>Two "diggers" panting, waiting for the time
>Of daylight, fresh air, and end of slime.
>
>The frequent quarrels, false alarms and folly,
>   The harsh indictment for the vaguest little fault,
>The keyed-up nerves exploding in a volley
>   Whenever prudence called the necessary halt,
>   And too much interest focused on Veano Vault.
>The hunger after weary hours of striving
>   'Gainst giant rocks and possible dirt fall,
>The evening jokes when everyone's surviving
>Despite the carbon-poisoning and Roll-call.

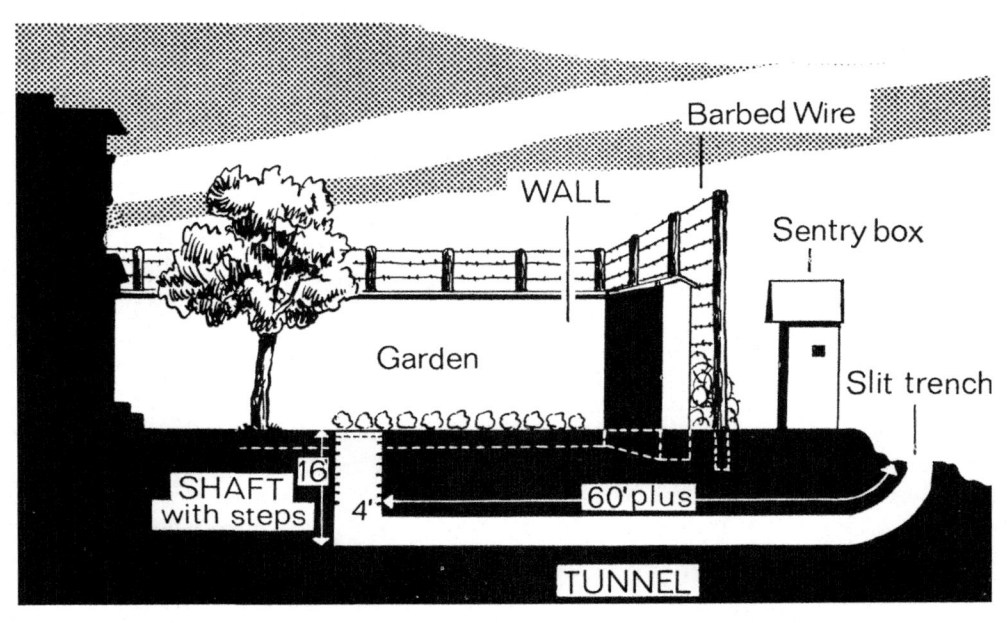

Above: *another illustration from Bransom's book, showing the tunnel and its exit, carefully aimed at a slit-trench outside the compound so that the escapers would have shelter when they emerged (Gregg collection).*

Above: *a remarkable photograph, liberated by Gunner from the* **Commandante**'s *desk drawer after the 1943 armistice, and showing the Italian guards unearthing the entrance to the Veano tunnel the day after the escape (Gregg collection).*

> The final breathless evening at the opening of July,
>   When a dozen keen escapees in the queerest of attire
> Lay huddled in the blackness ready soon to fly
>   Beneath the strolling sentries' field of fire,
>   With darkness for these walls of stone and wire,
> For midnight and just after safely passed out eight.
> Then shooting gave alarm and sealed the fate
> For those at the rear – it was too late.
>
>   It was beyond their ken,
>   With help so near to them
>   Why those mad Englishmen
>   Won't tolerate this den.

The tunnelling activities were concealed by other prisoners working in the garden above, where most of the excavated soil was dispersed. Concealing the entry and exit of the diggers was key to maintaining the tunnel's secrecy.

> It seemed impossible that we could have kept our tunnel a secret, but we did, for six whole months. I know we were not digging all the time, but we kept the tunnel a secret... The lid of the tea-chest had earth on it, and when the two diggers had gone down the lid was put on – and there they were shut in for two or three hours, or however long the shift lasted. There were leaves and earth on the trapdoor so the guards could not tell that there were people working down below.

Another danger was that a roll-call would be held whilst diggers were underground; the Italians would then have instigated a thorough search which might have found the tunnel or, perhaps worse, trapped the diggers underground for days whilst the guards turned the camp upside-down looking for them.

> We had to delegate an officer to watch the Commandant's office. Only the Commandant decided when to have our *apello*. His procedure was to send his Orderly to the Bugler's room in the barracks. When the Bugler was found he took time to dress and so on before he went to stand outside the Commandant's Office waiting to be ordered to blow his bugle. As soon as the Orderly was seen to leave the Commandant's Office, the diggers would be called up. The few extra minutes gained by this procedure were often vital.
>   All this seems a lot of trouble to gain a few seconds or even minutes to get these diggers out of the tunnel. But imagine you were forty feet along the tunnel and you had to crawl backwards to get out. The helpers had to prepare for you to get out; they had to have a coat or something for you to

put on, because you would be in working muddy overalls. If you could do it, and if there was time, you would nip across to the showers, so as to come to the roll-call fairly clean. Only twice were we unable to get the diggers up. On those two occasions we had to 'fudge' the roll-call.

The tunnel, sixty feet long, was aimed at a slit-trench near a sentry post beyond the wall and barbed wire.

> We couldn't actually see this slit-trench from inside the camp, but we could see other sentry-posts which had slit-trenches, and we knew there was a sentry at this point because you could look down from a little garden window.
> We'd given Hil Evans the key job, with a prismatic compass, of breaking out of the tunnel into the slit-trench, getting the direction absolutely right, the tunnel's arriving in exactly the right part of the slit-trench – not an easy task. He used a lot of methods to try and measure distances. His main problem was working out how deep it was down. You will see from the photographs which the Italians took that he was spot on, absolutely bang on, right in the corner of the slit-trench.

Conditions down in the tunnel were atrocious, and Gunner's description of them makes for humbling reading:

> Down in the tunnel there would be one person working on the face, digging with his hands or a tool, filling the sacks: the other would be at the base of the shaft. Each digger had his own favourite digging-tool. Mine was a piece of iron that I had bound with rope to give a good grip to your hand. You would prise the soil away and then put it in a sack underneath you. When the sack was full, the chap at the base would pull it back. Each sack had a loop on it and we hung them on the walls of the shaft. We tried to fill six sacks a shift.
> The tunnel was only as broad as your shoulders and under three feet high. When you were digging you were lying flat on your belly, and it was awful as the floor was usually very wet mud. It sounds pretty horrific and it was, especially for those like me: I am rather claustrophobic. I had to force myself to go and work there. I would look up at the roof and think, "Christ, this is going to come down on top of me."

Light was provided by a home-made lamp, which created its own problems:

Above: *another photograph in the same series, showing the slit-trench (at right) in which the tunnel emerged, just beyond the sentry-walk bordered by two barbed-wire fences, the inner a considerable barrier (Gregg collection).*

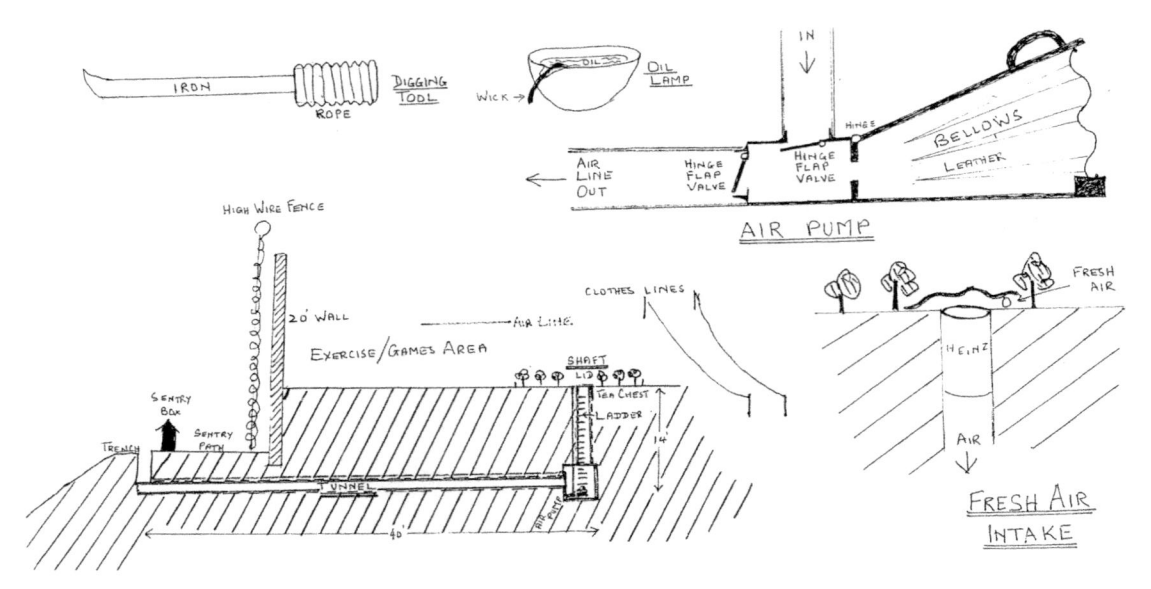

Above: a similar view to that drawn by Bransom, this time sketched by Gunner; it includes details of a primitive lamp powered by Italian hair-oil, Gunner's digging-tool, and the concealed air-pump which Donny helped to manufacture (Gregg collection).

All that we had underground was a smoky Roman-type lamp with a wick, which we filled with Italian hair-oil. The trouble was that although it gave light, it gave off much more black smoke, which was filthy.

In the cramped confines of the tunnel, such fumes could have been not merely inconvenient but fatal. Even though Donny was not allowed to dig, he and Gunner devised a solution to the ventilation problem.

We had to build an air-line down from the surface. At the base of the shaft we had an air pump, like a pair of bellows, which Donny helped me to make. The pump had two "flap-valves". When you pressed it down, one valve closed, the other one opened, and the air was forced down from the surface, through the pump and then along a pipe to the face where the digger was working. We made the air-pipe quite simply by using Red Cross soup-tins. As the tunnel progressed we put in more soup-tins. Each tin was held in position by mud. We thus made an air-line to give fresh air to the digger working on the face.

Without Donny's skill the vital valves would not have been possible:

Donny showed great ingenuity in designing and fabricating the two "flap-valves" which were the most tricky part of the job.

The pump helped the digger, but not his partner:

The chap digging was all right because the fresh air came from the pipe beside him. All the filthy smoke went back to the poor chap at the bottom of the shaft who was pumping and it got very, very thick there. We should really, I suppose, have had another pump to pump the bad air out.

Of course, the air-line had to be connected to the surface, which was useful in that it gave the diggers a means of hearing instructions from the surface, but also provided a weak-spot in that a curious Italian might stumble across it.

The only communication the diggers had was through the air-pipe. Where the air-line came to the surface we placed a cabbage leaf. That worked very well: the air could get underneath and it also covered it up if the "ferrets" were looking.

Other problems included getting in and out of the tunnel without being spotted – here the washing-lines provided cover for the vital moments when the tunnel's shaft was opened – and disposing of the sacks of soil dug out during a shift.

> When you dig a tunnel often the soil you dig up is a completely different colour to the surface soil. Then you would have to store the soil in the attics of buildings or some equally unsatisfactory solution. Luckily the lower soil at Veano was much the same colour as the soil on the surface, so we were saved one more problem.
> When the digger came up (and you would choose the moment when there were no guards about) certain officers would come along and they would put the sacks underneath their greatcoats and would walk around the exercise ground spreading the spoil about. I suppose we raised the height of the exercise ground by six inches or more. There was also a small garden near the main building; we raised the height of that as well.

All this activity above ground in support of the diggers required a complex organization.

> We had a large number of helpers. There were only six diggers but there were quite an army of people to do various work above ground. You required an organization to arrange for the getting rid of the soil, to organize men to work in the vegetable patch, to open and shut the tunnel entrance, to put the blankets up, to distract the Italians who were around, to keep the air-intake clear, and to help the escapees make their get-away clothing.

Gore was the man responsible for co-ordinating all this, in return for which he had been promised a place on the break-out itself. But although Donny had been refused permission to join the escape, he proved equally useful to the tunnellers. We have already seen how he helped Gunner to make the air-pump; but he had other tasks as well. As an excellent Italian speaker (his background in Classics was a great advantage), he helped to keep the Italian "ferrets" away from the tunnel, by offering them coffee and cigarettes from Red Cross parcels. Having become friendly with them, he got them involved in black-market trading with the prisoners, providing eggs, fruit and the like.

> We were ruthless in our dealings with the guards. We blackmailed them. Once we involved them in trading coffee or chocolate for anything that we might want, we had them at our mercy. If a man did not do as we wanted we would threaten to tell the Commandant, which would get the man posted to the Blue Division on the Russian front – a very cold death.
> Donny achieved results very quickly. As soon as they started to trade with him, the two "ferrets" were at his mercy. Donny then blackmailed them with threats of reporting them to the Commandant. The first thing that Donny demanded was a time-table for the local bus service. He also wanted the time-table of the main-line through-trains from Parma to Rome. This information I needed and used in my escape to Rome. Donny also achieved a real coup: he arranged for the "ferrets" to provide us with wireless valves to improve the quality of the BBC news reports which kept us up to date with the progress of the war. In this regard the prisoners of war were far better informed than our guards. Two Royal Signals officers had made a radio, which was well-hidden. The wireless valves which Donny produced helped them to improve the quality of the reception of the BBC news.

* * *

The tunnellers had not only to come up with a viable mechanism to get out of the camp, but also a plan for what they would do thereafter.

> As well as digging, the six of us had to do a tremendous amount of preparation. Every single detail had to be thought out – but that was all right, because we had a lot of time on our hands. As you can imagine, we had to make our plans as to what we were going to do when we got out. Out of the six, five decided they were going to go north, because the nearest place they could get their freedom was Switzerland.

Switzerland might have been closest, but only a tiny handful of Allied prisoners managed to escape from an Italian camp and make it to Switzerland before the Italian Armistice of September 1943. Two of them – Brigadiers James Hargest and Reginald Miles – had escaped to Switzerland from the "Generals' Camp" PG12 (Vincigliata) in March 1943.[5] Ironically Gunner, the tunneller who might have been expected to be keenest to get to Switzerland, had different plans.

> I had decided to go south to Rome. I had very good reason for that: I wanted to get to the Vatican, which was neutral territory. If I could get to the Vatican I would be home and dry, because I had been born in Dublin – I had an Irish passport as well as an English one.

The Republic of Ireland, of course, was neutral, and so Gunner hoped that the Vatican authorities – who were extremely helpful to Allied escapers – would be able to get him out of Italy.

> From Rome, I would be able to get back to Ireland, and then to England and my Regiment. So I decided to head south.

For the journey to Rome, Gunner planned to rely on a different part of his upbringing, his experience of the Hitler Youth. Far from pretending to be a neutral, he planned to travel openly as a uniformed Fascist.

> As for my cover story, I was a member of the Dutch *Hitler Jugund*. As I had been at school in Germany I knew a lot about the *Hitler Jugund*. On the other hand, my German was not good enough to convince real Germans that I was a German, so I decided to be a Dutchman. My story was that I was going down to Rome for a political meeting with various Italian Fascist youth organizations. I carried forged letters, passports and documents so that if and when I was stopped I could produce all the necessary documentation. I also had letters written in Dutch which I had purportedly received from my parents. My cover story took a lot of preparation.

Gunner of course knew Afrikaans – the South African form of Dutch – from his childhood there. The chances of meeting a real Dutchman in Italy in 1943 were remote, and it would therefore be very unlikely that Gunner's disguise could get him into trouble. He considered that his travel documents, thanks to Clayton and the Escape Committee, were flawless.

> As I was going to travel by rail, I needed the railway timetables, which Donny got hold of. I planned to get to a certain village in the mountains and then to catch a bus to the railway station. I needed a timetable for that and for the bus to make sure I would end up in Parma. The main line ran from Parma to Bologna, through Florence and finally to Rome.

Donny helped with the preparation of Gunner's Hitler Youth uniform, which was simply shorts, a khaki shirt, and a scarf. Donny embroidered the swastika and *Nederland* insignia, and also helped to make up the escapers' emergency rations.

> By the time we were due to go I felt fairly confident. To succeed I would need an awful lot of luck, or, to put it another way, I needed to avoid a bit of bad luck.

* * *

The tunnel was ready at the end of June 1943. By now, Allied troops were poised to invade Sicily, where landings would take place on July 10th. This the prisoners could not know, and their plans, so long in the making, remained unchanged. The stress of the hard work underground, careful concealment of their plans, and imminent risk to life and limb had taken its toll on them all.

> Just before we were going to make our break-out, Footie asked me if I would take with me, concealed in my boot, a letter which he wanted to send to his girlfriend and did not want the Italian censor to read. It seemed very strange to us young men that an officer as senior as Footie should have a girlfriend and not a wife – but he was probably only in his thirties.
>
> I asked him why he was entrusting the letter to me and not to one of the other escapers, most of whom had been in Seventh Tanks with him. He said that knowing my escape plans he considered that of all the escapers I had by far the best chance of making a home run. This gave me great confidence at a time when all of us involved in the escape were feeling very nervous and frightened.
>
> That night in bed I realized that Footie's excuse about the censor was balls – he couldn't have cared a damn whether or not the Italians read his letter. He was actually trying to bolster my morale, which was absolutely typical of Footie.

At last it was time to break out.

> When the tunnel was completed, we arranged for a cinema show in the exercise area on the day we wanted to go. We had seats and the screen where we wanted them, masking the entrance to the tunnel. We escapees never saw the film – probably a propaganda film made by the Germans or the Italians – but we wanted to have everyone watching and listening to it while we got down the tunnel. We got in our escape clothes, and put overalls on because it was pretty muddy down there and we did not want to ruin our nice uniforms or whatever different clothes we were wearing. We each had a bottle of water, obviously, because it was going to be pretty claustrophobic and rather hot down there.

The six tunnellers had agreed that with the exception of the leading man – Evans – they would draw lots for the order in which they would go down the tunnel. It was a privilege to be near the front of the queue, since the longer that the tunnel's exit was open, the more likely it was that it would be discovered. The further ahead in the queue one was, the more time one would have to make one's getaway before the alarm was raised. Gore, whose role had all been above the surface, drew number three; Gunner, who had been an active digger, drew number four.

Different accounts of the tunnel give different numbers of escapers who went down the shaft that night. Bransome stated twelve in his poem; Desmond Young stated eleven; Gunner remembered it as six. Whatever the number, in the end, only four made it out.

On the night of the escape, under cover of the film screening in the courtyard, the escapees assembled and opened the lid of the tunnel.

> At about 2200, while the film was on, we all went down.

But now, in the tension of the moment, Gore panicked:

> He was a very large man and had never been down the tunnel. On the day, when we were all dressed for it, he turned up with a huge chest strapped on his back. And I thought "God, why have I got him in front of me?" We were there with the lid open, and he started to go down, and suddenly shot back and said "I can't fit in! I can't fit in!" I said "Good" and kicked him out of the way and dropped down. Four of us broke out through the tunnel in the end: Johnnie Maclean, Hill Evans, Ian Bransom and myself.

The remaining escapers – Williamson being the fifth, behind Gunner – clambered down the shaft and waited in the dark, stuffy surroundings they knew so well. According to Desmond Young, above them Italian officers were sitting oblivious in deck-chairs close to the tunnel shaft.

***Above:** an Italian officer at right gives scale to the tunnel exit visible at left.
Gunner crawled out of this hole and waited in the slit-trench for the signal to move (Gregg collection).*

The escapers did not plan to push through the tunnel immediately, but to wait until the cinema screening was finished and the camp was quiet and still. The Italian guards might be expected to be less vigilant in the small hours of the morning.

> Once we were down there, the lid was left partly open. It was dark, remember. I was extremely frightened about sitting in the dark tunnel for hours, because I thought we would all end up being suffocated or the roof would collapse. My nerves were pretty well on edge. However, I was determined to escape after having spent six months planning, digging and preparing for the big day when I would be free.
>
> We waited in there, I think it was for about three hours, until about half-twelve, which was when we had decided was the time to go.

However, they would need more air if they were to last until then, and the noise of the film would help to cover the sound of the tunnel breaking out through the surface. If Evans had done his calculations correctly, the tunnel would surface in a slit-trench beside one of the sentry-posts outside the wire.

> The man at the front was Evans, the key man who was going to open the tunnel for us to get out. The first thing that he did was to break through from the tunnel. He had already worked out that he was near a slit-trench, but was not quite sure where, so he slowly and very carefully removed the soil. He wanted a flow of air otherwise we would die of suffocation. The air would come in along the tunnel and up the shaft. We were not quite sure that it would work – but it did, thank goodness.

Evans had done a superb job: the tunnel surfaced exactly where planned, in the bottom corner of a slit-trench. This meant that the escapers would be in cover as they left the tunnel. However, the perimeter of the camp was guarded by sentries, one of whom was very close to the slit-trench (the trench was in fact for the sentry to dive into in case of an air-raid). The tunnellers had foreseen this problem, however, and were still being supported by their helpers inside the buildings. A simple system told the tunnellers when it was safe to emerge into the darkness outside the camp.

> We came out very, very close to where the sentry was normally standing. You could not get out of the slit-trench with the sentry still standing in front of his box. But we had worked it out very carefully. Luckily, they used to have to patrol – there was a path going all the way round the camp right in front of the sentry-boxes –and they walked up and down or went to speak to other sentries. Each escaper had to wait for the sentry to move away on his rounds before he could climb out of the slit-trench. When the sentry started to walk away from his box, that would be the time to climb out of the slit-trench and go down the slope. The ground sloped down from the camp into a field of maize.
>
> For an escaper in the slit-trench to know when the sentry was walking away from the sentry-box, we had an officer in a window of the main building. He had glued two narrow cardboard tubes together. One tube had a torch fitted into it. The other tube was used to aim the torch at the slit-trench, so that the sentry would be unable to see the light. When you put your head out of the tunnel, all you had to do was to look up and to the right. If you saw a light, you knew that the sentry was walking away and that you were safe to climb out of the tunnel. We could never be sure that any of the things which we planned would work, but luckily this did work – it was one of the reasons the escape was so successful.

In the tunnel, the five men sat in the darkness and waited for Evans to make his move.

> We waited with our hearts in our mouths. We were sitting crouched in this tunnel, sitting rather like men rowing, with our backs to where we were going to go out, and the man following you leaning on your knees. We had to be very quiet, obviously. We could not talk, because the sentry was only a few feet away from us and any noise coming from a slit trench that was supposed to be empty would make the sentry highly suspicious.

At around 0030, Evans decided that it was dark enough to begin the break-out:

> Evans looked up, saw the light and climbed up. He went down the slope and was away. Then it was Number Two's turn to watch for the light, and he did the same thing. When Number Two had gone it raised our spirits. Then Number Three – and now, as Number Four, I was next. I can tell you, my heart was in my mouth at that moment, because I thought that someone might shoot me in the next ten minutes. There was a pause, and no light showing to let me know that I was safe to come out.

As Gunner crouched in the mouth of the tunnel, keyed up to run for the shelter of the maize, the escape began to unravel:

> Suddenly there was a shot, fired by one of the sentries. It came from somewhere down to the right; I think it may have been the chap in the watch-tower because he was in the best position to see what was going on. He was shouting and yelling and shots were being fired. Then all the sentries started shouting at each other, and I did not know what was happening. The escapee behind me [Williamson] went back up the tunnel and disappeared into the camp.

It is unclear what had happened: the signal-lamp was still functioning, and Gunner had not been spotted, but something had alarmed the guards. However, the chaos in fact worked in Gunner's favour; it took the sentries away from the slit-trench, and the accomplice inside the camp building flashed the 'all clear':

> I looked up at this point, and saw the signal-light. The guards had all gone down to where the alarm had been given. I therefore crawled out of the slit-trench and down the bank into the field of maize. By this time all hell had broken loose: search-lights were on, everyone was shouting, people were coming out of the barrack-room. I meanwhile was crawling down into this field and trying to hide in the middle. I thought I would stay there until the hubbub was over. I could not tell what was going on, but I did have a peep and there were a lot of people around 'our' sentry-box, so they had obviously found the exit by then.

Four of the six had escaped, and although the escapers would have preferred the tunnel to have remained undiscovered until after the morning roll-call, they had been luckier than many tunnellers. As he lurked in the maize, Gunner knew that three of his comrades were making their way to freedom, and that every minute took them further from the camp.

> I stayed in the field for an hour, possibly two. By this time the Italians were patrolling everywhere, and I think they were actually coming through the corn, because I heard rustling on both sides. But I was right in the middle, and they obviously did not go right through.
>
> When it had all calmed down, I crawled away from the camp and crossed over the road to Ponte dell'Olio. I was on a terrace above the camp, in a vineyard. I looked down on the camp, and I had the most incredible feeling – it was unbelievable. I had never experienced anything like that before, or since. I had made it. It was unbelievable: there they were shouting and yelling – and I was out. I savoured that for some time; I wanted to shout and yell, and I am sure I was laughing aloud.

This was always a dangerous moment for an escaping prisoner. The euphoria of actually being outside and free often blinded escapers to the need to get as far away as possible whilst they could. Having been keyed up and pumping with adrenalin for the period of the escape, prisoners often felt lassitude and inertia at this vital moment. Gunner had enjoyed his moment of triumph; now his professionalism re-asserted itself and he began the next stage of his escape: avoiding re-capture.

* * *

Escape was one thing; evasion another. In a totalitarian state like Fascist Italy – no matter how badly that totalitarianism was compromised by Italian carelessness – the task of an escaped prisoner was made difficult by the vigilance of the authorities in every area of life. Furthermore, most prisoners attempted to disguise themselves as civilians, a difficult task for British or New Zealand personnel in a Mediterranean land. For the time being, dressed in his Hitler Youth costume, Gunner stuck out like a sore thumb as he crossed the remote Italian countryside in the small hours of the morning.

> I started to head south by north up into the hills where I wanted to go: I was working on a compass and I had studied the map in detail. I arrived at the village I was heading for – some ten or fifteen miles away – before it was light, and I was very lucky because there were quite a lot of cliffs, especially where they had cut out roads. The Italians are very good at road-making and I very nearly stepped over a precipice and could have been killed. I had something to eat – I had lots of rations – and then I had a good kip, shave and wash. On the second night I walked to where I had to wait for the bus.

So far his luck was holding.

> When I got on the bus to Parma no-one took any notice of me, even though I must have been a funny-looking sight.

Gunner had chosen his disguise carefully. A British officer masquerading as a civilian would look out of place in Italy; but although a Dutch member of the Hitler Youth would look just as incongruous, that incongruity could be explained – Gunner's disguise actually took advantage of his 'difference'. In a bureaucratic state where obedience to the authorities was expected, Gunner's papers could be expected to satisfy officials who got in his way. In many respects, Gunner might reasonably consider himself safe enough if he could board a train.

> At Parma I got on the earliest train. I had the tickets, and thought everyone would be staring at me, but they were not particularly interested; they were all pre-occupied with going to work or whatever.

> The train went down the main line as far as Bologna. We had a very long wait there. I did not know what was happening, and much to my disgust suddenly a whole lot of German soldiers, in uniform with packs and everything, got on the train into my carriage. I thought "That's done for me", but in point of fact it was the best thing that could have happened. I pretended to be asleep, and most of the Germans went to sleep, so I fitted in. Twice the police came round and looked at my tickets and documents. I believe that the police thought I had something to do with these Germans.
>
> We went down to Florence – again, I had a very long wait – then on down the spine of Italy through Tuscany.

To while away the time, and to allay suspicion, Gunner read German propaganda magazines belonging to the soldiers on the train.

* * *

Although Gunner did not know it, Bransom and MacLean had already been recaptured (Evans would stay out for four days in total). When Bransom returned to Veano, he was publicly harangued by the Italian regional commander, as the Swiss recorded when they visited the camp at the beginning of September:

> Colonel Younghusband... especially reported to us the case of Major Harold Ian Bransom RA. The latter, after attempting to escape, was recaptured at Piacenza on July 2nd 1943. When he returned to the camp, the Commandant [of the area], General Messina, who was there for inspection, spoke to him in front of all the other officers and rated him violently in terms which the interpreter apologetically translated as:
> "Major Bransom, the General is sorry you have come back with your face not smashed in."[6]

As usual, the escapers were punished with thirty days *rigoroso*.

The Italians had been impressed with the tunnel, and took photographs of its entrance and exit. Gunner would later help himself to these when he found them in the Commandant's desk drawer.

* * *

The Italians knew by now exactly who they were looking for – though, as we shall see, they thought that two more prisoners had escaped than was really the case. Descriptions of Gunner and Evans had been circulated widely, and unfortunately modern telecommunications meant that Gunner had not outrun the hue and cry. His luck ran out less than an hour from Rome.

> When we were about twenty-five miles from Rome, two *Carabinieri* suddenly entered the compartment. They came straight towards me, and I had a pretty shrewd feeling that they knew that an escaped prisoner-of-war was about. The word of an escape had got around on the police net. The escape of prisoners was something that the security forces took fairly seriously. They had a look at my papers; they went through everything I had. I was taken to another carriage where they virtually strip-searched me, and I realized then that the game was up.

Re-captured prisoners of war were in an awkward position. They were not in military uniform and theoretically might be shot as spies. If they thought that they could bluff it out, then they would try to do so; but if their disguise was pierced, it was wise to establish as quickly as possible that they were escaped prisoners of war rather than secret agents or saboteurs. Realizing that he had failed, Gunner admitted his identity.

> I was taken to a police station, and later on to a train to make the return journey to Piacenza. There I was put on a small little tramway (rather like a railway) to Ponte dell'Olio, about two miles from Veano, and taken to the local police station.

Gunner would later have the immense satisfaction of capturing Ponte dell'Olio from its Fascist garrison – but for now he was at the mercy of a very excitable guard.

> I was handed over to a *Brigadiere* [Corporal] of *Carabinieri*. He was very excited, and started yelling and shouting at me, but I did not take much notice of him. In the end I think that annoyed him, because he picked up a round ruler and hit me on the head with it. Whether he was trying to make a point I do not know. Anyway he and another policeman took out their revolvers and said *"Avanti"*. I was absolutely convinced that in the march back to Veano I was going to be shot, with the report saying that I had been killed trying to escape.

But the guards restrained themselves, returning Gunner to the camp safely and handing him over to the camp authorities.

* * *

The Italians in fact had no idea exactly who had escaped through the tunnel, and were still looking for two men who they believed had made it out. These two prisoners had actually become what prisoners-of-war referred to as "ghosts". Desmond Young explained:

> The tunnel would hold at most eleven... Why not conceal two more within the camp and let the Italians assume that they also had got away? It would at least confuse the tally; it might be convenient to have two spare workers not subject to roll-calls.[7]

In other camps, ghosts served the useful purpose of attending roll-calls on behalf of inmates who were busy tunnelling; if an escape was successful but undetected, by attending roll-calls they could also conceal the escape so that the authorities did not even know to start looking for escapers.

The Veano ghosts were Majors Jonathan Pumphrey and Robert Fieldhouse.[8] Their problem was that the Italians made regular searches of the camp, and when these occurred the ghosts needed to be well hidden. Young explains how this was achieved:

> From the second floor there ran down a laundry chute to the washroom on the ground floor. There were small doors in the wall on the first and second floors. These were kept locked, but we had naturally made keys for them, as for nearly every other door in the building. The chute was just wide enough to admit a thin man. If we fitted platforms at each floor level, two men could stand, one above the other, with their faces opposite the door.
>
> They need only take refuge there during roll-calls and searches and *carabinieri* inspections. The nights they could pass under their empty beds. During the day, there would be no serious risk in their mingling with the rest... provided they were not seen outside. Before roll-calls we would lock them in the laundry-chute. For additional security we fitted snibs on both doors, which they could close from inside.[9]

* * *

Like his fellow escapers, Gunner was reprimanded by the Commandant and sentenced to thirty days' *rigoroso*, denied contact with the other prisoners. However, the inmates of PG 29 had been delighted by the escape attempt, which was considered by most to be 'one in the eye' for the Italians, and Gunner received many smuggled messages of congratulation and commiseration, including one from Donny. Even more welcome were the gifts of condensed milk and chocolate which Donny sent in to the punishment block. Veano was nothing like Capua; the four failed escapers were not even held in solitary confinement, but spent their month of internal exile playing poker and bridge, and enjoying the fact that they were exempt from roll-call parades. They were unaware that their captivity was about to come to an abrupt end.

CORRIERE DELLA SERA

ARMISTIZIO

Le ostilità cessate tra l'Italia l'Inghilterra e gli Stati Uniti

Il messaggio di Badoglio

Ecco il messaggio letto ieri sera alla Radio alle ore 19.42 dal Maresciallo Badoglio:

"Il Governo italiano, riconosciuta l'impossibilità di continuare l'impari lotta contro la soverchiante potenza avversaria, nell'intento di risparmiare ulteriori e più gravi sciagure alla Nazione, ha chiesto un armistizio al gen. Eisenhower, comandante in capo delle Forze alleate anglo-americane.

"La richiesta è stata accolta. Conseguentemente, ogni atto di ostilità contro le forze anglo-americane deve cessare da parte delle forze italiane in ogni luogo. Esse, però, reagiranno ad eventuali attacchi di qualsiasi altra provenienza".

STALINO SGOMBRATA

Violente battaglie in corso ad ovest di Carcov e di Conotop - Bruxelles attaccata dall'aviazione inglese

Chapter Twelve
Release

Since Donny had left the North African desert in July 1942, the whole course of the war had changed. There would be no more humiliating evacuations, no more embarrassing defeats. The Battle of El Alamein in October and November 1942 had marked the "end of the beginning", as Churchill put it, and the Eighth Army from Egypt and the First Army from Algeria had between them squeezed the Germans and Italians into a smaller and smaller pocket of North Africa until, on May 12th 1943, the southern shores of the Mediterranean had been swept clear of Axis forces. It was a worse defeat for the Axis powers than Stalingrad: 230,000 German and Italian troops were captured.

The Americans did not particularly want to follow this victory with an invasion of Italy, but the British believed that this would provide a short cut to the southern borders of the Reich. In fact, it would take the Allies until April 1945 to smash the German armies in Italy and to force their way to the Austrian border. Canadian, American and British troops landed in Sicily on July 10th 1943, and completed the conquest of the island by August 17th. This was quickly followed by British landings on the toe of Italy on September 3rd and Allied landings at Salerno, south of Naples, on September 9th.

Since the Axis defeat in Tunisia, relations between Mussolini and King Victor Emmanuel of Italy had been growing strained, and the king had begun to intrigue to depose Mussolini. On July 23rd, the Fascist Grand Council had passed a motion of no confidence in Mussolini, who was then sacked as Prime Minister and arrested; his place as Prime Minister was taken by the distinguished soldier Marshal Badoglio. Badoglio had resigned from the Italian general staff after the Italian army's poor showing in Greece in 1940. Now he and the king began secret peace negotiations with the Allies.

The new Italian government claimed in public that it would remain an ally of Germany, but the Germans were not fooled and began to take precautions against an Italian defection. Hitler had been persuaded that the best policy to adopt in Italy was for the Germans to make a stand as far south as possible and to give ground only slowly. This turned out to be excellent advice, and Field Marshal Kesselring would make the Allies fight for every inch of the Italian peninsula.

The armistice between Italy and the Allies was officially signed on September 3rd; the Allies made the news public on September 8th, but unfortunately did not give Badoglio the chance to warn the Italian armed forces. Individual commanders were forced to decide whether to remain loyal to their former allies, or to fight them. The lack of a concerted front meant that some Italian units were disarmed by the Germans and others massacred; many simply evaporated as the personnel deserted and rushed back to their homes. The king and Badoglio fled Rome on September 9th as the Germans took over the city. On September 12th, Mussolini was rescued by German forces, who then set him up as figurehead of a puppet Fascist government in the north of Italy. Badoglio's government formally declared war on Germany on October 13th. Italy was divided: its inhabitants now had to make the best they could of the terrible situation. The Italian civil war had begun.[1]

Commonwealth prisoners in Italian camps had no prior warning of the armistice, and when the announcement came on the evening of September 8th Gunner was still in *rigoroso*. His guards knew nothing for certain, but passed on the rumours.

> The guard told us that the King had arrested Mussolini and made an armistice with the Allies.

As the inmates sat down to their evening meal, the Italian Commandant summoned Colonel Younghusband to his office. Mander reports what Younghusband said when he returned to the dining-hall:

> "Well, gentlemen, the *Commandante* appears to have heard the rumour too." He went on to explain that a girl-friend of one of the camp NCOs was a telephone-operator in Piacenza, and she had told the *Sergente* that an Armistice had been signed in Rome and that Marshal Badoglio would broadcast an announcement at 7.30 that evening... In view of the fact that it was now 7.25 he suggested that everyone should go into the yard and listen to the announcement. Afterwards all ranks were to assemble in the dining hall for further instructions.[2]

The Italian guards and prisoners thus listened to the broadcast together. Everyone cheered at the news; Italians could be seen throwing their hats into the air, hugging one another, and even dancing little jigs of joy. One of the inmates, Captain Philip Tower, recorded the reaction of the inmates:

> We went back into the hall, finished our dinner, and then listened to a sentimental and impractical speech by the Senior British Officer that finished with us all singing *God Save the King*. We were told that we would all spend the night as usual in the camp, and that perhaps some of us would go out the next morning. The guards, too, would remain in position. In the morning, there would be a Thanksgiving Service before we packed our kits and awaited the train to take us down Italy to freedom.[3]

Younghusband announced that the British high command had ordered prisoners-of-war to stay in their camps, hoping that Italy's collapse would be rapid and that the prisoners would be better off where they were. Unfortunately, the Germans moved rapidly to take over the camps, and sent many prisoners north.

Gunner was released from *rigoroso* and immediately met up with Donny to consider their options. They knew that they had to get away quickly:

> Nothing was going to keep us in that camp.

Younghusband did not remain entirely inactive, however. At 2230 the store in which the prisoners kept their spare Red Cross food items was opened and they were allowed to take what they wanted. They were told to pack their belongings and be ready to evacuate at a moment's notice. Men were posted to watch the guards and to take over from them if necessary. The clandestine radio set was manned permanently in case the BBC transmitted further orders for the prisoners.

* * *

On September 1st, the Swiss had made what turned out to be their last inspection visit to Veano. Their records thus tell us how many prisoners were in the camp when the Armistice was announced.[4]

	Officers	**NCOs**	**Men**	**Total**
British	197	1	56	254
South African	–	–	1	1
Australian	–	1	1	2
New Zealand	3	–	–	3
Canadian	1	–	–	1
Polish	1	–	–	1
Irish	4	–	–	4
Maltese	–	–	2	2
Army	200	2	56	258
Navy	–	–	4	4
Air Force	6	–	–	6

On the day following the announcement, September 9th, the 268 inmates of Veano obeyed Younghusband's orders to remain within a thousand yards of the camp, so that in an emergency they would be able to hear the bugle alarm-calls which had been agreed. Tower went for a walk with his friends:

> It was about 1100, a lovely Italian morning, that Nigel [Beaumont-Thomas], Andy [Howard], Peter Lewis, Dick Kerr and I went out to walk up the path which we had so often travelled under armed guard. It was grand to be able to go off the path and walk in the field as one wanted, to be able to run on or lag behind, to pick a flower or talk to a man or woman working in the field – just as the spirit moved one – for the first time in fifteen months.[5]

Younghusband announced that the Commandant had promised that he and his guards would defend Veano if Germans arrived to take the prisoners away. Younghusband and his men knew just how little reliance they could put on that promise, and so the SBO announced that those who wished to sleep outside the camp that night would be at liberty to do so, as long as they told the camp authorities where they would be.

The inmates tore down the barbed-wire fence which had hitherto hemmed in the southern yard, an action both symbolic and practical, since it made it easier for them to escape in a hurry. They also built a barricade across the access road to the camp in order to slow down any approach by German troops.

Italian deserters poured into the area all day, bringing the news that Piacenza was already under German occupation. The sight of these Italians, fleeing for their homes, suggested that the country had simply fallen to pieces. The effect on the Italian guards was profound as well: two-thirds of the four hundred or so disappeared overnight.

Tower and his party were among those who remained outside the camp on the night of September 9th:

> We slept in the woods above our road-block: our first free night! It was grand to be under the stars with an exciting and unpredictable future, and to be our own masters again.[6]

* * *

On September 10th, Younghusband announced that he no longer considered himself bound by the official instructions to stay put, and told the prisoners that they had his permission to scatter: the Germans were coming.

The Commandant had given Younghusband enough Italian money to provide every prisoner with a small amount for immediate expenses. Queues formed as this was issued; lunch was served; and the prisoners streamed away from the camp – some in uniform, some in civilian clothes, all carrying everything which they thought that they might need for their journey.

The Germans arrived soon afterwards, as Mander described from hearsay:

> We were told later that they fired random shots into the surrounding woods, ransacked the buildings, and failed to find a single prisoner. It was said that Colonel Younghusband went round with the Germans pretending to be the Italian doctor's assistant, and that another officer, Colonel De Salis, who had hidden a large quantity of Red Cross parcels and some good books in a haystack just outside the wire, went and his undetected in the stack like a broody hen sitting on its eggs. He watched the whole performance from his rick-side seat, as it were, and then, getting bored with the length and the Teutonic thoroughness of the search, he lit a pipe and set fire to his rick.[7]

* * *

Gordon Lett explains the choices open to the inmates of PG29 as they scattered into the surrounding countryside:

> We had three courses of action to choose from – to make for the Italian coast and await the Allied invasion, which would probably take place at Genoa or Leghorn; to cross the frontier into Switzerland; or to go south to meet our advancing troops.[8]

Those who chose simply to wait would be disappointed: it took the Allies until April 1945 to reach La Spezia and Piacenza.

Lett recalled his departure from the camp with two 'other ranks', Sergeant "Bob" Blackmore and Rifleman "Mick" Micallef:

> A young *Bersigliere* sentry, Gianni Pancrioli... an hour before my departure, [had come] into my room at the prison and insisted on giving me forty *lire* and the address of his home in Parma, suggesting that I should make for that city to find shelter. It was a friendly gesture, and the last that I had expected... Bob, Mick and I passed through the open gates as in a dream, knowing that we were about to throw ourselves on the mercy of ordinary Italian citizens, of whom we knew nothing.
>
> The sentry boxes were empty. On one of them the last occupant had scribbled in chalk the slogan *Viva gli Inglesi*. Outside was the country road which wound its tortuous way up to the camp from Ponte dell'Olio. Our Italian commandant, leaving in a car bound for the south, waved as he passed us. The war had taken a strange turn...
>
> [From PG29] we had left the road and followed a narrow track leading to the woods. According to the map I had made in camp, a trek along the crest of the hills should lead us to the main range of the Apennines, and once we had crossed that, we should be within sight of the naval base of Spezia, and the sea. A month of travelling brought us to this point – a month walking through endless forests of chestnut trees. The weather had been warm and fine at first, so we slept in the open... We studiously avoided contact with the mountain peasants; we had no idea how they might feel towards us. But at last, when the Red Cross stores we had brought with us were exhausted, desperation made us approach a humble, isolated cottage to beg for food.
>
> The place was poorer in appearance than any we had yet seen. At first there was no response to our knock on the battered wooden door, but just as we were about to continue on our way, we heard shuffling footsteps. An old woman opened the door a little and peered into my face. She mumbled a remark in a dialect difficult to understand. Then two younger peasants emerged from the gloom inside. For a moment all three stared at us in silence. Then the man spoke:
>
> "*Siete Inglesi?*"
>
> "Yes, we are English," I replied. "We have escaped from the prison camp at Veano."
>
> They showed no surprise.
>
> "Welcome to our house," said the peasant. "Come in."[9]

That simple kind welcome was repeated thousands of times in the length and breadth of northern Italy in the autumn of 1943.

Lett and his men ended up in the mountains to the south-west, and organized resistance to the Fascists; they were assisted for some time by another former Veano inmate, Lieutenant-Colonel Lowry-Corry MC.[10] Lowry-Corry had left Veano with "Gussie" Tatham and "Friar" Tuck, but shortly afterwards had met another group consisting of Colonel "Dicky" Richards and two rather unfit Indian Army officers. Tatham elected to stay with them, and Richards took his place. The trio travelled south up the Val Nure; the Nure flows north from Ferriere in the mountains, past the town of Bettola, and down to join the Po east of Piacenza. The Val Nure led nowhere except the chestnut woods; by contrast, the Val Trebbia, the next major valley to the west, was an important and strategic crossing of the Appennines, used by Hannibal, Napoleon and, of course, the Germans.

Lowry-Corry's group skirted Bettola because they had been told that it contained Germans. Travelling across country, the party made very slow progress:

> We were about ten days doing a march which really could have been done in about four hours.[11]

They finally crossed the Nure well south of Bettola on September 21st and lay up in an area where charcoal-burners were active and other evaders were hiding.[12] It was the same region in which Donny and Gunner were to hide that winter. But by mid-November Lowry-Corry and his companions had joined Lett in the area of Rossano.

Lett and Lowry-Corry were not the only ones who decided to help the Allied cause by fighting where they were. Major Tony Oldham ran a partisan band in the mountains nearby; Major d'Arcy Mander evaded as far as Rome, where he joined the resistance until liberation. Oldham, Mander and Lett were all later awarded the DSO for their work behind enemy lines. Colonel De Salis also spent some time fighting for the partisans near Piacenza before making his way to Switzerland:

> That most undisguisedly English figure hoodwinked his former captors by calmly proceeding by bus and bicycle through their midst into Switzerland, in time to take part in the last operations against Germany.[13]

Major Hugh Clifford had intended to leave Veano with his friend Gerard Porter, but had missed their rendezvous and instead spent his first night of freedom in a pig-sty with fellow inmate Captain Harold Fairley. They headed up the Val Nure to Bettola, where they linked up with a New Zealand Sergeant who had escaped from prison hospital in Piacenza. After a winter in the mountains near Bardi, Clifford joined the partisans of the Val di Taro and Monte Penna, whom he considered useless. He and another officer tried to organize them and in June 1944 liberated the Val di Taro; however, they were over-run by the Germans later in the year and Clifford crossed the Allied lines in December 1944.

Not content with mere escape, these former prisoners had made positive contributions to the Italians' attempts to take control of their country's destiny and dissociate themselves from the Fascist past.

* * *

Other parties from PG29 set out to make the long journey south. If they were quick, escape was almost ridiculously easy in the chaos of Italy after the Armistice: Mander's batman from Veano apparently boarded a train to Naples, and then cycled south until he met Allied troops. He was home in five weeks. However, few showed this level of initiative, and made pitifully slow progress on foot. Tower was one of a group of six, of whom only he and Nigel Beaumont-Thomas made it to Allied lines.[14] Tower described the help which they received from Italian peasants during their two-month, five hundred mile trek south as being "beyond praise". Tower was wounded by a land-mine as he crossed the lines, but on recovering fought at Arnhem in September 1944. He survived, and escaped capture, but Beaumont-Thomas was killed there.[15] Andrew Howard and Peter Miller were re-captured whilst making their way south, as was another of the evaders, Peter Lewis.[16]

Mander's escape party which made its way south from Veano was originally four strong: himself, Major Bill Syme, Major James Marshall, and Trooper Maddox. Marshall was one of the three companions who had sneaked out of the Tobruk perimeter with Donny when 2nd Camerons had surrendered in June 1942. Mander, as we have seen, made it to Rome; but he was the only one who escaped successfully. Maddox was recaptured and taken to Germany. As for Marshall and Syme, they tried to make their way through the mountains in the depths of the winter of 1943-1944, but both were killed in an avalanche in the Gran Sasso mountains east of Rome.[17]

It is estimated that of the eighty-thousand Allied prisoners in Italy at the Armistice, some fifty thousand left their camps, but that only four thousand completed a successful evasion from Italy. Many from Veano found themselves in German prison-camps, such as *Oflag* VIIIF at Märisch Trubau in Czechoslovakia, where in 1944 there was a significant Veano population.[18]

Others were successful: Gunner's fellow tunneller, Hil Evans, trekked south as far as Vallepietra near Rome, where he hid with escaped submariner Loftus Peyton-Jones DSO, before making good his escape across the Allied lines.[19] Major Ross McLaren, who also headed south, joined up with a comrade from his own battalion who had escaped from PG49 at Fontanellato (Eric Newby's old camp); they were re-captured attempting to cross the lines on December 13th 1943, but after four days in a cell escaped through a window and went into hiding near Lecce di Marsi. On April 30th 1944 they and some companions began a four-day journey to cross the lines; two of the party were wounded by anti-personnel mines and the group came under Allied fire, but they made it to safety. Major the Hon. Simon Ramsay of the Black Watch also made a successful 'home run'.[20]

* * *

Corsica, separated by miles of sea from the Italian mainland, may seem an improbable destination, but it was already under Allied control and several did make it that way. From PG29, New Zealander Major Kedgley was one of those who went into hiding in the mountains to the north-east of Genoa, whence organized evacuations by sea to Corsica began in October 1943. On February 19th 1944 Kedgley and thirteen other evaders left in a small vessel and reached Corsica two days later.[21] Gunner's former tunnelling partner, Gerry Gore, also made it to Corsica; he was then posted to command an RAOC depot in Palestine. Gunner records the sequel:

> After the war, he was given the job of dumping in the sea all our unwanted arms. He had a Jewish Major working for him. It was discovered that most of the arms were not dumped but were put in boats run by the Jewish Stern Gang. Gore and his Jewish Major were court-martialled and both went to jail.[22]

Another officer from PG29, Lieutenant J.Y. Ferguson, also made an escape by sea. He had left Veano with Lieutenant N.C. Johnston, but became separated from his comrade and took shelter in a monastery at Fonte Avellana. There he met a Major Cauldwell (Montgomery's son-in-law) and discovered that two escaped British Generals were in the area. Ferguson volunteered to go down to the coast with a friendly Italian, and to steal a fishing-boat. On October 16th the two men set sail from Cattolica, and by October 20th Ferguson was at the headquarters of 'A' Force, the organization tasked with getting escaped prisoners-of-war and downed aircrew back to Allied lines in Italy. A successful operation later rescued the two generals. Meanwhile, Johnston had also made it safely to Allied lines.

* * *

Like many others, Donny and Gunner planned to walk towards Switzerland, though this would involve crossing the formidable obstacle of the River Po. Gunner, of course, knew Switzerland and had relations there. Others from PG29 had similar plans, and if they moved swiftly found little difficulty in making the journey north in the chaos which followed the armistice. For example, Lieutenant-Colonels "Tishy" Lister, de Salis and de Bruyne left the camp together, and were joined on second day by the camp's padre, Henry Rogers. Having headed south into the hills, they lay up until October 11th, looked after by wonderfully kind Italians. On October 12th they set off north, leaving Rogers behind, and on November 13th met up with Younghusband. The group caught a train from Piacenza to Como, and crossed the Swiss frontier shortly afterwards.[23]

Some of the Swiss escapes were co-ordinated by a fellow former inmate of PG29, Lieutenant-Colonel Norman Boddington, but without the help of friendly Italians nothing could have been achieved. Major Bob Orr, for example, hid near Veano for a while, and was then helped northwards; he too crossed the Swiss border safely in November. Those who successfully made the same journey included four more Lieutenant-Colonels (Bush, Cooper, Norman, and Reynalds) and Major Tony Dobson.[24]

Donny and Gunner had collected food and clothing from the Red Cross stores at PG29 before setting out. Gunner chose their route, having been outside before.

> As we walked out of the camp, I thought ruefully that there had been no reason for me to have spent five months digging a tunnel.

After an initial move into the mountains, up the Val Nure away from Piacenza and the Germans, the two friends attached themselves to a group of fellow evaders who also had Switzerland as their objective: Bob Foote, Ian Bransom, Jock McGinlay, Johnnie MacLean, and two of the batmen from the camp.
One of those Italians who helped the PG29 evaders was Franco Pareti, who was, according to Gunner,

> an excellent man, from a good family who had a house in the main square in Bettola [the main town in the Nure Valley]. Before the war he had held an important job as a development engineer with FIAT. He was very anti-Mussolini. In spite of that, and because he was so well-qualified, he was commissioned on being called up into the Italian artillery. At the time of the Italian armistice he deserted and returned home. I knew him well, as he was one of my partisans for over a year. Britain owes Franco a large debt for what he did.

Pareti later recalled his first encounter with Gunner and Donny:

> I met [Gunner] immediately after the Italian armistice, in the mountains around Ferriere, near Piacenza. At the time I was a Lieutenant of anti-aircraft artillery and a deserter from my unit – and he was a fugitive from his prisoner-of-war camp. During that difficult period immediately after the armistice he always maintained a calm and reasonable outlook, even in the most trying of circumstances.
> He was with six other former prisoners-of-war, amongst whom were two Lieutenant-Colonels, a

> Major, two other ranks and the late lamented Captain Mackenzie. I organized food and somewhere to sleep for them for two months until the end of October 1943. But life became ever more difficult as the Germans and Fascists reasserted their control.[25]

Thanks to Pareti, Foote's party made it safely across the Swiss frontier. A photograph exists of the party in the Italian mountains in October, dressed in civilian clothing – though, as Gunner remembers, their disguises were far from convincing.

> Footie led his party across the Po, through Milan and across the frontier into Switzerland. This was most creditable, although he quite rightly gave much of the credit to Franco Pareti. They didn't look much like a lot of Italian civilians – however, they made it, and they all eventually arrived back in the United Kingdom.

However, Donny was unwell, suffering from a fever which was never identified but which Gunner suspected to be malaria, contracted in Palestine, as well as from dysentery. Weak, running a temperature, and fit only to go to bed, Donny could not have made the gruelling journey north. Had he been well, Donny and Gunner would probably have travelled north with their friends to Switzerland, and their futures might have been very different.[26]

> If it had not been for Donny developing malaria, he and I would have gone with Footie's party; I would have met up with my Swiss family in Bern, and Donny might be alive to this day.

Foote and his group made good time; by late November 1943 they had sent word back aong Pareti's escape line that it was safe to use, and on November 22nd a party of nine other former guests of PG29 – including Captain D.E. Field and Majors Dennis Whitehead and "Bill" Bailey – assembled for the daylight railway journey to Turin. When they set out on November 25th they had got no further towards Piacenza than the railway station at

Below: *"Footie" (standing, centre) with his unconvincingly-dressed party of evaders. Standing at left is Jock McGinlay; between him and Foote is Gunner's fellow tunneller Johnnie MacLean; and to Foote's right is another of the RTR tunnellers, Ian Bransom. The other two obvious non-Italians are unidentified. It was this party with which Donny and Gunner would have travelled to Switzerland had Donny not fallen ill (Gregg collection).*

Bettola when they were arrested by a local official, *Tenente* Zanoni, who initially mistook them for Italian deserters. Whitehead and Bailey managed to escape and to hide up in the hills once more. The next time that they tried to make it to Piacenza, the driver of the lorry in which they were travelling delivered them both straight into Zanoni's hands.

Zanoni had a bad reputation, which he now lived up to. First of all he put the two prisoners in front of a firing-squad; then he called off the execution and simply had them both beaten with leather whips.[27] Whitehead and Bailey were then lucky enough to be handed over to the Germans, but their run for Switzerland was over. It would not be until 1945 that they were released from captivity.

It was not only the prisoners who headed for Switzerland, as Mander recalled:

> The first escaper from our camp to reach Switzerland went to a very crowded hotel for a meal. When he got there he was asked by the manager if he minded sitting at a table with some Italians. Having no objection, he was shown to a table, where he sat down to lunch with the *Commandante* of *Campo 29*, who had just beaten him to Switzerland by a short head.[28]

* * *

Whilst Pareti made arrangements for the rest of Foote's party to head north, Donny and Gunner agreed to stick together in the local area, and wait until Donny recovered sufficiently to make the move into the high mountains. Donny was running a very high temperature, and needed treatment, and so Pareti suggested that Gunner go for help to Travo in the Val Trebbia, where there was a house belonging to Signor Antonio Osti and his family. The son of the family, Eugenio, who was training to be a priest, lived with his mother and grandfather, refugees from Genoa.

Pareti and Gunner took Donny to the farm-house, where they put him into bed with a mass of hot-water bottles.

> They were very brave to take Donny and myself in – and they were delighted when we opened our Red Cross parcels, as they hadn't seen either coffee or chocolate for ages.

An anonymous account in the partisan archives of Piacenza gives an Italian perspective:

> Mak [Donny] fell ill almost immediately with amoebic dysentery, a dangerous tropical disease which he had contracted in Africa, and was taken in first by Don Amasanti, parish priest of Groppo Ducale, and then by a family living not far from Pontedellolio. For the entire duration of his illness, Ganna [Gunner] did not leave him for an instant: he got hold of a dictionary so as to communicate with the family as best he could, but he had not previously been well-disposed towards Italians and in fact had never wanted to learn our language before. He was not the only one, moreover, who thought that way. Many British, in spite of everything, continued to consider us enemies and to show reluctance even when we searched them out to help them.[29]

Although those who helped escapees faced dreadful punishments, a doctor was found who was prepared to treat Donny. He gave the invalid some pills and an injection, which seemed to do the trick, as Donny recovered rapidly thereafter, helped by the Red Cross food. Within a week Donny was able to climb the stairs, and was made to walk up and down them to help him recover his fitness.

Meanwhile, Gunner had been keeping an eye on the camp "across the way". He saw a German patrol with an armoured car and motor-cycle combinations check the camp, only to go away when they found it empty. One night Gunner went over and raided the stores, loading a hand-cart with Red Cross parcels, clothing, four Italian carbines, pistols, and a good supply of ammunition. These he hid in a shed.

A month or so after leaving the camp, Donny was much better, but still did not feel sure that he was up to a crossing of the Po and the journey to Switzerland. Therefore he and Gunner decided to stick with their plan of hiding in the mountains. Even this climb would have been impossible in Donny's weakened condition, and they enlisted the help of a farmer who owned a horse and cart, and who used to make the run up into the mountains to buy charcoal from the charcoal-burners – *carbonari* – who lived there (it could be sold at a premium in Piacenza). This man was just one of the Italians who showed Donny and thousands of other escaped prisoners the greatest of kindness. The farmer took them – under cover of darkness and along back-roads – to the head of the Val Nure, near Ferriere. Donny and Gunner now found themselves with the charcoal-burners. In the woods there were also many deserters from the Italian forces, hiding from the conscription being imposed on the Italians by the Germans. Donny was initially the better Italian speaker, though he and Gunner quickly picked up the local dialect. The *carbonari* lived in tunnels hewn from the mountains by their counterparts under Austrian occupation hundreds of years before. There the two escapees stayed for a month, living almost entirely on chestnuts (of which Gunner had a loathing ever afterwards). Their Red Cross parcels did not go far, though their hosts were again delighted by the cigarettes, coffee and chocolate which the British officers shared with them. The Italians christened their new friends "Mac" and "Ganna".

Chapter Thirteen
Resistance

When Mussolini's original Fascist government collapsed, and Italy surrendered, there was an interregnum before the German-backed Saló Republic took over. In the autumn of 1943, the mountains of Italy were filled with Italian deserters and Allied evaders like Gunner:

> For a month or so after our Veano escape of three hundred officer prisoners, Italy was in chaos. Everyone was on the move. Almost all the men in the large Italian army deserted and were trying to get home. The Fascists and their *Carabinieri* had not the authority nor the inclination to detain any escaped prisoners-of-war. The Germans were fully preoccupied with moving as many fighting units as possible to hold back our forces in the south.

In a small village at the head of the Nure valley, upstream from Veano, one teenaged girl had particular reason to hope that the war would soon be over: Anita Cavozzi had grown up in England and been marooned in Italy by the outbreak of war. In 2007 she wrote to Gunner with her memories of those days:

> I am British-born of Italian parents. On May 7th 1939, when I was twelve years old, I left London and went to live in Italy with my Auntie – and there I stayed for seven years. The village was called Cassimoreno, in the *Comune di Ferriere*. It was rich, with pure fresh water running everywhere, and plenty of chestnuts, and in the woods were the charcoal-burners.
> It was a remote and peaceful village where I lived, until Italy capitulated on September 8th 1943. Because of the lack of communication, we thought the war had ended. It had for us, you could say, just started. We found ourselves with lots of Italian and some English soldiers trying to avoid being captured by the Germans or Fascists. Nearby the village where I lived, there was a derelict house where some English soldiers took refuge.[1]

When the Fascists began to re-assert themselves, the locals suffered, as did the many deserters sheltering in the hills and villages. The Germans and their Fascist minions began to round up men of military age, giving them a stark choice: a labour camp in Germany, or military service in Italy against the Allies. Neither choice appealed. Another inhabitant of the upper Val Nure, Natale Grassi, later recalled the hardships of the winter of 1943:

> The food inspectors arrived, and we were to hand over most of our grain… We were poor, but we had a crust of bread and a hunk of cheese. Our mothers baked bread, and we would go around distributing it to all and sundry, partisans and non-partisans.[2]

* * *

Italy was now experiencing what many other European nations had suffered for years – German occupation, supported by a puppet régime. Most Italians were sick of war, and unwilling to fight for the Fascist government. Instead, political groups opposed to Fascism began to form a resistance movement. At first this was spontaneous and disorganized, resistance groups being formed by the *Partito d'Azione* (republican liberals), Christian Democrats, Communists and Socialists. Gradually the various parties agreed to co-operate and formed the Committee of National Liberation (*Comitato di Liberazione Nazionale,* CLN), which acted as a point of contact and co-ordination for the disparate groups in their dealings with the Allies. Eventually, the partisans settled into three main political groupings: the Garibaldi brigades (Communist in allegiance); the *Giustizia e Libertà* brigades (loyal to the Action Party); and the Matteotti brigades (Socialists). However, the partisans remained riven by political feuds which limited their effectiveness.

In the Val Nure, a fledgling resistance movement emerged at the head of the valley in the aftermath of the 1943 armistice, centred on the village of Peli di Coli on Monte Aserei, just across the watershed in the Val Trebbia to the west. Peli was an ideal spot for resistance, being isolated but with easy access both to the Val Nure and Val Trebbia. The young local priest, Don Giovanni Bruschi, opened his presbytery to any who wanted to join the resistance, and it was effectively the headquarters of the Peli partisans; Don Giovanni later became Chaplain to the Val Nure partisans.

As the autumn of 1943 went on, those who wanted to fight the Fascists drifted to Peli. One prominent member of the Peli group was an anarchist, Lorenzo Marzani, code-named "Isabella" – most Italian partisans adopted such *nommes de guerre*. Marzani brought with him a Catholic lawyer, Francesco Daveri. Cesare Baio, a young student from Bettola, helped former prisoners-of-war to reach Switzerland, and brought in the first weapons to Peli; he was assisted by a fellow student, Luigi Broglio. When Gunner later reached Bettola, he based himself in the Baio family home.

The Communist Aldo Bellizzi ("Paolo") ran a carpentry workshop in Piacenza which was a centre for collecting weapons; another Communist involved in the movement was Antonio Cristalli ("Tonio"). Italo Londei, who later led partisans in the Bobbio area, recalled how weapons were smuggled to Peli:

Above: *some of the key players in the Italian resistance in the Val Nure, photographed at Donny's funeral in October 1944. Second left is "Pino Montenegrino" (Dusan Milic); bearded to his right is "Aquila Nera" (Pietro Inzani); partly obscured by the priest's hand is Emilio Canzi; the priest is Don Giovanni Bruschi; and furthest right is Lorenzo Marzani, known as "Isabella" (Gregg collection).*

Arms were taken out to Bobbio by mail van, thanks to help from a friendly driver, and left at Celso Agnelli's restaurant near the Piazza Duomo. Celso's relations from Coli dropped in there on market days. They picked up the weapons and carried them back to Peli through tracks in the fields and woods, steering clear of the main roads.[3]

But one of the leading lights in the original Peli group was Emilio Canzi, who reached Peli late in September 1943. Canzi was a native of Piacenza, where he had been born in March 1893, and a veteran of the First World War, having served both in Libya and northern Italy, rising to the rank of Sergeant-Major. Canzi had then become an anarchist, and by 1921 had joined the anti-Fascist paramilitaries, the *Arditi del Populo*. In the following year, after the death of a Fascist in a street confrontation, Canzi had fled to Paris to avoid arrest. Returning to Piacenza in 1927, he had been arrested, but talked his way out of prison; his passport was, however, confiscated, and in April 1928 he fled Italy without it. He remained in exile – with his wife and children – until September 1936, when he joined Italian volunteers fighting against Franco in Spain. By June 1937 he was in command of

Below: *Emilio Canzi in the hills above the Val Nure (Gregg collection).*

36 International Brigade, but on June 16th 1937, at Huesca, he was seriously wounded in the hand by shrapnel. In September 1937 he returned to Paris, where he was arrested by the Germans on October 26th 1940.

After three months in prison, Canzi was transferred to a concentration camp at Hinzert, near Cologne. From there, in March 1942, he was extradited to Italy, where he was tried and sentenced to five years internment. This sentence he began on the island of Ventotene, but after the fall of the Fascist government in the summer of 1943 he was transferred to the mainland camp of Renicci D'Anghiari, in Tuscany. The armistice had given him the chance to escape, and he had returned to his native Piacenza.

Canzi, Donny and Gunner would become colleagues and friends, and Gunner later reported to SOE on Canzi in the following terms:

> Private address: 29 Rue de Coq Francais, Lilas, Seine, Paris.
> Canzi is a man of about forty-five years old, who has been in active opposition to the Fascists since 1922, [and] has suffered imprisonment and persecution as a result of his democratic beliefs. During the Spanish Civil War he commanded a Brigade fighting against Franco. At the time of the fall of Mussolini, he was in a political concentration camp in Italy, from which he was released. Since then he has been working for the CLN of northern Italy, organizing the partisan movement in the province of Piacenza.[4]

A typical member of Canzi's band of resisters was a deserter called Giovanni Agnelli ("Vanon"), who lived near the church in Peli:

> I returned by mule through the mountains from Pontremoli, where I had been a soldier, around mid-September. I got home in the evening to find Canzi already there. In the morning, he came up and told me: "Look, I'm going to need you."[5]

Another Peli partisan was Alberto Grassi ("Berton"), who joined the group because of his anger at the Fascist authorities:

> I was hopping mad, because they'd shipped me off to war without consulting me.[6]

In October 1943, the increasing activities of Fascist informers meant that the Peli group's weapons had to be moved from the church there to hidden caches in the area; Grassi helped with this. Agnelli was warned that the authorities had their eye on him:

> They found out from spies that I had a mule and that I was wearing an army uniform, so the *Carabinieri* arrived to tell me that I should turn myself in for stealing a mule from the army. So I told Canzi what had happened to me, and he said to me: "Take it easy. There won't be anybody coming up here."[7]

However, in November 1943, Marzani was arrested, and in December the Germans moved against the Peli group, which was forced to disperse. Cristalli was arrested; Daveri and Don Bruschi fled; Cesare Baio and his father were arrested, and died in a concentration camp near Cologne. Canzi, who had escaped to Parma, then returned to Piacenza, but was arrested by the Fascists on February 14th 1944.

However, there remained the weapons caches put together by the original Peli resistance group, as another member of the Grassi family, Albino, recalled:

> The arms remained hidden there until March, when the first people from the *Stella Rossa* showed up.[8]

The *Stella Rossa* – "Red Star" – unit was originally made up of students from Parma and Piacenza, and men from the Val Nure. Their leader was a Yugoslav, known as "Pino Montenegrino", but whose real name was Dusan Milic. Milic had been a Lieutenant in the

Yugoslav Royal Army, and had been captured early in the war. When the armistice came, he had escaped from the camp where he was being held at Cortemaggiore, near Piacenza, and had taken to the mountains. Described by Gunner as a brave man, he was also a 'loner' (though one with a keen eye for the local girls), and never gained the following which Donny and Gunner had. Well aware that the Communist Marshal Tito would come out of the war in charge of Yugoslavia, Milic was concerned to establish his credentials as a leader of Communist partisans so as to gain acceptance back home after the war. As a result, he later tried to ingratiate himself with the Italian Communist leadership and later even referred to himself as Chief of Staff of the partisans in the Val Nure; however, the authorities instead always consulted Donny and Gunner about military matters. Milic managed to avoid most of the heavy fighting later on, but made sure that he was prominent in photographs – for example, those of Donny's funeral.

Early in 1944, however, Milic/Montenegrino was in command of the only armed partisan band then operating in the area. Anger at the Fascists was growing. Even in the

Below: *"Pino Montenegrino" (Lieutenant Dusan Milic), whilst serving with the* **Stella Rossa Brigade** *(Gregg collection).*

remote Val Nure, the hand of the occupiers was not light. In January 1944, for example, the Germans had murdered three of the four Spinelli brothers, who were from Pistoia but were hiding in Farini di Sotto; a villager there had reported to the authorities that one of the brothers had killed a German soldier. The fourth brother, Guido, eighteen years old, was spared because he was disabled.

Montenegrino's unit did not, however, last long. On April 28th 1944 another Fascist anti-partisan sweep – a *rastrellamento* – hit Peli, as Albino Grassi remembered:

> The partisans would have numbered about ten, no more, and they had but few weapons. Along came the *rastrellamento*, and they set up a machine-gun... One machine-gun versus an army! [The Fascist] Captain Zanoni's hundred men showed no mercy; they murdered the elderly Cesare Mulazzi and dragged him on a sledge, blood pumping from him, as far as Coli... Four of us escaped into the mountains, but another squad of Fascists closed in from the other side, and we were trapped... In order to frighten me, they threatened "Come over here, so we can kill you" – and then beat me up. Then they took us [Albino Grassi and Primo Agnelli] away to Piacenza, and we found Canzi in a cell there.[9]

Primo Agnelli remembered their captivity with Canzi:

> I spent a month in Piacenza sharing a cell with Canzi. He used to buoy up our spirits and tell us not to sign anything or they would ship us off to Germany – and to rest assured that there would be an exchange of prisoners.[10]

When fresh resistance was contemplated, Peli was again to be its source. Two attempts had failed; a third was to be more successful. But this time, it was to be led by professional British army officers: Gunner and Donny.

* * *

After the long winter of 1943 to 1944, the presence of Donny and Gunner in the Val Nure brought fresh courage to the locals. The focus of the local farmers' hatred and fear was the Ferriere garrison of Sicilian and Calabrian *Carabinieri* – it was the Fascist government policy to police communities with outsiders. The many Italian deserters around Ferriere feared that the *Carabinieri* would round them up and force them into Mussolini's army.

Donny and Gunner were invited to a farmhouse in Peli to discuss the prospects for armed action with Montenegrino, who had escaped the April *rastrellamento*. Another of those present at the meeting was a university student, Gianmaria Molinari, one of the sons (or grandsons) of the socialist mayor of Fiorenzola. One of the mayor's sons had been murdered by Fascists in 1921; another, Giovanni Molinari ("Piccoli") had already founded a partisan unit.

> When, at the beginning of spring, Mak's state of health was up to it, he took himself up higher into the mountains, where he was looked after for many days by the partisan Giosi, who offered him his house and every assistance, so that the Scot joined the patriots... He was a pleasant, friendly man, differing from his friend Ganna, who was more reserved and distant.[11]

The Italians wanted the professional advice of the British officers, and hoped that their presence would give the resistance credibility and perhaps even access to military supplies from the Allies.

When asked sixty years later why he and Donny had not left the valley and made for Allied territory, Gunner found it hard to explain. He said that did not really occur to them to do so: the possibility was never mentioned. Had it been suggested, he felt, they would have refused: the operation in which they had involved themselves was going well; they

Above: Gianmaria Molinari, one of the leading lights of the partisan movement in the Val Nure (Gregg collection).

had a duty to people whom they now looked on as "theirs"; and it gave them a good opportunity to do the enemy real harm and hamper their operations elsewhere. Gunner had seen his parent unit, 3RTR, decimated at Calais, in Greece, and again in the Western Desert. Donny's battalion had been forced to surrender to enemy forces which had been superior in number but inferior in quality. Perhaps the two officers felt that this was their chance to 'get their own back', and use their leadership skills to make a real difference to people who needed their help.

The Peli conference immediately bore fruit. When Donny and Gunner discovered that the Ferriere *Carabinieri* numbered only two or three men, their first thought was:

> Surely we can deal with those.

And thus the liberation of the Val Nure began.

* * *

The armed band which set out for Ferriere one evening that spring comprised Donny, Gunner, Molinari, Montenegrino, and four sons of local farmers. Gunner and Donny's small party was armed with four carbines, pistols and shotguns. Surrounding the police station, they yelled for the occupants to come out. The policemen, however, were too scared to leave the building, and so the partisans contented themselves with firing through the windows. The next morning, a young boy reported that the *Carabinieri* had fled during the night, and the partisans returned to find the police post empty. It was an exhilarating moment:

> We suddenly found ourselves owning quite a lot of real estate in the middle of German-occupied Italy.

As well as control of the area, the raid on Ferriere had provided a bonus: weapons sufficient to arm their followers properly:

> We'd started with the four carbines and a good supply of ammunition which I'd raided from the Veano camp. We'd brought those up to the Ferriere area, and used them on our first raid on the police post. All the farmers had shot-guns for hunting, and we used them in the beginning. We did not like them, as they were not much use for partisans, and we did not use them again. Had we been able to get solid shot it might have been different. The Ferriere police station yielded quite an armoury – mainly carbines and automatic pistols – and a very good supply of ammunition.

One of the Italians, Alfrede Colombo, obtained a map of the area from the local school to help Donny and Gunner to plan their next move.

Donny was sure that the enemy would retaliate, and the pair decided to prevent vehicular access to Ferriere, which was in those days only possible from the north. As an infantryman, Donny had more training in this sort of fighting than did Gunner, whose background was in armour, even though Gunner had seen more action.

> He was a damned good infantry soldier. I learned a lot from Donny.

The group moved two miles north of Ferriere, to a point where a small bridge crossed a stream, and acquired explosives from local quarrymen. The plan was that if an enemy vehicle appeared, they would destroy the bridge and ambush the enemy from positions overlooking it.

Two lorries full of Fascist soldiers soon appeared, having driven up from the garrison at Bettola, the main town of the Val Nure. The lorries were widely-spaced, which may well have been a precaution against ambush, and since the partisans lacked automatic weapons they could only really hope to damage the leading vehicle. As the first lorry reached the bridge, the charges were blown and the vehicle overturned; Gunner recalls that all on board were killed. As the second lorry appeared, the ambushers engaged it with small-arms fire – it made good its escape, though not without casualties. This success, coming so quickly on the heels of the first, made heroes of the British officers, and secured their grip on Ferriere. The Fascist troops had no appetite for a stiff fight to recapture a dead end in the mountains.

> That was the last we saw of the enemy trying to occupy that area.

The locals found this situation "very satisfactory", though the local priest demanded to know who would mend the bridge. From then on, Donny and Gunner carefully cultivated the good-will of the local priests, since the Church was anti-Communist and had great influence over the local population. As the partisans were nominally Communist, their support might be eroded if the Church spoke out against them.

The news of the active commencement of resistance spread rapidly, and Italians of spirit flocked to join the two British officers. One of the first to arrive was Franco Pareti:

> As soon as Franco heard that we had taken over the village and had formed a band of partisans, he came and joined us. He was a natural leader, and he must have much credit in building up the group of fighters which became my band: the *Squadra di Ganna*. I really treated him as my Second-in-Command.

* * *

The two British officers now had a stroke of luck. Although the Allied advance was stalled in front of Monte Cassino, far to the south, and the Anzio landings near Rome had not provided the break-through for which the high command had hoped, there were Allied troops in the mountains. The Special Operations Executive (SOE), whose task was famously to "set Europe ablaze" by encouraging sabotage and resistance in occupied territory, had cheerfully got to work in Italy and the Balkans. Under the name No.1 Special Force, it operated from headquarters at Monopoli, near Bari, and was trying to assess the level of armed resistance which could be expected from the Italians in the north of the country.[12] During the summer of 1944 No.1 Special Force sent out various "missions" consisting of a "British Liaison Officer" and a radio-operator. The concept of the BLO was a simple but effective and economical one. The presence of such an official provided a communications link with the Allies, a means for the Allies to set the partisans' agenda and to channel supplies to those who needed them, and a confidence-boost for the partisans.

A representative of No.1 Special Force now showed up in Ferriere, a South African working under the name "Staff Sergeant Smith". Gunner remained grateful for the stimulus which Smith's visit provided:

> His arrival was really the making of our partisan force. Apart from anything else, he provided us with some British Sterling and American dollars; this hard currency was very welcome to the Italians, who knew that the Fascist *lire* were rapidly becoming valueless.

Smith told the two British officers the whereabouts of a radio-operator, some twenty miles to the south-west, who could send messages on to HQ No.1 Special Force. The radio transmitter was at Albareto, in the area controlled by former PG29 inmate Major Gordon Lett, who was commanding another force of partisans in the area around Rossano, near Pontremoli.[13] His operations had been given official status – he was the only escaped prisoner to be appointed a BLO in the field – and allocated the SOE code-name Operation Blundell Violet. For administrative purposes Donny and Gunner were considered to be part of Blundell Violet, though they had little or no contact with Lett. Messages to and from Lett's radio station were always carried by their courier, Tony Bosci.

From SOE files, it is clear that No.1 Special Force considered Donny to be the "unofficial British Liaison Officer" for the Val Nure. Gunner and Donny were escaped prisoners-of-war, not trained SOE personnel, and were under no obligation to work for No.1 Special Force – but it seems odd that Lett, in a similar position, was accorded official BLO status whilst Donny was not.

Smith arranged with Donny and Gunner that they would set up a supply dropping-zone on the slopes of Monte Capra, near Leggio, and asked them to suggest a code-phrase which they could listen out for on the BBC news broadcasts to Italy. Honouring his Irish roots, Gunner chose the Italian for "the Emerald Isle": *la isola e verde*. Smith told them that if they heard this phrase, they should prepare their recognition fires and symbols on the dropping-zone, since a supply drop would be imminent. Smith then went on to organize matters elsewhere, though he did return from time to time.

This access to Allied supplies gave Donny and Gunner great status locally. Although not all the drops were successful, the partisans were supplied – among other things – with the boots, Sten guns, ammunition and land-mines which they had requested.

> We never received as many drops as we would have wished, but we did have an early one which gave us a good supply of Sten guns and considerable 9mm Sten ammunition, as well as other goodies.

With their growing forces of partisans, Donny and Gunner now moved northwards to liberate the rest of the Val Nure. They adopted a methodical and effective strategy to capture the towns and villages which lay along the road from the head of the valley towards Ponte dell'Olio and Piacenza. They first by-passed each objective, and found the nearest bridge between it and Piacenza. The bridge was then blown, cutting the garrison off from reinforcements. Fighting was not then necessary; the garrison of each village knew that to remain was to court annihilation, and could usually be trusted to flee without a struggle.

> We went slowly down the valley, taking Ferriere, then Farini d'Olmo, and then Olmo.

At Farini d'Olmo, the garrison of *Repubblichini* – conscripts to Mussolini's new army – had low morale, and as elsewhere proved ineffective. After Olmo came the chief town of the Val Nure, Bettola. As befitted its status, Bettola had not only a road towards Piacenza but also a small railway, the *Littorina*. Like its smaller neighbours, Bettola was first isolated, then taken over without a fight.

> When we got to Bettola, again there was very little resistance. The *Carabinieri* deserted their post, and we occupied it.

* * *

The liberation of Bettola early in July 1944 was an important moment, since it placed Donny and Gunner in control of a major centre of population. This now had to be defended

Below: *Donny and two of his partisans; Donny has retained an Italian carbine, whilst his men are armed with Sten guns supplied by SOE (Gregg collection).*

and administered. It was time to take stock of their position and to assess what could be achieved with the forces at their disposal.

The limiting factor on the size of the partisan forces was not man-power, but weapons and equipment. Donny and Gunner eventually formed their men into two units *(squadra)* – the *Squadra di Mac* and the *Squadra di Ganna*. These two formations became the main combat arms of the partisan forces in the valley for the rest of 1944. Both *squadra* were initially about eighty men strong, growing to some two hundred as the year wore on. The partisans dressed in a mixture of Italian, German and British uniforms, though Donny and Gunner always wore British clothing, with red scarves to establish their Communist credentials. The mixture of equipment used by the partisans is evident in photographs which survive from this period, as is their pride in what they were doing. Officially-authorized partisans wore numbered badges with a Communist star: Gunner kept his badge, which has a low issue number.

The *squadra* were sub-divided into sections, averaging seven men:

> We operated with small fighting groups of from six to ten men each. That was the most suitable force for ambushes and hit-and-run attacks. Seven men formed a very useful size little 'battle group', with

Below: Gunner's partisan badge, a treasured possession (Gregg collection).

Above: *although the top of Gunner's head has been cut off by the photographer, this excellent picture taken in the summer of 1944 shows him with a section of the Squadra di Ganna. The rear rank are armed with three Sten guns; the seated partisan at front left holds a German 7.92mm Mauser Kar98k, whilst his prone companion is equipped with a Breda 30 LMG in 6.5mm calibre. The mixture of clothing includes Italian and German issue items (Gregg collection).*

one machine-gun, one or two Italian carbines, and the rest armed with Stens, British hand-grenades, and pistols.

The Sten gun has been much maligned over the years for its inaccuracy and tendency to go off accidentally, but Gunner thought it an excellent weapon for partisans, since it fired a compact cartridge which could be carried in bulk, was capable of great accuracy when used properly, and could also lay down a large volume of suppressive fire. However, the automatic-fire option was one which Gunner taught his men to avoid:

> I insisted that my lads use single-shot rather than automatic: my partisans were not allowed to fire it from the shoulder using the very crude and wasteful automatic mode. Instead, I made them practise holding the gun tightly against their stomachs. They then had to fire one ranging shot low. The second shot could then be fired by moving the whole rigid body. This was very economical on ammunition, and it was more lethal. We used to train by throwing a log or something twenty yards ahead and hitting it with our second shot.

The reason for this attempt at economy was very simple:

> Partisans had to make every round count. Once our machine-gun and Sten magazines were empty we had no reserves of ammunition at all. As a result, all our weapons were on single-shot, not automatic. Should we use a bullet to kill a man, we had no replacement for it until the next arms drop or until we managed to capture more weapons and ammunition.

Gunner was deeply impressed by the quality of the material with which he had to work when he commanded the *Squadra di Ganna:*

> If anyone tells you the Italians aren't brave, you can tell them it's nonsense. There was nothing wrong with their fighting capabilities; they just had bloody awful officers. Both the officers and their men were really badly trained conscripts, and the Italian army suffered from party-political interference.

By contrast, Gunner and Donny worked hard to earn the respect and trust of their men. They did so by acting in accordance with their British training: they treated their men as equals, lived and slept with them, and did without servants (Italian officers of the period allegedly had two, one just to polish boots). The inhabitants of the Val Nure wanted to treat the two officers as honoured guests, and Donny and Gunner could have lived like kings. They chose not to.

> Every house you went into, they welcomed you, they fed you, they spoiled you; you could sleep in their barns. And what they always did, they offered Donny and myself their best bedrooms, which we never accepted, because we wanted to make the point that we worked, lived, slept, ate, and fought with our soldiers.

To deserters from the Italian armed forces, such conduct was a revelation, and had huge benefits for morale and confidence.

During that summer of 1944 Donny and Gunner's partisan forces took many prisoners. Of these, good numbers of Italian soldiers were recruited into the partisans, but Germans and die-hard Fascists were incarcerated in prison-camps. This, more than anything else, shows the extent to which the Val Nure had become a liberated enclave in what was still ostensibly enemy territory.

> We had a prison camp, in a little village in the Monte Obolo area, and we had very few guards there, because the prisoners all knew that if they escaped they'd be in danger of having their throats cut by the locals.

By the time that Gunner left the Val Nure at the end of November 1944, there were three prisoner-of-war camps, as he reported to SOE:

> During the past year the partisans accumulated 312 Germans and about the same number of Fascists; this includes Black Brigade, 10th Flotilla MAS, MM, etc., but does not include *Alpini*, etc., who were all conscripted during *rastrellamenti* and who have always been a good source of recruits and supplies to the partisans. These prisoners are held in concentration camps at Groppo Ducale, Farini D'Olmo and at Ferriere. These prisoners are well fed and, considering everything, well treated. Their main use to us is as hostages and for exchange.[14]

Prisoner exchanges were made when a partisan was captured, the exchange rate being five Fascist prisoners for the release of one partisan. As a result, the Fascists and Germans did not shoot captured partisans out of hand, as they were useful bargaining counters.

> All the partisans knew that if they were taken prisoner, Donny and I would do everything to get them back. Morale was in consequence incredibly high. They were very proud and self-confident.

* * *

It was not only the partisans who showed their loyalty to Gunner and Donny. The two officers and their men were now effectively the government in the Val Nure, and as well as conducting military operations they had to maintain law and order:

> The countryside was full of Italian Army deserters. Most of them had thrown away their rifles but kept their pistols. We disarmed them, as there was a certain amount of brigandage, to which we put a stop.

The pair were careful to maintain good relations with the local community, the poor peasant families – *contadini* – who scraped a living among the mountains:

> Donny and I had an excellent relationship with the farmers, who were all feeding the black market of northern Italy. I'd try and protect the farmers who were doing that. Many of them were very short of labour, as their sons were in many cases in prison-camps in England and elsewhere – also, many were fighting for the Blue Division with the Germans in Russia. The vast majority never returned, and were killed or frozen to death at Stalingrad.
>
> This is where Donny and I were able to help. The small mountain fields were hell to cultivate. The work was mainly done with *sampari*, which were rather like the army's entrenching tool. Where we thought we could help, Donny and I would turn up and do the work for them. This, needless to say, was very good PR.

Within the liberated area there remained no Fascist sympathisers or informers, as far as Gunner and Donny could tell; certainly, they never feared for their lives, despite the price on their heads – literally. Even ordinary escaped prisoners were worth money to those who betrayed them: the Fascists had originally set the reward for the capture of an escapee – dead or alive – at 5000 *lire;* at the end of November 1943 they added a bonus of two months' ration of food and tobacco; in December they had announced that anyone who helped an Allied evader would be shot in the back as a traitor.

The loyalty of the Italians to their new leaders, however, went deep. Testimony to this is a stone monument on the road between Farini and Olmo, where two partisans were

Below: *Gunner, flanked by one of his partisans and the youth's proud father (Gregg collection).*

War prisoners who have evaded from concentration camps
Foreigners who are wandering in the impervious regions of Italy

REMEMBER!

The Italian Army has been thoroughly reorganised and you will soon discover what a frightful fate is hanging on your heads.

Should you be caught while in possession of arms, or should you have joined a gang of "partisans", you will be considered franc-tireurs and as such you will be tried in accordance with the laws of war.

Why, then, will you still put up with hunger, defy danger and suffer all sort of discomforts? Why should you prolong your suffering for the sak of what is a hopeless cause?

Surrender to the Italian Military Authorities who will treat you as well as they did formerly and will again recognize you as war prisoners.

Only following this course will you be able to avoid being condemned and to hope to see again your Fatherland and the dear ones who are anxiously awaiting your return home.

Above: a Fascist leaflet, air-dropped over the mountains in November 1943, showing the concern which the large numbers of Commonwealth personnel at large in Italy gave the authorities (copyright holder unknown).

tortured to death by the Germans for their refusal to divulge where the partisans were hiding. Fresh flowers are still laid there to this day. As Gunner later wrote,

> I am alive today because the locals, who were brave Italians, refused, even under torture, to divulge to the Germans the *posizione della squadra di partigiani*... Donny and I had a very high price on our heads. The Prefect of Piacenza would have loved to have captured us or at least have us killed. But there was no danger of that. Thanks to the loyalty of all the locals, nobody ever claimed the reward. Donny and I never felt in danger of betrayal, as we knew that the loyalty of all the locals was to everyone who was fighting the tyranny of the Germans.

And, of course, we should remember that it was not only the men who worked for the liberation of the Val Nure. All the inhabitants of the valley had experienced the injustice and oppression of the Fascist regime, and many women were prepared to risk their lives to help with the liberation of Italy. One such woman was the mother of Maria Luisa Sandys, who in 1944 was a child in Farini d'Olmo. In 2008, Maria Luisa wrote to Gunner as follows from her home in Exeter:

> My late mother was a partisan courier. Once I did go with my mother on a mission from Farini to Milano. Mother would meet contacts; she would be advised when it would be safe to get a lift, maybe in some trailer covered over with straw... However, once in Piacenza, a small boat would, in the pitch of darkness, carry one across the River Po. By following the railway tracks once on the other side, if it were safe, one would walk along the tracks towards *La Stazione Centrale dei Treni di Milano* – or one had to walk in the ditches.
>
> Mother's duties were to take messages on the well-being of 'boys' (partisans) to their families. She would only call on one or two families; in turn the families would pass, by word of mouth, the news on to their other relatives. Mother would take back to the boys warm socks, woollen hats and medicine.
>
> Mother had some very bad times with the Germans... She was stopped and searched, and all that she had on her was taken by the Germans; it happened at Piacenza train station.[15]

* * *

As well as giving Gunner and Donny an administrative burden for which they were ill-equipped, the occupation of Bettola presented them with a military problem. Standing on the main south-north artery of the Val Nure, the town also lay on an east-west route from the Val Trebbia through to Salsomaggiore. Gunner and Donny were convinced that, owing to the height and inaccessibility of the area, the enemy would not be able to recapture the liberated territory without a major operation, which they would probably not consider worth the effort required. However, the partisans could not afford to take any risks.

Gunner and Donny decided to split their forces into their two bands: the *Squadra di Mac* and the *Squadra di Ganna*. Gunner was to protect the western flank of the Val Nure, which was threatened by the enemy forces along the Trebbia. His task was to disrupt enemy use of the Val Trebbia, making a nuisance of himself without provoking the Germans to the extent that they would embark upon a major *rastrellamento*:

> My problem was the road running down the valley of the river Trebbia, and the town of Bobbio. Neither the town nor the road were garrisoned, although the road led all the way to the coast. In its day it had been used by both Hannibal and Napoleon. My *squadra* were therefore offered many small, vulnerable targets – staff cars, small parties of perhaps three or four vehicles, and the like. Very often they were lost and were looking for a quick way north. Usually the Germans had not been informed that the road might well be controlled by partisans. My *squadra* therefore had many more targets to attack than Donny's: so we killed or captured many more vehicles and arms and the like than the *Squadra di Mac*. Also I did not have a garrison like Ponte dell'Olio's to deal with.

Donny was to watch the east (a less likely avenue for attack) and the north (the direction of the main threat). The gateway to the plain in the north-east was Ponte Dell'Olio, then garrisoned by about forty men of the Italian Fascist forces – in Gunner's opinion a "pathetic lot" who

> offered no threat to Bettola or the upper Nure valley. They did not wish to fight, and they stayed in their barracks. Donny discovered that they and their officer would have been only too happy to surrender, but Donny did not want to take Ponte as it would have meant his *squadra* becoming involved in a defensive war, which is not what a partisan force wants. Instead, Donny wanted to attack the Via Emilia, which was part of the Germans' main line of communications for all their forces fighting in southern Italy. Donny's problem was that the German supplies were always in large convoys with very large escorts. Donny's target therefore had to be very selective and vulnerable. Donny obviously had the much more dangerous job.
>
> The Germans were incredibly sensitive about the Via Emilia. Donny and I could have blown up bridges on the Via Emilia or bridges on the railway line, but if we had done that we would have had the wrath of the whole German front-line army descending on us, and they would have cleaned us up. So we had to take just enough people off the Via Emilia that it didn't provoke the wrath of the Germans. We had to be a nuisance, but not a bloody nuisance. We didn't want to spoil our whole set-up there, when our main objective was to defend the Val Nure. We didn't want to do anything which would really arouse the Germans. They only had what are called "L-of-C" troops [Lines of Communication troops], the Mongols; they'd put them there mainly for that reason. Ponte itself was held only by these *Repubblichini*, which the Germans were happy with because it denied Ponte to the partisans.

Until now, the two British officers had been very much on their own. But this was now about to change.

Above: *Donny Mackenzie and two of his partisans, summer 1944 (Gregg collection).*

Chapter Fourteen
Liberation

After Bettola fell to Donny and Gunner's partisans, at the beginning of July 1944, the official co-ordinating body of the Italian resistance, the CLN – *Comitato Liberazione Nationale* – made contact:

> Donny and I were concerned to hear that the CLN in Milan was sending a man named Emilio Canzi to take over the *Comando Unico* of all the partisans in the Province of Piacenza. We suspected that the Central Committee of the Italian Communist Party had it in mind to change the command from two English public schoolboys to one dedicated Communist.
> Canzi informed us that the Committee had decided that we should become a regular partisan brigade – the 61st *Garibaldini* Brigade – which we thought was great.

Gunner always remained adamant that he and Donny commanded 61st *Garibaldini* Brigade: however, his own report to SOE in December 1944 stated that they ran 60th *Garibaldini* Brigade. The inconsistency arose when the Italian government awarded Gunner a medal in 1945, and the certificate named his unit as 61st *Garibaldini* Brigade. The Italians were very confused, and remain so, about the titles and commanders of their various units. They simply got this wrong – not that it matters, since in reality, despite all the grandiose titles which the Italians used, the partisans of the Nure consisted of the *Squadra di Ganna* and the *Squadra di Mac*.

* * *

Canzi had been freed from Fascist captivity in a prisoner exchange on June 24th 1944, and the CLN immediately sent him to Bettola as a political commissar, under the *nom de guerre* of *Commandante* Ezio Franchi – though he was usually just called "the Colonel". With him were a few members of the original Peli group of 1943, such as Lorenzo Marzani ("Isabella"), Canzi's bodyguard Alberto Grassi, and Giovanni Agnelli, who recalled how

> Canzi used to tell us that he had been interned by the Fascists for years, and that now they were going to pay for it.[1]

As well as his 'shadow' Alberto Grassi, Canzi always had another companion:

> We never slept at home, and moved around only at night, hither and thither, covering the entire province... He frequently wandered off alone at night without saying a word. And he always had a dog with him. A dog that he had found here. An intelligent dog too... I don't know how many times he picked up the sound of the Germans before we could. Ah, Canzi never made a move without his dog.[2]

Canzi was a compromise candidate for the post. A previous front-runner had been a former army officer, the Communist lawyer Wladimiro Bersani – known as "Capitan Selva" – from Lugagnano in the valley of the Arda, to the east of the Val Nure. The CLN had decided against him because of his clear Communist tendencies, which would have alienated many partisans; his death in action on July 19th 1944 neatly solved the problem of how to break this news to the Communists. Canzi's candidacy had been aided by the support of Francesco Daveri, one of the original Peli group.

On July 7th 1944, the partisans of the *Giustizia e Libertà* Division liberated the town of Bobbio in the Val Trebbia, immediately establishing a civilian administration, the "Republic of Bobbio". But on August 27th, after only fifty days, the Germans re-took Bobbio; as Gunner and Donny had already realized, the Val Trebbia was far too important a communications route for the Germans to allow it to fall into partisan hands. The commander of one of the brigades (7th *Alpini D'Aosta* Brigade) in the *Giustizia e Libertà* Division, Italo Londei, later recalled that Canzi passed through Bobbio on the day that it was captured:

> He greeted us and said "Daveri will be over the moon now that you've liberated Bobbio."[3]

This provides an accurate date for Canzi's first meeting with Donny and Gunner, since he headed straight across to Bettola. He made a good impression from the very start of their working relationship.

> Shortly after he arrived, Donny and I invited him to visit our *squadra* and meet all our partisans. This he was delighted to do, and he made an excellent speech to them. He praised them for their bravery, loyalty and efficiency as soldiers. He told them that all Italy could be proud of what they had done and that they could hold their own in any company.

As Gunner got to know Canzi, the Italian unbent and explained his motivations and worries. He could trust the two British officers in a way that he could not necessarily trust his Italian subordinates, riven as they were by political differences and plans for their own self-aggrandizement. To Gunner and Donny, he confided his conviction that the Italian communists wanted rid of him.

> When Emilio arrived we were agreeably surprised that he turned out to be a distinguished-looking white-haired man with a reputation of having been a very brave, hard-fighting soldier in the Spanish Civil War. We were even more surprised when he told us that he was a lifelong and dedicated anarchist, who disliked the Communists as much as they hated him. He explained to us confidentially that, as an anarchist, he believed in the minimum amount of government, while the Communists demanded the maximum amount of government for everybody. He once told me that his ideal was the democracies set up by the city-states of ancient Greece. He was in favour of democracy and prepared to work honestly and openly with the British and American forces.
>
> He also confided in me that he was pretty sure that he had been sent to the wilds of the Appennines to get rid of him from Milan. The Central Committee of the Italian Communist Party were really concerned that Canzi was earning considerable respect and that he was becoming a real threat to the Communists' control of the CLN. It was they, therefore, who devised a complicated and ingenious way of getting rid of him from Milan and sending him to the Appennines.
>
> Canzi told me that he had many powerful enemies in the Communist Party. It is obvious from the way that they arrested him and eventually killed him. He always knew that was what would happen. His enemies were the Stalinists in the Communist Party HQ; it seems that they did not like the Anarchists. They must have been their rivals.

Despite his anarchist beliefs, Canzi seems to have tried hard not to antagonize either his apolitical British comrades or the different political factions within the Piacenza partisan movement. Many partisans did not know of Canzi's personal political beliefs, recognizing only his patriotism: even Alberto Grassi, his 'shadow', said that

> I never really got a handle on what party Canzi belonged to... A man of few words but many deeds, he scarcely ever talked politics, but just said what needed doing.[4]

Gunner's final report to SOE in late 1944 expanded on Canzi's qualities as an honest broker and someone with whom the Allies could form a stable and productive relationship:

> When the *Comando Unico* of Piacenza was formed, the CLN made him Commandant. He is a man of great sincerity, integrity and strong conviction in his principles. He has considerable tact, but lacks the higher qualities of an organizer. This deficiency, however, is not greatly felt, as he is surrounded by several men capable in this respect... Emilio Canzi is very pro-British and American, and is a man to whom it will pay to give all possible support.[5]

But although Canzi was a man with whom Gunner and Donny could work, a more sinister arrival appeared at around the same time: a man known simply as "Rus" – "Red" – about whom Gunner remained uneasy seventy years after they had met: indeed, Gunner specifically asked that his remarks about Rus not be published until after his own death.

> Rus was a mystery to Donny and myself. He arrived at Bettola about the same time as Canzi and dressed like most partisans. In the holster on his hip was a .45 revolver, one of the most powerful small-arms made. Within a day or two of his arrival, he asked Donny and myself if he could join us in an ambush which we had planned about ten miles away on the Via Emilia and for which we had combined both *squadra*. Rus said that he wanted to learn how we operated.
>
> There was something about him that made you feel scared – even slightly frightened. He was a very hard and ruthless man. You felt he was devoid of any of the normal emotions. He was also a fanatical Communist. We thought that he would ask to join either Donny's *squadra* or mine, but he never did; he was a loner and always seemed to keep himself to himself.
>
> I asked Canzi who Rus was and what he was doing in Bettola. His answer shocked us: we were told that Rus was one of the Communist Party's executioners, and that he had probably been sent by the Central Committee to report on what Canzi did. Furthermore, Canzi said that when he had served his purpose, Rus would be ordered to kill him – of that, he was certain.
>
> Donny and I even contemplated putting a bullet in the back of his head. On our way to the Via Emilia, when we stopped for a rest, Rus came to Donny and myself, took both our hands, and said:
>
> "I know you are both one of us [Communists], and you can always count on me as a friend."

Gunner and Donny, of course, were far from being Communists, despite what Rus thought. Although they were in command of partisan forces nominally affiliated to the Communist Party, the two British officers were not politically motivated (though British Communists were very active in SOE in the Mediterranean):

Below: *a typical specimen of Communist propaganda produced on printing presses in the Val Nure after liberation in 1944 (Gregg collection).*

> Rus considered [us] to be serious Party members – which obviously was not the truth. We were in fact both very ordinary conventional Conservatives, typical products of our class and the schools which we had attended. Donny was, like me, I suppose, a natural born Conservative. We simply didn't discuss politics.

Although towards the end of 1944 political power-struggles within the Italian partisan movement did much to decrease its effectiveness and credibility, politics were irrelevant to most active partisans, who were fighting to free Italy from Fascist and German forces:

> Nominally, Canzi said we were a Communist brigade, but few of the peasants were. They respected property – their own farms! I never heard any of our partisans talking about politics.

* * *

Canzi's biggest surprise on arriving in Bettola was to discover that the huge partisan forces which he had expected to command were in reality figments of the fertile imaginations of their commanders, as Gunner recalled.

> Canzi had been flattered by being given an 'order of battle' of many dozens of partisan 'brigades' – most of which turned out to be fictitious, which fact he only discovered when he arrived at Bettola. He also discovered that the only fighting and well organized partisan unit in the area was the two *squadras* of Donny and myself. As a result, Canzi was content to take all advice on military matters from Donny or myself.

Canzi took over the day-to-day running of liberated territory, freeing Donny and Gunner to carry out military operations.

> We were also delighted with the arrival of Emilio in that he was able to take over the civil administration of the villages that we liberated, and which expected Donny and me to deal with many of their problems. All this was interfering with what we considered to be our main duty – that is to say, providing military protection from Germans or Republicans who might wish to recapture our valley.

One should remember that in the summer of 1944, Bettola and the Val Nure were totally free of enemy control, and that running such an extensive area was a full-time job in itself. The partisan government ran its own newspapers and radio station, and even produced petrol for the partisans' large fleet of motorized transport, as Gunner reported to SOE later that year:

> A clandestine radio station, *Radio Piacenza Libertà*, transmits partisan and Allied bulletins, and also anti-Fascist and German propaganda, from Bramignano, near Bettola. These transmissions are listened to throughout all the province of Piacenza, including Piacenza itself and perhaps even further afield. The hours of transmission are at 1230 and 1930 hours CET, on a wavelength of 42 metres...
> The partisan newspapers printed in our area are *Il Partigiane*, *L'Unanità Nuova*, *Il Grido del Popolo*, and *Il Ribelle*. Also many propaganda leaflets were printed in Bettola and Bobbio for distribution among the *Alpini* and other *Esercito* [army] units. These were very effective in inducing desertions...
> In the partisan-controlled area there are three petrol-producing areas:
> a. Veglea: production 1500 litres a day.
> b. Monte Cino: production 500 litres a day.
> c. Monte Ciaro: production 1000 litres a day.
> The petrol is not good, but you can run a car on it. The manager says that with some new drilling materials he could increase production tenfold.[6]

Food was plentiful in the fertile Val Nure – indeed, one of the reasons why the liberation of the area was so galling for the Fascist authorities was that Piacenza depended on food from the valley:

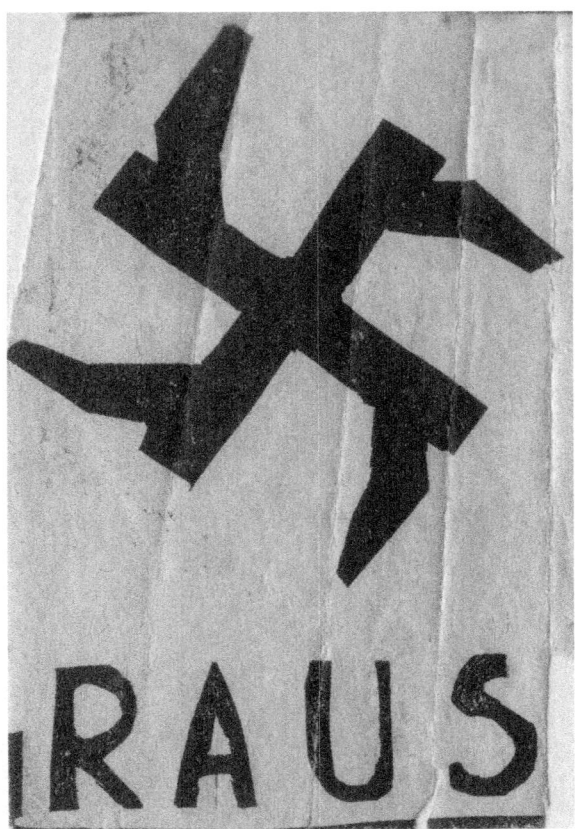

Above: two small propaganda sheets produced on the presses in the liberated Val Nure and intended to be scattered in Piacenza where German troops might encounter them. That at left says "Finished", that at right "Get Lost" (Gregg collection).

The province of Piacenza is very rich in agricultural produce, and as a result food conditions are moderately good, especially as due to partisan occupation the Germans and Fascists have not been able to carry away the wheat harvest. The only serious deficiencies are salt, soap, sugar, oil, fats and green vegetables.[7]

[Food] was one of the least of the problems for Donny and myself. The Val Nure was one of the main producers of food in the province of Piacenza. It produced the famous *Prosciutto di Parma* and Parmesan cheese. There is also beef and pork in abundance. It was the source of much of the black market food in the area. Every farm was well-stocked with pasta, chick-peas, olive oil, polenta and much else, including wood mushrooms, which were sun-dried to make *funghi secco,* which sold for a bomb...

Only during the first couple of months were Donny and I hungry, and had to depend on boiled chestnuts – yuck... Once we were were living with the *contadini,* we ate like lords.

* * *

By the end of November 1944, as Gregg reported to his superiors, the partisans south of Piacenza were well organized. They had been divided into two 'divisions', theoretically totalling some ten thousand men. Partisan unit titles were always more grandiose than their numbers warranted; units known as 'brigades' were usually no more than a light infantry company in strength and equipment, and the two 'divisions' in the Piacenza area were far short of the strength or fire-power of regular army units. However, these two formations do seem to have been better than the average, even though Gregg counselled caution when dealing with any post-war source on the Piacenza partisans:

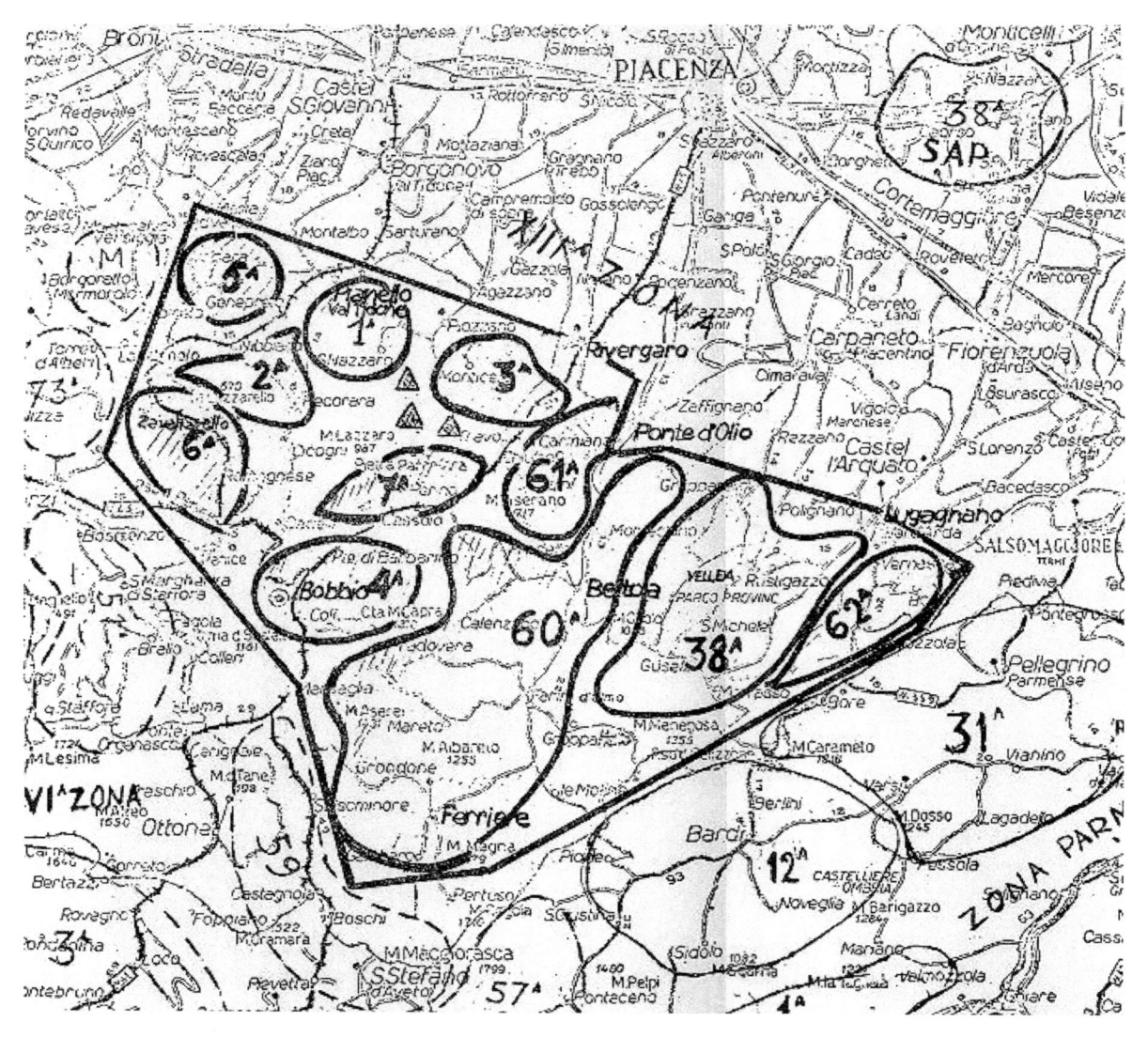

Above: *an Italian map showing the zones controlled by Canzi's Comando Unico in Bettola as at September 1st 1944: each partisan brigade's area of operations is indicated by the brigade's number. As can be seen, Donny and Gunner, commanding 60th Brigade, had the largest area (ANPI, Piacenza).*

Italian sources are interested in building up the Italian contribution to the forces that fought the Germans and Fascists. I'm afraid much of it is inspired by wishful thinking and a powerful imagination. They show an order of battle and command structure which would have been able to liberate Europe, much less the valley of the river Nure. The Italian map showing the situation at September 1st 1944 is ridiculous, and really comic. It shows, in what was our area, eleven brigades of partisans, seven of which were *Giustizia e Libertà*, and four Communist. The only partisan forces that were doing the actual fighting were Donny's and my *squadras* (60th Brigade as shown in the map). The truth is that the only two fighting units that liberated the Val Nure were Donny's *squadra* and mine. Even our 'brigade' was only made up of our two *squadras*, each of which consisted of not more than about two hundred men.

Command of the two divisions was exercised by Canzi from his headquarters at Bettola. The 'Unified Command' (*Comando Unico*) included two representatives from the *Giustizia e Libertà* Division, which operated in the Trebbia Valley to the west. There was also one representative from each of the four brigades within the *Garibaldini* Division. These six men reported to Canzi through his Chief-of-Staff (*Capo di Stato Maggiore*), *Tenente* Pietro Inzani, nick-named "Aquila Nera" (the Black Eagle). He was a local man – born in Monastero di Morfasso, east of Bettola – who had deserted from the army, become one of the earliest partisans in the Arda valley, and had then helped to found 38th *Garibaldini* Brigade. Gregg clearly admired him, and he was an official with whom he and Donny had close contact:

> For a long time second-in-command to Canzi; a regular *Alpini* officer; cool, ironical, brave, and the man, in fact, who controlled all military matters in the *Comando Unico*. No political interests; only an anti-Fascist.[8]

Inzani was later captured near Ferriere in 1945, when the Germans made a determined attempt to crush the partisans; by then he was commanding the Piacenza partisans' re-named *Valnure* Division. He was executed by his captors.

Canzi's secretary was "Filippo",

> a twenty-three year old university student, [and] the person responsible for all clerical and administrative work of *Comando Unico*.[9]

The *Comando Unico* gained a political commissar in October 1944: Remo Polizzi ("Venturi"). He and Canzi did not see eye to eye, since of course Canzi was unsympathetic to the Communist Party. Polizzi, he knew, had been sent to keep him 'on message'. Canzi's anarchist beliefs led him to exercise control with a light touch, stressing personal responsibility and self-discipline – and this, of course, did not always go down well with the Communists (though it was an approach which made him a pleasure for Donny and Gunner to work with).

The *Comando Unico* also had an intelligence section, which clearly did excellent work, as Gunner explained in his official report:

> **"Dedalo"**
> Formerly *Cancillire* of Borgo Val di Taro, and later Bettola. He ran our military information section, and used to co-ordinate and systematize all the information arriving from many sources.
>
> Among the people working for him was the *Capo di Stato Maggiore* of the Fascist Division *Littorio*, [and] also a Fascist working in the *Ufficio Politico* of Piacenza. The two men, who organized and sent out many spies (mostly women), were Antonio Borsi (of Riva, Piacenza), and *Ingeniere* Nicolo Contu (of Via Santo Marco, Piacenza). This latter is a Jew of considerable intelligence, who has worked very hard and well in getting information. His agents used to return with all the information of divisional signs, equipment and material of Fascist and German troops in the area.
>
> All the intelligence reports compiled by "Dedalo" were sent on to OSS Mission Oliviere... Some of the information was always sent on to Mission Roberto (OSS) and to "Alfonso" of the No.1 Special Force Mission Blundell.[10]

* * *

The references to other Allied missions and agents in the paragraph above raises an important issue. By the late summer of 1944, there were so many different Allied organizations sending missions into the mountains that it took a great deal of time and effort simply to establish who was genuine and who was not. Gordon Lett, in Rossano, once accepted an agent as genuine because he brought him a bottle of Scotch whisky. Not only were SOE – as No.1 Special Force – sending in Liaison Officers and agents, but there were also representatives of 'A' Force (the organization responsible for extricating former prisoners of war and downed aircrew) and of the OSS (Office for Strategic Services), the American equivalent of SOE.

Although "Oliviere" is described Gunner's SOE report as being part of an OSS Mission, it is clear from elsewhere in Gunner's report that Oliviere's status (and that of his companions "Walter" and "Nenno") was unclear to the partisans – and that no one was entirely sure who these agents were working for:

> ["Oliviere" and "Walter"] came under the command of a man who gave his name to me as "Nenno". They all lived together near Gropparello.
>
> "Oliviere", who is only twenty years old, presented himself to the partisans, when they first arrived, as a British officer. He promised the partisans unlimited parachute drops of arms and supplies, which never materialized. He was given a car by Prati [commander of 38th Brigade]. He then proceeded to enjoy himself, spending money like water. The partisans soon got very dissatisfied with him, and there was a very general feeling that he was a German agent.
>
> When the *Comando Unico* Military Intelligence Section was formed, Dedalo sent all his reports to Oliviere for transmission. *Comando Unico* became very dissatisfied with Oliviere, as all the places we requested to be bombed were never touched. This led to the general belief that Oliviere's W/T [radio] set was not operating...
>
> "Walter" lived and worked together with Oliviere. During this summer [1944] he married a German woman. He continually spread reports that he is going to Milan on a mission.
>
> This mission of three are looked upon very unfavourably by the partisans of the area, and as far as we could gather did no other work than transmit the intelligence reports sent them by *Comando Unico*. Oliviere spends his whole time in the company of women.[11]

In September 1944, suspicions about Oliviere came to a head, leading to a bizarre incident:

> In September, the CLN of Milan sent us written instructions to arrest Oliviere, without any explanation as to the reasons for this action. He was arrested on my responsibility.
>
> The same day Nenno, whom I had never met before, arrived at the *Comando Unico*, Bettola, and said that he was an Allied agent and that Oliviere was working under his orders. He said that if Oliviere was not released immediately, he would radio to Allied HQ and have Bettola completely destroyed by Allied bombardment.[12]

This seems a highly unlikely threat for an Allied agent to have made.

> Oliviere was retained under arrest, and I sent a message back by W/T asking for information and instructions. The reply, signed Macintosh, said that Oliviere was an Allied agent working for the *Comando Unico* Bettola. Oliviere was then released.[13]

The 'Macintosh' who sent this signal was Major Charles Macintosh, of No.1 Special Force Tactical HQ, with whom Gunner later became friendly and who was, in effect, Gunner's commanding officer during this period.[14] The problem with his reply, of course, is that it was the *Comando Unico* of Bettola who had asked Macintosh who Oliviere was; for SOE to reply that Oliviere was working for the *Comando Unico* seems more than a little confused.

* * *

Canzi's *Giustizia e Libertà* Division was commanded by *Comando Capitano* "Fausto", whose full name was Fausto Cossu. Fausto was – as the unusual ending of his surname suggests – a Sardinian (from Sassari), and a lawyer by training. Having been recruited into the *Carabinieri*, he had been sent to the Balkan front in 1941; when the armistice was signed in September 1943 he had been imprisoned by the Germans in the Kaiserstaeinbruch concentration camp in Austria. He had escaped in November 1943 and had returned to Italy. Whilst in the Piacenza area he had found several groups of *Carabinieri* who did not wish to collaborate with the Germans or Fascist authorities, and arranged for the *Carabinieri* in the Val Trebbia and Val Tidone to desert *en masse* in February 1944. These men were then organized into a 'Patriot *Carabinieri* Company'. This in turn formed the core of the *Giustizia e Libertà* Division, which was established in June 1944. Gunner wrote of Fausto that

> after he formed his division the CLN officially promoted him Captain. A man of considerable nervous energy, [he is] honest and an intense patriot. He is over-interested in fighting against the Communist element among the partisans. In his Division, no one is allowed to give the Socialist clenched-fist salute, or to carry a Red Star. When a Republican [i.e. Fascist] deserts to him, he believes his story too readily, and, if he happens to have been an officer before the Armistice, he will give him a responsible position. Because of this, it is possible that there might be a secret Fascist element in his division.[15]

The *Capo di Stato Maggiore* of Fausto's division was a man known as "Bandiere", who was in reality a former *Alpini* officer called Avvocato Patrigiani. Bandiere claimed that he had been an SOE agent in charge of Mission Quercia, and had entered Italy from Switzerland to conducy sabotage on the Via Emilia. Having lost his radio set, he stated, he had joined the *Giustizia e Libertà* Division. Gunner respected him, but considered that he was too interested in politics:

> A very capable and level-headed man, brave and with some idea of military tactics and strategy.... His political opinions are sound and democratic, but he is rather too interested in fighting against the Communists.[16]

SOE were very surprised to hear Bandiere's claims when Gunner reported them – it seems that Bandiere had exaggerated somewhat.

An example of Fausto and Bandiere's anti-Communist priorities came on June 5th 1944, when "Piccoli" (Giovanni Molinari) and three of his partisans, who were active and effective anti-Fascists in the Val Tidone and Val Trebbia, were murdered by Fausto's forces. Such in-fighting bedevilled the Italian partisan movement, and in later years Gunner had little good to say about the *Giustizia e Libertà* Division:

> They were very, very ineffectual, and contributed little to the resistance to the Germans and the Fascists of Mussolini's forces.

That said, it must be remembered that Fausto's men did achieve one major coup, the liberation of Bobbio on July 7th 1944. After the recapture of Bobbio by German forces on August 27th, Canzi immediately suggested recapturing the town, but Italo Londei persuaded him to use more traditional guerilla tactics:

> When the *Alpini* from the Monterosa unit re-occupied Bobbio, winding up the experiment with a republic, Canzi approached me along with Prati, Fausto, "Bandiere" and Pippo Panni. They wanted to mount an attack on Bobbio. Prati was there because the *Val D'Arda* Brigade had mortars, whereas we here in the Val Trebbia had none.
>
> In order to avoid injury to civilians and to other towns, I suggested that we stick to the tactics we had been following for weeks, blowing up the bridges in order to isolate Bobbio, and mopping up *Alpini* positions by night so as to capture men and weapons which might swell the ranks of the resistance. They agreed with me, and returned to their bases.[17]

However, Fausto's partisans moved back into Bobbio a month later, at the end of September 1944, only to be evicted again by the Germans in November. Writing in December, Gunner described the situation in the Val Trebbia as follows:

> **Area**
> HQ Pecorara; Pianello; Rocca de Giorgi; and Bobbio, a town of about four thousand inhabitants where, in consideration for the civilian population, we do not stabilize any administrative headquarters; but

we do use the printing press and the very efficient modern hospital. Fausto's area is all the province of Piacenza west of the Trebbia valley.[18]

The composition and strength of the *Giustizia e Libertà* Division were summarized in Gregg's 1944 report:

The Division is divided into six brigades [a partisan map dated September 1st 1944 shows seven, however], each with its various companies. In this division, however, there is a stronger central command than in any of the other partisan divisions that I have known...

Strength, Armament, Transport
Total strength of division 4000 men; 3 x 81mm mortars; 1 x 20mm MG; MGs; LMGs; German, Italian and British rifles, hand grenades, etc.; about forty vehicles – but since the September *rastrellamento*, when many bridges were blown, transport can be used to a very limited extent.

Political Tendencies
Democratic, monarchic, anti-Fascist and anti-Communist.

Activities
This division has done much good work on the main road between Piacenza and Castel S. Giovanni, and one brigade in particular – led by an Italian Lieutenant named Paolo[19] – has done several actions inside Piacenza, including on one occasion kidnapping the *Prefetto* himself and taking him up to the mountains, where he is still prisoner. He is employed sawing wood, and has to chant *"Duce, Duce"* while doing so.[20]

As for Fausto, he eventually rose to command the *Piacenza* Division, a post which he held until the liberation of Piacenza in May 1945; he was then appointed the first Chief of Police of the liberated city.

* * *

The second of Canzi's 'divisions', the *Garibaldini* Division, was composed of four independent brigades: 38th *Wladimiro Bersani,* 60th *Stella Rossa,* 61st *Giuseppe Mazzini,* and 62nd *Luigi Evangeliste.*

62nd *Luigi Evangeliste* Brigade was commanded by another Yugoslavian officer, Lieutenant Jovan B. Grkavac, known as "Giovanni lo Slavo" (Giovanni the Slav). Gunner described him thus:

An officer of the Jugoslav navy, an escaped POW with a considerable capacity for organization, and a very good guerilla leader. He is inclined to treat his Italians with rather too much contempt.[21]

Giovanni lo Slavo's men held the north-east flank of the *Garibaldini* Division:

Area
On either side of the main road from Pellizone; Bore; Vernasca; Mugagnano. This area has many roads leading in different directions, and has always been dangerous to hold.

Strength, Armament, Transport
One thousand, of whom eight hundred are armed; MGs; LMGs; rifles; grenades; etc.; seventy-eight vehicles, ranging from heavy lorries to small cars.

Political Tendencies
All partisans carry a Red Star, but this is really no indication of their political leanings. Giovanni was thinking of his own career in Jugoslavia after the war when he adopted this sign.

Activities
This brigade has done more than any other in disturbing German troops and supply movements on the Via Emilia around the area of Fidenza.[22]

38th Brigade was named after Wladimiro Bersani, who had run the unit in the Arda valley until his death in action at Tabiano di Lugagnano on July 19th 1944. Thereafter, the brigade was commanded by Giuseppe Prati, known at first as "Liberatore" and then, simply, as "Prati". Prati had been an officer in the *Alpini* before the Armistice, after which he had returned to his native Morfasso. From January 1944 he became an active partisan. He was not a Communist, and was frequently at odds with the *Comando Unico* – though he would later extricate Canzi from an awkward position, as we shall see. A later BLO with the Val Nure partisans described Prati as

> a soft-spoken skinny little man, with his pointed beard and pointed hat, he could have sprung straight from a renaissance canvas. Prati's allegiance, and thus that of his men, lay firmly with the Pope... I liked him.[23]

Gunner described him as

> a good soldier, inclined to be lazy, and... easily influenced by a stronger personality.[24]

Regrettably, that stronger personality could only be found in the person of *Commissario* Renato, the Communist political commissar of 38th Brigade:

> One of the most dynamic men in the province of Piacenza; a Communist, and only interested in Communist propaganda and intrigue.[25]

Typically, 38th Brigade also had a Chaplain: *Don* Giuseppe Borea, the parish priest of Obolo. Gunner summed up 38th Brigade's military capabilities thus:

Area
Between Monte Mengosa, Morfasso, Groppo-Ducallo, Groparello, Castel Arquata; roughly the area between the Arda valley and the Vezzeno river.

Strength, Armament, Transport
Twelve hundred, of whom nine hundred are armed; 1 x 20mm MG; MGs; LMGs; rifles, etc.; about fifty vehicles, ranging from heavy lorries to small cars.

Political Tendencies
While the partisans have not yet developed any definite political ideas, the heads of this brigade are only thinking in terms of the inevitable battle for power between the Communist and Democratic parties, which is expected after the liberation of northern Italy.

Activities
This brigade has done some very useful work on the Via Emilia, and has captured a considerable amount of German transport and supplies.

Morale
Good, but too much of the organization and command in the field depends on the individual detachment commanders.[26]

The remaining two brigades of the *Garibaldini* Division both operated in the Val Nure, and were effectively two arms of a single force, since 61st *Giuseppe Mazzini* Brigade seems to have been an off-shoot of the original units formed by Donny and Gunner. It was badly led by its senior officer, "Pippo" Panni:

Above: *three partisans of 61st* Giuseppe Mazzini *Brigade: their* nommes de guerre *seem to have been Portos, Sift and Tarzan* (ANPI, Piacenza).

> A regular Italian *Alpini* officer; a figurehead, who was made Brigade Commander by *Comando Unico* when "Istriano" left the majority in Val Nure and went with a handful of his partisans to do sabotage work in Liguria...
>
> Morale [is] not very good, due to the fact that the detachment commanders are all very ignorant peasants, who were excellent guerilla fighters but have not the ability to command the situation that later developed when we found ourselves occupying larger areas.[27]

Gunner's report glosses over the reasons for "Pippo" having replaced "Il Istriano" (judging from his name, another Yugoslav). It seems that Montenegrino and Il Istriano had fallen out, and that, in order to calm the situation, Canzi had sent Il Istriano to the Genoa area on a "special mission".

The brigade's political commissar, Baffini, seems also to have been ineffective, if we read between the lines of Gunner's report:

> A Communist, conscientious in his duties as *Commissario*... Political tendencies [of unit] as yet very indefinite.[28]

61st Brigade was some 550 men strong, with around forty vehicles and the usual weaponry – Gregg stated that they were equipped with 12mm heavy machine-guns, medium machine-guns, light machine-guns, and rifles.

* * *

Above: *a fine study of Gunner and men of his* **squadra** *sitting on the crest overlooking the Val Trebbia: the bridge in the background is believed to be that at Travo (Gregg collection).*

The last of the units of the *Garibaldini* Division was 60th *Stella Rossa* Brigade, officially commanded by Montenegrino, though led in reality by Donny and Gunner. Gunner was very clear that he and Donny were not military advisors but active commanders.

> My position was not that of Liaison Officer but of commander in the field.

The nominal commander, Montenegrino, had other concerns:

> [He was a] capable and brave commander when we were fighting in the mountains, but after we had captured Bettola in July 1944 he thought only of women and enjoying himself.[29]

Canzi did his best to keep Montenegrino under control, but essentially by-passed him and dealt directly with Donny and Gunner:

> Montenegrino was doing as he pleased, but once Canzi got back... it was a different story, and he quickly pulled him into line.[30]

Because the *Stella Rossa* Brigade was politically neutral, Canzi decided to treat its political side with the very lightest of touches: its political commissar was none other than Canzi's own nephew, Pino:

> Sharing his uncle's views on politics, as yet he is too young to be a great influence in partisan activities.[31]

Above: a group of unidentified partisans believed to be members of 60th Stella Rossa Brigade, Donny and Gunner's unit (ANPI, Piacenza).

As befits a report on the unit which he and Donny had raised and led into battle, Gunner's assessment of 60th Brigade was very positive. Although he was biased, it is clear that he and Donny had created what was in effect a competent light infantry battalion:

Area
The Val Nure from Ferriere to Ponte dell'Olio.

Strength, Armament, Transport
Eight hundred well armed men. 1 x 81mm mortar; 12mm MGs; MGs; LMGs; grenade-throwers; rifles, etc. About forty vehicles.

Political Tendencies
A brigade more interested in fighting than talking about politics. More than any other brigade, it has been commanded by Britishers.

Activities
Until October 1944, this brigade was engaged in clearing the enemy out of the Val Nure and in capturing the towns of Ferriere, Bettola and Ponte dell'Olio. After the capture of this last town, the brigade was able to operate on the plain, and finally on the Via Emilia east of Piacenza.

Morale
Good. It has the best fighting spirit of any of the brigades in the province.[32]

* * *

Control of these disparate forces, separated as they were by high mountains and political differences, was facilitated by good communications, a mixture of reliable and secure telephone lines, and unpredictable radios, which could be subject to enemy eavesdropping:

> A telephone exchange at Morfasso enabled all the brigades of *Garibaldini* to be in communication with *Comando Unico*. As well as this, there was another telephone line between Bettola and Bobbio [thus linking the Comando Unico with the *Giustizia e Libertà* Division]... Fausto is directly responsible to *Comando Unico* at Bettola, with whom he is in touch with two-way radio as well as by telephone from Bobbio to Bettola... W/T [radio] communication is maintained between Pecorara (Fausto's HQ) and Bettola. Bettola is also in W/T communications with the right-hand brigade of the *Garibaldini*: Giovanni the Slav, who keeps his set at Pellizone. All messages sent by W/T are sent in cipher.[33]

Canzi's headquarters did its best to keep the various partisan units under some sort of control, not an easy task:

> One of the main causes for the rapid development and good organization of the partisan movement in the province of Piacenza was... the good work that the Comando Unico did in instilling mutual confidence and a sense of co-operation between the different brigades. This was very important, as generally there is considerable intrigue and jealousy between the heads of the various formations.[34]

As we have seen, Montenegrino and Il Istriano had fallen out, which had put 60th and 61st brigades at odds; Prati and Giovanni lo Slavo were also on bad terms, thus fuelling antipathy between 38th and 62nd brigades; and Fausto was disliked by all Communists, owing to his murder of Giovanni Molinari. Luckily, Canzi was a man whom all could respect, and whom it was no shame to obey.

* * *

Meanwhile, there was no doubt at Allied headquarters that the Italian resistance was doing valuable work. In May 1944 a report was written at Field Marshal Alexander's headquarters, which stated:

> Assistance to the Italian partisans has paid a good dividend. The toll of bridges blown, locomotives derailed, odd Germans eliminated, small groups of transport destroyed or captured, small garrisons liquidated, factories demolished, mounts week by week, and the German nerves are so strained, their unenviable administrative position taxed so much further, that large bodies of German and Italian Republican troops are constantly tied down in an effort to curtail partisan activity...
> If anyone is ever heard saying "Those partisans are just an infernal nuisance" or "What do the partisans do, anyway, beneath all this swagger?" he might be asked "Have you thought just what it would be like if we had them to cope with instead of the enemy?" Large areas over which we could never motor except in protected convoy; in which no small body of men would dare to camp alone; a constant unnerving trickle of men who just disappear from the unit; all roads liable to be mined; bridges blown; supply and troop trains derailed from coast to coast; the necessity of strong guards on every installation; the exhausting business of combing hills far in the rear for an enemy whose earth is never stopped and of whom nothing may be seen or heard but a sniper's bullet now and then.

Donny and Gunner played a difficult game in pursuit of this aim. They wanted to hinder the enemy's war effort, and were within striking distance of two important arteries for German supplies – the Val Trebbia and the Via Emilia outside Piacenza. Pin-pricks on these routes could directly undermine the morale of the German armies in Italy. Gunner's own assessment of the impact of his activities chimed very closely with that made by Allied high command:

> The partisans' real and great strength was that they made the enemy scared witless. They soon thought that behind each tree was a partisan. Little did they know how few we were and how inadequately we were armed, with no reserve of ammunition. All the enemy knew was that when they posted a sentry he was usually dead by the time his relief arrived; that any small recce patrol which went out looking for information did not return; that if a man went to pee in a wood he never returned; that the replenishment vehicles never arrived; that any unescorted staff-car never arrived.

Some worthwhile targets were beyond the partisans' capabilities. For example, Donny and Gunner decided against one particular raid on an enemy position beyond the Val Nure – but later Gunner had even better reason to be glad that they had rejected the suggestion.

> Near Salsamaggiore, which was some little way away to the east of us, the German signals had set up a relay transmitting station, which allowed their forces down in the south to send signals back to Germany. It was exactly the sort of target which partisans like ourselves could usefully attack, and it was suggested that we should have a go at it. But the station had a very strong defence unit, including a troop of the same eight-wheel armoured cars we'd encountered in the desert. They were far too strong for us, we decided in the end – too tough a nut. I found out after the war that one of the signallers in there was my old friend Klaus Beckers. I'd gone to see him in Cologne, and when he described where he'd been, I told him where I'd been. Incredible.

After the liberation of Bettola, Donny sent raiding parties down to the main German transport artery, the Via Emilia, and hi-jacked lorries of valuable supplies:

> When we had established ourselves… we were able to ambush soft targets on the Via Emilia and on the road up the Trebbia Valley. Sometimes you had a jackpot, like the time Donny captured a lorry almost full of Belgian-made 9mm automatics, each with a fifteen-round magazine.

According to one source, Donny personally carried out a raid on an armoury in Piacenza itself, driving a lorry through the town: unfortunately, the anti-tank guns which he and Gunner wanted had been removed by the Germans. The only major raiding undertaken in the Trebbia valley, on the other hand, was the capture by Gunner of a large convoy of ox-carts laden with sugar, which was very welcome in Bettola:

> This delighted our locals when we sold the sugar, very reasonably, to fill Emilio Canzi's coffers. You must remember that the farmers on the whole were pretty well off, having spent the war selling their food on the black market.

But it was vital not to make themselves so much of a nuisance that the enemy had to intervene in the Val Nure, for the Germans were beginning to feel that the Italian partisans needed to be taught a lesson. They estimated that in June, July and August 1944, they lost thirty thousand men killed, wounded, missing or captured by partisan forces in Italy. By June, the German commander in Italy, Field Marshal Kesselring, was exasperated by the threat to his troops, as he later recalled in his memoirs:

> It was clear to me by June 1944 that the partisans might critically affect the retirement of my armies; I therefore tried to repair omissions by giving orders that the partisan battle was to be fought in the same way as the battle at the front. Weapons that had hitherto been used exclusively at the front – such as tanks, artillery and flame-throwers – were to be employed everywhere where there was a chance that with their help the danger might be quickly removed. The best troops were only just good enough to be used in fighting of this kind.[35]

On June 17th Kesselring issued an order which was to be used in evidence against him at the Nuremberg trial, since it seemed to authorize the atrocities which his subordinates were to carry out in their operations against the partisans:

> The fight against the partisans must be carried out with all the means at our disposal and with the utmost severity. I will protect any commander who exceeds our usual restraint in the choice of severity of the methods he adopts against the partisans. In this connection, the old principle holds good that a mistake in the choice of methods in executing one's orders is better than a failure or neglect to act.[36]

Such orders were eventually to rain horror on the Val Nure.

Despite Kesselring's orders, until the winter of 1944 most enemy offensives in the Nure were half-hearted and posed little threat. Whenever the enemy attacked, it was the partisan policy to fade away into the mountains, relying on the local knowledge of the partisans, who were, as Gunner put it, "like mountain goats". The enemy column could then be surrounded and eliminated on ground of the partisans' choosing – or allowed to go on its way if it seemed too strong to deal with.

The first major alarm came shortly after Bettola fell to the partisans in June. To the amazement of the British officers, reports arrived that a mountain battalion of *Repubblichini* had appeared at Ferriere. This unit must have slipped in through the mountains, at that time without roads. Gunner rushed to the scene with his *squadra*, ferried in lorries. Contacting the enemy Colonel, he informed him that the *Alpini* were surrounded, and demanded a meeting. The *Alpini* officer was terrified, and pleaded to be allowed to leave unharmed with his men.

> Early on, we needed heavy machine-guns. The problem was partly solved when the Republican *Alpini* suddenly appeard near Ferriere. The CO was a useless, very frightened little man. I believe it came as a surprise to him that he was met by an organized, well-trained unit like our partisans. All he wanted was to get away, and we let him go. However, it cost him six heavy machine-guns.

In fact, Gunner got more than he asked for: the *Alpini* left the machine-guns, and half the battalion simply disappeared back the way they had come. But at least fifty men – and one girl – deserted to the partisans.

> These *Alpini* were excellent material, and came mainly from the Treviso area. They had been rounded up by the Germans and been trained and organized in Austria.

The girl attached herself to Donny's *squadra,* and made it clear that she thought a great deal of him – though when her advances were turned down she quickly found an Italian boyfriend.

Desertions of this sort were commonplace in the summer of 1944, as Gunner explained in his SOE report:

> Desertions from the voluntary Fascist units *(Brigata Nera;* X *Flottiglia* MAS; SS *Italiana;* GNR; MUTI) are almost nil, because they know that they would be given no mercy by the partisans. However, the non-Fascist units (like the *Alpini, Monte Rosa,* the *Littorio* Division, etc.) are only too ready to come over to the partisans, and they have done so in large numbers. In the province of Piacenza alone this year there have been about a thousand. Most of these soldiers at some time or other have been interned in camps in Germany, and are very bitter against the treatment they received.[37]

Below: *"Alpini Girl" – one of the unexpected spoils of the repulse of a Fascist probe over the mountains above Ferriere – and the Italian partisan boyfriend whom she found after being rebuffed by Donny (Gregg collection).*

Above: *"Mongol" deserters from 162nd (Turkistan) Division (ANPI, Piacenza).*

The second main enemy operation against the Nure partisans came when a "Mongol" battalion stationed near Piacenza – part of 162nd (Turkistan) Infantry Division – carried out a drive through Ponte dell'Olio. These troops had been recruited by the Germans owing to their hatred of Communism, but they proved ineffective on this occasion.[38] The partisans, as normal, let them advance unopposed, only for the Mongols to turn off into the Trebbia valley. The partisans sniped at them as they left, but the enemy unit was not seeking a major confrontation: indeed, several of the "Mongol" troops actually deserted to the partisans.

> We were certainly bothered, but they never made an all-out effort.

A third and more serious threat came in the summer of 1944:

> Suddenly a whole regiment of self-propelled guns arrived – German. And we thought, "Oh God, they're going to clean us up." And we then discovered that they were there on R-and-R, because they'd been doing a lot of fighting down south... Quite obviously, the local *fascisti* in Ponte had asked them to attack the partisans.

Gunner took his *squadra* down to face the threat. They dug in on a road bend south of Ponte dell'Olio, where they thought that they could stage an effective ambush if the enemy armour advanced further. But the Germans showed a remarkable lack of resolve, perhaps owing to the fact that they had been in continuous combat further south for a long time:

> The SP guns came and they took up positions around Ponte. I remember that I watched it all from a trench just near the road. All they did was fire and set alight about eleven farms, which of course had exactly the opposite effect to that intended. The locals had very few casualties because they'd just left their farms. That's all the Germans did, thank God.
> We were more effective. The Germans had a *Hauptfeldwebel,* which is the RSM, and he came a bit too far into the woods. He thought it was quite peaceful, but what he didn't realize, as he went round one building, was that he'd meet two of my chaps, and soon end up with a Sten in his ribs.... They put

a Sten-gun to his back, and they captured him. He was absolutely scared stiff, because he thought he'd be shot straight away. He was brought to me and Donny. I've never seen anyone more relieved to see British officers.

The German RSM was later exchanged for partisans who had been captured – but his fate had been an object lesson in the dangers posed by the Italian partisans.

> You can imagine what the effect would be if the RSM of a British battalion suddenly disappeared while on active service. It could only create fear in the minds of most of the men.

The *Hauptfeldwebel* had in fact been captured by another Briton, an escapee called Roland (possibly surnamed Hewitson), who came from Nottingham and was known as "Rolando" to the partisans; Gunner considered him extremely valuable. He was one of many escaped prisoners in the area, some of whom helped Gunner and Donny. However, others had simply settled down on Italian farms with local girls and were waiting for the war to end. One nameless individual volunteered to fight, but then tried to rejoin his Italian girlfriend. Unimpressed, Gunner let him go – after a severe thrashing:

> I had no alternative but to do what I did. The lad had been a batman at Veano. When we walked out of the camp, he moved into a farm and was soon sleeping with the daughter. The farmer dug a 'priest's hole' under the pig-sty in the event of a search. One day the man arrived at my *squadra* and asked to become a partisan – which he did. After a little while, he wanted to return to his bird's bed and attempted to desert. I was left with no alternative but to take drastic action. If one man deserts he could easily remind some of the others that they too would like to return to their girlfriends' beds. I therefore had to give him a hiding and kick him out. There was too much at stake. All the other partisans agreed with the action I had taken. It's also relevant that he was English: I did not want my other partisans to think that I was showing favouritism.
>
> That was not the end of the story. Very soon the frightened girlfriend came to see me with a long letter she had written. She thought, because of what happened, she and her boyfriend had made serious enemies of the partisans and that we might wreak vengeance on her family. I told her that she had nothing to fear, and that she should look after her man until the war was over.

Above: Stella Rossa partisans Vittorio Bersani ("Atos"), Giovanni Castignoli ("Fra Diavolo"), and Andrea Molinaroli ("Biondo"). All three carry Sten guns supplied by SOE. According to one Italian source, Fra Diavolo commanded a detachment of Garibaldini in the attack on Ponte dell'Olio (ANPI, Piacenza).

Chapter Fifteen
Ponte

Ponte dell'Olio stood at the lowest point in the Val Nure before the plain of the Po, and marked the absolute limit of the advance which Gunner and Donny had set for themselves. As we have seen, Donny had been keeping an eye on the community and its small garrison, whilst Gunner had taken responsibility for the western flank overlooking the Val Trebbia:

> We'd split up, and Donny was looking after the north. He wasn't in Ponte, but he had it virtually surrounded. Meanwhile I was down in Val Trebbia, in a lovely farm with two very pretty daughters, one of whom Montenegrino was always sleeping with – but that's another story.

There was no military reason to take Ponte dell'Olio. For one thing, it was in flatter terrain in which partisans were at a disadvantage and in which the Germans could use armour effectively, as their previous actions with the self-propelled guns had shown. The partisans' existing liberated zone was such difficult terrain that the local German-led Mongol troops had little interest in trying to recapture it. Ponte, however, was so close to Piacenza that its occupation could not be ignored by the Fascist authorities – it had a symbolic importance far beyond its military value. Charles Macintosh at Tac HQ of No.1 Special Force had counselled Donny and Gunner against taking Ponte; he appreciated that partisans were not capable of taking and holding ground against strong opposition – and the capture of Ponte would force the Prefect of Piacenza to react strongly. Just as the capture of Bobbio in July 1944 had touched a nerve and forced a violent German reaction, so the capture of Ponte, so close to the major artery of the Via Emilia, might provoke a *rastrellamento* in the Val Nure.

Below: *Ponte dell'Olio as pictured in a pre-war postcard (copyright holder unknown).*

The garrison of Ponte was made up of *Repubblichini* – Italian Fascist forces, mostly conscripts. The garrison was there to deny Ponte to the partisans and thus protect the German lines of communication along the Via Emilia; it was not strong enough for offensive action, nor inclined to take it.

> Their nominal boss was the Prefect of Piacenza, but the Lieutenant commanding it was the son of one of Mussolini's closest collaborators. The people who were serving there, on the whole, were not local. They'd mostly come down from Rome or even southern Italy – all the local ones had deserted long before. The garrison were absolutely determined to surrender sooner or later; they didn't threaten anyone; they lived in their barracks. When they went out, they only usually went to try to capture some farmer's wife taking goods up into the Po valley and rob her of them. There had been one or two tentative offers from the Lieutenant – "Could we talk to you and come to some arrangement?" – and Donny didn't discourage him.

However, whilst he listened to the offers of surrender, Donny did nothing about them. As far as Gunner and Donny were concerned, the village could be left undisturbed: it was neither a threat nor a worthwhile prize. As Donny put it, Ponte dell'Olio was "withering on the vine": let it wither.

* * *

However, late in September 1944, Donny wrote to Gunner suggesting that they needed to discuss Ponte. It seems that he and other partisan units had attempted to 'bounce' the garrison out of the town, but had been unsuccessful, as one Italian partisan commander later explained:

> I personally took part in two military actions alongside Captain Mak, although I formed part of a different unit at the time. The first was in September 1944 against the Nazi/Fascist garrison at Ponte dell'Olio: unfortunately our action did not have a positive outcome, owing to the superior numbers of the enemy, and we were forced to withdraw.[1]

However, the garrison was in dire straits, and the inhabitants of Ponte were suffering as a result: none of the infrastructure was in working order, as the government did not want to provide anything from which the partisans might get a benefit; and there was a great shortage of food (the garrison had been reduced to living on pasta and chick-peas). It was too uncomfortable for them to remain in Ponte, but they were scared to leave: they were sure that the local peasants would massacre them. The partisans, they knew, had comfortable, safe prisoner-of-war camps in the hills. They had once again offered Donny their surrender, which he had refused thus far.

Gunner remembered the gist of Donny's letter:

> "I want to see you urgently. Would you come over to us, and go and pick up old Canzi on the way. I think we've reached the stage here where we've got to make a major decision: whether we take Ponte or not. Ponte is ripe for the taking – it'll be no problem at all. There are about forty to fifty *Repubblichini* in there, and they have no fight in them whatsoever. They are not a threat to Val Nure; they're not going to come out and capure Bettola or anything. There they are staying. But we've got to make a decision. Ponte gets in the way at the moment, because I have to keep it isolated. It's wasting man-power which we should be using for what we're really doing."

"What we're really doing" was raiding the Via Emilia and German communications, a role at which partisans could be most successful. It is interesting that Donny did not see the liberation of the Val Nure as an end in itself, but as a means to supporting the main Allied war effort further south. His letter continued:

> "We could take Ponte quite easily; no problem. But I can't do it entirely alone with just my *squadra* – I want your help, because I'll need extra people to arrest, disarm and take the garrison prisoner. When you and Canzi come over, we'll look at the problem and decide what we should do. I think that we'll have to take it, and we'll plan how we're going to do it. Once we've taken Ponte, it will become Canzi's problem, not mine any more."

Gunner collected Canzi and headed over to Ponte. The garrison was cooped up in its barracks in the town centre, which had been fortified, and the partisans were able to move fairly freely within the town itself, as well as beyond it towards Piacenza. Gunner had already made an excursion to the old camp at Veano, less than two miles away from Ponte. It was deserted, his tunnel just as he had left it, and he pocketed photographs of the tunnel which he found in the commandant's desk drawers. He had also visited the Osti family, who had first given him and Donny shelter. But now it was time to discuss the fate of Ponte itself.

> We went over to a hotel in a little village just beyond Ponte and discussed it all.
> If we took Ponte, it would force decisions on us. The person we were worried about was the Prefect of Piacenza. The key man was Canzi, who would have to run Ponte; he said that he might be able to arm some people and have a Home Guard there, but that he would have to ask Donny and me to give up some good solid partisans to form its nucleus. If we took the place, we had between us enough partisans that we could form a small force to protect it. But that could only be done by weakening Donny's *squadra* and my own.

In the end, the three men decided to capture the town, and to set up a farmers' market there which would enable the people of the plain to buy produce from the mountains.

* * *

Typically, even now Canzi was having difficulty controlling the various partisan groups under his nominal command, especially since so many different shades on the political spectrum were represented. In a letter dated October 4th 1944, the day on which Donny and Gunner were attacking Ponte, Canzi wrote to one of the officers in his area as follows:

> Distinguished Colonel di Brune,
> Captain Gregg has spoken to me on your behalf, passing on some rumours about alleged negligence on the part of this Headquarters regarding requests for air-drops.
> First of all I must tell you that this report cannot be anything other than unfounded. We have had and we still have need of weapons; it would have been therefore illogical and against our interests not to consider asking for them from those who can send them. As proof of our action we have sent, for your inpection, some statistics relating to this Zone, concerning the air-drops which we have agreed, transmitted and had approved by the Allies.
> The groundless and false report which is doing the rounds makes me think that there might be someone who, for personal or political reasons, is trying to discredit this Headquarters. Perhaps I am not wrong in thinking that one of those involved could be a certain Major of *Alpini* who answers to the name of Faggioli; in fact, I have information that the above-named Major has expressed this opinion. While I have refrained from any action against him for his dishonourable behaviour, or against anyone attempting to continue to act in so dishonourable a fashion, I authorize you, if you think that I am right, to pass on my opinions to his face.
> Yours sincerely,
> Long Live Free Italy!!
> Commander Ezio Franchi[2]

Under such circumstances, a successful outcome at Ponte was in Canzi's interests as well.

Canzi tried his best to co-ordinate efforts to take the town, and wrote to Fausto, commanding the *Giustizia e Libertà* Division:

> Dear Fausto,
> I am informed that Rivergaro has been cleared of Fascists. I request that you order your men to occupy the area. That will secure the flank of our line.
> On Sunday we surrounded Ponte dell'Olio. The Fascists received reinforcements of a hundred men, two 45mm mortars, an 81mm mortar, and several armoured cars with heavy machine-guns. Since we are short of ammunition, we therefore feel the need to know which of your men are in the area and prepared to come to our assistance.
> I await your reassurance. Best wishes,
> Your friend Emilio,
> Ezio Franchi[3]

Not all of Fausto's subordinates, however, were prepared to move: Paolo, for example, felt that to abandon his positions to assist at Ponte would be too much of a risk.

> HQ III Brigade, to HQ *Giustizia e Libertà* Division
> ...since the messenger was waiting for an immediate report I have informed the *Comando Unico* that in the area above Rivergaro in dispersed positions are four heavy automatic weapons, which I have sited, among others, to prevent the enemy from making use of the road from Rivergaro to Ponte dell'Olio, stretching from Rivergaro to Bassano.
> We would have followed up with a detailed report of our dispositions had we been sure of the intentions of the Germans who recently arrived at Bobbio. I have assured the *Comando Unico* that we will do our best to give effective assistance and I have informed them that there is daily contact between our patrols and those from the Val Nure.
> Dated October 3rd 1944 (1615 hours).
> Brigade Commander
> Paolo[4]

Gunner's own *squadra* was in position above Perino in the Val Trebbia, protecting the northern approach to Bettola, and if it was to contribute to Donny's attack at Ponte had to be replaced. Canzi asked Fausto to ensure that other units moved in to replace it:

> To the HQ of 2nd *Giustizia e Libertà* Division
> Dear Fausto,
> Please would you take action to ensure that Perino and its area, currently garrisoned by Ganna's detachment of the *Stella Rossa* Brigade, is taken over by a unit of a brigade under your command.
> As soon as your unit arrives, Ganna's detachment will move immediately.
> Commanding Officer,
> Ezio Franchi[5]

Gunner and his *squadra* moved in the expectation that Canzi's request would be honoured, but the promised replacements did not in fact take their place:

> **Transfer of Various Detachments**
> Although I made a promise to Commander Fausto and although agreement was reached with Paolo concerning the transfer for a concerted effort, at the moment it is impossible for me to effect such a move. This is for various reasons which I explained to Commander Fausto on one of the days during my visit.
> Commander Ganna came to this Headquarters during my absence and explained to Lieutenant Pino his intention to move into the Val Nure. He got confirmation from Pino himself that I would guard the area currently held by him. This was in accordance with my own wishes and I believe also those of the Divisional Command.
> It is indeed true that the *Alpini* may stay in Bobbio if kept under siege, but if you allow them, as yesterday, to carry out actions which are risky for them but which tend to undermine the security of

the Division, then the area guarded by my unit will remain under direct threat from them, on the right side of the River Trebbia.

It is my intention and duty to hold the area from San Salvatore down to the lower Val Trebbia opposite Travo: I would like to keep command of the two detachments which Paolo left uncommitted, as I do not have sufficient troops.

I will provide a clearer picture of my dispositions and, as I said, I will do that in person.

In recent days many of my misfits and those who went off with the American have returned once again to my Brigade.

Long live Free Italy.

Political Commissar   Commander 4 Brigade
Candiani   Virgilio[6]

* * *

The Battle of Ponte dell'Olio between October 3rd and 5th 1944 will never feature in any list of the decisive battles of history: it was short, noisy, and almost entirely bloodless. Modern Italian sources are almost wholly unreliable on the action; one account, the romantically-titled *Ballad of Mac and the Iron Monster,* Gunner viewed as "poppycock". (Appendix C contains a partial translation of this work of fantasy: it actually states that Gunner left for Allied territory just before the battle, which is demonstrably untrue – yet the story contains a touching scene of farewell between the two men. Given such a fundamental inaccuracy, it is hard to take the rest of it at all seriously.)

In particular, the Italians claim that the battle was fought by huge forces of partisans of all denominations:

> The detachments of *Garibaldini* were positioned to the rear of the town, on the hills which overlooked it from the east. For their part, the *Stella Rossa* and *Mazzini* brigades were to the front of Ponte dell'Olio. Mac led the *Stella Rossa* Brigade; the *Mazzini* Brigade was under the command of "Pippo" Panni. The two detachments of *Garibaldini* were commanded by Fra Diavolo.
>
> The Fascists – surrounded, and barricaded into their barracks and the primary school – numbered slightly fewer than eighty, but were well armed with automatic weapons. There were about five hundred partisans: Communists, Democrats, Socialists, Actionists, Anarchists, and Monarchists, all united by their desire to fight the Fascists.[7]

Gunner dismissed such claims as wholly untrue, stating that the only units involved were his own and Donny's, a total of fewer than a hundred men.

> I had about forty or fifty men with me; Donny had about the same, perhaps fewer. I had to send some three or four men off to secure where we were going to spend the night. We were going to capture and disarm the enemy and move them off to a village which we used for our prisoners.

The reason for the discrepancy is simple: Communist propaganda.

> The Communists built up into something rather special. The Communist papers were saying "The people are rising! They are destroying the Fascists! The Communist Party has led the attack!" A load of bloody rubbish. Absolute nonsense. They did nothing. But every commander of every semi-fictitious 'brigade' wanted to claim some of the credit for the capture of Ponte.

With only a hundred or so men, but confident that they could take Ponte with ease, Gunner and Donny set out for their last battle.

> I upped sticks and left seven men – one of my battle-groups – to look after the road down into the Val Trebbia, just so we weren't surprised. We went over; Canzi joined us; and we made our attack, coming in from all angles.

The two British-led units carried out a pincer attack: Donny came in from the north and east, and Gunner from the south-west. There was a good deal of gun-fire, mostly inaccurate blazing away by the terrified *Repubblichini,* who then surrendered.

> Like most of these sort of 'armies', there was a tremendous amount of firing, but it never came to actually fighting. They don't do that. But there was an awful lot of wild shooting. The *Repubblichini* weren't military in any meaningful way; they were just absolutely lost. The outcome was that we took it; it was a walk-over. Proof that there was no proper fighting – there was not a single casualty. Donny didn't have a single casualty; I didn't; the bloody *Repubblichini* didn't. There was only one person who was hit, probably by a bullet fired by one of the garrison: a boy of fourteen. The only one.

Bizarrely, the boy was treated by a doctor from the nearby German airfield at San Damiani:

> That is absolutely true. He was put in a car, and they took him to a German medical unit down near the Via Emilia. It wasn't life-threatening or anything, but he had a bullet in him somewhere or other. The only bit of blood which was spilt in this tremendous 'battle'.

In fact, although Gunner insisted that the boy was the only casualty, there had been one other, though he made light of it:

> I wasn't really wounded, not properly. Most of the fire was going up in the air, but something flying around hit me in the right hand, and you can see the pit in my palm just at the base of my little finger. Thank God it hit between the bones because otherwise it might have smashed them. I thought at first that it had gone right through, but it hadn't – so it probably wasn't a bullet, maybe a ricochet or a stone. I suppose I was wounded, but only slightly. Nothing compared to the other times. It didn't need any treatment, though we may have put a dressing on it – it did produce a hell of a lot of blood. I bleed well. But I was walking around normally.

However easy it had been, the capture of the town gave the partisans "a wonderful feeling of success", as is evident in a photograph of Gunner's *squadra* taken immediately after the attack.

Below: *the triumphant* Squadra di Ganna *after the fall of Ponte: Gunner is at centre with upraised hands. At right wearing a beret is another British soldier known as Rolando (Gregg collection).*

That night we had a party – lots of singing and dancing, plus plenty of *vino* and cognac.

The capture of Ponte had another most welcome sequel, since the Germans evacuated the airfield, as Gunner later reported to SOE:

After the capture of Ponte dell'Olio, the nearby airport of San Damiani fell into our hands. This airport is one of the biggest in northern Italy. However, it had been demolished by the Germans and it would require much work to clear a strip. We found four thousand bottles of rum and brandy bricked up in one room.[8]

Gunner and Donny now positioned their men to beat off any counter-attack which might be made: again, Gunner took the west, watching the road and river, and Donny the north and east. Attack was, as usual, most likely from the north. Canzi, meanwhile, set up his civilian administration in Ponte itself. He was immensely pleased with the success of the operation to take Ponte:

To HQs: 2nd Giustizia e Liberta Division
38th Garibaldi Assault Brigade
60th Garibaldi Assault Brigade
61st Garibaldi Assault Brigade
and, for information, to:
CLN Piacenza
CAI & HQ Delegation Em. Sett.

Subject: Liberation of Ponte dell'Olio

The liberation of Ponte dell'Olio took the form of an important military operation.
    The Fascist garrison, a force which normally numbered about a hundred men, armed with one mortar, and quite a lot of light and heavy machine-guns, enjoying the advantage of very favourable ground, were well entrenched in a fortified village house. Every day armoured cars came up from Piacenza and added their support to the fire of the defenders.
    Our very warmest congratulations therefore to the men of the *Stella Rossa* and *Giuseppe Mazzini* brigades, who, during six days of siege, in the mud, undergoing rain and enemy fire, forced the garrison to yield, capturing the entire force.
    This headquarters wishes to pass on to these two courageous units all the admiration and thanks of the anti-Fascist population of our province.

Political Commissar   Commander
Savio   Ezio Franchi[9]

* * *

The early signs were propitious, but the fall of Ponte had provoked a reaction. The Germans were not interested, but the Fascist authorities in Piacenza had felt the blow to their prestige most acutely. They scraped together what forces they could to make a reconnaissance – their credibility among the populace, low as it was, would only suffer if they let this setback pass without some visible action. The Prefect of Piacenza, a man called Graziani, decided to make a retaliatory attack.

Early in the morning of October 6th, whilst Gunner remained in position on the road, Donny decided to conduct a reconnaissance of his own, moving north across the river to make sure that the enemy were not in the area. He set out along the eastern bank of the Nure down-stream from Ponte dell'Olio with two companions, partisans called Giuseppe Carini (a native of Ponte) and Pietro Merli (from S. Giorgio Piacentino). Reconnaissance patrols are always small, relying on stealth rather than fire-power. Their movements that morning were covered by thick mist.

According to Gunner's recollection of events, Donny then made to cross the river over one of the wide banks of stones and rubble which punctuated the channel, near the hamlet of Vigolzone. But as he, Carini and Merli reached the half-way point, the mist lifted, leaving the men vulnerable at just the wrong moment.

> In the letter which Donny had sent me, he had said "We must watch out for the reaction of the Prefect of Piacenza". In point of fact that's exactly the people that shot Donny. By a most unfortunate freak coincidence, the Prefect of Piacenza had come out, guarded by some armoured cars and lorries loaded with soldiers. They'd come round the road on the western bank of the river, which was about thirty or forty feet above the level of the river: and when the mist rose, poor Donny and his two men were exposed, right in the middle – just bare rocks. They couldn't get away and didn't have a chance to put up a fight. There they were killed by machine-gun fire from an armoured car.

Donny was two weeks short of his thirtieth birthday. Across the valley, the sound of the shots echoed in the still morning air, reaching Gunner as he and his men relaxed in the afterglow of their victory.

> I was the other side of Ponte. Suddenly we heard this firing going on, and we rushed across to that side, and I saw the three bodies on the rocks. The Prefect and the *Fascisti* and the armoured car had gone; there was nothing there at all. I asked the local villagers what had happened, and they said "Oh, the Prefect got us together and made us a speech, saying that this was going to happen to all the partisans. And then he pushed off in a hurry back to Piacenza."
>
> Donny was dead. There was not a question of him being wounded. I picked up Donny, and I carried him to that single-track railway, and we took him up to Bettola on a trolley-car. A doctor looked at him, but he was dead.

Gunner had lost friends at Calais, in Greece and in the desert; he was no stranger to death and the horror of war. In the years since the end of the war he has lost some of his nearest and dearest friends and relations – yet he still describes Donny's death as

> the saddest moment of my life.

* * *

To confirm Donny's death for the authorities, Gunner took a photograph of his dead friend, which he kept. His collection also included a drawing made at the time:

> I had a partisan called Neri who drew a picture of him in death. I had a lot of trouble later trying to decide whether to show that to Donny's mother – which I didn't.

Although the author possesses copies of both, it seems best not to publish the photograph.

* * *

There was more cause for sorrow. Two other partisans, Giuseppe Magnaschi (from Carpaneto) and Sergio Gasperini (from the Friuli region) had also been surprised by the Fascists at Vigolzone whilst they had been preparing a corn distribution there. They too had been killed.

In Bettola, Donny and his four partisans received burials fit for the heroes that they were. First, their bodies lay on public display for people to pay their respects:

> Donny lay in state in the church in Bettola for a couple of days, and the whole population of the valley walked past him. Thousands, thousands of people.

Above: *Donny Mackenzie in death, as drawn by local artist and partisan "Neri", and labelled "Bettola, Sett 1944": "Sett", short for September, must be an error in the stress of the moment (Gregg collection).*

On October 8th came the funeral service in the church of Bettola itself, before Gunner and his comrades carried Donny's coffin in procession through the town, Gunner dressed in his best battle-dress and RTR beret. Donny and his partisans were laid to rest in graves set into the high walls of the enclosed cemetery of San Bernadino in Bettola.

> Concerning the death of Captain Mak I can state the following. He died a hero alongside two patriots, Merli and Carini, in an ambush carried out by the enemy near Ponte dell'Olio, and if I am not mistaken it was on October 7th 1944. His remains were taken to Bettola, placed in a larchwood coffin, and interred in a grave in the cemetery of S. Bernardino together with his other fallen comrades.[10]

> All the people and the Mayor arranged the funeral. The word got around, and everyone turned out, from all the villages in the valley. There were thousands if not tens of thousands of people. The women were all crying, loads of the men were crying – and I was crying too.
>
> We had the church service first of all. It was a Catholic service, and the bells tolled the whole time that day, and there was a lot of incense. Then we had this procession, which went on a mile, and went right the way through the town and ended up at the cemetery. I was the first person on Donny's coffin, and I had two men behind me and there were three on the other side. They were Donny's partisans. Then we had the interment, and there was a lot more chanting from the priest. Needless to say, it was Hell – a very sad moment for me.

An extraordinary sequence of photographs shows the huge turnout at the ceremonies which were conducted, and bear witness to the popularity which Donny had enjoyed and the grief which his death brought to the inhabitants of the Val Nure. The author makes no apology for reproducing them all here.

The fact that such a funeral could be held, freely and without fear of interruption from the enemy, shows just how much Donny and Gunner had achieved.

> All the valley had the freedom to turn up for that funeral, because they had our protection. No wonder we were popular. They trusted us. Mind you, if they'd had Communists running the thing it would have been different, more political. We weren't a bit political. We were purely fighters to protect them. That was our job – to save them from occupation, to save the men from being sent off to Germany or Russia and the women to the brothels or whatever. They knew that, and they know that still today.

Below: *mourners in their thousands queue in the main market square of Bettola (Piazza Colombo) to pay their respects to Donny and his comrades, who were lying in state in the church of San Giovanni. Today the trees are taller, but the statue in the right foreground still stands: it commemorates Christopher Columbus, whom local legend claims as a son of Bettola. The striped campanile at extreme right already bore the appropriate inscription AI CADUTI DELLA VALNURE ("To the Fallen of the Nure Valley"). The half of Bettola on the west bank of the Nure is known as San Giovanni, and the eastern half as San Bernadino (Gregg collection).*

Above: *the funeral procession prepares to move off from Piazza Colombo, with a guard of honour of armed partisans. That such a gathering could take place openly in 'occupied' Italy is testament to the achievements of Donny, Gunner and their comrades (Gregg collection).*

Below: *from San Giovanni, the funeral procession crossed the river to the eastern half of town, for a burial ceremony in the San Bernadino cemetery (Gregg collection).*

Above: the funeral cortege is here seen just after having crossed the bridge over the Nure. From there it moved north-east along what is now the SS654 Via Vittoria (Gregg collection).

Below: although the church of San Bernadino is only just across the river, on the Via Europa, the burial ground is over half a kilometre away. Here the funeral procession turns east from the Via Vittoria towards the cemetery: the campanile of San Bernadino is just visible in the centre background. To the left of the figure in the light-coloured coat in the foreground is Montenegrino, almost obscuring Gunner, whose RTR beret is just visible (Gregg collection).

227

Above: the rest of the procession following behind: the campanile of San Bernadino can be seen more clearly in this shot. The whole area is much more built up now (Gregg collection).

Below: for the final stretch of Donny's journey to his grave, Gunner took over part of the burden of his coffin (Gregg collection).

Above: *behind Donny followed the coffins of the four Italian partisans who were also being buried that day (Gregg collection).*

Below: *the cemetery is little changed (though the main arch with the crucifix here has been knocked through), and some of the grave-stones visible here can be picked out by a modern visitor. As can be seen, it was standing-room only for the ceremony (Gregg collection).*

Above: *the prominence of the priests in all these photographs shows how little impact Communism had really made on the hearts of the Italians. Here, the priest without a hat at top left is Don Giovanni Bruschi, chaplain to the partisans: to his left, with a moustache, is Emilio Canzi (Gregg collection).*

Below: *second left is Montenegrino; bearded to his right is "Aquila Nera" (Pietro Inzani); partly obscured by the priest's hand is Emilio Canzi; the priest is Don Giovanni Bruschi; and furthest right is Lorenzo Marzani, known as "Isabella" (Gregg collection).*

In tribute to Donny – Capitano Mak – a local writer penned the following poem, which survives in the partisan achives in Milan.

> You have dyed my land with your blood,
> Alongside my brothers, and for the same ideal.
> Even death has seen you victorious.
> With your bright eyes open to eternity,
> With your proud face simple and serene,
> You passed us that last time
> Just as you did every day, my fair Captain.
> "Forward!" the partisans shouted,
> Holding their weapons ready for battle,
> Battle in which they saw you leading bravely;
> "Forward!" with your example and in your name.
> You still have two comrades with you,
> And the grieving people saluted
> A good soldier from far away,
> Just and loyal: "Farewell, our brother;
> You have brought great honour to your country!"
> My people will always come to your tomb
> Bringing a wild flower and a prayer;
> Mothers will come to bring a lament
> On your own mother's behalf, with the same love.[11]

Chapter Sixteen
Farewell Val Nure

Donny's death left more than a personal vacuum for Gunner; it left the *Squadra di Mac* leaderless and demoralized, and Gunner now the sole British officer in the Val Nure. The immediate problem of leadership could be solved – Gianmaria Molinari, one of the original six Italian partisans of the Ferriere raid, who had been acting as Donny's second-in-command, now took over the unit. The partisans had reached the edge of the lowlands south of Piacenza, and were in a position to do real harm to Axis forces there and along the Via Emilia. But the real question remained: what next?

Part of the problem lay in the Allied plans for the Italian campaign. The push north from Monte Cassino in May 1944 had resulted in the fall of Rome on June 4th, and there had been high hopes of a speedy advance to the Alps. On June 7th, the Allied commander, General Alexander, had issued a proclamation to the partisans in the north, ordering them to prepare for the final battle of liberation. But the Germans had managed to stabilize the front in the Apennines, on the Gothic Line. As the Allied advance ground to a halt, the role of the partisans was re-assessed. On November 13th, Alexander made a radio broadcast stating that partisans should scale back their activities and go to ground until the spring.

> The following directive has been issued by the Allied High Command to all partisan formations in northern Italy... During the coming months, winter conditions and the shortage of supplies will in many areas enforce a reduction in offensive activity by the partisans. The maximum effort must be made to use sparingly all present and future stores. Offensive operations should normally be limited to ambushes and sabotage, and true guerilla tactics must be adhered to.[1]

It was an error of judgement, opposed by SOE on the grounds that it showed a fundamental misunderstanding of how partisans operated. Alexander may have been trying to save the partisans useless losses and hardship, but his remarks actually had the opposite effect. Now that the Germans knew that the front line was safe until spring, they could deploy spare combat units for the task of crushing the partisans once and for all.

* * *

Although the official advice was that the partisans should go into hibernation, various Allied organizations which had dealings with them were stepping up their activities in order to ensure that the partisans were ready to play their part in battles to come. By the autumn of 1944, official Allied missions were becoming increasingly active in the Val Nure area, including American ones, as Gunner recorded in a report to SOE later that year:

> Roberto, [an] Italian parachute Lieutenant sent in by OSS... has collected a small squad of about fifteen armed men, among them Gunner Ronald J. Riches (64th Medium Regiment RA; 90 Dunscombe Road, Upper Holloway, London N19), an escaped British POW... who is doing very good work indeed.
>
> In the middle of October, Roberto reported to me in Bettola and said he had received orders to work in my area. I sent him over to the area of Bore and asked Giovanni the Slav to give him a car, a house, rations and every assistance in getting information...

Comando Unico used to send to Roberto their intelligence reports, and I have proof that he never transmitted a single fact until he had sent one of his own men to verify it.

Roberto is a very keen soldier, and while he was in my area he worked very hard, being as enthusiastic for the partisan cause as he was in collecting military information. The partisans had a very high opinion of Roberto and his Mission.[2]

Gunner was in contact with the headquarters of No.1 Special Force through the Blundell Violet mission run by Gordon Lett, though he did not visit the transmitter in person, sending instead his runner, Tony Bosci:

At the beginning of October, the radio of this mission was put at my disposal. It is situated at Albareto (near Borgo Val di Taro), and from Bettola it requires a seventy-five kilometre car ride and then a seven hour walk. This made it very difficult for me to use efficiently.[3]

The radio station of the Blundell mission was manned by "Alfonso", whose real name was Giacinto Lazzari. He and his assistant had reached Lett's mission in July 1944, and had been hidden in Albareto so as to prevent the feuding political factions of the Rossano area from taking over the radios. Their sets worked well without interruption until they broke down shortly before Christmas 1944.

Alfonso and his operator Bianchi were very hard-working and keen on their job. He got on very well with the partisans, and Canzi always had a very high opinion of his capabilities.[4]

Lett's own report for SOE records that Gunner paid a visit to the Rossano headquarters of Operation Blundell Violet on October 12th, in the aftermath of Donny's death:

Captain Gregg arrived from Piacenza area [and] requested to be put in touch with base as various missions in his area had failed to make contact.[5]

* * *

As we have seen, Franco Pareti had been active in helping Allied evaders to reach Switzerland, and he was not the only Italian who gave succour to Allied evaders:

The population in the mountains are almost 100% anti-Fascist and pro-Ally. They do anything in their power to help escaped British or American POWs. *Tenente* Franco Pareti of Bettola himself guided forty-two ex-POWs across the Po valley, past Milan and on to Switzerland.[6]

But as well as such unofficial escape lines, the organization known as 'A' Force was specifically tasked with aiding the evasion of downed aircrew and escaped prisoners back to Allied territory. 'A' Force (or IS9) was an off-shoot of the famous MI9, and it was active in the mountains of Italy during 1944. As well as liberating territory, Donny and Gunner had been helping 'A' Force to run an extremely efficient escape route which escorted Allied personnel southwards over Monte Carrara. Along this route at least 126 aircrew, mainly Americans, were escorted through the Val Nure and back to Allied territory between September and November 1944 alone. An Italian source makes it clear that this success was mostly Gunner's work:

After Mak's recovery, if Ganna settled at all it was at Villanova for some time, until he stationed himself at Bettola. Tall, fair, of distinguished bearing, he grabbed people's attention and there were many who offered him hospitality, all people worthy of respect – such as Nicola Cantu, Antonio Bosi, Signor Slavieri, and others. But he decided to set up his headquarters in the house of Signora Baio, who had been left on her own after the deportation of her menfolk, believing that he would find greater peace and quiet there.

Ganna commanded a fighting unit, but dedicated himself almost exclusively to the repatriation of Allied prisoners-of-war. He repeatedly hosted all the partisan leaders of the Piacenza area: Prati, Fausto, Istriano, Montenegrino, Giovanni the Slav, Clini ("Falstaff"), Patrignani ("Bandiera"), and got on well with them. Then one day, not far from Bettola, there landed a small aircraft, piloted by a Sardinian Captain, on a mission tasked with communicating with Ganna about the transportation of Anglo-American evaders out of the confines of occupied Italy. From that day, Allied prisoners continually flowed into the Baio house, for whom Ganna gradually arranged passage of the lines by means of guides. He then passed through the lines successfully himself and managed to get home safe and sound.[7]

The branch of 'A' Force nearest to Donny and Gunner was based at Bardi, to the east of the Val Nure; it was code-named "Vermouth".[8] The Val Nure partisans were essential to 'A' Force's escape line, because they had plenty of food and good transport. Just the repatriation of these skilled aircrew would have been a vital enough contribution to the Allied war effort, even without the partisans' other activities. Since Donny had been busy at the northern end of the Val Nure, most of the burden of running the partisans' contribution to the escape line had fallen on Gunner.

> I worked in very close touch with this mission, in that I used to send out partisan patrols to contact British and American escaped POWs or pilots. These parties, in all about seventy British and Americans, were collected at Bettola, where they were fed and accommodated at the expense of the *Comando Unico*, and then given transport on to Bardi. All the other members of the mission were very hard-working, and since September 1944 have sent through the line over 130 ex-POWs and pilots.[9]

One of the aircrew who passed through Gunner's hands was called Schaeffer, of the fountain-pen family; he gave Gunner his watch in gratitude.

A flavour of the experiences of the aircrew who passed through Val Nure at the time can be gained from one de-briefing report, dated November 11th 1944:

> On July 23rd 1944, source [1st Lieutenant Harry R. Ernst, 348 Squadron, 99th Bombardment Group] was piloting a B-17 on a mission to bomb a tank factory in the Milan area. About two hours from base, fourteen miles north of Genoa, No.1 engine developed a runaway prop and caught fire. The propeller would not feather. After a few minutes No.2 engine overheated and started throwing oil. The ship was losing altitude rapidly. So over the area, forty miles N of Genoa, bombs were salvoed and the plane headed for base. Over the Adriatic [*sic* – actually the Ligurian Sea], in the Genoa area, No.1 engine caught fire. Source turned inland and over the Carrosio area (44° 40'N – 40° 43'E) ordered the crew to bail out. All 'chutes opened. Source, who was last man out, landed "west of Carrosio", injuring his knee, and made straight for the woods. Source had been fired at from Carrosio with small arms on his way down, so realized he had been spotted...
>
> While in the woods, source was contacted by an Italian peasant who collected food from a nearby village and exchanged source's flying jacket for civilian clothes which he put over his own. Another civilian arrived and took source to a nearby village where he spent the night in a barn. On July 24th 1944 source and his Italian companion traveled by train to a house in Genoa, where source stayed for three weeks, never even going outside the house. While at Genoa, the Italian contacted other Italians (believed to be working with American Forces) who arranged another hiding place for source in Pedemonte. On about August 14th 1944, source cycled with his Italian helper from Genoa to the outskirts of Pedemonte (44° 30'N – 8° 55'E) where they left the cycles and walked to a hut in the mountains. Here source lived for about six to seven weeks with an Italian family. By this time, source's helper had got into some trouble with the Fascists, so about October 1st 1944 he took source to a partisan house in Pedemonte. From there, he was taken north by partisans to the area of N. Antola (44° 46'N – 9° 10'E) where he joined a small partisan band who gave him news of an American parachute troop in the area. Source traveled to the vicinity of Pradello (44° 46'N – 9° 30'E), reached middle October 1944. Contacted the American paratroopers and also 1st Lieutenant John W. Martin, 1st Lieutenant Vincent J. Bracha, and 2nd Lieutenant Curtis L. Willis. All American pilots of the 12th Air Force.[10]

Pradello lies some two miles west of Bettola, and thus the four American pilots were now in the Val Nure, safe in the territory controlled by Gunner and his partisans. The American paratroopers mentioned were probably the men of OSS Mission "Walla Walla" – of whom more will be said later.

> While with the paratroopers, they obtained instructions on the radio to enable the airmen to escape...About October 22nd 1944, source, a British soldier (Private E. Joyce) and his three American companions traveled south to the area of Bardi (44° 36'N – 9° 43'E) where they contacted a South African Sergeant working with a British escape organization [Sergeant Fick of "Vermouth"]. Here source and his party was joined by 2nd Lt J.N. Girling (USAAF), Petty Officer Joseph Cahalone (HMS Submarine *Sahib*), and Sapper Robert Bexley (Royal Engineers). At this point, Private Joyce decided he would not attempt to reach Allied lines himself and returned to the American paratroopers near Pradello. Source and his companions, together with 1st Lieutenant John W. Martin, 1st Lieutenant Vincent J. Bracha, and 2nd Lieutenant Curtis L. Willis, traveled along an arranged route as far as Aulla (44° 10'N – ?° 10'E), reached 2/3 November 1944. From here the official guide left and the party traveled from one partisan group to another until they reached Raggio (44° 8'N – 10° 19'E) on morning of November 5th 1944. Here they were joined by an American and partisan patrol of about fifteen men under American Lieutenant McCory. The whole party climbed Monte Altissimo (44° 1'N – 10° 12'E) (November 7th) with a shepherd as a guide, to the Giardino Valley (where the shepherd left them). Thence to Rudsina (43° 58'N – 10° 15'E) reached morning of November 7th 1944. Here they contacted 92nd American Division. The American and partisan patrol went to their headquarters at Forte Dei Marni. The remainder of the party traveled to Vareggio, where 12th Air Force personnel left them. The two British men went to Leghorn, where source left them and came in to Bari.[11]

We know that all four American airmen mentioned in this report met Gunner as they passed through the Val Nure, and that at least one of them got on well with the young British officer: Second Lieutenant 0756775 Curtis L. "Red" Willis, of Arizona, wrote to Gunner in July 1945:

> Dear Gunner,
> You won't, perhaps, remember me very well, but I am one of the four American pilots who paid you a short visit in October 1944. They called me "Red".
> I have wondered very much what happened after we left, so would certainly appreciate hearing from you. I would like to know if the artist [perhaps the man called Neri, who sketched Donny] ever finished his book on the activities of the people there.
> It is rather hard to write anything due to military restrictions. I hope they will soon be lifted.
> The four of us fellows made out quite well after leaving you. The food was rather scarce at times, but no one had any great difficulty.
> I was the only one of the four who managed to see anyone in your behalf and I don't think I did very much good. They did tell me, however, that they sent a small plane over shortly after we left to check the situation. (I hope you can make head or tail out of what I talking about.)
> John Martin saw Lester Joyce [perhaps the Private E. Joyce mentioned in the above Escape Statement] in Naples after we had been there awhile. I was certainly glad to hear that he made out okay.
> I remember you mentioning your *fiancée*; I trust you are a happily married man by now.
> Do you find it hard to go around without a pistol in your belt and a Sten gun on your back?
> Sincerely yours,
> Curtis L. Willis ("Red")[12]

Unfortunately, this letter took a year to reach Gunner – though by the time that it did, he was indeed a "happily married man", though not to Pamela Scott, the girl he had mentioned to Willis (though he insists that he would never have referred to Pamela as his *fiancée*). By the time that Gunner was able to reply, "Red" Willis had moved on from the address given. Gunner never heard from Willis again, which always saddened him.

At the end of October 1944, Adrian Gallegos, an Anglo-Spanish operative of SOE, crossed the lines into Allied territory. Gallegos had been involved in SOE's Corsican operations but had been captured late in 1943 and, after escaping, had assisted Lett's partisans in the Rossano area. When Gunner visited Lett's mission on October 12th, he spoke at length to Gallegos, whose report to SOE soon afterwards had the following to say about the activities of Donny, Gunner and the Nure partisans:

> "Zona X" covers a large area of the hilly country to the south of Piacenza. To the west it is bounded by the Piacenza-Ottone road; its northernmost town is Ponte dell'Olio (which was captured by the partisans a short while ago), and I am not quite sure how far it extends to the east and south. There is a *Comando Unico,* at the head of which is a man by the name of Emilio Canzi. The HQ is at Bettola.
>
> Captain Mackenzie used to be the unofficial British Liaison Officer. He was killed in the Ponte dell'Olio fighting, and was succeeded by Captain Tresham Gregg. Both these officers were at one time POWs in Italy.
>
> Gregg has no W/T [radio] set, and came over to our area to send a signal requesting supplies. He asked me to give information about his area to whomsoever might be interested. Briefly, it is this:
>
> His area is very large and very rich – food, above all, is to be found in abundance. There are ten thousand partisans, eight thousand of whom are armed. He assured me that they were all very good men, but I am inclined to think that he was trying to paint too much of a rosy-coloured picture. The area includes many roads under partisan control and, in fact, he motored seventy kilometres before setting off on foot to reach us. The partisans are in control of oil wells producing 3,500 litres per day, of a wireless broadcasting station, of a newspaper, of a large model hospital, and of over a hundred lorries and cars. The Germans don't seem to bother them much, but I expect that the bother will start when the front line gets nearer to their area.
>
> Gregg is a young Irishman of the active and impetuous kind.[13]

Gunner insisted that he never claimed that there were 10,000 partisans – his *squadra* and Mac's numbered at most five hundred – and cheerfully took issue with the final sentence:

> I am Irish, but I don't think I'm impetuous.

Another SOE report of much the same date stated that Lett was exhausted and finding it hard to get hold of food, but that Gunner was in fine fettle:

> Captain Gregg is organizing the partisan movement in the area of Piacenza. He is also responsible for the landing strip at Bettola and personally leads a band of partisans believed to form part of the 21st Brigade [sic] of the *Piacenza* Division. He is enthusiastic and therefore considers his zone of highest importance. Although prone to exaggeration, he is doing good work. Living conditions very good.[14]

* * *

On November 9th, SOE Headquarters replied to Gunner's message of October 12th, and Lett forwarded their reply by courier, as he recorded in his official report:

> Alfonso left to contact Captain Gregg, Piacenza.[15]

The round trip took over a week – Alfonso returned on November 17th:

> News received at Sassetta that Alfonso had returned from the Piacenza area with messages and information from Captain Gregg for transmission to base.
>
> Squad of British ex-POWs passed through area under 'A' Force guide for front line. Included Sergeant Strachan, 3rd Coldstream Guards, with letter from Unified Command, Piacenza, and information from Genoa area (Sixth Zone).[16]

The letter referred to had been signed by Gregg and Canzi, and is also in the Blundell Violet file, though only in translation. Dated November 12th 1944, it reads:

Unified Command of the Volunteer Patriot Formations of the Province of Piacenza.
To the Allied Command.

This Unified Command of the Patriot Formations of Piacenza once more makes an appeal to the Allied Command in the hope of obtaining the indispensable aid necessary for the continuation of the struggle which for so many months has been waged with great heroism.

The Patriots of Piacenza have succeeded, almost entirely with their own means, in forming an organized and disciplined force of about ten thousand men which, with Allied help, could be doubled in a short space of time.

Three quarters of the province has been liberated.

The approach of the front line and of the winter makes urgent the despatch of light and heavy war material, munitions – of which there is a grave scarcity – and warm clothing.

The Allied Commaand has given many promises, but so far none of the them have been kept, and it is hard to understand the reason.

In the name of the people of Piacenza, whose every energy is strained to the task of throwing off the yoke of German and Fascist oppression, this Command re-affirms to the Allies its steady purpose to continue the struggle, but at the same time makes clear the absolute necessity of immediate aid.

Commander of All Formations
Franchi Ezio

Allied Representative with the Unified Command
Tresham D. Gregg
Captain, RTR[17]

* * *

Supplies of material were now beginning to reach the partisans in significant amounts, but from OSS rather than SOE:

In the middle of November, Roberto asked me to find a dropping area one kilometre by one kilometre for a mass drop of arms and ammunition. This area we found in the Muri valley above Farini D'Olmo. However, before we even had time to transmit its location, we received a message saying the planes were on their way. The planes came over at mid-day and dropped their loads in small packets, scattered all over the mountain area of the province of Piacenza. After a lot of trouble all the containers were collected, but over three-quarters of their contents were destroyed due to the parachutes not opening.

A week later we received a daylight drop at Pellizone, when 357 containers and four bodies were dropped. This drop was one hundred *per cent* successful.

On November 29th 1944, the day I left the area, Roberto was expecting another daylight drop of heavy arms.[18]

Among these "heavy arms" were the sort of weapons necessary if the partisans were to deal with enemy armour such as that which had killed Donny:

In November, four bazookas arrived by parachute. Rather than distribute one to each Brigade, I arranged that a mechanized anti-tank unit should be formed under *Comando Unico*. These four anti-tank weapons were put in two lorries and, in the event of tanks attacking any one Brigade, they were switched to the threatened area. This unit came under the direct command of the *Comando Unico*.[19]

Another OSS mission which had by now appeared in the Nure was Mission "Walla Walla". This, the first of OSS's armed missions to the partisans, consisted of two officers and thirteen men. They had parachuted on to to Monte Aiona near Genoa on the night of August 11th 1944, and spent a total of nineteen weeks behind enemy lines. The Americans had been misinformed about the situation in the area. Expecting to lead a small group of partisans into action, they had instead found themselves in a liberated zone, assisting partisans whose main needs were training and weapons. Walla Walla had busied themselves arranging supply drops, and had travelled through the Apennines investigating the possibilities for assistance to the partisans. By the time that they reached the Val Nure, they were exhausted:

> Captain Wheeler, [with] Lieutenant Smith and thirteen American GIs... is very tired and dispirited, due to the small number of drops he has been able to arrange. In November he sent a man over to me to ask if I could arrange with 'A' Force Mission "Vermouth" near Bardi to have him sent back through the front line. Captain Wheeler has since received a drop which has made him change his mind about crossing the line.[20]

More importantly, Commander Holdsworth at HQ No.1 Special Force had now decided to upgrade Gunner's area from an off-shoot of Blundell Violet to a full mission in its own right. The decision was therefore taken to send a trained SOE officer, Captain Stephen Hastings, to take over from Gunner.

* * *

Hastings' orders, dated November 25th 1944, survive in the National Archives.

> Intention: You will establish a liaison mission with partisan formations in the Piacenza area.
> Method: You will be in command of the mission consisting of yourself, Lieutenant Insom and Sergeant Scott.
> You and your party will be dropped by parachute to reception to the west of Monte Caramato (Sheet 72 Ref. 6374) on the night of 26th November 1944, or as soon after as possible. This reception is organized by the OSS mission "Nembo." The leader of this mission is named Emilio Lombardi.
> On arrival you will ask to be conducted to Captain Gregg, an escaped British POW who is at present working with the *Comando Unico,* Zona "X" (Piacenza), with HQ at Bettola (Sheet 72 Ref. 5185).
> You will explain to Captain Gregg the nature of your mission and will hand him the letter addressed to him which invites him to become a member of your mission under your command.
> Having discussed local conditions with Captain Gregg you will make contact with the *Comando Unico* of Zona "X" and explain to them that you have been sent as British liaison mission to the partisan formations in the Piacenza area, and that your mission has the support of both the Italian government in Rome and the *Comitato Liberazione Nazionale Alt'Italia.*
> When you have established your mission in a safe place you will open up W/T contact with this HQ and report on your exact location and on anything else of immediate interest.
> Your next task will be to investigate the landing ground two kms. south of Bettola (Sheet 72 Ref. 5283) and to make the necessary arrangements for the landing of a Lysander or other aircraft on this ground. When these arrangements are complete, you will signal full details to this HQ.[21]

Hastings was ordered to enforce the recent "Alexander Directive" by preventing the partisans from making any major efforts, encouraging them instead to husband their resources ready for the spring:

> Incompetents and hangers-on should, if possible, be eliminated from the bands. During the period of reduced offensive activity, emphasis should be on the building up of a reliable information service and on the organization of anti-scorch methods.[22]

"Anti-scorch" was the Allied code-name for preventing the Germans from destroying infrastructure as they retreated; partisans could and did play an important role in such precautions against German vindictiveness.

However, these operations orders were out of date, and Hastings was not parachuted in until the night of February 2nd 1945. HQ No.1 Special Force at Bari were making plans which had been overtaken by events, since Gunner and the forward Tac HQ in Florence had already been in communication. Gunner was coming home.

* * *

Tac HQ, No.1 Special Force, was run by Charles Macintosh, who had asked Gunner to see to the construction of several landing-strips in the Val Nure and Val Trebbia in preparation for increased activity there over the winter. Such airfields might be used by Dakota transport aircraft or by the much smaller Lysanders, which were only useful for ferrying personnel but had a superb short-field capability. An SOE report described one such landing-field, in the valley bottom south of Bettola (that mentioned in Hastings' orders):

> A landing strip has been constructed at Bettola under the supervision of an Italian engineer who was employed in the construction of Piacenza aerodrome. The strip lies on the east bank of the Torrente Nure. The present length of 900 yards will be increased to 1000. The strip, which runs roughly north and south, has been seen by RAF officers, who agreed that aircraft of the Lysander type can easily be used on it, but transport aircraft [only] with discretion, because of the lack of dispersal areas if a number of aircraft were employed at a time. Approach to the landing ground is difficult and has to be made in a valley on a slight curve. Strict aerodrome control would therefore be necessary. The surface is of small gravel, but its present condition after rain is not known. The hills on each side are approximately 1500 feet high.[23]

This landing strip had been cleared of large stones by prisoners-of-war. Gunner described it as follows in his own SOE report:

> We made a six hundred metre landing strip in the Nure valley above Bettola. It has a good firm runway, but a small hill to the south which makes take-off difficult. We have been working for twenty days on a 980 metre landing strip near Perino in the Val Trebbia.[24]

Macintosh told Gunner that he was sending in a Lysander carrying a new radio-operator, who would be dedicated to serving the communications needs of the Nure partisans. He ordered Gunner to board the aircraft himself and fly back to Florence to report on the situation in the Val Nure, and to discuss how the partisans could be used during the final Allied push to the Po. Macintosh also told Gunner that he had an important job lined up for him. The makeshift airfield was prepared for the reception of the aircraft.

> I received a message from Charles Macintosh that the RAF had photographed it and were prepared to make the trip on a certain day. We were ready for them with a smudge-fire and lights, but the plane never came.

Gunner was later told that the aircraft had been shot down by an American fighter, which had mistaken the Lysander for the superficially similar German Henschel 126. This story appears to be true: on November 22nd 1944, 148 Squadron Lysander III T1456 was indeed shot down in error by an American P-51 Mustang.[25]

Gunner was ordered instead to hike out through Carrara along the escape route which had been set up to aid evaders. With Gregg were to come an excellent South African, Warrant Officer "Johnny" Beukes, who had done sterling work with the partisans but now wanted to re-join his regiment,[26] as well as two outstanding Italian partisans – Franco Pareti and Toni Bosco:

Above: Gunner's comrade and trusted friend Franco Pareti, who earned the gratitude and respect of all the Allied troops whom he met and assisted. Born in Bettola on November 16th 1921, Pareti was an engineering student in Milan when he was conscripted into the Italian Army in 1941. Having served as a Lieutenant in an anti-aircraft unit, he deserted after the Armistice, taking to the hills above his native Bettola, where he assisted many Allied evaders to Switzerland (copyright holder unknown).

> Franco was a great lad; he was the best type of Italian. Charles Macintosh and I had plans for him – we thought he'd make a bloody good agent, a proper SOE agent. He had the brains, he had the courage, he had the sense: he was a leader.

The Italians were to be trained by No.1 Special Force, and it was intended that Pareti would become a fully-accredited 'A' Force agent; Toni Bosco, Gregg's courier, had volunteered to become an SOE radio-operator.

Pareti, as we have seen, had helped many of the Veano inmates to make their way to Switzerland. By January 1944, at least eighty former prisoners-of-war owed their freedom to him. But it had come at a bitter personal price: that month, his mother, uncle, aunt and cousin had all been arrested by the Fascists for assisting evaders. Pareti had rushed to Milan, where he had stayed until April, when he secured his mother's release. Returning to the Val Nure, he had joined the partisans and worked particularly closely with Gunner.

* * *

Leaving Molinari and Canzi in charge, Gunner moved off from the Val Nure on November 29th 1944. He and his companions sneaked past German patrols to make contact with the American 92nd (Negro) Division. Gunner crossed the Allied lines at Monte Altissimo, near Serravezza, on the night of December 5th-6th 1944.

> When we climbed down the cliff on the other side we began yelling to let them know that we were British – we didn't want them thinking we were Germans. "Is anyone there?" we were shouting. But

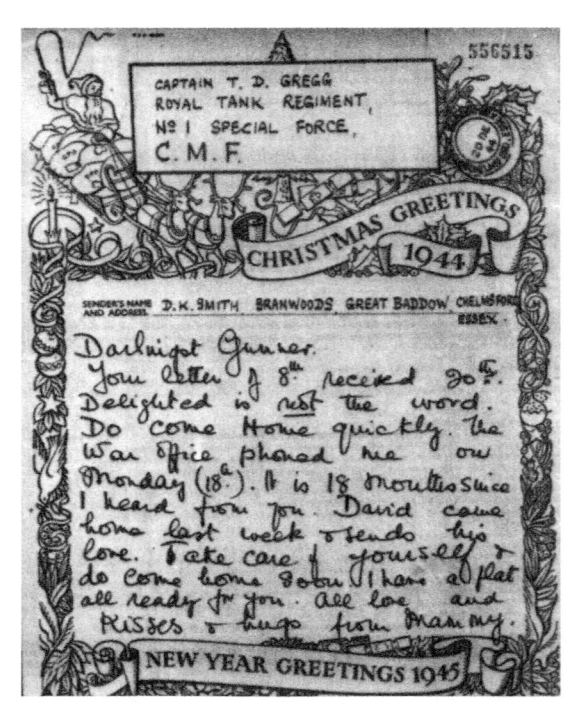

Above: the delight of Gunner's mother at knowing him to be safe and well shines through even in the short letter which she was able to send (Gregg collection).

we got no reply at all. We were exhausted, and so we leaned against a wall for shelter and had a bite to eat which we had with us. Suddenly two black faces appeared over the wall just above our heads. We said "We're British" and they replied: "You've gotta be real careful here. You's in the front line now."

Gunner remained amused at this welcome; where he was sitting seemed considerably less dangerous than what he was used to. He also used to sigh happily at the memory of the bliss of the hot shower which the Americans provided for him.

Almost Gunner's first action on reaching safety was to write to his mother. His letter was sent on December 8th, and arrived on December 20th. It was the first direct contact between mother and son in eighteen months. Gregg treasured her reply, on an armed forces Christmas aerogramme:

[To] Captain T.D. Gregg	[From] D.K. Smith
Royal Tank Regiment	Branwoods
No.1 Special Force	Great Baddow
C.M.F.	Chelmsford
	Essex

Darlingst Gunner,
Your letter of 8th received 20th. Delighted is <u>not</u> the word. Do come home quickly. The War Office phoned me on Monday (18th). It is 18 months since I heard from you. David came home last week & sends his love. Take care of yourself & do come home soon. I have a flat all ready for you. All love and kisses & hugs from Mammy.[27]

* * *

From the front line, Gregg and his companions were taken to see Macintosh in Florence; the whole party then flew to No.1 Special Force headquarters at Bari, where they arrived on December 11th. There they were to be de-briefed, and were expecting to make preparations for the final liberation of the Po valley.

Above: *Gunner's South African colleague "Johnny" Beukes, whose exploits with the partisans (see footnotes) read like something out of Hollywood (copyright holder unknown).*

> At Bari, Charles Macintosh spent several days debriefing me, and even longer discussing what the partisans' main problems were, and trying to work out what he could do to help.
>
> On one day we had a visit from several officers from Operations and Plans, who wanted to know how and to what extent our partisans could assist should it be decided that the Allies would advance north over and through the Apennines. It was soon obvious to me that these officers had little idea how partisan forces should best be used. [They asked whether we could] capture and hold a particular mountain pass for twenty-four hours, by which time the advancing British troops should have arrived.
>
> My answer was *NO*. We had neither the men, support weapons, reserves of ammunition, or training for that sort of warfare. Partisan fighting was completely different. Once our machine-gun and Sten magazines were empty we had no reserves of ammunition at all. We would either be killed or forced to run away.

Gunner was issued a temporary pass in Bari on December 14th 1944, the same date as that on his official report about the operations in the Val Nure. Gunner's report – of which we have already read extended extracts – was considered excellent, as a memorandum in the Blundell Violet file from SOE headquarters shows:

> This report is exceedingly interesting and adds one more piece to the picture being built up of partisan activity in occupied territory. Certain portions will be useful for the Foreign Office, especially those which touch on the political colour of the groups or the individuals forming the groups. The Foreign Office have got it into their heads that the only really active bands are the Communists.[28]

As a result, it was decreed that from then on all SOE reports from Italy were to include a summary of the political aspects of operations. A copy of Gunner's report itself was forwarded to the Foreign Office.

> This is to certify that Capt. T.D. Gregg R.T.R. behaved himself very well while fighting with the Partisans.
> Although he was continuously encouraged by the women he took no advantage of it.
> I hereby wish to recommend him, and in my opinion I reckon he will make a very good HUSBAND. (Although a bit slow in doing things.)
> Signed: Johnny Beukes.
> 17 Dec. 1944.

Above: an amusing note produced at SOE HQ in Bari whilst Beukes and Gunner were being de-briefed and writing their official reports (Gregg collection).

No.1 Special Force specialized in what was called "irregular warfare", and its cavalier approach had in the past got it into trouble with the bureaucrats who trailed in the wake of the Allied armies. One of the many organizations involved in the Italian campaign was the Prisoner of War Repatriation Unit, which was responsible for processing all those prisoners who made it back to Allied lines. No.1 Special Force had had its knuckles rapped on previous occasions when it had rescued prisoners from behind enemy lines and then allowed them to by-pass the usual channels in their understandable desire to return to Britain as quickly as possible. It is amusing, then, to read the following scrupulously polite letter to No.1 Special Force concerning Gunner's presence in Bari.

Captain Gregg
CSM Beukes – UDF

It is understood that the above, recently returned from EOT [enemy-occupied territory] where they have been working for Major Macintosh, will return to EOT to continue the good work they have been doing.

We shall be glad to know if it is your intention to absorb the above in your W/E [war establishment] as in the case of those mentioned in your J/2160 of 26 Nov 44 and if their position has been regularized with the P/W/ Repatriation Unit.

We hope to have the pleasure of seeing both Capt. Gregg and CSM Beukes before they return to EOT as they have much information of interest to us and we should like to arrange their interrogation by an officer of the Repatriation Unit in Bari with the knowledge that their position has been regularized.

(Illegible)
Wing Commander[29]

Gunner did indeed undergo such an interview, and was asked to fill in forms listing his war service, movements since capture, and next of kin. From these forms the authorities were also able to discover such vital information as his medical category (A1), weight – 168 pounds – and religion (Church of England). Gunner listed his spoken languages as "German (good); Italian (good); English."

* * *

Macintosh now told Gunner the real reason why he had been brought out – he was to return to London to represent Macintosh in conferences at a high level.

Some very senior member of the government (Churchill?), on hearing of the Italian partisans and their success, asked the following question:

> "If the Italian Communist partisans have been so successful, are they going to do a Tito on me? Is there any danger that they might try to emulate Tito and the Jugoslav partisans and try to take over the government by force after the war?"
>
> Charles Macintosh and I knew that there was absolutely no chance of this, but London did not. After long discussions they had decided to send for Charles, who knew more of the Italian partisans than anyone. When Charles heard this, he blew up. He explained that the war was just ending, and this could be the most critical moment, and that his knowledge was of supreme importance in ensuring that the situation did not get out of hand. Charles suggested that he could send a British officer who had long experience as the commander of a successful partisan unit. He also sent a report giving his views on the subject. Furthermore, he asked Franco Pareti to write a report on me (without my knowledge) as to why I was well-qualified to be questioned about the Italian partisans in place of Charles. Franco's report is most flattering, but remember that Charles intended it to convince London that I was well qualified to stand in for him.

Gunner was devastated; he had promised his partisans that his absence would only be temporary, and that he would come back to them to be in at the finish. Macintosh promised Gunner that should fighting begin again in northern Italy he would recall him at once, since it was possible that an Allied attack might be made along the Trebbia valley.

The question of reward now arose. Many of the officers and men who served with the Italian partisans received medals from the British government in recognition of their efforts; Gordon Lett would be awarded the DSO for doing much the same work in Rossano as Gunner and Donny had done in the Val Nure. Other former prisoners-of-war received the same award or the BEM for their services, or an MC or MM simply for their successful evasion after the armistice. Gunner felt strongly that both Donny and Franco Pareti deserved some official recognition for what they had done:

> I asked Charles if it was possible to obtain any decoration for Donny. Charles replied that since he had been killed in action, that left only the Victoria Cross – which obviously was not on.
>
> I also tried to get some award for Franco Pareti for all he did guiding so many British and Commonwealth officers to freedom. [Bob Foote later] told me that his party would never have made it to Switzerland without Franco's help. He had also tried to get Franco some British decoration, but the Foreign Office told him that it was difficult because Franco had officially been a deserter at the time – as were about 90% of the Italian army at that point.

Pareti received no award. However, 'A' Force appreciated his qualities and after he crossed the lines with Gunner he was immediately employed by them, being attached to Field Headquarters in Florence. His file in the National Archives shows that he was considered to have very good knowledge of the Lombardy and Emilia regions, good knowledge of Turin, and fairly good knowledge of Udine and the Veneto. Since he was expected to return behind enemy lines, early in 1945 he was issued with false documentation in the name of Carlo Ferrara of Bologna: a *Carta d'Identica* from the *Comune di Pesaro,* a German *Arbeiterausweis* (work-permit), and a travel permit notionally issued at Bologna on January 10th 1945 and valid until March 11th. However, the war in northern Italy took a different turn, and on May 8th 1945 Pareti was demobilized from British service and given a travel permit back to Milan: there, on June 6th, he reported to the *Servizio Informazione Segreto* (SIM, the Italian Secret Service).

* * *

Whilst gunner had been concerned to obtain recognition for others, Macintosh tried to arrange an award for Gunner himself:

> When we arrived in Bari, Charles very kindly said to me: "After eighteen months with your partisans, you deserve a DSO. I'll do my best to get you one."

Unfortunately, the war was just ending and No.1 Special Force was preparing to disband. Everything was in chaos, as was probably all their paperwork. After Charles and I had finished our discussions, he had a long talk with Franco Pareti, which I thought was to vet him. Franco told me afterwards that he was asked to write a report on me, and that he should use the word "citation". So it looks as if Charles was doing his best to keep his word to me. As I heard no more about a medal, I just chalked it up to one of the disappointments we all have to face from time to time.

Pareti's report on Gunner has survived in the SOE Blundell Violet file. It makes interesting reading, since it tells us what an experienced member of the Italian resistance thought of Gunner and his achievements. Interestingly, it does indeed begin with the word "citation", suggesting that Macintosh indeed intended it to be evidence in support of the award of a medal.

Citation

Permit me to draw to your attention the activities of Captain Gregg, a British officer in the Royal Tank Corps, subsequently a prisoner-of-war, and then a distinguished commander of partisans after his escape from the prisoner-of-war camp at Veano (Piacenza) on September 8th 1943.

I met him immediately after the Italian armistice, in the mountains around Ferriere (Piacenza), when I – a Lieutenant of anti-aircraft artillery – was a deserter from my unit and he was a fugitive from his prisoner-of-war camp. Even during those difficult days immediately after the armistice he always maintained a calm and reasonable outlook, even in the most trying of circumstances.

He was with six other former prisoners-of-war, amongst whom were two Lieutenant-Colonels, a Major, two other ranks and the late lamented Captain Mackenzie. I organized food and somewhere to sleep for them for two months until the end of October 1943. But life became ever more difficult as the Germans and Fascists reasserted their control. Captains Gregg and Mackenzie were taken into the house of a young man called Eugenio Osti, at Stoppa (near Rivergaro, Piacenza), who provided for them and sheltered them until they joined the partisans right at the start of April 1944.

I decided to send the other five, who had stayed put, to Switzerland, and that was one of the first groups of British prisoners-of-war which I took to Switzerland, where they formed part of an overall total of eighty-two whom I sent there.

Captain Gregg, on joining the partisans, adopted the nickname "Gunner" (Ganna), and, together with the late Captain Mackenzie, became one of the best partisans. He became commander of a detachment of the *Stella Rossa* Brigade, commanded by Montenegrino, and became one of the best members of the unit. In the course of many actions, he distinguished himself by his courage, daring, and disregard for his personal safety. Whenever he led his partisans in dangerous actions, he was always the first into battle and always the last out of it. The partisans themselves developed a deep love of their commander, and had so much affection for him that they would have risked their lives for him, whatever happened. He therefore selected a detachment of the best men, hand-picked by him, who would never desert him under any circumstances.

Gregg distinguished himself in quite a few actions, contributing by his intelligence to their speedy and successful outcome. He attacked German columns on the Genoa-Torriglia-Bobbio-Piacenza route, capturing equipment and MT, and taking prisoner quite a few Germans.

Gregg always worked really hard to improve the lives of his humble partisans, to make them aware of the importance of their task, and to ensure that their morale was always improving. He busied himself, towards the end of his time here, in establishing a secure link between Allied forces and the partisans. He had to seek help from other English officers nearer the front line, and established a system of communications for obtaining air-drops of equipment, weapons and clothing for the partisans. His work bore excellent fruit, in that within a few days air-drops were carried out in the Piacenza area for the units which needed them.

Gregg was a constant help to the partisans, and provided moral support for many commanders in the more troubled periods of our hard lives. Nazi and Fascist forces were conducting *rastrellamenti* practically every week, keeping the partisans in a continual state of nervous tension. He always managed to appear calm himself, thus inspiring in his partisans a feeling of confidence about the future. What impressed me in the operations which I conducted with him were the calm and intelligent daring with which he was able to bring about a favourable outcome, the courage and exuberance of his physique, his uncompromising treatment of all those who were crooks, and his honourable conduct towards the enemy. He hated dishonest people, and was ferocious towards those who used force to settle their own personal scores. In fact, he was able to stamp out every wicked tendency among his partisans, and thus managed to give a profound sense of purpose to the partisan formations of the province of Piacenza. His youth notwithstanding, he was always able to remain even-tempered in his manner, to such an extent that I often marvelled at the maturity of his mental outlook. He could see things which so many others could not, and was always able to command respect.

Because of his reliability, his courage, and the repeated examples of his bravery, right there among his partisans, where a man's potential really shows itself, I believe Captain Gregg to be one of the best officers whom I have ever met. Upright in character, he was a very good soldier, capable of explaining his activities to high command. I, along with Warrant Officer Beukes – his companions in the partisans over such a long time – believe him deserving of a high award for his bravery in battle, since he risked his own life with whole-hearted and selfless courage in pursuit of the victory of Righteousness and Justice.

Lieutenant of Artillery FRANCO PARETI, of Milan[30]

Gunner had no idea of the wording of this citation, or that it still existed, until it was drawn to his attention by the author in 2009.

* * *

In the meantime, however, Gunner found himself on a flight back to RAF Northolt, where to his surprise he was met by George Millar,

an old escaping friend of mine from Padula – the best escaper of the lot. He had become a very, very successful commander of the French Resistance in north-east France. He took me to the Cavendish Hotel, where he was staying, and I remained a guest of Rosa Lewis for a month.

The legendary Rosa Lewis – later to be immortalized by the BBC television series *The Duchess of Duke Street* – was famously kind to service personnel (often adding their bills to those of richer guests), and as a close friend of Millar's from pre-war days she made Gunner most welcome.[31]

Rosa was a wonderful person. She had been a family friend of George since he was a boy and had even escorted him to Eton for his first term. Rosa gave me a fabulous welcome at her hotel, and she said that I could stay at the Cavendish for as long as I liked – free of charge. Staying there was a fantastic experience and the greatest fun. But when they made the television series they totally miscast her; they made her a chirpy little Cockney girl and she wasn't – she was tall and so elegant, and if anyone looked like a duchess it was Rosa.

But life in London was not all pleasure:

George took me to SOE HQ in Baker Street, where for almost a month I was interviewed and cross-examined repeatedly by their senior officers. One of them was Maurice Buckmaster, the famous head of their French Section. They were very interested in how effective the Italian partisans had been, where and how they operated, and which areas they had liberated.

The government had ordered George to write his book *Maquis* to boost the reputation of the French resistance. He was writing night and day to get the book finished as quickly as possible, and I helped him with the editing there in the Cavendish.

Gunner was also summoned for two meetings in the Foreign Office, which was interested in the question of whether the Italian Communists would attempt to stage a take-over in the wake of liberation.

I met a small unofficial committee who asked me many questions. I gave them three good reasons why the Italian Communists would not emulate the Jugoslavs. They were:
1. The Italian people had had enough of being governed by a dictatorship.

2. The Italians had no natural, charismatic leader like Tito, Castro, Franco, Hitler, etc.
3. The Italians are a very religious people, and they would not want to be governed by Communists, who were atheists.

These were the same reasons given in Charles' report. As I now know, the committee also had Franco Pareti's report about me.

* * *

The question now arose of Gunner's future with SOE. He was expecting to return to Italy, but London seemed to have other ideas:

> SOE also wanted to know if, when the Allies moved against the Japanese and tried to recapture Malaya, I would be interested in going behind the lines again there. They told me that there was an arm of SOE called Force 136, operating behind the lines in Burma and northern Malaya. I was pleased that SOE were thinking ahead, and the offer was tempting. But I knew that as a regular RTR officer, my future lay in conventional fighting with my regiment, and that I should really return to regimental duty. On the other hand, I had promised my partisans that I would return and Charles had promised that he would make this happen.

In fact, the commander of No.1 Special Force, Commander Holdsworth, had sent a letter back to England urgently requesting that Gunner be returned to Italy as quickly as possible:

> The above-named officer, recently arrived at this Force from the field, is an escaped POW who has been working with this Force behind the lines since September 1943.
> Now that he has come out of the field, he will have to be evacuated to the UK through PW Repatriation Unit. We are most anxious to secure the services of this officer and have arranged for him to report on arrival to Major A.H. Flynn at Room 238, Hotel Victoria.
> May steps please be taken through London to obtain the posting of this officer to this Force as soon as he can be released from [the] War Office, and for his return to this theatre immediately after a short period of leave in the UK.
> A Medical Certificate and Certificate of Willingness duly completed by this officer are enclosed, together with full particulars as furnished by him on his arrival form, [a] copy of which is attached.[32]

Gunner made a formal application to become an official BLO with No.1 Special Force, submitting at least two different sets of forms. Amongst other things, these included spaces for his bank details, presumably so that his bank could be asked about his spending habits and potential as a security risk – though one wonders how much activity there had been on his account since December 1941.[33] There was also a space for interests and hobbies, against which Gunner wrote:

> Small boat sailing.
> Bee-keeping.
> Rugby & Athletics.

Gunner considered himself to have a working professional knowledge of wireless (able to read and transmit Morse code); a working amateur knowledge of photography; and competence in map reading, field sketching, lecturing and demonstrating, propaganda and navigation. He stated that he could ride horses and bicycles, drive cars, trucks and motorcycles, swim, sail, mountaineer, shoot and run – but that he could not ski or fly an aeroplane. To the question "For what particular war work do you think yourself best suited?", Gunner replied

> BLO to partisans, etc.

The form also asked "Are you interested in office or administrative work?", to which Gunner tactfully answered:

> For very short period for my information and experience.

On January 19th 1945, Gunner underwent his SOE interview in London, and on January 30th, he was accepted "for work in the field", according to his SOE personnel file. But no word reached Gunner of his return to Italy and the Val Nure. Gunner wrote to Macintosh:

> I reminded him that he had promised to have me flown back to Italy, No.1 Special Force and my partisans as soon as they let me go in London.

Gunner received Macintosh's reply in March. Its contents were a sad disappointment, because they gave no definite information and suggested that the process of getting Gunner back to Italy had completely stalled.

> TAC HQ, No.1 Special Force, CMF
> 2.3.45
>
> Dear Gunner,
> Thank you very much for your letter. I regret my reply has been so long delayed but I was away when it arrived. I have asked my base to help me get you back soon and I hope you will hear from us.
> We have some photographs and Oscar's address here for you, and we are always hearing from people who knew the "Gunner".
> Peter Mac and his boys are all well settled now [Colonel Peter McMullen, leading SOE Mission Clover 1 near Genoa], and we would very much like to join them as life here is rather dull.
> Please excuse this short note and hurry back here where we would very much like to see you.
> Cheers,
> Charles Macintosh[34]

In fact, on February 20th Gunner's posting to SOE had been cancelled: he was no longer required. The end of the war in Europe was in sight, and the speed of the Allied advance over the Po made it unnecessary to drop him back into the Val Nure. Furthermore, the main Allied attack was made up the east coast towards Trieste, rendering the Val Nure a backwater. When Piacenza was liberated in April 1945, however, it was by the partisans – but Gunner languished in England until the war's end, and did not witness the final triumph of what was left of his and Donny's men.

Above: *Gunner in 1945 (Gregg collection).*

Chapter Seventeen
Victory

What of the partisans whom Gunner had so unwillingly abandoned, the men whom he still calls "my partisans" and "my men"? By the time that he had left them at the end of November 1944, the partisans in the Val Nure had been undergoing re-organization:

> [The *Garibaldini* Division] previously consisted of four independent brigades under *Comando Unico* which, when I left the area, were being formed into one division named *Divisione Mack*, after Captain A.D. Mackenzie.[1]

But Gunner had not expected this reorganization to last for long. The conclusion of his SOE report, dated December 14th 1944, proved all too prescient:

> While the partisan movement in the Apennines assumed very large proportions during the summer, I believe that during the coming winter it will very nearly die out of existence. The reasons for this are:
> a. The lack of munitions, food, supplies and clothing needed to last a winter in the mountains.
> b. The very large scale operations which the Germans are carrying out and planning against areas held by partisans.
> c. The lowering of morale due to the apparently immobile state of the front line in Italy. On three occasions they have been told by British radio to rise and smite the Hun, as the day of liberation was at hand; on each occasion they attacked, but found themselves no nearer liberation.
> The partisans, I think, will split up into small bands of about thirty to fifty men.[2]

Italian partisans had already begun to be affected by the in-fighting which bedevilled the resistance in 1945 and led to it becoming, in the eyes of many, a political rather than a military force. Gunner had seen evidence of this, as he explained in the assessment of Canzi which he wrote for SOE:

> Politically, he is a democrat of the Action Party. He has been honestly trying to work for the equality of all political parties, and in doing so he has had to frustrate an attempt by Renato, *Commissario* of the 38th *Garibaldini* Brigade, to set up an organization to secure for the Communists, on the liberation of Piacenza, the control of all stores, police and all executive jobs in the administration.[3]

As if such squabbling were not enough, the winter of 1944-1945 had been a difficult time for the partisans. As the Allies waited for the spring, German forces from the front line operated freely against the partisans to their rear. On November 23rd 1944, just before Gunner's departure, a determined *rastrellamento* had begun in the Val Trebbia and Val Tidone. 162nd Turkistan Division, supported by tanks and artillery, targeted the *Giustizia e Libertà* Division. Fausto's men, outnumbered two to one and lacking the fire-power to stop the German forces, dispersed after a few days.

By the end of November 1944, German attacks on areas all around the Val Nure had caused devastation and hardship, as Gunner had seen for himself as he walked out of occupied territory:

> On my return journey along the Apennines after I had passed Bardi, the condition of the partisans and the civilians was becoming desperate, because of Germans burning the villages, carrying away the cattle and murdering or deporting the civilian population.[4]

Early in December, overwhelming German forces advanced into the Valu Nure from both sides. Canzi hoped to prevent the Germans from breaking through the mountains to Bettola, by conducting blocking actions at Coli – near Peli – and in the Cerro pass, but these were brushed aside. As a result of this German offensive, the OSS Walla Walla party changed their minds about staying put: they passed through Gordon Lett's area on December 21st 1944 and set out for Allied lines the next day. One cannot help feeling that they abandoned the Italians just when they most needed help – but there was nothing which a half-platoon of tired American soldiers could have done to stem the tide of horror which was breaking over the area.

As the Germans and Fascists entered the Val Nure, they carried out their usual atrocities, as the inhabitants later recalled:

> They burned houses in Averaldi [between Peli and Farini], and captured two lads from Sant'Angelo Lodigiano who had been dodging the draft and been hiding out there. They kicked them to death. Touching their skulls was like touching a bag of rice...They passed through my arms because we buried them here alongside the partisan Baciccia, who was killed in the fighting. All of us men slipped away until there were none left. One old man stayed behind on his own, and they butchered him. They also carried out outrages against the women. In Costiere, quite close by, there was a school-teacher and her sister. They tried to rape them both. They put up quite a fight, so they sat them on a red-hot stove.[5]

> They carried everything away – pigs, chickens, cows – and they left nothing. They left us with nothing.[6]

Gunner's successor in the Val Nure, Captain Stephen Hastings, later saw evidence of the German atrocities:

> I was shown a photograph of twenty or thirty grinning German soldiers grouped around the body of a woman they held naked and spatchcocked between them, while an NCO posed above her body with a long dagger ready to strike; another of a girl, her hands tied behind her, hanging on a meat-hook like the carcase of a pig. They had died in the *rastrellamento*.[7]

Further attacks in January 1945 forced Canzi to give the order to disperse; many of the Val Nure partisans withdrew to Parma. Canzi was suffering from pleurisy and was in hiding in Alberto Grassi's barn in Averaldi; Fausto and Prati had vanished; and Gianmaria Molinari, standing in for Donny and Gunner in command of the old *Squadra di Ganna* and *Squadra di Mac,* was captured and killed on January 5th 1945. The citation for his award of the Italian Silver Medal for bravery reads:

> Having already repeatedly distinguished himself in the partisan conflict by his leadership qualities and personal courage, in the course of a fierce engagement he daringly pushed forward into the German positions in an attempt to drag to safety a wounded partisan officer. Surrounded, he returned fire until, running out of ammunition, he was hit by hostile gun-fire. Overwhelmed, imprisoned and brutally tortured, he maintained a proud composure, revealing nothing of his men's positions, scorning any possible chance of being allowed to live. He faced death heroically in the name of Italy.[8]

His memorial stands in Rompeggio, Ferriere:

> This mountain stone
> With its pure white gleam
> Dedicates to the fatherland
> The supreme sacrifice
> Of the partisan
> Gian Maria Molinari,
> Chief-of-Staff of the Val Nure area
> Apostle and martyr

For Christian and human freedom.
November 11th 1922-January 5th 1945

"Aquila Nera" – Pietro Inzani – Canzi's former Chief-of-Staff, now commanding the *Val Nure* Division, was captured on January 6th and executed at Ferriere on January 8th; he was a local man, from Monastero di Morfasso. Like Molinari, he was posthumously awarded the Italian Silver Medal of Valour. His citation read:

> Inzani distinguished himself in partisan warfare as a tireless organizer and as an able and willing commander. He repeatedly experienced heavy fighting and difficult situations. During a *rastrellamento*, whilst commanding in the field, he fell into enemy hands. He was then beaten and is reported to have suffered serious injury. With exemplary courage, he told the Germans that he was proud to be a partisan and to fight for the freedom of his country. He was tortured and put in front of a firing squad, dying bravely.

A statue of him stands in the front hall of the local school in Ferriere.

Don Giuseppe Borea, Chaplain to 38th Brigade, was captured on January 27th and, after torture, was shot by the Fascists on February 9th 1945. He refused the offer of a chair and of a blindfold and is said to have forgiven his executioners; with the words "I offer my life for peace and the glory of my country", he removed his priest's habit and shouted *"Viva Gesù, Viva Maria, Viva l'Italia."* The eight bullets of the firing-squad failed to kill him, and he had to be finished off with a bullet to the back of the head.[9]

By the end of January 1945, the Piacenza partisans had suffered in one month more casualties than at any previous stage of their existence.

* * *

When Hastings parachuted into the Apennines area on February 2nd 1945, as the head of SOE Mission "Clover II", he found the situation in the Val Nure totally transformed from that of the previous autumn, when Donny's funeral in Bettola had seen thousands of Italians gather freely without a thought of enemy interference:

> We made our way down to the Val Trebbia, crossed Highway 45 and up over the mountains to Val Nure, which marked the rough boundary between IIIrd and XIIIth Zones. All the bridges had been blown this high up in Val Trebbia and Val Nure. The country was nominally controlled by partisans, although there was a risk of enemy foot patrols on the main roads. We crossed the Nure river, skirting round Ferriere, and climbed steadily... Headquarters of XIIIth Zone was reported to be in the small mountain village of Groppallo. After two days' march we reached it... To the west a narrow road snaked down to the Val Nure, where it joined the broken highway leading north down the valley some ten kilometres to Bettola, a frontier village on the way to Piacenza. This place had changed hands more than once, and was currently occupied by a Fascist outpost.[10]

Canzi was no longer in command, his place having recently been taken by a Colonel Marziolo; of Canzi's former *Comando Unico* staff, there remained only the Political Commissar, Remo Polizzi ("Venturi"). Hastings tried to find out what was going on, but it seems that political in-fighting had been rife in the wake of the partisans' defeat:

> Neither the duties nor indeed the allegiance of this *Commisario* [Venturi] were clear to us. He appeared at all our meetings and seemed to regard himself as a political consultant *cum* intelligence officer, or in other words a general snooper, collector and purveyor of gossip and rumour, most of it alarmist and much of it inaccurate... The atmosphere in Groppallo was one of suspicion and uncertainty... Morale was indeed low.[11]

Above: *the Brigata Mak, named in honour of Donny, which participated in the liberation of Piacenza on April 28th 1945 (ANPI, Piacenza).*

Hastings gained the impression that much of the fault for this low morale lay with Canzi. As we know, Canzi and the Communists did not see eye-to-eye, and the Communists were now in the ascendant. Hastings formed a very one-sided view of Canzi's abilities and behaviour, and probably arrived in the Val Nure with a mind already poisoned against the Anarchist commander.

> A main cause [of Marziolo's difficulties] lay in the machinations of a man called "Franchi" [Canzi's *nom de guerre*, Ezio Franchi], his predecessor in command, it turned out. I had been warned about Franchi; he was reported to be useless as a military commander, but a dangerous intriguer and far from honest. He and a small band of cronies were still about in the Piacentino trying to gain support by stirring up trouble for poor Marziolo. There was a strong suspicion that Franchi had condoned what amounted to banditry, the harsh treatment and bullying of the local mountain people on whom some of the defeated partisans had battened for food and shelter. Moreover, it was even rumoured he had made a deal with the Fascists by which his partisans agreed to cause no trouble if left alone. It was impossible to establish the facts.[12]

This is so at odds with the picture of Canzi painted in Gunner's report that one wonders if Hastings had ever seen a copy. If he had not seen Gunner's report, one has to ask why not: it would, after all, have been the most sensible document to have read before approaching the Val Nure. And who had "warned" Hastings about Canzi? One suspects some Communist skulduggery at HQ No.1 Special Force (one only has to read David Smiley's *Albanian Assignment* to see how biased in favour of Communists SOE headquarters at Bari was).

Late in March 1945 the resistance fighters were re-organized into the *Divisione Valnure* (one of the three brigades of which was named "Mak" after Donny). However, the political in-fighting continued: it was effectively an argument between those who believed that resistance was the important thing, regardless of political persuasion, and those who wanted to politicize the whole movement. Canzi was too apolitical, and the bizarre upshot was that in April 1945 Venturi had him arrested. The arrest had been ordered by the CLN and approved by Hastings, as he reported back to his superiors:

> With the disappearance of these two [Canzi and a man called Aceti], the intrigue, weakness and suspicion which have eaten into the partisan formations of this zone will disappear.[13]

On April 20th 1945, a partisan commander called "Salami" and a group of deserters from 162nd Turkistan Division surrounded the *Comando Unico* headquarters in Groppallo, and arrested Canzi and his companions. Lorenzo Marzani was there:

> It was shortly after noon. Present in the mess hall where we were having the usual frugal lunch were Emilio Canzi, Judge Brescia, Corsello, yours truly, and several others. Absent 'with good reason' (maybe because they had foreknowledge of what was about to happen) were Marzoli, Venturi and Mosaiski.
> Into the place stepped commander "Salami" together with a platoon of men with guns at the ready, among them a number of Mongol ex-prisoners. In the blinking of an eye, we were disarmed. Canzi put up a vigorous fight, but was forcibly dragged outside, bundled into a truck waiting in the street, and removed to an unknown location.[14]

Canzi was imprisoned in Bore and interrogated, but was soon released by Prati's partisans. He was thus able to take part in the liberation of his home town, Piacenza, on April 28th, though only as an ordinary partisan.

Many of Donny and Gunner's former partisans were with the liberating forces which took over the city that day – for example, Renato Cravedi, who in August 1944, aged seventeen, had joined the *Stella Rossa* Brigade and had served with the unit until it had dissolved in the face of the great *rastrellamento* of December. It was a proud moment for the Nure partisans, and for Hastings and his British liaison staff, but how much prouder it would have been for Gunner – and Donny.

Below: Fausto Cossu welcomes American forces to Piacenza, May 5th 1945 (ANPI, Piacenza).

Above: the funeral of Emilio Canzi, Piacenza, November 1945 (ANPI, Piacenza).

Canzi was soon restored to his post as Colonel on the *Comando Unico*, but he did not long survive the war's end. His death may have been engineered by the Communists, since Canzi was resisting their attempts to hi-jack the partisan movement and turn it into a political party. Both he and another anarchist, Savino Forsinari, died in separate incidents, both being run over by Allied vehicles. Canzi, whilst riding a motorcycle, was struck by a British army truck in Piacenza on October 2nd 1945; his leg was amputated, and he died of bronchial pneumonia on November 17th. He was buried in Peli di Coli. Two of the Grassis were there:

> Canzi wanted to be buried here because he found folk from our parish who wished him well, every last one of them.[15]

> I buried Canzi here in holy ground in Peli. And, as he had requested prior to his death, we placed a rock from these mountains under his head as a pillow.[16]

A bronze statue at Averaldi, not that far away, shows Canzi standing looking into the distance towards Bobbio, a Sten-gun slung over his shoulder.

* * *

Gunner's DSO never materialized, but on September 20th 1945 he did receive small recognition for his services. Unusually, his name appeared twice in the same issue of the *London Gazette*, with two mentions in dispatches – the first for Calais. The second 'mention' reads as follows:

> The King has been graciously pleased to approve that the following be Mentioned in recognition of gallant and distinguished services in the field:
> R.T.R.   Capt. (temp.) T.D. GREGG (85707).[17]

It is not clear who made the recommendation for this second 'mention', since Gunner's SOE file contains the comment "not put up through us." But the recommendation survives in the National Archives, dated July 9th 1945 and signed by the Director of Military Intelligence at the War Office, a certain J.A. Sinclair. Sinclair, on retiring from the army in 1952 as a Major-General, became head of the Secret Intelligence Service, MI6 (1953-1956). His recommendation was endorsed on July 13th with a terse "I agree" by the Military Secretary to the Secretary of State for War, Lieutenant-General Colville Wemyss.

Gunner's citation for his 'mention' is interesting more for its innaccuracies than the information which it gives us about his activities:

> Captain (Temporary) Tresham Dames Gregg (85707)
> HQ Squadron, 3rd Battalion, RTR, 4 Armoured Brigade, 7th Armoured Division.
>
> On 23 Dec 41, a week after his capture near Benghazi, Captain Gregg escaped from a column of prisoners. He was however discovered two hours later. Transferred to Italy he was imprisoned at Capua, Padula and Veano (Camp 29). At Padula he helped to dig two tunnels but both were discovered before they could be used. During July 43 he and seven other officers escaped from Veano camp through a tunnel they had made. As he emerged within three yards of a sentry, Captain Gregg was shot in the head, but he succeeded in getting away, only to be caught on a train bound for Rome.

It has to be pointed out that had Gunner been shot in the head during the escape, he would probably have remembered: one wonders how this myth arose and became 'official'. Regrettably, when his obituary was being researched by the *Daily Telegraph* in 2014, this mistake was included on the basis of the citation in the National Archives.

> After his release on 9 Sep 43, Captain Gregg went with one other officer to Rivergaro, where they decided to await further news. Captain Gregg's companion fell ill. Upon his recovery in March 44, the two officers went south. After only one day's journey they were persuaded to try to form a partisan band. Captain Gregg served as a commander until October 44 and as a personal assistant to one of the Italians for a further month.
>   At the beginning of December 44 he was guided through the lines to American forces near Seravezza.[18]

Ten days after his 'mentions' were gazetted, Gunner also received an honour from the Italian Ministry of Defence.

> I'm both delighted and satisfied that the Italian government did me the honour of presenting me with an Italian decoration, of which I am very proud.

Gunner's framed certificate stood on the table in his front hall.

> *Ministero della Difesa-Esercito*
>
> *Il Capitano T.D.*
> *Gregg, Tresham*
> *della 61A Brigata "Garibaldi"*
> *avendo partecipato alla lotta armata contro*
> *i tedeschi e contro i fascisti, e autorizzato a*
> *fregiarsi del distintivo d'onore istituto per i*
> *patrioti Volontari della Libertà.*
> *Decreto Luogotenenziale 3 Maggio 1945, n.350*
> *Roma, li 30-9-1945* [19]

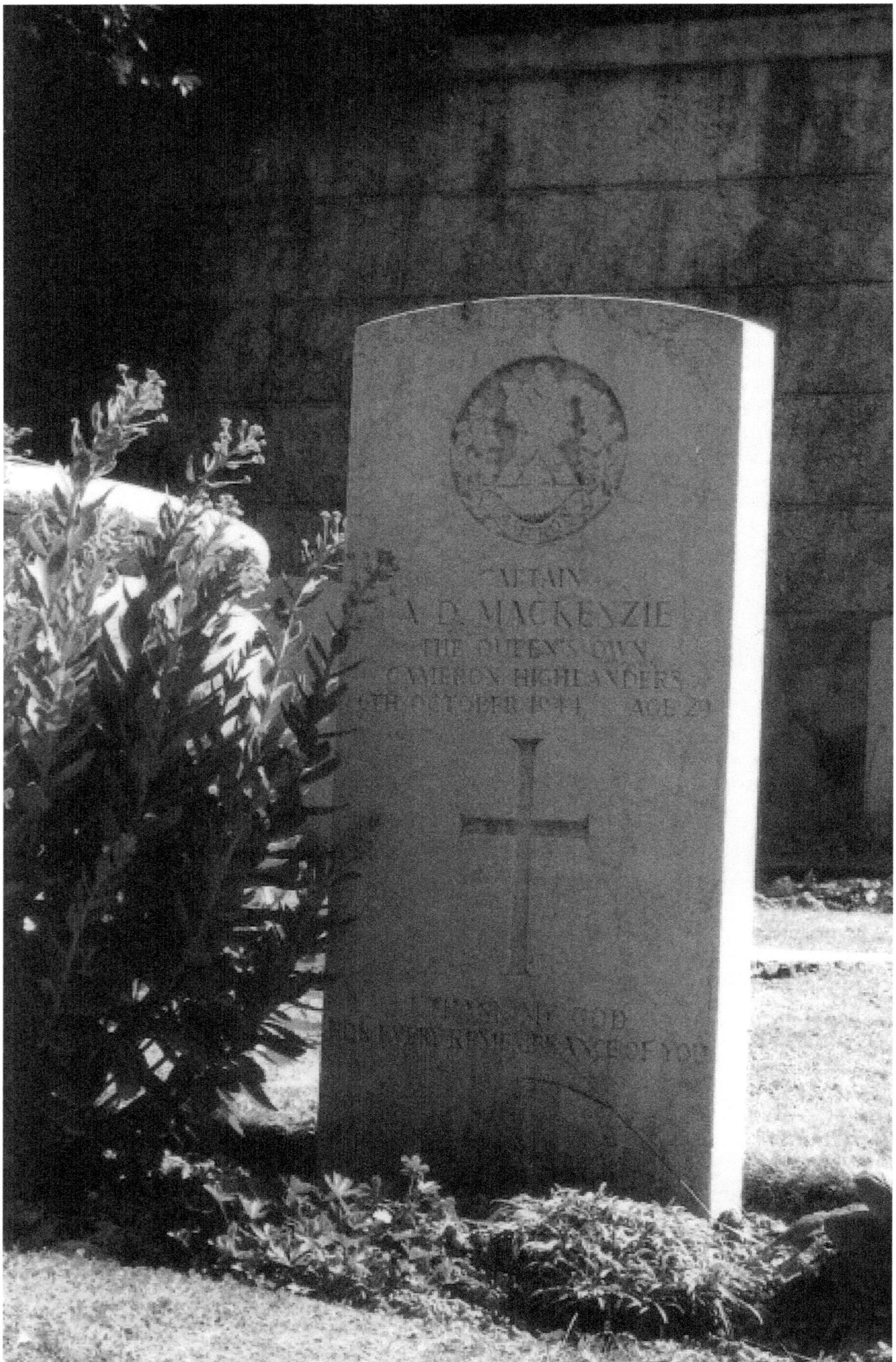
A. D. MACKENZIE
THE QUEEN'S OWN
CAMERON HIGHLANDERS

Chapter Eighteen
Remembrance

Donny's death was officially announced in *The Times* on February 5th 1945; no hint was given of how or where he had died, his listing stating simply "Mackenzie, Major A.D., Queen's Own Cameron Highlanders." His family inserted a fuller notice in the "Deaths" column of the same edition:

> Reported killed in action with Italian patriot forces, Major A.D. Mackenzie, Queen's Own Cameron Highlanders, only child of the late Lynedoch Archibald Mackenzie, Capt., RE (TF), died of wounds in Gallipoli, and Mrs Mackenzie, Rosefield, St Cyrus, Montrose, *fiancé* of Sarah Tomlinson, aged 30.[1]

It must have been a terrible blow for Dor Mackenzie to have lost her only son in much the same fashion as she had lost her husband all those years before. Donny's relatives Gervase and Tim Yates had been left to live with her, and many years later Gervase described her as

> almost a mother to us throughout the war. She had had a very sad life, but was wonderfully cheerful and stoical about it... As with her husband, Dorothy Mackenzie lost her only son hardly having seen him after the start of the war.[2]

As head of his family, Donny had held the title to Rosefield, in which his mother lived. With typical consideration for others and characteristic forethought, he had taken the precaution of writing and hiding a will shortly after beginning his partisan activities. Gunner had done the same:

> Luckily, we'd both done our wills after we escaped. Donny had left all his estate to his *fiancée* Sarah.

The wills had been written on scrap paper on May 4th 1944 – Gunner and Donny witnessing each other's will in the absence of anyone else – and buried in a tin box under the floor of the Osti house in Travo. The wills were recovered in July 1945 by Allied forces, and Donny's wishes were carried out, as his cousin Brian recalled:

> Donny's will... bequeathed 'Rosefield' to his mother for her life-time, and then to me; so, in 1953... this charming little 1815 stone-built house, that I had known so well since I was five, became my property... I have no reason to suppose that the will was not honoured fully in respect of Sarah Tomlinson... Donny's will made no provision for his personal possessions.[3]

* * *

Soon after his return to England, Gunner contacted Dor Mackenzie, and in mid-March 1945 they finally met in Brown's Hotel in London to exchange memories of the man for whom they had both cared so much. They were together over the course of two days, and Gunner showed Dor almost all the photographs and material relating to her son which he had collected; not, however, the drawing and photograph if her son in death. He did, however, present her with copies of the photographs of her son's funeral in Bettola. In return, Dor gave Gunner two photographs of her son, which he treasured.

Also present at the meeting was a family friend, an officer called A.C. Campbell, who then wrote to the Colonel-in-Chief of the Camerons to tell him what had happened to Donny after his escape. The letter differs in some details from the information provided by Gunner for this account. It does, however, confirm the favourable impression which Gunner and Donny's achievements made on senior officers who heard their story: they clearly considered it worthy of being put on public record. The fact that Campbell wanted an account published in the regimental magazine shows that he considered that Donny had acted in the highest traditions of the regiment.

> I have just seen Mrs Mackenzie, Donald Mackenzie's mother, and with her met Captain Gregg, who was with him in Italy up to the time he was killed.
>
> I don't know if any details have come your way, but to be on the safe side I gave Gregg your address and mine, and he is going to try and get hold of a written account of Mackenzie's activities with the partisans, which he wrote and is now in possession of the Political Warfare Bureau, Rome. It appears that they were in a camp in the mountains south of the River Po at the time of the armistice. The Italian commandant opened the gates and let everyone free. The two of them decided to get away and spent a night at a farm, and were then guided up to a charcoal-burners' camp higher up in the hills, where they spent about two months.
>
> At the start of the winter they returned to the farm and there Mackenzie was ill with dysentery, so they stayed there three or four months till he was fit, then decided to make for Naples, where our troops then were. This would have been about February 1944. The first day out they met a Yugoslav officer, who was trying to organize a force of partisans, so they decided to join forces with him and not continue their journey, as the local population was strongly anti-Fascist. They then started forming a band, which presented no difficulties as plenty of arms were hidden at the time of the armistice, and the chief trouble was the selection of the most suitable men. Further arms were obtained by disarming the local police and other bands which had been formed of local brigands which were doing a lot of harm in the district. They were also joined by other escapees and later got arms and supplies dropped by plane.
>
> Their bands then started carrying out sabotage, increasing their activities as their strength grew. Finally they controlled most of a province, having eliminated the pro-Fascist elements. One instance Gregg quoted was that Mackenzie carried out a raid on an armoury in Piacenza, driving a lorry through the town itself: unfortunately, the anti-tank guns which they wanted had been removed by the Germans, but it shows the sort of thing they were doing.
>
> By this time their band had expanded into two, led by Gregg and Mackenzie respectively.
>
> Their largest operation was in November '44 when the two bands, about eight hundred strong, surrounded the town of Ponteloso (my spelling is probably at fault), captured and held it for three days. During the time they were holding the town, Mackenzie took out a small patrol to watch for a German counter-attack which was expected, and was killed during the resultant action. Gregg was able to recover his body, and he was buried in the village where they had originally raised their band and where their headquarters was, a crowd of some four thousand people being present.
>
> I thought it might interest you to have these details, and I wanted to record them while they were still fresh in my memory. I hope, however, that Gregg may produce something which could later be published in "79th News".
>
> Mrs Mackenzie also told me that she was anxious to give her son's uniform, including full-dress uniform, to an officer joining the Regiment.[4]

Gunner and Dor Mackenzie never met again.

* * *

2nd Camerons had certainly not forgotten Donny. Lieutenant-Colonel Duncan, who had commanded the battalion at Tobruk and had subsequently been held in Veano, had been released from captivity at the end of the war in Europe. He resumed his interrupted command of the battalion on October 11th 1945, at Madonna Di Campiglio, north of Lake Garda. From there, he set out to find out what had happened to his former subordinate:

> On November 20th Lieutenant-Colonel Duncan visited Bettola for the purpose of seeing the grave of Captain A.D. Mackenzie and in order to make inquiries into the events leading up to his death. Donald Mackenzie, a former 2nd Battalion officer of great promise, had been taken prisoner by the Germans at Tobruk. On leaving his POW camp, after the Italian armistice, he had joined the partisans. After becoming a leader of the Red Star Brigade, which operated in the Bettola-Piacenza area, he had met his death in an enemy (Fascist) ambush. Donald Mackenzie was the finest example of a regimental officer; he possessed great charm, coupled with more than ordinary ability, and his death under circumstances which could not fully be ascertained was deeply mourned by all who knew him.[5]

It was British policy to consolidate the graves of its war dead in official cemeteries in the country of death, usually as close as possible to the original site of burial. By carrying out such concentration, the authorities would better be able to look after the graves in perpetuity, as the mandate of the Commonwealth War Graves Commission demands. On November 27th 1945, Donny's body was removed from its grave at Bettola.

> In the spring of 1946, when the undersigned was in the *Guardia Comunale* in Bettola, two British officials appeared in the town, with instructions which told us that his remains were to be taken away and buried in the cemetery of Staglieno in Genoa.
> At the opening of the grave, which was still intact, I personally arranged for the assistance of Signor Pietro Scarpetta, a decorator in Bettola, and father of a missing brave partisan who had been a member of the unit commanded by Captain Mak. When the corpse was removed from the grave, it was placed in a groundsheet and loaded on to a Jeep which headed for Genoa by way of the Cerro Pass. May I be permitted to add that it was a moment of great emotion, not only for me but also for Signor Scarpetta and for all those who had in any way had the chance to appreciate Captain Mak's gifts. He was a great soldier, a hero who belonged to a different nation but fell for the freedom of Italy, who left the land steeped in his selfless blood. I am certain that all those who had the chance to meet Captain Mak will preserve in their hearts the memory of a soldier who died a hero.[6]

He now rests in grave I.A.5 of the Staglieno Cemetery, Genoa. The inscription on his tombstone reads:

> I thank my God for every remembrance of you.

This is a quotation from St Paul, *Letter to the Philippians* I.3. Who chose it: Dor, or Sarah?

* * *

In 1949, Donny's paternal uncle (Lieutenant-Colonel Daniel Barton Mackenzie) attempted to have his nephew's distinguished service officially recognized by the British government. He sent supporting documents to Gordon Lett, who had notionally been, as one official letter put it, "Captain A.D. Mackenzie's CO in Italy"; Lett was by then British Vice Consul in Tripoli, and had been awarded the DSO for his own work with the Rossano partisans. Lett passed Colonel Mackenzie's dossier on to the Military Attaché at the Rome embassy in 1950, with

> a strong recommendation for recognition of Mackenzie's services.[7]

When questioned about this in 1952 – Colonel Mackenzie having enquired what was being done about his nephew's award – the officer who had been Military Attaché at the time stated, in effect, that he could not remember the dossier in question and that if it had existed he had probably forwarded it to the War Office. There the matter seems to have fizzled out – though Colonel Mackenzie (according to his son Brian),

> was furious at the loss of a file that he had entrusted to the Embassy in Rome.[8]

As we have seen, Dor Mackenzie had been busy during the war looking after two of her Yates nephews. In September 1944, the rest of the family had returned to Scotland from Ceylon, as Kit Yates recalled:

> Fortunately, 'Rosefield' is a fairly large house, and the four of us also moved in with Aunt Dor. It must have been a very difficult time for her, having so recently lost her only son, and now saddled with an additional two adults and two pre-teen children in her home.[9]

Dor died, alone, in 'Rosefield' in 1953. The house was clearly, for many of the extended Mackenzie family, a haven in a peripatetic existence, as Brian Mackenzie recalled:

> Its remoteness, comparatively, made me wonder if it was compatible with our roving military life; but then I found that it was so important in my daughters' minds as a stable factor in their lives that I joyfully decided to keep it. Letting to the United States Navy filled the gap until I retired.[10]

Brian Mackenzie lived at 'Rosefield' from 1975 until the Nineteen-Eighties.

> Our eldest daughter, Fiona, was married in the open air on the cliff-top at St Cyrus, with the fulmars gliding about and the gulls calling. We go back quite frequently...
> This letter has drifted a long way from Donny, but his room was always "Donny's", and I am sure that he would have approved of our alterations.[11]

The family kept Donny's memory alive in other ways as well, twice visiting the Val Nure:

> On our way motoring home from Libya, my wife and I visited Bettola and Ponte dell'Olio, and met people who had known him there, including the Mayor of Bettola, who had lost two sons fighting with the Communists. There was a sense of outrage locally because the War Graves Commission, when they took his remains away from the tomb in Bettola, had discarded the expensive coffin that the Bettola folk had used.
> Later, about 1963, when I was serving in Germany, my wife and I took our three daughters to Bettola, and then across the hills, by Columbanus' beautiful monastery at Bobbio, to visit Donny's grave in Genoa.[12]

* * *

Donny was remembered with respect and affection in the Val Nure long after his death. In 1957, for example, one of the partisans wrote as follows to the Mayor of Bettola:

> Even though it is not easy to agree willingly when asked to talk of a fallen partisan, I am convinced that anything which can be done to bring alive for men the sacrifice and heroism of those who selflessly gave their lives for freedom is a very valuable task.
> To talk of Captain Donald Mackenzie ("Mak") and of his gifts as a man and as a soldier, of his loyal and brave fighting, it would be necessary for me to be a different person. As it is, I will try in simple language, as far as I am able, to remember the actions and events in which he took part and of which I am aware.
> Captain Mak was part of the *Stella Rossa* Brigade, in which there fought men of all political persuasions, and commanded a detachment. His name truly became well known to all, since he displayed gifts which were humane and uncommon in a soldier. He had very advanced social ideas and never missed an opportunity to help the weak, bringing his message of encouragement and hope. Although language posed a great obstacle, nevertheless he was easy to understand.[13]

The Italians officially recognized Donny's sacrifice in 1969, when they erected a memorial to him and the two partisans who died at his side, at Albarola, near Ponte dell'Olio. The memorial was erected as part of a ceremony which celebrated the twenty-fifth anniversary of the liberation of Ponte dell'Olio. Sadly, as so often after the war, the event

Above: *the Albarola memorial to Donny, Merli and Carini, which was unveiled in 1969 (courtesy Signor Claudio Oltremonti of Piacenza).*

seems to have been hi-jacked by the Communists for domestic political reasons, and the account exaggerates the party's role in the liberation of the Val Nure. The following passage is a loose translation of an article which appeared in the Italian newspaper *Libertà* in November 1969.

> A memorial on the hill of Albarola commemorating the sacrifice of three partisans was inaugurated on Sunday morning in the presence of dignitaries and the British Consul, wishing to honour the memory of the legendary "Capitano Mac".
>
> The memorial was solemnly unveiled... in memory of all those who sacrificed their lives in the Val Nure, in particular three partisans who died on the spot – Carini, Mackenzie and Merli... The understated ceremony was moving and produced a deep effect on the hundreds of people present, amongst whom were many former partisans.
>
> The ceremony was organized by the Italian Partisan Association and began with a reception in the town hall of Ponte dell'Olio in honour of the British guests – the Consul, Vice Consul and Attachés with their wives – who by their presence confirmed the bonds which had been formed during the war between the partisans, civilian population, and ex-prisoners of war, who all fought for freedom against the invader in the Val Nure. A long procession, headed by the band of Ponte dell'Olio, wound its way under the morning sun from the main street of the town to the bridge, and then on to the road which leads to the caves of Albarola. Behind the standards of various communities, the banner of Piacenza and the flags of service associations, walked the civil and military dignitaries and representatives of the Resistance movement. With them were the guests: the Consul-General from Milan, Mr J. Plant; the Vice-Consul, Mr Frank C. Unwin; the Commercial Attaché, Mr A. Ian Harris; Senator Spigaroli; On. Tagliaferri; the Prefect, Dr Nicastro; the Head of Police, Dottore Rocco; Colonel Giallanella of the Carabinieri; Comm. Freschi; and the mayors of Ferriere, Farini d'Olmo, Bettola, Ponte dell'Olio, Vigolzone, Caorso and Monticelli.
>
> Everyone was moved when the British and Italian National Anthems were played. This was followed by the blessing of the memorial – the first to be dedicated to the fallen of the resistance movement in the Val Nure – by the vicar of Vigolzone, Don Massari. In his speech, Mayor Guarnaschelli stressed

Above: *unfortunately, the memorial spells Donny's name incorrectly: "Cap. Mak Donal McKenzie"*
(courtesy Signor Claudio Oltremonti of Piacenza).

the importance of the liberation struggle, which was still an important factor in the life of the country, and he appealed to the young in particular to learn from the example.

A speaker recalled the events of October 4th 1944, their immediate consequences – namely, the greater confidence instilled in all the units operating in the Val Nure – and the historical importance of the event as a symbol of a united Europe. In his speech, he described the personalities and the courageous actions of the three partisans, recalling in particular how Capitano Mac – after his escape from the camp at Veano – chose to fight on Italian territory rather than undertake the more comfortable journey to a safe shelter in neutral Switzerland. Also pointed out to the young in particular was the importance of the causes which inspired resistance against the ruthless invader, issues still important for the country's progress.

After the official part of the ceremony had come to an end, the crowd lingered for quite some time round the memorial, where the Italian flag and Union Jack were flying, and greeted the guests with great friendliness. Mr Unwin, the Consul, was wearing his war decorations... He explained that he too had been a prisoner-of-war at Arezzo, and that he had managed to escape, and after six months had nearly reached the Allied lines at Cassino after an exciting journey which ended, however, with his recapture and dispatch to Magdeburg in Germany. Much admired, in fact almost besieged by youths and girls seeking autographs, was Mr Ian Harris, Commercial Attaché at the British Consulate in Milan; very tall and blond, he was wearing a Scottish kilt and jacket. The grey and black tartan was that of the Menzies clan, to which the young diplomat's mother belongs. His traditional Scottish costume was completed by an elegant black jacket with gilt buttons and a full frilled white cravat.

The Consul and the Vice-Consul expressed their admiration of the population and gratitude for the hospitality which their countryman had received during their stay in the Val Nure in the war.[14]

Twenty-five years on from that ceremony, Donny's name was still famous in the Val Nure. In 2008, Peter Wright visited Veano and Bettola, following in the footsteps of his uncle, Major Nigel Beaumont-Thomas MC, who had been an inmate of PG29 with Donny and Gunner. Mention of the prisoner-of-war camp still sparked Italian memories of Donny:

In Bettola, in response to my inquiry... an enthusiastically helpful group pointed across the piazza, indicating the left side while saying "banco" and then pointing right. I didn't understand, but when seventy-five yards down the piazza and in front of the bank, I saw opposite a photo shop, and inquiring of a young, attractive sales assistant *"Piero, photo, partigiani?"* was led back up the piazza. At about the mid-point, she pushed an intercom button beside a large, dark brown door. After a beep, she spoke into the intercom. Soon we were buzzed in. The assistant conferred on the dark stairs with an elegant man with a neatly trimmed beard and my stomach began to quiver. Within half a minute, he was convinced of my sincerity, and he invited me into his home. I was left alone in his office while he went into the back for his collection. In ten minute, he returned with seven portfolios from which he produced dozens of 12x18s, all black and white, of Mac, Emilio Canzi, the Partisans, their lives. He had photos of "Montenegrino", an officer from Montenegro who also had chosen to stay and fight. There were photos of Mac alone; Mac and Montenegrino holding guns; Mac with his girlfriend; Montenegrino with his two girlfriends; and finally Mac's funeral. There were combat shots, including one I had seen on the monument at the pass. But there were no photos of any other prisoners from Veano.[15]

Nor has the official recognition ceased. The sixty-fifth anniversary of the liberation of Ponte dell'Olio by Gunner and Donny was celebrated with yet another ceremony. On Sunday October 18th 2009, Colonel Michael Onslow of the Royal Regiment of Scotland – the unit into which the Cameron Highlanders has been absorbed – visited Vigolzone. A meeting was held in the town hall of Vigolzone; in the chair was the President of the Piacenza branch of the National Association of Italian Partisans (ANPI); the opening address was given by the Mayor of Vigolzone; there was a slide-show of period photographs; and afterwards a laurel wreath was laid at the memorial at Albarola.

* * *

And what of Donny's *fiancée*, Sarah Tomlinson? As we have seen, she had still considered herself engaged to him when his death was announced in The Times in March 1945. Like so many other women, she had lost a man she held dear. Luckily, she was able to find happiness with someone else. She married George Patrick O'Neill Pearson (of Cartmel, Lancashire)[16] on March 23rd 1946, at St Paul's Church, Knightsbridge. The ceremony took place, as the announcement in The Times put it, "quietly". Their first child, Christopher

Above: *Colonel Michael Onslow, Royal Regiment of Scotland, at the Albarola memorial, October 2009 (ANPI, Piacenza).*

Rait O'Neill Pearson, was born in May 1947; their second, Diana Katrina O'Neill Pearson, in 1949; their third, Hilary Sarah O'Neill Pearson, in 1955 (a fourth daughter had been stillborn in 1954). George predeceased his wife in December 1982; Sarah Diana O'Neill Pearson died on March 29th 1992.

Full lives, fully lived. Donny would surely have been happy for them.

* * *

Gunner lectured several times on his wartime experiences to the Cumbrian Historical Society and to raise money for the Royal British Legion. He and his second wife, Joan, visited Greece in the autumn of 2005 as part of the "Heroes Return" programme which encouraged veterans to re-visit the theatres in which they served during the Second World War, and as a result Gunner's story was published in the *Cumberland News* in November 2005.[17] The article, mentioning Donny, was the first that the present author knew of Gunner, and eventually made this account possible.

In the autumn of 2006, having met and interviewed Gunner at his home in Cumbria, the author delivered a lecture on Donny's career with the partisans to pupils and staff at Winchester College. One of the staff mentioned what he had heard to a relative, the author Edward Marriott, who in his turn interviewed Gunner and wrote an article on him for *Saga Magazine*.[18] Because of the publication of this article, Donny's relatives were able to make contact with Gunner through the magazine and to thank him for what he had done after Donny's death in 1944.

Furthermore, two wartime inhabitants of the Val Nure – women who had been children there in 1944 – also read the *Saga* article and, through the magazine, sent letters to Gunner. Mrs Anita Basini, of Slough, had in 1944 been a resident of Cassimoreno, near Ferriere, and wrote as follows:

> Whether you recall my village or not, I can assure you that all that region – Ferriere, Farini D'Olmo, etc. – much appreciated the courage you showed and the sacrifices you made to rid us of the Germans. I know, because I was there. Thank you.[19]

Gunner did indeed remember the village of Cassimoreno; one of the partisans in his *squadra*, Alberto Columbo, had come from there. Another letter came from Maria Luisa Sandys of Exeter, originally from Farini D'Olmo:

> Could you fix it for me to meet one of the brave men who contributed to the liberation of my valley...? The article about your heroic days... has brought my life in Farini during the war back to me as if it were yesterday. Thank you so much for what you did for us, and I am so very sorry that many brave men have lost their lives to save ours.[20]

Gunner subsequently met Mrs Sandys. It is heart-warming to think that Gunner's time behind enemy lines in the Val Nure still sparks gratitude in the people whom, for a time, he and Donny liberated from Fascist domination. In his long and distinguished career, perhaps that was his finest hour.

Gunner remained a modest man, who tended to dismiss any suggestion that he had achieved anything special. He took a great deal of persuading that his story was in any way worth recording.

> I'm just bloody lucky to be alive. Don't make me out to be some kind of hero. Everyone of my generation went through similar experiences. Everyone has a story to tell.[21]

Nevertheless, Gunner was pleased that the *Saga* article had achieved one of his most deeply-felt wishes:

> I am determined that the world should know what a fine man Donny was, and how bravely he lived and died, and what a credit he was to his friends, the Cameron Highlanders, Winchester and Scotland.

This work owes its existence to that determination; Gunner allowed his story to be told so that Donny's might also be put on public record.

Below: *Donny's memorial in Winchester College's stunning War Cloister. Passing these inscriptions on his way to work every morning, the author determined to discover the stories behind all of them – which led to a valued friendship with Gunner, and ultimately, to this book (author's collection).*

Many years ago, Donny's Winchester College obituary ended with the following words:

> A letter from the [Communist] Mayor of Bettola and an obituary notice in a Communist paper printed in Piacenza bore striking testimony to the inspiration which his... partisans found in their "Capitano Mac", to their admiration for his courage and high spirits, and to their grief at his death.
> As a boy, thanks to his cheerfulness and courage, he had always been at his best in times of difficulty. Evidently he had carried this quality with him to the end.[22]

The writer of the obituary – most likely Donny's former housemaster, the Jacker – judged his comments well. The boy whom he had known and shaped had indeed risen above the obstacles which fate had placed in his path, and had as a result forged an enduring memory.

But Gunner deserves to have the last word on his friend:

> Donny now has a memorial which the Italians erected to him near Ponte dell'Olio. However, his real memorial is in the hearts of the people who live in the valley of the river Nure. They will never forget him. Neither shall I.

* * *

Colonel Tresham Dames "Gunner" Gregg died at his home in Cumbria on March 17th 2014. His funeral was held in the small church just yards away in Walton, near Brampton. He received full obituaries in both the *Daily Telegraph* and *The Times*, as well as in the Piacenza newspaper *Libertà*. Belatedly, therefore, he received some of the recognition which he so richly deserved.

RESISTENZA - Ufficiale dell'esercito britannico, era arrivato a Veano come prigioniero di guerra catturato in Libia dai tedeschi

Addio a capitan Ganna, eroe partigiano
Con la brigata Stella Rossa nell'ottobre 1944 aveva liberato Pontedellolio

Addio a capitan Ganna protagonista del movimento partigiano e brillante ufficiale dell'esercito britannico.

Venerdì scorso a Walton, nella regione inglese di Cumbria, si sono svolti i funerali del colonnello Tresham D. Gregg, 93 anni, più noto nella storia della Resistenza piacentina con il nome di "Ganna", contrazione di "Gunner", cannoniere. Il colonnello Gregg era nato a Dublino il 7 aprile 1920.

Catturato dall'esercito tedesco in Libia, vicino a Tobruk il 15 dicembre 1942, fu consegnato agli italiani e trasferito in Italia. Più volte fuggito dai campi di internamento venne infine rinchiuso a Veano, la residenza estiva del Collegio Alberoni trasformata in campo di prigionia per gli ufficiali anglo-americani.

Con l'armistizio dell'8 settembre 1943 avrebbe potuto riparare in Svizzera, dove si trovavano alcuni familiari, ma il suo più caro amico e compagno di prigionia, il capitano Archibald Donald "Donny" Mackenzie, il capitano "Mak", dei Cameron Highlanders, era malato di malaria; decise così di rimanere con lui per curarlo. Insieme furono ospitati alla Stoppa di Ancarano. In Valnure si stabilirono con un gruppo di carbonai. Nella primavera del 1944 Gregg e Mackenzie furono contattati dai primi elementi della Resistenza che cercavano aiuti per combattere i nazifascisti. I due soldati inglesi si unirono a loro e condussero con successo una serie di azioni che portarono alla liberazione di un territorio che arrivava fino a Bettola. Gregg e Mackenzie erano diventati comandanti della Brigata Stella Rossa. Stabilirono contatti con l'intelligence britannica, in particolare con la missione dello Special Operations Executive "Blundell Violet". Grazie a quel collegamento arrivarono i primi rifornimenti di armi e viveri aviolanciati. Il coraggio e le capacità di comando di Gregg e Mackenzie suscitarono l'ammirazione e l'affetto dei partigiani che si legarono ai propri capi indissolubilmente. All'inizio di ottobre del '44 fu liberato Pontedellolio, ma il 6 ottobre 1944 ci fu l'epilogo drammatico con la morte del capitano "Mak", insieme ad altri due partigiani, intrappolati dai fascisti mentre si trovava di pattuglia nei pressi di Albarola. Diverse foto del funerale di "Mak" ritraggono Gregg che sorregge il feretro del compagno nel suo ultimo viaggio e la grande partecipazione dei valnuresi come estremo gesto di affetto e riconoscenza verso l'ufficiale inglese. Gregg raggiunse le linee alleate il 5 dicembre 1944. Dopo la fine della guerra fu dislocato in India ed a Singapore, ritornando in patria nel 1949 all'Army Staff College. Fu nuovamente inviato in Italia, a Trieste, al quartier generale delle truppe britanniche. Successivamente servì come "squadron leader" nel 6° Royal Tank Regiment in Germania, comandante di compagnia a Sandhurst e del 1° Royal Tank Regiment a Hong-Kong ed in Germania. Il suo incarico finale fu quello di colonnello del Recruiting Northern Command a York.

La notizia della morte di "capitan Ganna" è stata trasmessa all'Anpi di Piacenza dal professor Shaun Hullis, docente di latino alla St. Benedict's School di Ealing, amico della famiglia Gregg e autore di un libro su Donald Mackenzie che sarà a breve pubblicato in Inghilterra. L'ufficiale sarà ricordato con i partigiani morti negli ultimi dodici mesi durante la celebrazione del prossimo 25 Aprile. Il colonnello Gregg era tornato a Bettola nel giugno del 1969 ed aveva incontrato i compagni partigiani: Giuseppe Posatini (Pinein), Alberto Rossi (Berton), Antonio Ferrari (Saetta), Domenico Rossi (Leone), Angelo Albertelli (Cirillo), Luigi Segalini (Ginetto) e Celeste Bernazzani (Bruto). Con i familiari aveva visitato il Collegio Alberoni di Veano e la Stoppa, ad Ancarano.

Maria Vittoria Gazzola
mariavittoria.gazzola@liberta.it

Il colonnello Gregg; a fianco regge la bara dell'amico "Mak" morto ad Albarola

Appendix A
Lineage of Tresham Dames "Gunner" Gregg

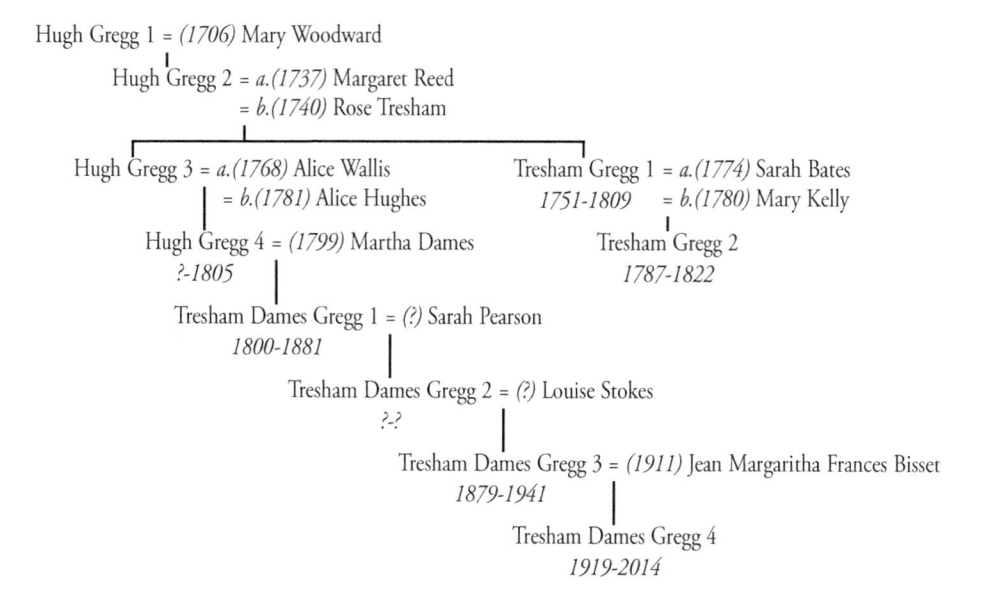

```
Hugh Gregg 1 = (1706) Mary Woodward
       |
    Hugh Gregg 2 = a.(1737) Margaret Reed
                 = b.(1740) Rose Tresham
       |
Hugh Gregg 3 = a.(1768) Alice Wallis          Tresham Gregg 1 = a.(1774) Sarah Bates
             = b.(1781) Alice Hughes          1751-1809       = b.(1780) Mary Kelly
       |                                              |
Hugh Gregg 4 = (1799) Martha Dames                Tresham Gregg 2
?-1805                                             1787-1822
       |
Tresham Dames Gregg 1 = (?) Sarah Pearson
1800-1881
       |
Tresham Dames Gregg 2 = (?) Louise Stokes
?-?
       |
Tresham Dames Gregg 3 = (1911) Jean Margaritha Frances Bisset
1879-1941
       |
Tresham Dames Gregg 4
1919-2014
```

Hugh Gregg (1), from Dublin, married Mary Woodward on January 2nd 1706 (or 1707) at St Andrew's Church, Dublin. The couple had one son, Hugh.

Hugh Gregg (2), of Nicholas Lane and St Mary's Abbey, Dublin, married twice. His first marriage was to Margaret Reed, whom he wed on September 3rd 1737 at St Werburgh's Church, Dublin. His second marriage was to Rose Tresham (daughter of Thomas Tresham, of Cornmarket, Dublin); this was celebrated at St Andrew's Church, Dublin, on September 11th 1740. It was by this marriage that the name Tresham entered the family.

Hugh (2) and Rose had two sons before her death in May 1766: the elder was christened Hugh Gregg (3), and the younger was baptized Tresham Gregg (1) on July 17th 1751. Tresham rose to be governor of Newgate Prison, Dublin, in 1796. Like his father, he also married twice: firstly, in 1774, he married Sarah Bates; in 1780 he re-married, this time to Mary Kelly. By the time that he died in 1809, Mary had borne him a son, Tresham Gregg (2). But this son (born in 1787) died without issue in 1822: thus the name Tresham Gregg might have come to an abrupt end.

However, all was not lost. Hugh Gregg (3), elder brother of Tresham Gregg (1), married twice: his first wife, Alice Wallis, on August 26th 1768; and his second, Alice Hughes, in 1781. By this second marriage, he had one son: Hugh Gregg (4). This son married Martha Dames, daughter of Gilmore Dames, on November 9th 1799 (Martha Dames Gregg re-married on July 3rd 1816, this time wedding Gregor von Feinagle, of Luxembourg. She died on December 14th 1874). For some reason, the fourth Hugh Gregg broke with tradition and named his eldest son Tresham.

* * *

Tresham Dames Gregg (1), the first to bear the name, was born in 1800 and educated at Trinity College, Dublin, where he was awarded his BA in 1826 (MA, 1830). He went on to become a Doctor of Divinity (1853). As the Reverend T.D. Gregg, he became Chantry Priest of St Nicholas-within-the-Walls, Dublin; this church, having fallen into disrepair, lacked a roof, and only a side chapel, dedicated to St Mary, continued in use until the church was abandoned in 1867. The title of Chantry Priest, however, continued as a sinecure until 1882, as his great-great-grandson, Gunner, explained:

> He had no parishioners; his duties were theological. He lectured in Britain, but also in America, and was the author of about thirty books, copies of most of which are in the Library of Congress and the Library of the Royal Dublin Society. When he was born, Dublin was entirely Protestant; when he died, the population was mainly Catholic. Many of his books and lectures were very anti-Catholic; he even wrote a play called Bloody Mary! He was very well known in his day. I think that he must have been rather like Ian Paisley.

The Reverend Gregg was indeed a trenchant Protestant theologian, and member of the Dublin Protestant Association. He was the author of many works denouncing Catholicism (or Papism, as he termed it): they include *Protestant Ascendancy vindicated, and national regeneration, through the instrumentality of national religion, urged; in a series of letters to the Corporation of Dublin* (1840); and *Free Thoughts on Protestant Matters* (Dublin, 1846). In the preface to the second edition, the Reverend Gregg expressed his antipathy

> to the infatuated workings of the late unprincipled Prime Minister,

whom he went on to call "Sir Rotten Peel". Peel's crime had been to support an increase in state support to the Catholic seminary at Maynooth, a decision which sent up howls of protest from Irish protestants such as Gregg, who saw it as the thin end of the wedge. In 1849 Gregg visited the historian Thomas Carlyle in London, hoping for his support in stemming Catholic influence. Carlyle recorded the visit in a letter to his mother:

> This morning I had a visit from a most fiery Irish Protestant Priest, a "Revd Mr Gregg" of Dublin, — who, if he could but interest "Thomas Carloile" in his ideas, would quickly get them disseminated over all the world: — but this, I doubt, will be very difficult to do!
> (Thomas Carlyle, letter to his mother, Chelsea, March 19th 1849)

Somewhat less controversial was a later book of Gregg's: *A Methodization of the Hebrew Verbs, Regular and Irregular, on an original plan* (1861).

The Reverend Gregg had married Sarah Pearson, from North Yorkshire; she was the daughter of the squire of Pannal Ash, near Knaresborough. Reverend Gregg died on October 28th 1881; his widow died on May 1st 1902.

* * *

The couple had also had a daughter, Adeline Beatrice Gregg, and we should briefly follow her fortunes, since Gunner was proud of his relatives from that branch of the family. Adeline married the Reverend Edgar F. Hutchings MA, vicar of Haynestown, County Louth. The couple had one child, a daughter, Irene. Irene Hutchings married the Reverend John Pim Barcroft: the Barcrofts were an aristocratic Lancastrian family from Barcroft Hall in Cliviger, near Burnley. On January 5th 1917 Irene gave birth to a son, who would go on to become the Reverend Ambrose William Edgar Barcroft. (Irene Hutchings died on August 20th 1959.)

Ambrose Barcroft was educated at St Columba's and Trinity College, Dublin, from which he graduated with a BA in 1940. Between 1941 and 1946 he was Curate of Drumachose in County Derry, gaining his MA in 1946. He then joined the Royal Navy as a Chaplain, with which he served until 1970. He then retired from the Navy and became Rector of Pitlochry in Perthshire. In June 1950 he had married Hazel Bigg (daughter of John Bryan Bigg), and the couple went on to have four children: John Pim Barcroft (1952), David Stafford Barcroft (1953), Heather Anne Barcroft (1957) and James Thomas Barcroft (1963). His second wife was Sheila, a school-teacher from Pitlochry who remained a good friend of Gunner and Joan.

* * *

The next Tresham Dames Gregg (2), Gunner's grandfather, was secretary to the Reverend Gregg – which, given the latter's prominence and prolific writings, must have been a busy task. The son married Louise Stokes, whom Gunner described as follows:

> A very powerful lady in every way. Her father was the master and skipper of a four-masted tea-clipper which sailed regularly to ship wool from Australia and tea from China.

The couple had two children, Mabel and Tresham Dames Gregg (3). But Tresham (2) died very young, and his widow re-married. Her second husband was Horace Shaw,

> a first cousin of George Bernard Shaw. He was head of the Irish Land Commission, the purpose of which was to

buy up the estates of English absentee landlords and hand them on to Irish tenants. In the family, he was known as "The Pater" and his wife as "The Mater".

With Horace, Louise had two more children, Fredrick and George Shaw. Her daughter Mabel married a doctor from Northern Ireland, J.W. Houston. They had three children, Violet, William, and Robert ("Bob").

> My closest relation was my father's sister's son, Bob Houston. He was an RAMC doctor on Malta for several years during the war. He moved to British Columbia after the war after a spell in Nigeria as a member of the Commonwealth Medical Service; he loved this job, as his main hobby was birds. He resigned after independence, when corruption took over.

Fredrick Shaw fathered two children (Pat and Helen), and George also became father of two (John and Jane).

* * *

Tresham Dames Gregg (3), Gunner's father, was born in 1879 in Dublin. He was educated at the Blue Coat School in London, more properly known as Christ's Hospital, which is now on a site near Horsham. From there he went on to read Classics at Trinity College, Dublin, before going out to South Africa. He was a fine horseman, who twice rode with distinction in the Dublin Horse Show.

Appendix B
Tank Types used by 3RTR 1939-1941

VICKERS MEDIUM TANK

The Vickers Medium Tank had been designed in 1921 and was in production from 1924, with the Mark I replaced on the production lines by the Mark II in 1925. The last Mark IIs were updated in 1934 and they were phased out of service in 1938-1939. They were ungainly vehicles, with poor protection for their crew of five, who would have been vulnerable to anything larger than a light machine-gun. The petrol was stored in the main crew compartment, increasing the risk of catastrophic burns if hit. They were tall, increasing their vulnerability, and slow at 13 mph. Their main armament was one 3-pounder (47mm) gun and two .303-inch Vickers machine-guns.

LIGHT TANK MARK VIB

The Light Tank Mk VI was produced by Vickers-Armstrongs and intended as a scout vehicle. It was mechanically reliable, though its lively behaviour cross-country made it difficult to fire from on the move. Its crew of three (commander, gunner and driver) were protected by armour 4-14mm thick, making the tank proof only against small-arms fire. The commander operated the radio set, whilst the gunner controlled the two Vickers machine-guns in the turret (one .303-inch and one .5-inch). The tank weighed around five tons and its 88hp engine could drive it at 35mph on roads and 25mph across country. It had a range of 130 miles.

CRUISER TANK A9

The A9 tank (Tank, Cruiser, Mk I) had already been designed by the time that the 'cruiser' tank concept was developed, but it was compromised by cost-cutting measures. Its armour was thin – no more than 14mm, and in places only 6mm – and mostly vertical (though it was known that sloped armour provided better protection). In 1937 it was ordered into limited production as a stop-gap measure pending design of a better tank. The A9's armament was a 2-pounder (40mm) gun in the main turret, with a co-axial Vickers .303-inch machine-gun. Either side of the driver were two small turrets, each containing a further Vickers .303-inch machine-gun. This required a crew of six (commander, gunner, loader, driver and two hull-gunners). The 2-pounder main gun could only fire armour-piercing shot, though High Explosive rounds were needed if the tank was to engage anti-tank guns effectively. A 'close support' version was developed which had a 3.7-inch howitzer for just such an eventuality, but this weapon did not have armour-piercing shot for emergencies.

The A9 had an 150hp AEC engine designed to power buses; this could propel the A9's twelve tons for 150 miles at 25mph on roads, and 15mph across country. The A9 was mechanically unreliable and had a tendency to shed its tracks when turning corners – quite a disadvantage in combat.

CRUISER TANK A10

The A10 (Tank, Cruiser, Mk II) had been designed as an Infantry tank version of the A9, but proved unsuitable for the role – so it was re-designated a 'Heavy Cruiser', neither one thing nor the other. Like the A9, its turret held a 2-pounder and a .303-inch Vickers machine-gun. The A10 lacked the hull-turrets of the A9, and instead the hull was fitted with a BESA machine-gun, which was an excellent weapon but used a different calibre of ammunition to the Vickers (7.92mm); eventually the turret Vickers was replaced with another BESA. Again, a close support version mounted a howitzer in place of the 2-pounder. The crew of five (commander, gunner, loader, driver, hull-gunner) were protected by thicker armour than the A9 on almost every surface, to a maximum of 30mm, but because the AEC engine was the same as the A9 the A10 was much slower; it weighed fourteen tons, and could only travel at 16mph on roads and 8mph across country.

Its range was only one hundred miles. The A10 shared the A9's mechanical unreliability and ability to lose its tracks at the slightest provocation.

Second Lieutenant Dick Shattock, a comrade of Gunner's in 'A' Squadron of 3RTR, wrote thus of the A10:

> A10 tanks surely ranked as the worst in history. As an engineer, I quickly realized this. The tracks broke every few miles, literally. The engines, AEC ex-London bus engines, were installed with the radiator cooling-fan placed on one side of the tank but the radiator itself placed on the opposite side. The so-called cool air then passed over the over-heated engine via the red-hot exhaust through the radiator... The designers of the A10 must have been in the pay of the Nazis.
>
> (Shattock, quoted in Delaforce, *Taming the Panzers: 3RTR at War*)

Bob Crisp of 'C' Squadron also condemned the A9 and A10:

> They were ponderous square things like mobile pre-fab houses, and just about as flimsy. Their worst failing was their complete inability to move more than a mile or two in any sort of heavy going without breaking a track or shedding one on a sharp turn.
>
> (Crisp, *The Gods Were Neutral*)

CRUISER TANK A13

The A13 (Tank, Cruiser, Mk III & Mk IV) was the next design of cruiser tank. In 1936 British officials became interested in the American Christie system of tank suspension, which promised excellent mobility and high speed. Some of the most successful tanks of the Second World War – the German Panther and Soviet T-34 – used Christie suspension. The A13 wedded this suspension with the turret of the A9 and a 340hp Liberty engine, producing a vehicle capable of 40mph on roads (though speed limiters were fitted to keep this down to 30mph), despite weighing more than the A10; it could travel at 14mph off-road, but had a range of ninety miles. The tracks were better than on the A9 and A10, being less likely to fall off; the tank was on the whole reliable and popular with its crews. Production started in 1939, and almost immediately it was decided to increase the thickness of the armour (which was 30mm at its thickest). The vehicle had a 2-pounder in the main turret, together with a co-axial 7.92mm BESA (though early models had a Vickers .303-inch); there was no hull machine-gun, meaning that it only required a crew of four (commander, gunner, loader, driver).

LIGHT TANK M3 STUART (HONEY)

The American M3 Light Tank was designed as a cavalry-style vehicle to be fielded in complete regiments, much like the British cruiser tank concept. The vehicle was put into production in March 1941 and almost immediately supplied to the British under the Lend-Lease arrangement. The British officially named it the "(General) Stuart" but its crews referred to it as the "Honey" owing to its mechanical reliability. The tank was armed with a 37mm gun and five .30-inch Browning machine-guns (three in the hull, one co-axial with the main gun in the turret, and one pintle-mounted as anti-aircraft defence). The 37mm gun had an advantage over the British 2-pounder in that as well as Armour-Piercing shot it could fire a High Explosive shell, useful against anti-tank guns.

As well as being reliable the tank was fast – its official speed was 36mph on roads and 18mph across country, but in the desert speeds of 40mph are often mentioned by British crews. This speed compensated for relatively thin armour (13mm to 51mm) and the short range of the main armament. By the time that the Honey saw action the Germans had begun to use 50mm and 88mm anti-tank guns, enabling them to destroy a Honey at 2000 yards or more, when the Honey could only realistically strike back at 800 yards.

The vehicle had other faults. Its engine – a 250hp Continental radial – would have looked at home on an aeroplane but was thirsty and fussy about what fuel it used. This meant that the vehicle had a range of only 74 miles, a great handicap in the desert, especially since the British refuelled their vehicles manually from four-gallon tins. The internal layout of the vehicle was not what we would term ergonomic, the main transmission from engine to tracks running in a duct right through the turret floor, making it a bit of a dance to traverse. The turret was designed for two men, but the British preferred to operate it as a three-man turret (Commander, Loader/Operator, and Gunner) with only one man (Driver) in the hull. Indeed, the British crews made extensive modifications to their Honeys, on the basis of their combat experience. Sergeant Jock Watt describes what was considered necessary:

> A large number of modifications were carried out to satisfy our requirements, replacing many items we considered a luxury with racks for extra ammunition. A sling-seat was added for the commander; when the situation allowed he could sit suspended with half his body sticking out of the turret, instead of having to grope with his

feet to find a foothold whilst suspended on his elbows. All unnecessary tools were slung out; on each tank there were tools for a complete engine overhaul – what a waste. Imagine sitting in the desert trying to take an engine to pieces with a lot of angry men hell-bent on stopping you. There were many more tools and fittings we considered unnecessary, and we discarded them all, including four thermos-flasks neatly clipped to brackets on the wall. The net result of all this was to increase the ammunition capacity by about fifty *per cent.*

(Watt, *A Tankie's Travels*)

The tank was very compact, making it tall and easier to spot in the flat desert terrain, a flaw exacerbated by the British practice of placing pennons on the wireless aerials to identify sub-units and command vehicles.

The Honey's career as a main battle tank was brief, and after Operation Crusader it was soon relegated to reconnaissance roles.

Appendix C
The Ballad of Mac & the Iron Monster

Ermanno Mariani
(Translation by author & Gabrielle Hullis, with assistance from Sara Marani)

This is the true story of Archibald Donald Mackenzie, a Captain in the Cameron Highlanders, who was taken prisoner by Italian soldiers in Africa, brought to Italy, and held in the prisoner-of-war camp at Veano in the province of Piacenza. After the armistice of September 8th 1943, Mackenzie left the camp with his friend Tresham Gregg (an Irish Captain, who adopted the *nom de guerre* "Ganna"). Whilst in hiding in the Appennines south of Piacenza, Mackenzie fell ill with amoebic dysentery, a delibilitating tropical illness which he had contracted in Africa, and was sheltered during this period by Father Amasanti of Groppo Ducale, who was in close contact with the partisans.

The local people quickly developed a liking for Mackenzie. He passed his time telling stories to the children. Mackenzie was forty years old, tall, and slender; the only vanity which he had was that he dyed his greying hair black, and combed and smoothed it backwards. Perhaps he thought that by doing so he could become closer to his partisans, who were almost all in their early twenties. His partisans saddled him with a very simple nom de guerre: Mac. To all the partisans, the Scotsman was always just "Capitano Mac".

Mac was an able man, and above all inspired respect. He made a great effort to welcome and to offer shelter to escaped Allied military personnel from the camp at Veano as well as other prisoner-of-war camps in the area. Americans, British, Australians, Polish, Russians – all the escapees being hunted by the German and Fascist authorities very soon came across Mac. Thanks to his organizational skills, he had a network of friends which allowed him, during the winter of 1943 to 1944, to get to safety dozens and dozens of Allied soldiers. Provided with false documents and expert guides, they were escorted as far as Switzerland and, from there, were able to return to their own countries. Mac had every opportunity to walk out of the war whenever he wanted; the network which he had created had agreed to take him to Switzerland whenever he wished. But he did not want to leave the Appennines or his partisans. Deaf to any suggestion of leaving, Mac said:

"This is the perfect place for fighting the Nazis and Fascists. I'm fighting for freedom, and it seems to me that here behind the German lines, with these partisans, I can make my contribution to the struggle."

And so Mac stayed to fight, for the freedom of a foreign country, for a people he did not know. He was admired by all the partisans not only for his qualities as a human being, but also for his powers of leadership and organization. His capabilities were soon recognized and quickly he was unanimously acclaimed commander of the *Stella Rossa* Brigade, even though he was not Italian or, for that matter, a Communist. But he certainly played his part in the war.

The greatest of the operations in which he took part was the siege of Ponte dell'Olio, the most ambitious and the largest-scale military operation conducted by the partisans of Piacenza – and Mac was one of its main architects.

It was October 4th 1944, four days since the start of the siege and the fourth day of heavy rain. The lightly-equipped partisans in their soaking canvas jackets looked out over their machine-guns and watched the area below them; it was impossible even to light a cigarette. Below them, Ponte dell'Olio, on a low and chestnut-wooded hill, was the gateway between the plain and the Val Nure. The area, which had thousands of inhabitants, was entirely surrounded by the *Stella Rossa* and *Mazzini* brigades and two detachments of *Garibaldini* from the *Bersani* Brigade. 8mm Breda machine-guns were positioned on the hill-tops all around the town.

Water poured down onto the reed-beds in the valley. The roads were deserted. The shutters and blinds of the low, pastel-coloured houses were closed; the inhabitants were virtual prisoners. On the walls were bizarre patterns left by machine-gun fire, patterns etched hour after hour into the plaster. Dividing the area in two was the long bridge which spanned the Nure – a long, straight, stone-built arched bridge.

The detachments of *Garibaldini* were positioned to the rear of the town, on the hills which overlooked it from the east. For their part, the *Stella Rossa* and *Mazzini* brigades were to the front of Ponte dell'Olio. Mac led the *Stella Rossa* Brigade; the *Mazzini* Brigade was under the command of "Pippo" Panni. The two detachments of *Garibaldini* were commanded by Fra Diavolo.

The Fascists – surrounded, and barricaded into their barracks and the primary school - numbered slightly fewer than eighty, but were well armed with automatic weapons. There were about five hundred partisans: Communists, Democrats, Socialists, Actionists, Anarchists, and Monarchists, all united by their desire to fight the Fascists.

During the siege, Mac constantly kept watch through his telescope from a machine-gun nest overlooking the barracks and the school in which the Fascists were barricaded. The water on the lens of his telescope formed meandering streaks which obscured his view.

"Will it never stop raining?" muttered Biondo, one of the nearest partisans.

The Scotsman muttered between his teeth: "They've got to surrender. Why don't they surrender? They've been without water and light for four days now. Their food and ammunition must be running out by now."

The railway track which then connected Piacenza and Bettola and ran through Ponte dell'Olio had been blown up in several places. Provincial Route 654, which ran from Piacenza to Ponte dell'Olio, had been occupied by the partisans and had been sown with land-mines.

Suddenly, some of the *Reppublichini* in the barracks and the school began to sing '*Battaglioni del Duce*':

"Battalions of the Duce, battalions
Created from death for life,
Know that in the spring the Party and the
Lands bring forth fire and flowers.
To win, we need the lions
Of Mussolini, armed with courage."

From the hills the partisans replied aggressively with '*Urla il vento*':

"The wind howls, the storm rages,
Our shoes are broken, but we must go forth
To conquer the sweet springtime,
Where the sun of the future rises –
To conquer the sweet springtime,
Where the sun of the future rises."

After a few verses, the singing was drowned out by the low, throaty bark of machine-guns, which all began to rattle at the same time from their fixed positions, their bullets tracing new and strange patterns on the walls of the school and barracks where the troops of the "Black Brigade" of Lucca and the 630th National Guard of Piacenza had barricaded themselves. The continuous fusillade for a moment sounded like a howl on one long single note. Then, slowly, the scream of metal diminished in intensity - but it did not stop.

The people of Ponte dell'Olio had had no light and no water for four days. Barricaded in their houses, the people covered their ears, repeatedly asking: "When will it end?" Not even during the nights of the siege could they live in peace. With the aid of darkness, in fact, small squads of partisans, the very core of the partisan brigades, came down through the streets of the town, scaling the walls like cats. Arriving at the primary school and the barracks, where the *Reppublichini* were holed up, they hurled their hand-grenades and anti-tank mines, so as to ruin the sleep of the besieged. And those awoken with a start by the crash of explosions retaliated by machine-gunning furiously and indiscriminately, while the partisans, in cover behind the walls of the houses, had a good laugh - though not without a touch of anxiety about all that fusillade of shots.

Suddenly, the rain changed its intensity: the small drops of a short while before were replaced by a downpour. The machine-guns ended their staccato conversation.

Long minutes of silence. Capitano Mac, with his blue eyes, tried to peer through the dense raindrops. Nothing. Nothing. Everything was wrapped in a shroud. From the surrounding area one could see the terracotta roofs of the bedraggled houses, and the high tower of the church, which had stood unused for four days, ever since the siege had started. The priest, Don Tinelli, had hidden himself away like all his fellow-townspeople. Sticking one's head out into the open was not healthy. In the course of those four days and four nights, they had fired hundreds of thousands of rounds. The noise had been horrific. Incredibly, there had been only one casualty, called Topolino, a partisan runner, only fifteen years old, who had been hit in the back by machine-gun fire. No one has ever been able to work out whether the shot came from the Fascist positions or from those of the partisans.

Topolino was immediately brought into the country on a horse. A call was put through from Don Tinelli, the priest of Ponte dell'Olio, to a Luftwaffe doctor stationed at the nearby San Damiano airfield, and despite being enemies of the rebels, the German agreed to pass through the partisan lines under a white flag, and visited the boy. He said that there was nothing which could be done, and Topolino died shortly afterwards. The German returned safely to the airfield.

During the afternoon of October 4th, there came from the provincial road the unexpected sound of an engine.

"The vegetable wagon!" shouted the partisans.

This was a giant armoured truck, built on a Fiat 666 chassis, and used occasionally to escort trucks of rotten produce for composting – hence the nickname given to it by the partisans: the *Tullon della Verdura*. It was a steel monster: eight metres long and four metres high. It ran too quickly on the provincial road to be considered a tank; it was not tracked, but had truck wheels. From the head of this monster – a revolving turret – projected a powerful machine-gun, a 12.7mm Breda. In each side of the titan there were several loopholes, so that, if necessary, the machine-gun could shift its field of fire. It had nine millimeters of steel armour-plating, and was impervious to any machine-gun supplied to the partisan brigades.

The vegetable wagon ran quickly along the road towards Ponte dell'Olio. The road had been mined by the partisans, but miraculously the armoured car ran over the minefield without blowing up. There was a sigh of disappointment from the partisans who watched the road; maybe the mines were old or defective. As Mac caught sight of the metal monster, its intent was immediately clear.

"It's bringing food and ammunition to the garrison."

The Scottish officer exchanged a look of understanding with Biondo and Santo, his subordinates, and gave the order to open fire. Tracer bullets cascaded from the machine-guns without pause, but the armoured car continued to roll in the direction of the bridge. From the hills all around the road poured an inferno of fire, every machine-gun firing on the monster as it continued to move forwards regardless. The bullets hammered on its armour like a ferocious downpour of rain. Unstoppable, the armoured car reached the bridge, its course always marked by a hail of lead. From time to time the machine-gun in its turret retaliated with a burst, but did not do anyone any harm.

The *Tullon della Verdura* finally reached the school, and some of the Republicans courageously succeeded in transferring a few packages under partisan machine-gun fire. A risky, difficult task. Mac's men could not help but admire the courage of these soldiers. In the end, the monster was put into motion again and speeded up towards the bridge. Mac gave the command:

"We have to stop the thing. Open up with all the machine-guns." The Scottish officer knew full well that, if it made one successful run, the truck would be able to come back with fresh reinforcements. It had to be stopped, once and for all.

In the middle of the bridge, under a hail of red, yellow and blue tracer rounds, the armoured car stopped, pinned down under a heavy fire from Taspak's Bren-gun. The machine-gun consumed whole magazines as it aimed at the armoured chest of the beast, which by now was not moving and resembled a target in a shooting-gallery at a fun-fair.

From the hills there rose a yell of joy, and the partisans fitted magazine after magazine to their overheated and smoking machine-guns, firing every round they had. The bullets ricocheted in huge numbers from the turret of the monster, producing a sinister metallic clatter. The armoured car appeared disabled; a thick white pillar of smoke rose from the radiator, which had been riddled in many places. For the Fascist crew inside the turret, this was the worst moment in their lives.

Taspak's Bren, which had been sited to take the bridge in enfilade and which, therefore, had been the only one to fire directly on the *Tullon della Verdura*, suddenly jammed, at the very moment when its fire would have been most useful. A 'tac-pum' round had been loaded into the magazine (that is the nick-name which the partisans had given to the German Mauser rifle), and this had jammed the Bren. While Sceriffo and La Tigrona stripped the weapon, the *Tullon della Verdura*, with a monstrous roar, began to move – very, very slowly. The shattered wheels turned: all four tyres had been riddled with bullets. The iron monster staggered forwards at a walking pace under the furious torrent of bullets which gushed from the rebel machine-guns. From behind the shutters of their houses, the ordinary people watched this spectacular and terrifying display with dismay.

Drunkenly the armoured car lurched to the right, leaving the stone bridge and joining the Provincial Highway, followed all the while by a trail of bullets. The stoppage cleared, the Bren began to fire, but now its fire was not as effective. At this point Mac, Biondo, Santo and a small group of partisans came down from the hills. They had everything ready: an anti-tank grenade and Molotov cocktails put together in record time. For a few moments the machine-guns on the hill ceased fire. Mac could only his own heavy breathing and that of his companions, the rhythmic pounding of their hobnailed boots on the grass and then the road. As they got to within three or four metres of the armoured car, Mac flung his own petrol-bomb, which landed on the turret of the vehicle, knocking its cork out. The glass bottle bouced off onto the ground and shattered, spilling its petrol on the road. Immediately afterwards Biondo hurled his anti-tank grenade, which detonated on the rear of the armoured car with a deafening explosion.

At once the machine-gun turret fired a random burst. The partisans were already disappearing into a nearby vineyard, with only Santo bemoaning the loss of the heel of one of his boots, carried away by a bullet-strike. The armoured car had stopped again; the grenade had pushed it over the gently-sloping edge of the road. While the machine-gun continued to fire out of the four rear gun-ports, several of the Fascists quickly pushed with all the force at their disposal, as the driver tried to steer and the engine roared as it turned. Perhaps it was the pushing; perhaps it was that the machine was lighter without its crew; perhaps it was a skilful manoeuvre by the driver; perhaps it was a supreme effort by the engine – but whatever it was, the fact is that there was another miracle and the armoured car managed to set off again, juddering and smoking. As soon as it moved, the crew returned to the safety of the iron monster's belly. The sound of machine-gun fire once again pursued the armoured car as it managed to reach the last turning and safety.

The *Tullon della Verdura* did not come back. The Fascists in Ponte dell'Olio surrendered the next day to the partisans of the *Stella Rossa, Mazzini* and *Garibaldini* detachments. Mac himself had negotiated the surrender of the Fascists, offering them their lives and a safe conduct to Piacenza in return for their weapons. Don Tinelli had acted as intermediary between the Scotsman and the Fascist lieutenant who was in charge, and, thanks to Mac's guarantee, the Fascists had agreed to surrender. There were eighty-two *Repubblichini*, and they left as a gift for the partisans a veritable cornucopia of machine-guns, sub-machine-guns, rifles, pistols, hand-grenades, explosives and ammunition.

It was a great victory, but it was marred when Colonel Franchi arrived in Ponte dell'Olio; he was the commander of *Zona* XIII and therefore Mac's commanding officer. When the Fascists were laying down their personal weapons in the town square, Franchi ordered that they be kept as prisoners-of-war.

"They'll be useful as exchanges for our partisans held in Piacenza," was Franchi's final word on the subject, and he refused to allow debate.

It was a bitter pill for Mac to swallow. He had given his word of honour to the Fascists, to whom he had promised their freedom in return for their weapons. He found the decision hard to take. Annoyed, he took himself off with Biondo and Santo to meet a friend in a quarry near Albarola. The Scotsman and the two partisans, wrapped in their waterproofs against the curtain of driving rain, spotted just too late the glint of metal from the barrels of sub-machine-guns and rifles; they had bumped into a Fascist patrol, which took them by surprise. The three resistance fighters, surrounded by Fascist troops with levelled sub-machine-guns, had no choice but to put their hands up. Lieutenant Caruso – awarded the *Medaglia d'Argento* by the Republican government – gave the lead to his squad and shot Mac, killing him with a single bullet. Immediately the Fascist patrol opened fire on the other two partisans. The three resistance fighters were finished off with bayonets and stripped of their packs.

The partisans of Piacenza put Mac in for the *Medaglia d'Oro,* and their citation for the award read:

"He died heroically in a land which he had adopted as a second home and which he loved as profoundly as his native Scotland. He was a shining example to those fighting for the freedom of the people, and and unforgettable hero of the European resistance."

The *Medaglia d'Oro* was not then awarded, nor has it ever been. At the quarry in Albarola where Mac and his two partisan companions were killed, today there are three old pillars, spoiled by years of neglect. They are difficult to reach. The path, a bit like their memory, has been eroded by time.

Notes

Prelude: Veano

1 Italian prisoner-of-war camps had the official title *Campo concentramento di prigioneri di guerra* (abbreviated to 'PG'), followed by a number.

2 Several attempts have been made to tell the story of the liberation of the Val Nure by Donny Mackenzie and Tresham Gregg. An article about Donny (*The Amazing Story of Capitano Mac*) appeared in the *Glasgow Evening Citizen* in August 1959, but Gregg was not consulted and although he did not see it until 2008 he remained deeply unhappy about its mistakes: *Many of the statements in the article are just not true, or show a great confusion of what was true. I see no purpose in writing to the editor and pointing out the errors. However, I'm more than a little curious as to who* [its author] *John MacLennan is or was.* (Gregg, pers.comm. to author, March 2008.)

In 2004, Malcolm Tudor published *Special Force: SOE and the Italian Resistance 1943-1945*, which gave a brief account of the work which the two men did in the Val Nure. Drawn mainly from exaggerated Italian sources, it failed to satisfy Gregg. An opportunity to put the record straight came after a lecture by this author at Winchester College late in 2006. The writer Edward Marriott contacted the author and went on to interview Gregg and to write an article about him – *The Cumbrian Capitano* – for *Saga Magazine* (November 2007). Gregg was much happier about this piece, especially since it prompted several people to write to him: they included Donny's relatives and grateful Italians who had been children in the Val Nure during his time there in 1944.

2012 saw the publication of *A Spur Called Courage: SOE Heroes in Italy*, by Alan Ogden. Although it mentions many names which appear in this book, it is sadly awry on the story of Gregg and Mackenzie: on page 173 it states that *Captain Mackenzie MacDonald had led a similar existence after walking out of his POW camp in Piacenza in September 1943. Although he had been offered the chance to reach the Swiss frontier, he determined to remain in Italy and became deputy commander of the Garibaldi Valnure brigade, complete with red star sewn on his Bersagliari hat. In October 1944, while commanding a small group of Partisans gallantly holding up a German attack, he was killed on the banks of the Nure River near Albarola.* Readers are invited to assess the accuracy of this summary for themselves.

In November 2012, after interviewing Gregg, John Burland wrote a short but accurate article for *Cumbria* magazine, also called *The Cumbrian Capitano*.

After Gregg died on March 17th 2014, full obituaries were published in both *The Times* and *The Daily Telegraph*. Despite the family and this author's involvement in compiling these obituaries, both introduced unnecessary errors – such as the mistaken assertion that Gregg was shot in the head whilst escaping from Veano (a mistake with its origin in the citation for his Mention in Dispatches in 1945) – though Gregg would have been amused to discover that he commanded an "Artisan Brigade".

Chapter One: Gunner

1 *Supplement to the London Gazette*, December 30th 1995: *CBE To be Ordinary Commanders of the Military Division of the said Most Excellent Order: Colonel Tresham Dames GREGG (485734), late The Light Dragoons.*

2 According to an army report on his award, Lieutenant Tresham Gregg displayed *phenomenal command skills by successfully taking charge of a mixed vehicle and dismounted soldier troop during Op Panchai Palang. [He] led from the front as his reconnaissance vehicles cleared routes through important areas, often having to use choke points to progress. Insurgents attacked his troops on several occasions, but the officer did not hesitate to move his vehicles into the line of fire to protect his men. Although the group suffered a number of casualties during the offensive, Lieutenant Gregg demonstrated compassion and maturity beyond his years to maintain a high level of morale that proved inspirational to the rest of the battle-group.* His Military Cross citation read: "*His courage, forthright leadership and determination to complete the mission in the face of heavy casualties were pivotal to the success of the operation.*"

3 December 22nd 1983. Readers interested in the full Gregg lineage should see Appendix A.

4 His Italian comrades in 1943-1944, unable to pronounce "Gunner", called him "Ganna".

5 Quotations not otherwise attributed are taken from personal comments made by Tresham Gregg to the author between 2005 and 2012, both in writing and in the course of several face-to-face interviews in Glassonby, Cumbria; the most extensive took place in April 2010 and August 2011.

6   Emile Bisset (*née* Verpelat – the 't' is silent) was descended from a Huguenot who had escaped from Paris and become pastor of the Lutheran church in Thun, Switzerland. Her father was also pastor of the church. She later claimed that she was the first woman to attend a university in Switzerland; she studied languages at Geneva University, and went on to take a second degree in Boston. When returning from Boston by ship she met Walter Bisset, a director of the White Star Line, whom she later married.

7   The Dublin Lying-In Hospital was founded in 1745 as the first ever maternity training hospital. In 1757 the hospital moved to premises which it still occupies, becoming the New Lying-In Hospital, referred to as "The Rotunda". The Master in 1919 was Henry Jellett.

8   Gregg still has the trophy.

9   The British tennis player Winifred Alice "Freda" James won the women's doubles in 1933 at the US Women's National Championship (with Betty Nuthall), and at Wimbledon in 1935 and 1936 (with Kay Stammers). She played for Britain from 1931 to 1939.

10   Harold Geoffrey Owen "Tuppy" Owen-Smith was born in Rondebosch on February 18th 1909, and went on to play cricket as a right-handed batsman for South Africa (five test matches in 1929) and rugby as a full-back for England (ten matches between 1934 and 1937, captaining the side three times). At Oxford University he also proved himself a fine boxer and athlete, winning five 'blues'. He also captained the Barbarians. Having qualified as a doctor at St Mary's, he then returned to Rondebosch and became a GP. Owen-Smith died on February 28th 1990.

Denys Paul Beck Morkel was born in Cape Town on January 25th 1906, and was a noted right-hand batsman and bowler. He started playing first-class cricket in 1924-1925, and represented South Africa for the first time in a match against the MCC in Johannesburg in December 1927. Owing to ill-health, he last played for South Africa in 1932. He had settled in England, where in 1932 Sir Julien Cahn helped him to establish a business in the motor trade in Nottingham. Between 1932 and 1939 he played for Sir Julien's team, and made nearly ten thousand runs, also taking over four hundred wickets. During the Second World War he served in the army. Morkel died in Nottingham on October 6th 1980, just two weeks after his wife Margery.

11   Emile Verpelat was buried in Steffisburg, near Thun. Gregg later visited her grave in Thun and presented to the church there a slate engraving of the Last Supper, a gift from the Dean of York to the Swiss church.

12   Gunner is unsure now of their name, though they may have been the Squires.

13   Mabel Edeline Strickland OBE (1899-1988) was the daughter of Sir Gerald Strickland (later Lord Strickland), Prime Minister of Malta. She was the editor of *The Times of Malta* during the Second World War and in the Nineteen Fifties became a anti-independence politician, leading the Progressive Constitutional Party. In 1962 she was elected to the Maltese Parliament.

Chapter Two: Donny

1   Lynedoch Archibald Mackenzie BSc, AMICE, of Buglawton Hall, Congleton, Cheshire, was the son of Donald ("Don") Mackenzie, Writer to the Signet, of 12 Great Stuart Street, Edinburgh. His mother was Laura ("Louie") Augusta Mackenzie, daughter of Lynedoch Douglas of the Highland Light Infantry. The couple married on January 23rd 1912, at St John's Church, Buglawton. Dor Mackenzie was the daughter of Joseph Maghall Yates KC, and sister to Wykehamists Joseph Mervyn St John Yates ('I' 1892-1895) and Humphrey William Maghall Yates ('I' 1897-1900). A third Yates brother (H. Gervase N. Yates) did not go to Winchester, owing to illness, but became a tea-planter in Ceylon; two of his sons spent the duration of the Second World War with their "Auntie Dor" at her home, 'Rosefield', St Cyrus.

2   Later 2nd Battalion, the Cameronians.

3   Lieutenant-General Kenneth MacKenzie-Douglas had served in Wellington's army, and was rewarded with the title of Baronet Douglas of Glenbervie; the last of his line was the fifth baronet, Major Sholto Mackenzie-Douglas MC, Seaforth Highlanders.

4   Lieutenant-Colonel Daniel Barton Mackenzie MBE.

5   Born in Nablus in 1920, Brian Douglas Mackenzie followed Donny to Winchester College ('B' 1933-1938). He played for the Soccer XI and shot for the Bisley VIII before attending RMA Woolwich from 1938-1939. Commissioned into the Royal Engineers three months before war was declared, he went out to France on May 3rd 1940, just in time to meet the German invasion. He was one of the last to be evacuated from Dunkirk on June 2nd 1940: his party used their helmets to paddle to HMS *Halcyon*, one of the last ships to leave. He returned to Europe in 1944 in command of 202 Field Company, which

built twenty-six bridges in five months and finished the war in Bremen. Later he served in Hong Kong, Libya and Germany before retiring as a Lieutenant-Colonel in 1968. Subsequently he worked in schools, at Uppingham, Glenalmond and Ardvreck (as a piping instructor) and served as Deputy Secretary of the Highland TA&VR Association from 1975 to 1985. He was proud to be a shooting member of the Queen's Bodyguard for Scotland, the Royal Company of Archers. In 1943 he married Eileen West, who died in 1997; he himself died on September 7th 2012, aged ninety-two. He was survived by his three daughters.

6   Brian Mackenzie, *pers.comm.* to author, 2008.

7   The term 'public school' does not mean that the school is run by the state; quite the opposite. The term is synonymous with 'independent school', which is easier to understand, and implies not state supervision but the willingness of the school to accept any pupil who meets its entrance criteria. Many of the original public schools had originally been charitable foundations established for the education of poor scholars, but had gradually begun to accept fee-paying pupils in addition so as to fund better teaching and facilities for their core of scholars. In the Victorian period, such schools had become increasingly popular with the upper classes and with the newly wealthy upper middle class. The schools' curricula were based on sport and the classics. They may have omitted much which we would consider important in education today (such as science), but helped to prepare the sons of the elite – and those who aspired to be elite – for leadership, be it in government, the armed forces, the colonial service, or in business. But there had been problems, and in 1868 it had proven necessary to pass the Public Schools Act to put into good order the affairs of nine charitable foundations (Winchester College, Eton College, Charterhouse School, Harrow School, Merchant Taylor's School in Northwood, Rugby School, Shrewsbury School, St. Paul's School, and Westminster School. These had been given independence under boards of governors, and had under the stimulus of the Act's provisions begun to develop into modern, forward-thinking places of education which still lead the field today.

9   The foundation was intended to educate seventy 'poor and needy' scholars who would then go on to New College, Oxford, which William founded at the same time; there were also to be ten fee-paying 'noble Commoners'. Over the centuries, the staff of the College gradually recruited more and more 'Commoners', who by the Nineteenth Century numbered sometimes over a hundred. In the late Eighteen-Fifties, the construction of a series of boarding houses began; by 1905 there were ten.

10   Delaforce, *pers.comm.* to author, 2009. Jackson was born in 1884 and died in 1972.

11   Peter Revell-Smith, *pers.comm.* to author, 2009. Peter Norman Railing was the son of Norman F.H. Railing ('B' 1911-1916), who had been born Freudenthal but had changed his name on the outbreak of the First World War and gone on to serve with the Grenadier Guards. Peter Railing ('B' 1938-1942) also served with the Grenadier Guards, being Intelligence Officer with 4th Battalion in north-west Europe in 1944 and 1945. He then went on to New College, Oxford.

12   Sir Roger du Boulay, *pers.comm.* to author, 2010. Seymour James Gerald Schlesinger was at Winchester from 1933 until 1938, when he went on to Corpus Christi College, Oxford. He took a War Degree in Medicine, and trained as a doctor, serving in the RAMC from 1944 until 1947. He then undertook training in psychiatry, and after more academic work and practical experience in several hospitals and areas, in 1961 became a clinical lecturer at Oxford University. He worked at Oxford's Warneford Hospital from 1961 until retiring in 1985. He married Margaret Behn in 1944; he also changed his surname, to Spencer.

13   Tony Pawson OBE, *Indelible Memories*.

14   du Boulay, *pers.comm.* to author, 2010.

15   Brian Mackenzie, *pers.comm.* to author, 2008.

16   Revell-Smith, *pers.comm.* to author, 2009.

17   Delaforce, *pers.comm.* to author, 2009.

18   Delaforce, *pers.comm.* to author, 2009.

19   Revell-Smith, *pers.comm.* to author, 2009.

20   Revell-Smith, *pers.comm.* to author, 2009.

21   The eccentric system of naming for forms still survives in part, but in the Nineteen-Thirties the progression was Junior Part 2, Junior Part 1; Middle Part 3, 2, Science, and 1; Senior Part Science III, 3, 2, Science II, Science I, and 1; and Sixth Book 2, Science, 1b and 1a.

22   Jackson, summary of report on A.D. Mackenzie, in Moberley's House archives, Winchester College.

23   Jackson, *ibid.*

24   Jackson, *ibid.*

25   Brian Mackenzie, *pers.comm.* to author, 2008.

26	The *Geneva Convention relative to the Treatment of Prisoners of War* came into effect two years later.
27	Jackson, *ibid.*
28	Jackson, *ibid.*
29	Jackson, *ibid.*
30	Jackson, *ibid.*
31	Jackson, *ibid.*
32	Jackson, *ibid.*
33	Jackson, *ibid.*
34	These days, the game is normally referred to as "Winkies", but use of the term in interviews with Old Wykehamists has produced such a negative reaction that the author has not used it here.
35	Commoners comprised 'D', 'E', 'G', 'H' and 'K'; "Old Tutors Houses", also known just as "Houses", was made up of 'A', 'B', 'C', 'F' and 'I'. College fitted into neither faction and, having a far smaller pool from which to draw its players, was at a massive competitive disadvantage.
36	*The Wykehamist.*
37	*The Wykehamist.*
38	Jackson, *ibid.*
39	*The Wykehamist.*
40	*The Wykehamist.*
41	*The Wykehamist.*
42	Jackson, *ibid.*
43	He represented Winchester College against Bradfield on Saturday March 19th 1932, but lost his bout against H.M.C. Candy.
44	Winchester won the Ashburton in 1871, 1872, 1873, 1876, 1904 and 1937. At first, the Rifle Volunteers were self-financing and entirely independent of government control, although in 1868 the Winchester College unit became part of 1st Hampshire Volunteer Battalion.
45	Jackson, *ibid.*
46	The Bren was the standard light machine-gun of the British army, issued one per infantry section of eight men and intended to give covering fire in the attack and volume of fire in the defence. It was immensely reliable and accurate – perhaps too accurate for a weapon intended to rain bullets over a wide area – and had the great disadvantage that it was fed from a thirty-round magazine, thus requiring constant pauses to change the magazine in action. It was still in use with the British army in the 1982 Falklands War.
47	du Boulay, *pers.comm.* to author, 2010.
48	*The Wykehamist.*
49	'G' 1928-1933.
50	*The Wykehamist.*
51	Jackson, *ibid.*
52	Jackson, *ibid.*
53	Brian Mackenzie, *pers.comm.* to author, 2008.
54	Brian Mackenzie, *pers.comm.* to author, 2008. Colin Pitman (L.C. Pitman, 'B' 1930-1936) also went on to join the Cameron Highlanders (5th Battalion), and was killed in action in Tunisia on March 23rd 1943.
55	Brian Mackenzie, *pers.comm.* to author, 2008. Pearson had been a pupil at West Downs preparatory school in Winchester, so it is likely that the two young men met through a mutual acquaintance.

Chapter Three: Growing Up

1	Within a month of the death in 1916 of Lord Kitchener of Khartoum, a Memorial Fund was established by the Lord Mayor of London; within two years the fund stood at £500,000 (around £12,000,000 today). Eventually it was decided to use this money to offer university scholarships to the children of men who had served in the armed forces.
2	The motion was opposed, one must in fairness to Winchester point out, by a Wykehamist contemporary of Donny – Keith Richard Felix Steel-Maitland ('I' 1925-1931), of Balliol College; he became President of the Oxford Union in 1934. Somewhat ironically, he did not serve in the Second World War.
3	*Daily Express*, Saturday February 11th 1933.
4	Sir Winston Churchill, speech to Anti-Socialist and Anti-Communist Union, February 17th 1933.
5	Robert Bernays, quoted in *Hansard*, July 30th 1934.

6 Sir Bernard Melchior Feilden CBE, FRIBA was born in Hampstead on September 11th 1919; he was one of a pair of twin sons, and one of five brothers. Until the age of nine Feilden and his family lived in Canada for the sake of his father's health (his father had been gassed during the First World War). On his father's death the family returned to Bedford, where Feilden was raised by his aunts and mother. After being educated at Bedford School, Feilden followed in the footsteps of his maternal grandfather, an architect, and won an exhibition to the Bartlett School of Architecture in London. During the war he served in the Bengal Sappers and Miners, in Iraq, Iran, India and Italy, a pleasingly assonant selection of theatres.

After the war he finished his studies with the Architectural Association, and joined the London firm Boardman's. In 1954 a shooting accident cost him his left eye, and he moved to Norfolk to set up practice with David Mawson. Feilden and Mawson became, over the next forty years, a large and distinguished firm. Feilden won six of the company's fifteen major awards.

Feilden was called in as a conservation architect or consultant on important monuments across the globe: Norwich Cathedral, York Minster, St Paul's Cathedral, Hampton Court Palace, the King's Manor in York, St Giles Cathedral (in Edinburgh), the Al-Aqsa Mosque in Jerusalem, the Taj Mahal, the Sun Temple at Konarak, the Forbidden City in China, and even the Great Wall of China. For his work on the dome of the Al-Aqsa Mosque he received an Aga Khan Award in 1986. A Fellow of the Royal Institute of British Architects, he represented RIBA on the Ancient Monuments Board from 1962 to 1977, and was a member of the RIBA Council (1975 to 1977). He was President of both the Ecclesiastical Architects' Association and the Guild of Surveyors in 1976. From 1981 to 1987 he was President of the International Council on Monuments and Sites (UK).Between 1972 and 1994 he lectured on Architectural Conservation at the Unesco International Centre for the Study of Preservation and Restoration of Cultural Property (ICCROM) in Rome, serving as director from 1977 to 1981. He was also responsible for the campus of the University of East Anglia. He was appointed CBE in 1976 and knighted in 1985.

His publications included *An Introduction to Conservation* (1980), the magisterial *Conservation of Historic Buildings* (1982), *A Manual for the Management of World Cultural Heritage Sites* (1983), *Between Two Earthquakes* (1987), and *Guidelines for Conservation in India* (1989).

In 1949 he married Ruth Bainbridge, with whom he had two sons and two daughters. After her death in 1994, he married Tina Murdoch in 1995. According to his obituary in the *Daily Telegraph*, Feilden was *a gentlemanly, kindly man..., an avid reader of histories and biographies. He demanded much of himself, always setting himself targets and goals when there were difficulties to be overcome – his most recent being to live to see the American presidential election. After his formal retirement he continued to work as a consultant from his homes at Stiffkey and later at Bawburgh, Norfolk, where he enjoyed his hobbies of sailing, painting and fishing. He also served on the fabric committees of Norwich, Ely and St Edmundsbury cathedrals.*

7 Prince Alonso Maria Christino Justo of Orleans Y Bourbon, who was born in Madrid on May 28th 1912, was a member of the Spanish royal family. He was related to King Alfonso XIII, who had fled Spain in 1931 when the country was declared a republic. Alonso's father, HRH the Infante Don Alfonso, was Alfonso XIII's first cousin. Alonso's mother, Princess Beatrice Leopoldine Victoria, was the grand-daughter of Queen Victoria. On his father's side the Prince was descended from Louis Philippe (King of the French 1830-1848); indeed, many French monarchists still hold that Alonso's family are the rightful kings of France. The Prince, with his brothers Alvaro and Ataulfo, was educated at Winchester ('E' 1926-1930), and at the Zurich Federal Polytechnic, where he obtained a diploma in mechanical engineering in December 1934. This diploma, according to an obituary contributed to the *Times* by a Swiss minister, was *one of the hardest of its kind*. He was, according to his Winchester obituary, *an expert skier and a member of a Spanish team which distinguished itself in Switzerland. He loved Switzerland, its mountains and its people. And yet wherever he went it was he who, with his undaunted vitality, his entrain and joie de vivre, his sense of duty, and his pluck in adversity, seemed in his simple and modest way to give so much more than he received. He was interested in wireless, television, and music. The Prince's natural gifts reached a level far above the average. He spoke five languages, as well as Allemanic-Swiss, faultlessly... and was a good all-round athlete, and a perfect sportsman. Among the younger generation he was quoted as the type of young man no one could help but like and love. He had by no means an easy, care-free life; he had to start his fight to get through life from the very bottom, and he did it splendidly. Until he went to Spain, via Lisbon, to join Franco's insurgents in late October 1936, the Prince had been working as an engineer and draughtsman in a factory at Coventry, where he had been employed for fifteen months, patiently doing a job far below his remarkable qualifications.* He had joined the Coventry Aero Club in June 1935, and qualified as a pilot in August 1936. He was killed in an aeroplane accident on November 18th 1936, while fighting for General Franco's forces. He was twenty-four years of age. His brother, Alvaro, collected Alonso's

body from the crash site, and took it to Seville. Alonso was buried with full military honours in the family mausoleum at Sanlúcar de Barrameda, near Cadiz.

8   Oxford University Archives OT 4/3.
9   *London Gazette,* August 28th 1936: *Camerons – 2nd Lt. Archibald Donald Mackenzie, from Gen.List, T.A. 31st Jan. 1935, next above 2nd Lt. R.B. White.*
10 *The 79th News,* October 1936.
11 *The 79th News,* January 1937.
12 Yates, *pers.comm.* to author, 2008.
13 Donald "Don" Osborne Finlay won the Olympic silver medal in the 1936 Berlin Olympics in the 110 metre hurdles and went on to fly fighter aircraft during the war. He rose to be a Group Captain and was awarded the DFC and AFC, with at least four confirmed 'kills'. He captained the British team at the 1948 Olympics.
14 David George Brownlow Cecil, Sixth Marquess of Exeter, KCMG, had won the gold medal in the 400 metre hurdles at the 1928 Olympics. He remains the only man known to have completed the 367 metre run around the Great Court of Trinity College, Cambridge, in the 44 seconds which it takes the college clock to chime twelve, a feat which he completed in 1927 and which famously appears in the 1981 film Chariots of Fire, though credited therein to a different man.
15 The *London Gazette* contains four entries detailing Mackenzie's appointment to the staff, two of which are simply corrections of the previous two. His appointment to the staff was announced in the issue of December 17th 1937, and dated his appointment to October 17th 1937. This announcement was repeated in the issue of December 31st 1937. The issue of January 21st 1938 corrected the first announcement to read October 22nd as his date of appointment, and the issue of January 25th 1938 made the same correction to the second announcement. In short, *2nd Lt. A.D. Mackenzie, Camerons, is apptd. to a Spec.Appt. (Cl.HH) (temp.) 22nd Oct 1937.*
16 *London Gazette,* Febuary 1st 1938: *The undermentioned 2nd Lts. to be Lts. 31st Jan. 1938:- A.D. Mackenzie and remains secd.*
17 *The 79th News,* January 1938.
18 Sir Winston Churchill, speaking in the House of Commons on November 12th 1940.
19 Christian Johann Heinrich Heine (1797-1856) of Dusseldorf was one of the most important German poets of the Nineteenth Century. Many of his works have been set to music as Lieder by composers such as Brahms, Mendelssohn, Orff, Schubert, Schumann, Richard Strauss, and Wagner. Gregg here quotes from Heine's poem *Mein Kind, wir waren Kinder,* the first two verses of which might be translated as follows: *My child, we were just children,/ Two happy kids, that's all:/ We crept into the hen-house,/ And hid there in the straw./ We crowed like the cockerel,/ And all the passers-by/ Thought our "Cock-a-doodle-doo!"/ Was the real cockerel's cry.* Heine's poetry was burned by the Nazis because his parents had been Jewish, even though he was educated at Catholic schools. Presciently, in 1821 he wrote that *dort wo man Bücher verbrennt, verbrennt man am Ende auch Menschen.* ("Where they burn books, they will ultimately burn people as well.")
20 The Siebengebirge are a set of hills on the east side of the Rhine south-east of Bonn, not far from Königswinter.
21 Sir Winston Churchill, press statement, September 21st 1938.

Chapter Four: Phoney War

1   Gunner recalls the following anecdote which Feilden told him about his war service:
    His squadron spent the war building bridges, one of them over the Shatt al Arab in Iraq. Bernard then dived in to the water and swam the whole length of the bridge, being cheered – as he thought – the whole way by Arabs. Only when he reached the far bank did they manage to tell him that they'd expected him to be eaten by the sharks which swim up from the Persian Gulf to eat the dead animals which were swept down the river.
2   Descriptions of the different types of tanks used by 3RTR will be found in Appendix B.
3   'The Load of Hay' is now called 'The Augustus John.'
4   Field Marshal Sir Archibald Percival Wavell, 1st Earl Wavell GCB, GCSI, GCIE, CMG, MC, PC (May 5th 1883 to May 24th 1950). Wavell is buried in Winchester College; his tombstone reads simply "Wavell".
5   *The Wykehamist,* June 4th 1940.
6   William Murray "Bill" Leggatt was the second son of Ernest Hugh Every Leggatt, of the Indian Civil Service, and Jesse Leggatt (daughter of the banker Andrew Murray). Born on September 2nd 1900, he came to Winchester in September 1914 (C, 1914-1918). Leggatt had a clear head and was an excellent athlete. He was in Lords in 1917 and 1918, and in OTH VI in 1917-18, being captain in 1918. The

writer of his obituary in the *Wykehamist War Service Record and Roll of Honour* stated that he would never forget *an exhibition of kicking given by him and Rupert Potter for Old Houses VI vs. Houses*. He also spent two years in the soccer XI, as a fine full-back. He passed into RMA Woolwich in 1919, and was captain of the Academy's teams in cricket and football. In cricket, he won two matches against the RMC. In 1919 he took fifteen wickets, and in 1920 made 96 and 78 in a lowish-scoring match. As a full-back he was a worthy member of the strong Old Wykehamist football team which won the Dunn Cup for the first time in 1920. In 1926 he played for Kent with success, as a typical hard-hitting Army batsman. He also played for the Army in 1926, as well as every year from 1930 to 1934, when he was captain. On July 29th 1929 he married Connel Auld Mathieson, daughter of T. Ogilvie Mathieson; in 1931 they had a son, Michael William Leggatt, who also came to Winchester (C, 1944-1949). They lived at Hinton Place, Hinton St. George, Somerset. Leggatt was promoted Captain in 1933 and served as an instructor at the RMA from 1931 to 1935. In the latter year, he was appointed Adjutant of 16 Field Brigade, and rose to the rank of Major in 1938. He then served as a Brigade Major in Egypt until the outbreak of war. He was a GSO2 and then GSO1 at GHQ MEF from July 1940 to March 1942. After nine months in command of 11 (HAC) Field Regiment RHA with Eighth Army (during which period he fought at El Alamein, where he was awarded the DSO), he returned to GHQ as a GSO1, until August 1943, when he took command of 83 Anti-Tank Regiment RA. He had been twice mentioned in despatches. In May 1944, now a Lieutenant-Colonel, he returned to England, his health broken, to act as OC of 3rd RA Reserve Regiment. In April 1945 he was sent on a year's sick leave, but never recovered, and died of a heart attack in the smoking room of the Cavalry Club, Picadilly, London on August 13th 1946, aged fifty-one. He had been equally good at staff work and the command of men, and would have been sure of further promotion but for his ill-health. Everybody had been fond of him, and his death came as a great shock. He had possessed great gifts, and few strong men have been more gentle. His funeral was held on Saturday August 17th 1946, and he rests in the south-west part of St. George's churchyard, Hinton St. George.

7. Major-General Ronald Frederick King "David" Belchem CB, CBE, DSO (1911-1981) was the author of the excellent memoir *All in the Day's March* (1978). Commissioned into 6 RTR in 1931, he was a talented linguist (an interpreter in both Russian and Italian); he served in Egypt and Palestine from 1936 to 1939, and after attending the staff course in 1940 joined Wavell's intelligence staff in Cairo. In February 1941 he was posted as GSO2 (Operations) of 'W' Force, the Commonwealth contribution to the campaign in mainland Greece. After being evacuated, he became a Staff Officer with Eighth Army in the Western Desert until 1943. He returned to regimental duty as OC 1RTR in Tripoli and Tunisia 1943 before re-joining the staff as Montgomery's Brigadier General Staff (Operations) in Sicily and Italy. Belchem followed Montgomery back to England, performing the same role for 21 Army Group in 1944. After the war he was variously OC 6 (Highland) Infantry Brigade BAOR (1948); Chief of Staff to Montgomery (1948-1950); and OC 33 Armoured Brigade BAOR (1950-1953). He retired in 1953.

8. Brigadier Claude Nicholson CB was born on July 2nd 1898; his brother was Godfrey Nicholson, MP for Farnham ('D' 1915-1920). He was at Winchester College from 1912 to 1915 (in 'G'). A tall, dark-haired man, he entered RMC Sandhurst in September 1915, and obtained a commission in 16th Lancers, with whom he served in France until 1918. He became Adjutant in 1921, serving in Palestine, India and Egypt, and entered the Staff College at Camberley in 1929. In 1930 and 1931 he was a GSO3 at the War Office, and then spent two years in command of a company of Gentlemen Cadets at the RMC. He became a GSO2 at the Staff College, with the brevet rank of Major, in 1934. On December 31st 1935 he married the Hon. Ursula Katherine Hanbury-Tracy. The couple had a daughter, and their son – Richard Hugh Nicholson – eventually also went to Winchester ('G' 1950-1954).

With the brevet rank of Lieutenant-Colonel (January 1st 1938), he then instructed at the Staff College, before moving on to command his regiment (now 16th/5th Lancers) in India in 1938-1939. On his return he graduated at the Imperial Defence College. With his quick brain, vigour and determination he was marked out for speedy promotion to high rank. Airey Neave, who fought under Nicholson's command at Calais, described him in *The Flames of Calais* as *a true professional. He worked hard and was widely read. His ability was well known... By temperament, Nicholson was a perfectionist. Outwardly, he was the trained cavalry officer and a good horseman which he had dreamed of being as a boy. He was sympathetic and courteous. He was also sensitive, modest and very intelligent. There were some who thought him formal and orthodox, but to the rapidly changing situation at Calais he reacted with great swiftness of mind. He must have been deeply troubled by the conflicting orders which he received, but he was not a man to lose his head.* General Sir Hubert Gough – the distinguished First World War Army commander – thought most highly of Nicholson, and wrote of him as follows in *The Times*: *This nation has lost one of the finest of her sons... He had, however, lived long enough to impress all who knew him with his great qualities*

– a deeply-read student of war, a cool and thoughtful mind, well founded on those invaluable characteristics of firmness, decision and energy... As an Englishman, his broad-minded and noble character was an asset and a great example. Though his life was short, that example, like those of other true and gallant gentlemen, from whatever class they arose, will live and help in the creation of other English characters like their own. Nicholson died in a German prisoner-of-war camp (Oflag IX A/Z) on June 26th 1943, aged forty-four, and is buried in grave 7.71 of the Rotenburg (Fulda) Civil Cemetery, Germany.

Chapter Five: Calais

1 Toby Everett had been Senior Under Officer at Sandhurst.
2 The Adjutant was Captain George Moss.
3 Brigadier Hugo Craster Wakeford Ironside OBE was born in Northamptonshire on June 14th 1918 and educated at St Edward's, Oxford. He was awarded a Prize Cadetship to RMC Sandhurst and was commissioned into 3 RTR in 1938. After being captured at Calais, he was marched to Trier, and spent time in camps at Laufen (Stalag VIIC), Posen, Biberach and Warburg. When transferred to Oflag VIIB in Eichstätt, Bavaria, he joined in the construction of a tunnel which began in a lavatory. The existence of this tunnel was betrayed by a fellow prisoner (not everyone approved of escape attempts) but the Germans proved unable to locate the hidden trapdoor. On June 3rd 1943, sixty-five officers broke out through the tunnel; they were all recaptured, but it had taken 50,000 German troops, police and militamen to do so. Ironside evaded capture for two days before being captured by a famer with a shotgun when he entered a village looking for water. He was then transferred to Oflag IVC at Colditz Castle. He joined a Polish tunnelling attempt, which was attempting to break out through the sewers. He later recalled that *when you finished your shift, filthy and soaked you had to slide under a large electric cable. It scared me to death.* However, the Polish were removed from Colditz before the tunnel could be completed. Ironside was also involved with the construction of the famous glider in the Chapel attic.

After being released in 1945, Ironside married Tonita Harbord, with whom he had a son and a daughter, but this marriage was later dissolved. He commanded 8RTR in Germany from 1958 (the Adjutant claimed that he *gave a bit of style to what had become a rather prosaic affair),* and continued in command when the battalion was merged with 5RTR. In 1960 he was appointed OBE. He later served in the War Office and Ministry of Defence, retiring in 1968. From 1972 until 1982 he worked at the Central Office of Information. In 1977 he married Carolyn John, but she predeceased him, and in 2001 he married Jane O'Gorman *(née* Llewellyn). According to his *Daily Telegraph* obituary, *he was a man of great charm, and in retirement he enjoyed golf, flying kites, and taking cars to pieces.* He died on October 3rd 2008, aged ninety.
4 SS *City of Christchurch* had been built in 1915 as the *Aschenburg* for the German Hansa Line. In 1919 she was seized as reparations and in 1920 taken over by the Ellerman Line as SS *Lorenzo*. In 1929 she was re-named *City of Christchurch*. She was sunk by enemy aircraft on March 22nd 1943 off Portugal.
5 Trooper Bill Jordan, quoted in Delaforce, *Taming the Panzers: 3RTR at War.*
6 At this stage of the war, the British transported petrol in flimsy metal tins which often leaked, were difficult to pour from, and resulted in massive wastage of a precious fluid which had to be imported to Britain at the cost of thousands of merchant seamen's lives.
7 Director of Staff Duties.
8 Foote was attached to SD7, the RAC branch of the General Staff.
9 Foote, in Tank Museum archives.
10 Keller, report on the fighting at Calais, National Archives CAB106/233.
11 Foote, in Tank Museum archives.
12 This generation of the Davies-Scourfield family produced several outstanding officers, all Wykehamists. David ('B' 1924-1930) rose to command 3WG in Italy in 1944, winning the MC and being wounded twice. John ('B' 1929-1934), like David, played cricket for the Winchester First XI ("Lords") and joined the regular army before the war; he served with the Rifle Brigade until his capture in Libya in 1942, spending the rest of the war as a prisoner. Gris ('B' 1932-1936) joined the King's Royal Rifle Corps in 1938 after passing out top at RMC Sandhurst. He too was captured, at Calais in 1940, and spent the next five years causing the Germans as much inconvenience as possible; at one point he escaped for ten months, working with the Polish resistance, and upon recapture he was locked up in Colditz. His memoirs, *In Presence of My Foes,* make humbling reading. He too was awarded the MC.

13   A Bren-gun carrier was a lightly-armoured tracked vehicle (likened by American troops to a sardine-can on tracks) which was originally intended to bring mobile fire-power to bear on the enemy. In practice, the vehicles were used for reconnaissance, towing anti-tank guns, transporting supplies and ammunition, and any one of a multitude of tasks for which their mobility suited them. By the end of the war some had even been fitted with flame-throwers.

14   Davies-Scourfield, *In Presence of my Foes.*

15   *ibid.*

16   *Maid of Orleans* had been built in August 1918 and requisitioned from Southern Railways for use as a troop transport in 1939. After Calais, she made six voyages to Dunkirk before being badly damaged on June 1st in a collision with HMS *Worcester;* by then she had rescued five thousand men. In 1942 she became a Landing Ship Infantry, and saw service in the Normandy landings as HMS *Maid of Orleans.* However, on June 28th 1944, whilst returning empty, she was sunk by U988 off the Isle of Wight with the loss of five of her complement of ninety-eight.

17   Close, *A View from the Turret.*

18   Reeves, quoted in Delaforce, *op.cit.*

19   The fifty-five year old Colonel 3954 Rupert Thurstan Holland DSO, MC, was Base Commandant at Calais. In the decorations awarded for the fighting at Calais in September 1945, he was appointed CBE.

20   Keller, National Archives CAB106/233.

21   Lieutenant-General Sir Wellesley Douglas Studholme Brownrigg KCB, DSO (1886-1946).

22   Carpendale, quoted in Neave, *The Flames of Calais.*

23   Major R.H.O. Simpson, OC 'A' Squadron, in Tank Museum archives.

24   *ibid.*

25   Corporal Alan Woolaston, 'C' Squadron, in Tank Museum archives.

26   Simpson, Tank Museum archives.

27   Of O'Sullivan, Gregg states: *After the war, Barry commanded the newly-formed RAC Junior Leaders' Squadron at Bovington. Barry had a distinguished career both during and after the war. He was a keen sailor, but was drowned during the Fastnet race when most of the fleet of yachts was sheltering during the great storm. He saved the life of a civilian, but was drowned when he removed his life-jacket. He was given the Royal Humane Society's Gold Medal, which was presented to his widow at the Royal Hospital. My wife and I attended.*

28   O'Sullivan, statement in National Archives WO167/458.

29   *ibid.*

30   No member of 3RTR called Galbraith seems to have been killed at Calais, but the Price mentioned in the text is probably twenty-four year-old Trooper 7893872 John Edward Price, son of Harry Walter Price and Winifred Price, of Ealing. He rests in grave M.4 of Calais Southern Cemetery.

31   O'Sullivan, National Archives WO167/458.

32   O'Sullivan, summary of statement in National Archives WO167/458.

33   Nicholson, unfinished report, quoted in Neave, *Flames of Calais.*

34   Part of 58 Anti-Tank Regiment, Royal Artillery.

35   Davies-Scourfield, *op.cit.*

36   For a full account of the Battle of Calais, which deserves fuller treatment than this work can give, readers are referred to the excellent *The Flames of Calais* by Airey Neave, who fought there, or the more recent *Calais: 30 Brigade's Defiant Defence, May 1940,* by Jon Cooksey.

37   Quoted in Cooksey, *Calais.*

38   *ibid.*

39   British infantry regiments had long been known by their regimental numbers: the King's Royal Rifle Corps had been raised as the 60th. Thus the 2nd Battalion of the KRRC was often referred to as the "Second 60th".

40   Davies-Scourfield, *op.cit.*

41   *ibid.*

42   *ibid.*

43   *ibid.*

44   The "Rifle, Anti-Tank, .55in, Boys" had been developed by Captain H.C. Boys at the Royal Small Arms Factory, Enfield, in 1937. Boys died a few days before the weapon was approved for service, so he never saw it in action. Perhaps that was as well. It was a bolt-action rifle over five feet long and weighing thirty-five pounds. Its magazine held five rounds. Fired from the shoulder using a bipod, it packed an unpleasant kick – this, and its weight, made it very unpopular with men who had to use it. The Boys rifle was also very difficult to maintain, and ineffective against all but the lightest armour.

At a hundred yards it could penetrate 16mm as long as it hit square-on, but that sort of armour was found only on half-tracks and scout cars; the frontal armour of German tanks was impervious to it. And any firer who let a German armoured vehicle get to within a hundred yards before firing was a very brave man indeed.

45 Davies-Scourfield, *op.cit.*
46 *ibid.*
47 Quoted by Davies-Scourfield from *Annals of the King's Royal Rifle Corps*, Volume VI.
48 One destroyer – HMS *Wessex* – was sunk by air attack off Calais on May 24th, whilst a second – *Vimiera* – was badly damaged by air attack in the same area and put out of action for ten days. Swordfish biplanes of 812 and 825 Naval Air Squadron bombed German artillery positions on the high ground near Coquelles, but two Swordfish were lost and their four crewmen were killed. The minesweeping trawler *John Cattling* was sent to Calais to act as a radio link with the garrison, whose headquarters were now in the Gare Maritime. The destroyers *Wolfhound* and *Verity* went into Calais during the afternoon to take ammunition to the garrison, and *Verity* landed a party of Royal Marines to guard the harbour facilities and prepare them for demolition: MTB25 sped across to Calais with primers for the demolition charges. It is the only MTB reported to have visited Calais that day, and so it is possible that it was this vessel which picked Gunner up.
49 Evitts, quoted in Cooksey, *op.cit.*
50 Quoted in Neave, *op.cit.*
51 Quoted in Cooksey, *op.cit.*
52 *ibid.*
53 *ibid.*
54 *ibid.*
55 Holland, in National Archives WO217/2.
56 Quoted in Cooksey, *op.cit.*
57 Churchill, in *Their Finest Hour: The Second World War, Volume 2.*
58 Hoskyns 'A' 1909-1912; Bird 'E' 1929-1934.
59 Bampfylde 'G' 1933-1938; Wood 'I' 1923-1929; Parker 'E' 1926-1931.
60 Segar-Owen 'K' 1913-1918.
61 Sinclair 'I' 1931-1936.
62 Raikes 'H' 1922-1928.
63 Lieutenant Douglas Norman "Douggie" Moir, like Gregg, Ironside, Sinclair and Davies-Scourfield, became an inveterate escaper. Known to his men as "Ginger", he was born in India on August 24th 1918 and educated at Kelly College in Devon, where he proved a considerable athlete. After Sandhurst he joined 3RTR. His first camp was Stalag VIIC, at Laufen. As he was being moved from there by train in a cattle-truck, he and a comrade leaped from the moving train and evaded capture for several days. They were then sent to Warburg, where Moir was involved in the stunning "Warburg Wire Job" escape, in which sixty officers stormed the barbed-wire fences with scaling ladders whilst other inmates fused the lights and created a diversion. He and two fellow escapees were at large for nine days, travelling two hundred miles and crossing the Danube, before being recaptured and sent to Oflag VIIB, a castle at Eichstätt. Whilst in solitary confinement there, Moir made new plans for escape, and he and two Canadian officers shinned ninety feet down the walls on ropes made from knotted sheets. They were seen, captured, and returned to the cooler. But the Germans had now had enough, and sent Moir to Oflag IVC: Colditz. That did not stop him trying to escape. His first attempt was a fake one, his intention being that the Germans would punish him with imprisonment in the town jail, from which it would be easier to escape. Unfortunately, they simply put Moir in solitary within the castle. He then began work, with Ironside and others, on the famous Colditz glider. Colditz was liberated before this flew. For his unflagging determination to escape and to aid the escape of others, Moir was mentioned in dispatches in 1946. He then served with 7RTR in India during Partition. In 1958 he took command of the RAC's Junior Leader programme, before serving as a liaison officer with the Jordanian and Belgian armies from 1961. He retired in 1969 with the rank of Lieutenant-Colonel, and he and his wife Phyllis (*née* Wells) retired to Devon. They had married in 1945, and had two daughters. Moir died on May 6th 2008, aged eighty-nine.
64 It is often forgotten that the Dunkirk evacuation was not the end of the war in France, which continued until France's surrender on June 22nd. Large numbers of British troops remained in the country and in Norway, including 51st (Highland) Division, commanded by Wykehamist Major-General Sir Victor Fortune. He and his men were supporting French attempts to hold the line of the Somme, which the Germans crossed on June 5th, forcing 51st Division back towards the coast and

eventual capture at St Valery-en-Caux, a stand as glorious as Calais, and on a larger scale. British troops also remained in Norway, but the campaign had almost reached its end, and on June 8th the last were evacuated. However, the naval forces covering them suffered a dreadful cost, and that day the aircraft carrier HMS *Glorious* was sunk by German naval gun-fire with the loss of over 1400 men.

65 *Supplement to the London Gazette*, September 20th 1945. Corporal 7883962 Ralph Archer 3RTR was thirty-one when he was killed at Calais on May 23rd, and lies in grave 12 of the Ardres Communal Cemetery on the road between Calais and St Omer.

Chapter Six: Greece

1 Queen's Yarn was also known as Yarn Barton (Barton being the local word for a farm enclosure). The property had once been used for the making of flax yarn, and when Gregg's mother lived there the large stone water troughs used in the process were still there.

2 Keller was still in command; "Simbo" Simpson had 'A' Squadron; Bill Reeves (with a DSO for his outstanding work at Calais) had 'B' Squadron; 'C' Squadron was run by "Bimbo" Warren.

3 2nd Lieutenant 134975 Thomas Evance Eeley was commissioned into the RTR from 102 OCTU on June 15th 1940, as was Bob Crisp; Eeley had joined 3RTR on June 12th.

4 Robert James Crisp DSO, MC, was born in Calcutta on May 28th 1911, but grew up in South Africa. He was a superb cricketer, representing Rhodesia and Western Province before playing for South Africa in nine test matches in 1935 and 1936. In England in 1935 he took eight five-wicket hauls, including five for 99 at Old Trafford which gave South Africa its first victory in England. He then played for Worcestershire, and he remains the only first-class bowler to have more than once taken four wickets in four balls.

A journalist before the war, Crisp was commissioned into the RTR on June 15th 1940 from 102 OCTU; he joined 3RTR on June 15th and had a spectacular career as a tank commander. He was severely wounded on December 16th 1941 but by then had earned a DSO and an MC, as well as four mentions in dispatches. He later wrote two books about his experiences: *The Gods Were Neutral* (1961, about 3RTR in Greece) and *Brazen Chariots* (1959, about 3RTR in Operation Crusader). His other achievements were climbing Mount Kilimanjaro twice, swimming Loch Lomond, and spending a year walking around Crete having just been diagnosed with cancer. He had a long career as a journalist for *Wisden* and other publications. His last book was *The Outlanders: the Men who made Johannesburg* (1964).

5 Taunton Alexander "Tony" Viney was the son of Colonel A.D. Viney and Lucy Margery Viney of Parktown, Johannesburg, and obtained an MA from Cambridge before joining the army. He was commissioned into the RTR as 2nd Lieutenant 134497 T.A. Viney on June 1st 1940, and rose to the rank of Captain before being killed in Tunisia on April 8th 1943. He has no known grave, and is commemorated on face 3 of the Medjez-el-Bab memorial.

6 The Royal Mail Motor Vessel *Stirling Castle*, of the Union Castle line, had been built in 1935 by Harland and Wolff in Belfast to serve the south and east African routes. In 1936 she set a new record for the voyage from Southampton to Cape Town (thirteen days, nine hours). 680 feet long and with a weight of 25,550 tons, she could make twenty-one knots and was designed for 216 First Class and 508 Tourist Class passengers, as well as freight (much of it refrigerated). In 1940 she was requisitioned as a troopship, capable of carrying six thousand men, eating and sleeping in two shifts. In 1943 she carried troops from America as part of Operation Bolero, bringing US forces to England in preparation for D-Day. By the end of her virtually trouble-free wartime career, she had carried 128,000 men and steamed over half a million miles. She was scrapped in 1966.

7 WS4 was the largest WS convoy to date. Some ships left Avonmouth on October 31st; off the Mersey, these joined others which sailed from Liverpool section on November 1st. More ships sailed from the Clyde on November 2nd, and the whole convoy assembled off Oversay; there were originally sixteen merchant vessels in total, with a varying escort. The *Stirling Castle* was the ship of the convoy commander (the Commodore), and sailed at the head of the middle column of five. After a three-day stop at Freetown (November 14th-17th), WS4 set out for Durban, which it reached on December 3rd. The ships sailed again on December 5th, and *Stirling Castle* arrived in Suez on December 22nd 1940.

8 Perla Siedle Gibson (1888-1971) was born in Durban. She studied music, singing (she was a soprano), portraiture, and pottery in Europe and America from 1907. In 1917 she married Jack Gibson, returning to South Africa in 1923. She kept up her artistic interests, exhibiting regularly, but only became famous when she dressed in white to serenade the wartime convoys. In 1968 she lost an eye in an accident at home, but this did not stop her from pursuing her hobbies until her death three years later.

9   *Supplement to London Gazette,* February 18th 1941: *2nd Lieutenant T.D. Gregg (85707) to be Lieutenant RTR, WEF January 1st 1941.*
10 The first staff officer to arrive was Major GSO2 Belchem (Operations), who reached Athens on March 5th. He was joined by Major GSO2 Gurney, Donny and Captain GSO3 Street, along with four Captains GSO3 (Liaison): Johnson, Houghton, Page and Legge-Bourke.
11 *Bonaventure,* a *Dido* class light cruiser, had a short career. Launched in April 1939, she was not commissioned until May 24th 1940. Less than a year later, on March 31st 1941, she was torpedoed by the Italian submarine *Ambra* south of Crete, with the loss of 139 of her crew.
12 Watt, *A Tankie's Travels.*
13 *ibid.*
14 *ibid.*
15 *ibid.*
16 National Archives WO169/1411.
17 National Archives WO169/1411.
18 There were *Swiftsures* on both sides at Trafalgar; the French had captured an earlier '74' of that name which was recaptured at the battle and brought back into Royal Navy service as HMS *Irresistible.*
19 National Archives WO169/994B.
20 National Archives WO169/994B.
21 National Archives WO201/44.
22 National Archives WO169/994B. *1645 Telephone conversation Air Commodore Grigson – Captain Mackenzie. 1930 Telephone conversation Captain Mackenzie – Captain Street.*
23 National Archives WO169/994B.
24 National Archives WO201/52.
25 National Archives WO201/52.
26 Dennis Bartlett, OC 1 Troop, was awarded an MC for his part in this action.
27 National Archives WO169/1411.
28 National Archives WO169/1411.
29 National Archives WO169/1411.
30 1 Armoured Brigade war diary, quoted in Delaforce, *Taming the Panzers.*
31 Watt, *op.cit.*
32 Dale, quoted in Delaforce, *op.cit.*
33 The 7.92mm BESA machine-gun was the standard co-axial armament on most British armoured fighting vehicles of the Second World War. It was reliable, belt-fed, and had a high rate of fire. Its unusual calibre meant that it could fire captured German ammunition.
34 National Archives WO201/46.
35 National Archives WO201/46.
36 Two of them were Winchester contemporaries of Donny: Captain 66299 John Colpoys Haughton ('F' 1926-1932), of 106 (Lancashire Hussars) Light AA Regiment, RHA, had embarked on SS *Slamat* but was killed either when it was bombed or after being picked up by HMS *Diamond*. Killed at the age of twenty-seven, he is commemorated on face 3 of the Athens Memorial. Sub-Lieutenant Charles Altham Wood ('E' 1930-1935), who was serving on HMS *Diamond*, also has no known grave, and is commemorated in panel 61 of the Portsmouth Naval Memorial. He was twenty-four years old.
37 Before Pollux could depart, an inbound convoy called Zeus had to unload; it was composed of *City of Canterbury* and *Cape Horn*, which were to dock at 1200. Pollux was made up of the vessels *Bellray* (loading at 1030), *Rodi* (1530), *Lesbos* (1600), *City of Canterbury* (1630), *Popi Vernicos* (1700), *Rocos* (1730) and one escorting destroyer.
38 The *Rodi's* passenger list contained in the naval operations order in National Archives WO169/1334a gives a fascinating insight into the chaos left in the wake of the evacuation of Greece. The 654 passengers were to be: five "Maniadakis staff"; the "Polish Minister" and four companions; twenty-nine Yugoslavs; Alexander Perivari and one member of the British Military Mission; Lieutenant-Commanders Lambos RNVR (OC Ship) and Trevor; Majors Jerome, Juke, Low, and Mackenzie; Captains Compton, Mackay (NZ), Stewart, and Tydeman; Lieutenants Harris (RM), Richards (NZ), Scott (ADC), and Westall; Messrs Bell and Holmes, with four-hundredweight of packing-cases; seven women; six children; nine other ranks under Sergeant Ragless of the Field Security Section; one hundred wounded New Zealanders; 120 wounded from No.7 General Hospital; 353 "first priority" New Zealanders; and two couriers from "the Legation" called Pawson and March.
39 The 1594-ton cargo ship SS *Popi* had been launched as the SS *Cairnisla* in 1896 by Short Brothers in Sunderland: her single screw drive her at a top speed of nine knots, making her something of a

slug 259 feet long, until 1915 she sailed with the Newcastle-based Cairn Line, before transferring to Dixon Peter & Sons of Grimsby as SS *West Marsh*. In 1930 she was sold to Vernicos CN of the Piraeus in Greece, explaining why the British troops in 1941 knew her as the *Popi Vernicos*. She survived the war and sailed on with the Greek firm until 1956, when she joined her final owners, the Costa Rican Kansas Compania Naviera. Re-named once more, the *Mary K* left the northern Greek port of Stratoni on November 29th 1957 with a cargo of iron pyrites, bound for Constanza in Romania. On December 1st she sent a distress message announcing that her cargo had shifted, before sinking with all hands somewhere off the Dardanelles. One body and two empty lifeboats were recovered.

40   National Archives WO169/1334a. The order goes on to add that *four tons of baggage, the property of the King of Greece, will be handed over to Movement Control Officer (Shipping) Suda by 0900 hours 9 May for loading in SS Bellray.*

41   Caswell, quoted in Delaforce, *op.cit.*

42   Watt, *op.cit.*

43   Dale, quoted in Delaforce, *op.cit.*

44   Reeves, quoted in Delaforce, *op.cit.*

Chapter Seven: Crusader

1   The Polish Independent Brigade Group had been founded in Syria in 1940 and had been due for service in Greece until the rapid collapse of resistance there put an end to such plans. It then moved to Egypt, spending May and June 1941 at Mersah Matruh. In July it returned to El Amiriya near Alexandria, where it trained in preparation for duty at Tobruk. In the last week of August 1941 the Poles took over the western sector of the port, which Gunner later that year helped to relieve.

2   For details of Cairene life during this period, readers are urged to look at Artemis Cooper's excellent *Cairo in the War.*

3   Crisp, *Brazen Chariots*. A John Collins is a cocktail made from two parts whisky, one part lemon juice, and a splash of sugar syrup. For best results, shake the whisky, lemon juice and sugar syrup together with cracked ice before pouring over ice cubes, a slice of lemon, a slice of orange, and a Maraschino cherry, topping up with soda water.

4   The spelling is correct, although several sources refer to him as Ewins. Lieutenant-Colonel 27189 A.A.H. Ewin was mentioned in despatches in December 1942 for his conduct during Operation Crusader.

5   Thus when 3rd County of London Yeomanry (22 Armoured Brigade) formed up for Operation Crusader on October 26th 1941, its strength was 39 officers and 584 other ranks, equipped with fifty-two cruiser tanks and ten Daimler scout cars; but in addition it had sixty-eight 3-ton trucks, twenty 15-cwt trucks, eight utility vehicles, four 15-cwt water-tankers, two 8-cwt trucks, one 15-cwt office truck, one radio van, two 3-ton trucks for the use of fitters, one motor-cycle and two motor-cycles with side-cars – a grand total of 171 vehicles, two-thirds of which were not armoured.

6   Major Ewart W. Clay MBE, in *Path of the 50th*, the history of 50th (Northumbrian) Infantry Division.

7   National Archives WO169/1411.

8   Richard Stuart Roffey was commissioned from the RAC OCTU Sandhurst to be 2nd Lieutenant 117234 on January 21st 1940.

9   The commanding officer, Brigadier Alec Gatehouse DSO, MC, was one of the finest commanders of tanks in the desert war.

10   Full accounts of the fighting were written by several of those who served with 3RTR during Operation Crusader, and readers wishing to know more of the battalion's role can do no better than to read Bob Crisp's *Brazen Chariots*, Cyril Joly's *Take These Men*, or Jock Watt's *A Tankie's Travels*. An overview of the whole battle can be gained from the excellent *Crucible of War* by Barrie Pitt.

11   Watt, *A Tankie's Travels.*

12   Gabr is the Arabic for 'grave', and this place-name simply meant that there were burials at this point in the desert.

13   Lieutenant 218981 James Henry Owens was the son of James and Mary Ann Owens, and the husband of Edith Mary Owens. He was not a young man – indeed, at thirty-six he was very old for a Lieutenant – and hailed from Dudley in Worcestershire. The reason for his age was simple; he was a pre-war regular NCO, who had risen to the rank of SSM in the Bays, before being commissioned on August 21st 1941 and transferred to 3RTR. He now rests in grave 5.C.5. of the Halfaya Sollum War Cemetery.

14   Captain 95563 William Peter Colborne Williams MC, Second-in-Command of 'B' Squadron, had won his MC for his bravery at Calais, was still only twenty-two years old when he died. He was the son

of William Henry Williams and Gertrude Ann Williams, of Ponthir, Newport, Monmouthshire. He is commemorated in Column 20 of the Alamein Memorial.

Williams' crew had consisted of Corporal Jim Caswell (driver), Trooper Eastwood (wireless operator) and Trooper James (gunner). The shell which destroyed their tank hit the turret as they were ramming a German command vehicle; it killed Eastwood and seriously wounded James and Williams. Trooper 7927609 Harold Eastwood, aged thirty-three, was a Yorkshireman from Keighley. The son of John H. Eastwood and Ethel Eastwood, he left a widow, and is commemorated in column 22 of the Alamein Memorial.

15	Crisp, *op.cit.*
16	National Archives WO169/1411.
17	Close, *A View from the Turret.*
18	Crisp, *op.cit.*
19	National Archives WO169/1411.
20	Major 66189 Peter George Page MC was the son of Herbert and Helen Page, who lived in Bedford. Despite his rank and decoration, he was still only twenty-six years old. Page now rests in grave 2.C.12 of the Knightsbridge War Cemetery, Acroma.
21	National Archives WO169/1411.
22	National Archives WO169/1411.
23	Crisp, *op.cit.*
24	National Archives WO169/1411.
25	Crisp, *op.cit.*
26	National Archives WO169/1411. The two dead officers named were: Lieutenant 95223 Arthur Harry Edwards Stuart, aged twenty-three, of Alverstoke in Hampshire, was son of J.A.P. Stuart and Norah Stuart, and is commemorated in column 21 of the Alamein Memorial. Lieutenant 93098 Alan George Hickson was the son of Joseph F.X. Hickson and Alice May Hickson, of Birkdale in Lancashire. He is commemorated in column 20 of the Alamein Memorial.
27	National Archives WO169/1411.
28	Crisp, *op.cit.*
29	National Archives WO169/1411.
30	*The History of 4th Armoured Brigade,* written by Donny's great Winchester contemporary, R.M.P. Carver.
31	National Archives WO169/1411.
32	National Archives WO169/1411. Captain 121409 Kenneth Clyde Caldwell had been on attachment from 4th (Queen's Own) Hussars. Aged twenty-two when he died, he was Canadian: his parents (Lieutenant-Colonel Eugene Lloyd Caldwell, of the Royal Canadian Dragoons, and Winifred M. Caldwell) were from St John's in Quebec. He is commemorated in clumn 15 of the Alamein Memorial. Trooper 7908618 Francis Bell Ashton was also twenty-two years old when he died that day; like his officers, he is commemorated on the Alamein Memorial (column 22).
33	Bir Hatiet Genadel lies some ten miles south-south-west of the airfield at El Adem. It can be found on modern maps as Bir Hatiyat Janadil or Ahqaf al Jandal, just west of a noticeable north-south wadi.
34	National Archives WO169/1411.
35	National Archives WO169/1411.
36	This regiment had replaced the decimated 8th Hussars.
37	Crisp, *op.cit.*
38	Lieutenant 126634 Harry Gilmore Maegraith was a married man, his widow being Cecelia Evelyn Maegraith, of Coulsdon in Surrey. Maegraith was the son of Alfred and Louise Maegraith, and was twenty-six years old when he died. He is commemorated in column 20 of the Alamein Memorial.
39	National Archives WO169/1411.
40	National Archives WO169/1411.
41	The divisional symbol was a red eagle.
42	Millar, *Horned Pigeon.*
43	1st Buffs had been over-run on December 15th after two days of fierce fighting at Point 204; their commanding officer was Lieutenant-Colonel J.E. King. The unit had formed part of 5 Indian Brigade. King's last signal to Brigade HQ was *if you do not hear from me again you will know that I can no longer communicate.* The Buffs lost 531 men killed, wounded and prisoner; only the Quartermaster, Medical Officer, and sixty-nine other ranks escaped capture. The Germans captured twenty serviceable lorries at Point 204, one of which was presumably that in which Gregg now found himself.

Chapter Eight: Pericoloso

1. Morgan, *Only Ghosts Can Live*.
2. Gordon Lett, *Rossano*.
3. At this time, Italian rations for prisoners of war were on the following scale (all quantities are in grammes per day):

	Officers	*Other Ranks*	*Other Ranks (if working)*
Bread	150	200	400
Macaroni or rice	66	66	120
Fat or oil	10	13	13
Sugar	16	15	15
Cheese (cooking)	10	10	10
Cheese (table)	If available	30	43
Meat	14	34	34
Tomato purée	15	15	15
Egg	(1 a month)	–	–
Peas & beans	15	30	30
Coffee substitute	7	7	7
TOTAL CALORIES	780	1081	1821

   These rations could be supplemented by purchasing extras if facilities existed for doing so. Unsurprisingly, there was a lot of black-market trading with guards.

4. An Afrikaans folk song from the Boer war period, adapted from an American Civil War song, *Ellie Rhee*. The song begins *My Sarie Marais is so ver van my hart, Maar'k hoop om haar weer te sien.* ("My Sarie Marais is so far from my heart, but I hope to see her again.")
5. Bears are Bern's mascots (the city's name means "bears"), and bears have been kept in the city since 1480. Their pit, near the Nydeck Bridge, has been in the same location since 1513. In 2009 it was extended to make a more natural enclosure in keeping with modern views on animal rights.
6. National Archives WO224/113.
7. George Reid "Josh" Millar DSO, MC, *Chevalier de la Légion d'Honneur, Croix de Guerre avec Palmes,* was born in Scotland on September 19th 1910. According to his obituary in the *Independent* in 2005, written by the distinguished SOE agent, historian, and Wykehamist M.R.D. Foot, *as a small boy, George shared his cot with the family Airedale. The dog had to be put down in 1917, because U-boat attacks made it impossible to get meat enough to feed him; this did not make George love the Germans.* He was the son of an architect and studied the subject at St John's College, Cambridge, but instead became a journalist, first on the *Glasgow Evening Citizen* and then on the *Daily Telegraph* and *Daily Express*. In 1936 he married Annette Stockwell; the *Independent* commented that *he was tall, sturdy, cherub-faced, and always attractive to women. His first wife Annette, the daughter of an army Colonel, had set eyes on him twice before she abandoned her previous husband to live with him.*

   Millar then worked from the Paris office of the *Express*. He had already spent some time in France, and came to speak the language well. With his famous colleagues Alan Moorehead and Geoffrey Cox he covered the war in France until the country's fall, whereupon he joined the army as an officer in the Rifle Brigade. With 1st Battalion he served in North Africa until his Scout Platoon was over-run at Gazala in 1942. Having briefly met Rommel, he was like Gregg transferred to PG66 at Capua, and then to PG35 at Padula. His persistent attempts at escape were rewarded by a transfer to PG5 at Gavi. At the Italian armistice in September 1943, the inmates of Gavi tried to hide from the Germans who had come to transfer them to Germany, but Millar was discovered and put on a train bound north. Millar jumped from the train and made his way to safety by way of Munich, Strasbourg, Paris and Lyon. After three months on the run he made it across the Pyrenees into Spain. On his return to England, he dictated his impressions of his escape, which he later turned into a best-selling book, *Horned Pigeon* (1946). He was awarded the MC for his successful escape.

   Impressed by the SOE operatives whom he had met, he volunteered for service as an agent and was parachuted into France near Besançon in the run-up to D-Day, with the code-name Emile. The *Independent* recalled that *sixty years later, women in the Ognon valley who had worked for him would still cry "Ah! Emile!" when his name was mentioned, and lay a hand on their hearts.* Three months later the area was liberated and Millar returned to England, where he wrote the memoir *Maquis* (1945) whilst his memories were fresh. The award of the DSO was made in recognition of his work in France. The war had destroyed his marriage – the title *Horned Pigeon* refers to the cuckold's horns which Millar had been wearing unawares as he made his home run – but after his marriage was dissolved in 1945 he married Isabel Paske-Smith that same year.

After the war, Millar and his wife settled on a Dorset farm, making frequent yachting trips which Millar turned into books: *Isabel and the Sea* (1948), *A White Boat from England* (1951), and *Oyster River* (1963). He also wrote novels, including *My Past Was an Evil River* (1947), *Through the Unicorn Gates* (1945), *Siesta* (1950), and *Orellana Discovers the Amazon* (1954). Non-fiction works included *Horseman: the Memoirs of Captain J.H. Marshall* (1970), *The Bruneval Raid* (1975), and his autobiography, *Road to Resistance* (1979). His other interest was fox-hunting. His wife died in 1990, as the *Independent* obituary explains: *His life had a sharp jar in 1989, when Isabel was involved in a banal car accident from which she never recovered consciousness. He gave up their farm, and moved to a house near Bridport, where Venetia Ross-Skinner looked after his closing years. Once such a pillar of physical energy, he was reduced to a wheelchair, and went blind; his spirit remained glowing.*

8   Millar, *Horned Pigeon*.
9   ibid.

Chapter Nine: Tobruk

1   Sarah had been born on December 27th 1917. Her father, Thomas Symonds Tomlinson (November 1877-April 1965) was made a Knight Bachelor in the New Year's honours list of 1925 and served as Chief Justice of Zanzibar (1925-1928). He and his wife, Diana (*née* Hibbert), had five children: Dr Arthur John Hibbert Tomlinson (1916-1967); Sarah Diana Tomlinson; Merelina Symonds Tomlinson (1921-?); Penelope Anne Tomlinson (1925-?); and Elizabeth Selina Tomlinson (1926-?). The Tomlinsons were related distantly to Dor Mackenzie and the Yates family. Sir Thomas Tomlinson's wife, Diana Hibbert was the daughter of Percy John Hibbert (1850-1926) and Emily Augusta Diana Yates (1853-1942). Emily Yates was the daughter of Joseph St John Yates (1808-1887).
2   Roy Watts, 2nd Camerons.
3   Watts.
4   National Archives WO169/7629.
5   Anderson's report (National Archives WO169/7629) states, however, that 'Salmon' was commanded by Major J. Marshall. 'Trout' was under the command of Major P. Tower, who – like Marshall – would later be a prisoner-of-war with Donny and Gunner in Campo PG29.
6   Historical Records of the Cameron Highlanders.
7   Watts.
8   *Historical Records of the Cameron Highlanders*.
9   Watts.
10   Captain Faure Walker, 3rd Coldstream Guards.
11   Watts.
12   National Archives WO169/7629.
13   Major-General Henry Robert Bowreman Foote VC, CB, DSO, was born in Ishapore, India, on December 5th 1904. He was the son of Major Henry Bruce Foote (Royal Artillery) and Jennie Elizabeth Foote. When his mother died, he was sent at the age of four to a boarding school in England (St Cyprian's, Eastbourne). He then became a pupil at Bedford School (1918-1923) before going on, like Gregg, to RMC Sandhurst. In 1925 he was commissioned into the Royal Tank Corps. When war broke out he was serving on the staff, and formed part of the British army's mission to Washington DC in 1941. In the following year he took command of 7RTR, and at the Battle of Gazala performed the exploits which won him his Victoria Cross. It was announced in the *Supplement to the London Gazette* of May 16th 1944:

The King has been graciously pleased to approve the award of the Victoria Cross to: Major (temporary Lieutenant-Colonel) Henry Robert Bowreman Foote, DSO (31938), Royal Tank Regiment, Royal Armoured Corps (Edgbaston, Birmingham). For outstanding gallantry during the period 27th May to 15th June, 1942. On the 6th June, Lieutenant-Colonel Foote led his Battalion, which had been subjected to very heavy artillery fire, in pursuit of a superior force of the enemy. While changing to another tank after his own had been knocked out, Lieutenant-Colonel Foote was wounded in the neck. In spite of this he continued to lead his Battalion from an exposed position on the outside of a tank.

The enemy, who were holding a strongly entrenched position with anti-tank guns, attacked his flank. As a further tank had been disabled he continued on foot under intense fire encouraging his men by his splendid example. By dusk, Lieutenant-Colonel Foote by his brilliant leadership had defeated the enemy's attempt to encircle two of our Divisions.

On 13th June, when ordered to delay the enemy tanks so that the Guards Brigade could be withdrawn from the Knightsbridge escarpment and when the first wave of our tanks had been destroyed, Lieutenant-Colonel Foote re-organised the remaining tanks, going on foot from one tank to another to encourage the crews under intense artillery and anti-tank fire. As it was of vital importance that his Battalion should not give ground, Lieutenant-Colonel Foote placed his tank, which he had then entered, in front of the others so that he could be plainly visible in the turret as an encouragement to the other crews, in spite of the tank being badly damaged by shell-fire and all its guns rendered useless. By his magnificent example the corridor was kept open and the Brigade was able to march through.

Lieutenant-Colonel Foote was always at the crucial point at the right moment, and over a period of several days gave an ex- ample of outstanding courage and leadership which it would have been difficult to surpass. His name was a by-word for bravery and leadership throughout the Brigade.

Having returned to Britain in 1944 from Switzerland, he served on the staff again before being appointed Second-in-Command of 9 Armoured Brigade. Between 1945 and 1947 he was Brigadier in charge of the Royal Armoured Corps contingent in the Middle East, and from 1947 until 1948 commanded 2RTR. After a year in the Ministry of Supply, he commanded 7 Armoured Brigade and then 11th Armoured Division. Returning to staff posts, he was between 1953 and 1955 Director General of Fighting Vehicles at the Ministry of Supply. He then served as Director, Royal Armoured Corps, at the War Office from 1955 until his retirement in 1958, with the rank of Major-General. He died on November 11th 1993, and is buried in St Mary's churchyard, West Chillington. His Victoria Cross is held at the Tank Museum at Bovington.

14. National Archives WO169/7629.
15. *Historical Records of the Cameron Highlanders.*
16. Walker, *Iron Hulls, Iron Hearts.*
17. Watts.
18. *Historical Records of the Cameron Highlanders.*
19. Watts.
20. *Historical Records of the Cameron Highlanders.*
21. *ibid.*
22. Mitchell, quoted in *ibid.*
23. *Historical Records of the Cameron Highlanders.*
24. Michael B. Lloyd.
25. Heckstall-Smith, *Tobruk: The Story of a Siege.*
26. Elsewhere on the perimeter, for example, 180 men of 3rd Coldstream Guards had scattered, among them Captain the Hon. Michael Victor Brodrick MC (Winchester College, 'A' 1932-1938), who made it back to British lines, only to die at Salerno in September 1943.
27. Mitchell, quoted in *Historical Records of the Cameron Highlanders.*
28. *ibid.*
29. *ibid.*
30. *ibid.*
31. *ibid.*
32. *ibid.*
33. *ibid.*
34. *ibid.*
35. *ibid.*
36. *ibid.*
37. *ibid.*
38. *ibid.*
39. *ibid.*
40. Sergeant 2927301 Charles Paul Fisher was killed on August 24th 1942 at Benghazi, aged twenty-eight. The son of Isaiah Charles Fisher and Dorothy Nellie Fisher, of Hounslow in Middlesex, he rests in grave 7.D.27 of the Benghazi War Cemetery.
41. Major 58195 James Murray Marshall was the son of Major-General Francis James Marshall CB, CMG, DSO, and Alice Maud Marshall. He was from Inverness, and was actually not a Cameron Highlander but attached to 2nd Camerons from 1st Battalion, Seaforth Highlanders. Aged thirty-two, he died in Italy on March 3rd 1944, and is buried in grave XII.C.7 of the Moro River Canadian War Cemetery, near Ortona.

Chapter Ten: Veano

1. They included:
    Rifleman 6914050 John "Mick" MICALLEF, 2nd Battalion, Rifle Brigade. Micallef was born in Malta but had emigrated to England in 1937 and had joined the Rifle Brigade in 1938. He was wounded and captured at Sidi Rezegh on November 22nd 1941. He had volunteered to be an orderly at Veano on the assumption that being in an officers' camp would be more comfortable than where he was. In March 1945 he was awarded the MM for his service with the Italian partisans.
    Sergeant QX7647 Robert James Grierson "Bob" BLACKMORE, 2/15th Australian Infantry Battalion (captured near Derna on April 7th 1941). Blackmore was the NCO in charge of the orderlies in PG29.
    Private Patrick HANNAWAY, 1st Buffs (captured in December 1941 in the action previously described).
    Private JOYCE, Essex Regiment.
    Trooper J. MADDOX (unit unknown, but a tank crewman who had been disfigured by a wound in the desert).
    Driver MCENTAGERT (forename unknown), of 3RHA (captured at Sidi Rezegh in November 1941).
2. National Archives WO224/112.
3. *ibid.*
4. Private papers of R.G. McDowall, IWM 7949 98/29/1. He had been captured at Sidi Rezegh in November 1941, but was in PG29 only between August and November 1942.
5. Mander, *Mander's March on Rome*. Major 44131 D'Arcy John Desmond Mander was born in County Cork in December 1899, and educated at Charterhouse. He joined the Green Howards from RMC Sandhurst in 1929, and in 1939 married Dorothy Eileen Nichols; the couple had two daughters. He served in Belgium and France in 1940, being evacuated from Dunkirk. Mander then served in North Africa, and was captured whilst serving with 4th Battalion, Green Howards, at Gazala in June 1942. He and a few other officers were flown to Italy, and Mander suggested that they seize the aircraft in flight – but this was vetoed by more senior officers. After escaping from captivity in September 1943 he went to Rome where he made use of his fluent Italian and German and worked tirelessly in support of the Italian resistance, also helping Allied prisoners of war, until the liberation of the city. He supplied valuable intelligence to the Allies despite twice being arrested by the Gestapo. He was later awarded the DSO for his outstanding conduct: the citation included the statement that *the decision to carry out such work was entirely his own and in the conduct of it he was unassisted by any official Allied prisoner-of-war organisation. There is no doubt that this officer made an important contribution to the success of our espionage and counter-espionage efforts and it is recommended that his courage and resource should be recognised by the award of a DSO.* Mander enjoyed a successful post-war military career, attending Staff College in 1944 and serving with the Allied Control Commission in Germany. He served in India and the Sudan, and commanded 1st Green Howards in action in Malaya from 1950 to 1952; this earned him a mention in dispatches. Various staff appointments followed, ending with the job of Military Attaché in Vienna. He retired in 1963 with the rank of Colonel. He then worked for the civil engineering firm Sir Owen Williams & Partners until his retirement in 1974. The *Daily Telegraph* wrote of him that *he was a keen golfer and an enthusiastic, though lethal, cyclist until he finally abandoned his bicycle in his late eighties. His main passion, however, was gardening, and with the help of a niece who worked as a garden designer he created a new garden with a pond and orchard at the age of ninety.* He died in Surrey in 2001 at the age of ninety-one.
6. Admiral Sir Walter Henry Cowan, 1st Baronet, KCB, DSO & Bar, MVO (1871-1956) had fought at Omdurman in 1898 (winning the DSO) and in the Boer War; he had commanded a battleship at Jutland and fought the Bolsheviks in the Baltic in 1919; at the outbreak of the Second World War he had joined the Commandos as a Commander, seeing service in North Africa. When his Commando was disbanded, he attached himself to an Indian cavalry unit and was captured at the Battle of Bir Hakeim on May 27th 1942 whilst engaging an Italian tank with his revolver. He was repatriated owing to his age in March 1943, but went back to the Commandos and saw active service again in Italy. He was awarded a bar to his DSO, the two awards separated by over forty years. He finally retired in 1945.
7. Cowan, report in National Archives WO224/112.
8. *ibid.*
9. Mander, *op.cit.*
10. Colonel the Lord Clifford of Chudleigh (Lewis Hugh Clifford, 13th Baron Clifford of Chudleigh, OBE), in IWM 6784 78/19/1 *Experiences with the Italian Resistance 1943-1945* by Major Hugh Clifford, Devonshire Regiment.
11. Cowan, report in National Archives WO224/112.

12 Colonel 5875 George Edward Younghusband shared the post of SBO with another full Colonel, George Fanshawe (see below). Born in November 1896, he was the son of Major-General Sir George John Younghusband, keeper of the Crown Jewels from 1917. George Younghusband had been commissioned from RMC Sandhurst into 11th Hussars in November 1914. He then saw service with 3rd Hussars, and was on the staff of 2nd Armoured Division until his capture at Mechili in March 1941. Younghusband was made CBE in March 1945 in recognition of his services, and left the army with the rank of Brigadier. He lived in the family home in Wales (*The Neuadd,* in Crickhowell), and died in January 1970, aged seventy-three. He had a daughter in 1928.

13 Mander, *op.cit.*

14 *ibid.*

15 Cowan, report in National Archives WO224/112.

16 *The Prisoner of War,* June 1943.

17 *The Prisoner of War,* September 1943.

18 Colonel 13054 George Hew Fanshawe, of the Queen's Bays, shared the role of SBO at Veano with Colonel Younghusband. Born in January 1899, he married Mary Holme Wiggin in July 1926 in Sialkot, India. He had commanded his regiment from 1939 to 1940, and was appointed OBE in 1945 for his services in captivity (*Supplement to the London Gazette,* March 20th 1945). He retired from the army with the rank of Brigadier and the CBE. He died on April 27th 1974 in the Radcliffe Hospital in Oxford, aged seventy-five. The British artist with whom Cowan compares Fanshawe – Lionel Edwards (1878-1966) – specialized in the depiction of horses and English country life.

19 Cowan, report in National Archives WO224/112.

20 *ibid.*

21 McGinlay, in IWM 2391 93/11/1.

22 Cowan, report in National Archives WO224/112.

23 Mander, *op.cit.*

24 Cowan, report in National Archives WO224/112.

25 Later Colonel (Honorary Brigadier) 63052 Harold Ian Bransom CBE, DSO, TD. Bransom had commanded 287 Battery of 124 Field Regiment, Royal Artillery. From North Africa in February 1942 he had sent home some poetry ("written in Libya in the front line") to be bound and published, all profits to go to help members of the regiment who had been taken prisoner. This was published as *Inferior Verse of Fighting Men in the Western Desert* by Doig Brothers of Newcastle-upon-Tyne, and a revised and enlarged edition was published in January 1943. Bransom published a sequel, *Still Inferior Verse,* after the war, containing his poems written whilst a prisoner.

Bransom had won his DSO at Sidra Ridge on June 6th 1942 whilst commanding the artillery component of 32 Tank Brigade, which was counter-attacking German forces near Bir Hacheim. As the brigade's seventy-five Matilda tanks approached the German troops of 21 Panzer Division, they ran into an unexpected mine-field. Fifty of the Matildas were disabled, and Bransom's guns held the Germans off long enough for the survivors to escape, though Bransom himself was captured. After the war he was prominent in the Territorial Army and Army Cadet Force, as well as becoming a prominent solicitor.

26 Bransom dedicated the work *to my friend "Gunner" Gregg, one of our tunnel diggers, who later escaped and fought in the successful campaign to recapture Italy and on the way "collected" the tunnel photographs taken by our Italian guards.*

27 Major 140577 Alexander Oliphant "Jock" McGinlay MC of 7RTR was recommended for a DSO by his Squadron Commander after Operation Crusader. The citation attached to the war diary of 7RTR reads: *Lieutenant McGinlay was in action continuously from the night 21st/22nd November to the morning of 30th November. During this time he performed his duties with the utmost gallantry and was largely responsible for three successful attacks on enemy strongpoints. On two separate occasions he led the tanks to a start line on foot when under the most intense artillery and mortar fire, with a complete disregard for his own safety. He has acted as troop leader, liaison officer, reconnaissance officer and even FOO and at all times has been absolutely reliable. His magnificent courage and unquenchable cheerfulness have been unsurpassed. His leadership and advice have been first class at all times. Signed: Major J.R. Holden, OC 'D' Squadron, 7th Battalion, Royal Tank Regiment.* The recommendation for a DSO was declined (this medal was usually awarded to officers of a higher rank) and instead McGinlay was awarded an MC.

28 McGinlay, in IWM 2391 93/11/1.

29 *ibid.*

30   Officers known or believed to have been in the camp at Veano with Donny and Gunner are:
Major 72697 L.S. "Bill" BAILEY, RASC (mentioned in despatches, *London Gazette,* December 15th 1942).
Squadron-Leader 33018 Alfonso Rudolf Gordon "Porpoise" BAX, of 211 Squadron RAF (shot down over Derna on September 4th 1940). According to Mander, he made an attempt to escape from PG29.
Major 93266 Nigel BEAMONT-THOMAS, of the Bombay Sappers & Miners (captured at Tobruk, June 21st 1942).
Major 45446 Peter Lawrence BIRKIN, Royal Artillery. He rose to be a Lieutenant-Colonel, was awarded the OBE in 1954, and was mentioned in dispatches in August 1945.
Lieutenant-Colonel 793 Norman "Bodd" BODDINGTON OBE, Royal Engineers.
Major 63052 Harold Ian BRANSOM, Royal Artillery.
Lieutenant-Colonel 11109 William Edgar BUSH DSO, MC, OC 5th Battalion, Green Howards (captured at Gazala, May 31st 1942).
Major 147264 Patrick Andrew "Pat" CLAYTON DSO, of the Long Range Desert Group.
Major Lewis Hugh CLIFFORD, Devonshire Regiment.
Lieutenant-Colonel 107838 Loris Clyde COOPER, OC 4th Battalion, Green Howards, an Australian sheep-farmer in peacetime (captured at Gazala, May 31st 1942).
Lieutenant-Colonel 678 Gordon DE BRUYNE OBE, OC 1st Battalion, King's Royal Rifle Corps (having replaced de Salis, below, as OC January 24th 1942, de Bruyne was captured during the desert retreat of May 27th 1942 near Gobi. Soon after their capture, de Bruyne and RQMS J. Condon made a dash for freedom when they and their Italian escort came under shell-fire in the dark. Condon was hit, however, and de Bruyne ran back and stopped the bleeding. Condon later stated that *I would have died in a very short time if it had not been for Colonel de Bruyne's prompt action. He came to my assistance when actually making his escape, thus giving up his chance of making a certain get-away.*).
Lieutenant-Colonel 1830 Sydney Charles Fane DE SALIS DSO, OC 1st Battalion, King's Royal Rifle Corps (captured at Sidi Rezegh, November 22nd 1941).
Major 52585 Anthony Henry George "Tony" DOBSON, Royal Engineers, had been serving as Brigade Major of 150 Infantry Brigade when captured at Gazala on May 31st 1942.
Lieutenant-Colonel 18334 Colin Stuart DUNCAN DSO, OC 2nd Battalion, Cameron Highlanders (captured at Tobruk, June 22nd 1942).
Major 23291 Hillary Mervyn "Hil" EVANS, New Zealand Artillery (captured near Sidi Azeiz, November 1941).
Captain Harold Edward Melville FAIRLEY, Royal Army Service Corps.
Colonel 13054 George Hew FANSHAWE, Queen's Bays.
Captain 86454 James Yuill FERGUSON (Royal Corps of Signals); he was awarded the MC in 1944 (*London Gazette,* August 24th 1944) for "gallant and distinguished services in Italy". In 1946 he was appointed MBE, again for services in the field.
Captain D.E. FIELD, 4th Battalion, East Yorkshire Regiment (captured at Gazala, May 31st 1942).
Major 47054 Robert Ronald FIELDHOUSE, RASC. He was appointed MBE in June 1945.
Lieutenant-Commander David Alexander "Frosty" FRASER, RN.
Major GURNEY (?Major Richard Quentin Gurney, City of London Yeomanry).
Major 120694 Keith N. HILLAS, 16th Battalion, Durham Light Infantry, had been with his battalion since its formation, first as OC 'A' Company and then as OC 'B' Company (captured at Sedjenane, Tunisia, on March 2nd 1943). By 1945 he was prisoner 1426 in *Oflag* 79 at Braunschweig.
Andrew HOWARD, of 2 (Indian) Field Regiment, RA (captured at Bir Hacheim in May 1942).
Lieutenant N.C. JOHNSTON (unit unknown).
Major Joseph KAZAK, Polish Army.
Major E.G. KEDGLEY, 19th New Zealand Infantry Battalion, had been wounded and captured on June 28th 1942.
Dick KERR (rank and unit unknown).
Peter LEWIS (rank and unit unknown).
Lieutenant-Colonel Martin Douglas Bathurst "Tishy" LISTER, OC 6RTR.
Lieutenant-Colonel 3601 Henry Charles LOWRY-CORRY MC, Royal Artillery.
Major 44131 D'Arcy John Desmond MANDER, 4th Green Howards.
Major 58195 James Murray MARSHALL, of the Seaforth Highlanders, had been attached to 2nd Camerons and had been one of Donny's comrades in the unsuccessful attempt to reach the Egyptian frontier after the fall of Tobruk.
Major 140577 Alexander Oliphant "Jock" MCGINLAY MC, 7RTR

Major 38825 Ross Scott MCLAREN DSO, Durham Light Infantry, had been second-in-command of his battalion when captured. He had won his DSO whilst an acting Lieutenant-Colonel in 1940, and was appointed MBE in March 1945.

Major John Francis "Peter" MILLER, 6RTR (captured at Gazala in December 1941).

Lieutenant-Colonel 14022 Dudley Stewart NORMAN DSO, OC 4th Battalion, East Yorkshire Regiment. Actually an Irish citizen, he was captured at Gazala on May 31st 1942.

"Doc" O'NEILL, an Irish volunteer medical officer.

Captain IA354 Antony John "Tony" OLDHAM MC, 5th Mahratta Light Infantry.

Major "Bob" ORR, 20th New Zealand Infantry Battalion (captured near Tobruk, November 1941).

Gerard PORTER (rank and unit unknown).

Lieutenant-Colonel Jack PRITCHARD (unit unknown).

Major 47917 Jonathan Moberly PUMPHREY, 102 (Northumberland Hussars) AT Regiment, Royal Horse Artillery.

Major Stephen RADCLIFFE (unit unknown).

Major the Hon. Simon RAMSAY MC, 7th Battalion, Black Watch, was captured at El Nab in Libya during the push westwards towards Tripoli on January 21st 1943.

Lieutenant-Colonel 33558 Charles Reginald REYNALDS, OC 44RTR.

Lieutenant-Colonel "Dicky" RICHARDS (unit unknown).

Colonel Arthur ROBINSON, Royal Artillery.

Chaplain 30150 the Reverend Henry Richard ROGERS MA (Church of England).

Commander Bryan Gouthwaite SCURFIELD DSO, OBE, AM, KW, of HMS *Bedouin* (captured on Malta convoy, June 16th 1942, when his destroyer was sunk by enemy action); he was later sent to Germany and was killed by a strafing attack by an Allied aircraft on April 11th 1945.

Lieutenant-Colonel SINGLETON (unit unknown).

Major 47680 Keith SWETTENHAM, of the Highland Light Infantry, had been acting as DAQMG of the Guards Brigade when he was captured at Tobruk on June 21st 1942. His dancing is mentioned in David Niven's memoirs.

Major 70744 James Frederick "Bill" SYME, of 3rd Field Regiment, Royal Artillery.

Major 110124 A.H. TANDY, of the RASC, ran a camp store (called "Tandy's") in which inmates could securely keep surplus stores from their Red Cross parcels.

Lieutenant-Colonel Philip Robert ("Bolshie" or "Gussie") TATHAM was a Wykehamist of an earlier generation to Donny Mackenzie (K1912-1916). He had been captured whilst commanding Prince Albert Victor's Own Cavalry (11th Frontier Force) near Bir Hacheim in May 1942.

Major 71007 Philip Thomas TOWER, of 25 Field Regiment, RA (captured at Tobruk, June 21st 1942).

Lieutenant-Colonel P.G. "Friar" TUCK, Royal Artillery.

Major 26799 James Bryan UPTON, RHA; according to Clifton, *an equally rabid escaper and a most ingenious improviser of gadgets which were essential to our efforts.* He was appointed MBE in November 1945. Between 1960 and 1961, when living at Hotham House, Hotham, near York, he was High Sheriff of Yorkshire.

Major 71597 Harold Dennis WHITEHEAD MC, TD, 5th Battalion, Green Howards. He had been awarded his MC in July 1940 and had been captured at Gazala on May 31st 1942.

Brigadier 8787 Arthur Cecil WILLISON DSO*, MC, had been OC 32 (Army) Tank Brigade, which consisted of 1RTR, 4RTR and 7RTR. He had seen sterling service at Tobruk during the siege of 1941. The Swiss reported that Willison wanted to write back to Britain to recommend Foote for a VC, but was refused permission by the Italians. He retired from the army in July 1947 owing to a disability.

Major 34959 the Hon. Mervyn Patrick WINGFIELD, later 9th Viscount Wingfield, of the Royal Irish Fusiliers. His official Italian prisoner of war number was 3200.

Brigadier Desmond YOUNG MC. Young went on to write a famous biography of Rommel, which was filmed as *The Desert Fox* (on which Young advised).

Colonel 5875 George Edward YOUNGHUSBAND, 3rd Hussars.

31 Clifton, *The Happy Hunted*.
32 Brigadier George Clifton DSO**, MC, of the New Zealand staff, had then been sent to the punishment camp at Gavi. From there he was taken to Germany. His book about his wartime experiences, *The Happy Hunted*, is an inspiring read. All those who came into contact with Clifton, including Gunner's Padula friend Josh Millar, were filled with admiration for the man.
33 National Archives WO224/112.
34 Mander, op.cit.
35 *ibid.*

36   Cowan, report in National Archives WO224/112.
37   Clifton, *op.cit.*
38   One of the other officers involved in this attempt was Bryan Upton. The wounded man, Lieutenant-Commander David Alexander "Frosty" Fraser, was born in July 1907 in Woking. He saw service as a Midshipman on the battleship HMS *Malaya* until 1927, before taking his promotion course at RN College Greenwich early in 1928. From there he volunteered for service in submarines. He served on board *L26* in the Mediterranean and from 1931 served as First Lieutenant of the submarines *H33*, *L26*, *Swordfish*, and *Odin*. His first command was *L23* in 1936. After two years on the battleship *Rodney*, he returned to submarines in December 1939 as British Naval Liaison Officer to the Polish submarine *Orzel*; the Poles later gave him an award for his work. He took command of the British submarine *Oswald* in April 1940, but the submarine was lost on August 1st 1940 and Fraser was captured. The *Oswald* had sailed from Alexandria on its second patrol of the war, and spotted an Italian convoy whilst on patrol at the southern end of the Straits of Messina. The vessel surfaced to radio the information back to base, but the Italians detected the signal and sent four destroyers to hunt down the *Oswald*. The Italian *Ugliano Vivaldi* found the *Oswald* on the surface the next night, charging her batteries, and prepared to ram. Fraser was below at the time, and made it to the bridge just in time to see the enemy destroyer hit his submarine and drop depth-charges alongside. The damage was such that Fraser immediately gave the order to abandon ship. Fifty-two of the crew of fifty-five were rescued by the *Vivaldi*.

      After the war Fraser was court-martialled for the loss of the *Oswald* and docked two years' seniority (the court decided that he had had time to dive his submarine and had been negligent in not doing so). But he was also mentioned in dispatches for his attempts at escape. His post-war career saw him command *Campania* (a small aircraft-carrier) and *Hartland Point*, as well as serving as Executive Officer of the training ship *Worcester*, but he retired in 1952 with the rank of Commander. He died in Hampshire in 1978.
39   Mander, *op.cit.*
40   Clifton, *op.cit.*
41   Mander, *op.cit.*
42   Clifton, *op.cit.*
43   Mander, *op.cit.*
44   *ibid.*

Chapter Eleven: Vault

1   Mander, *op.cit.*
2   The Wooden Horse escape took place from *Stalag Luft* III at Sagan in Poland. It involved RAF Flight Lieutenant Eric Williams (who later wrote a book, *The Wooden Horse*, about the escape), Lieutenant Richard Michael Codner (RA), and Flight Lieutenant Oliver Lawrence Spurling Philpot (RAF). The tunnel entrance was close to the perimeter fence and its opening and closing were concealed by the placing of a wooden vaulting-horse on the same spot several times daily. The tunnel broke through on October 29th 1943, and all three officers made a 'home run' by way of Sweden. Philpot also wrote a book – *Stolen Journey* – about his experiences.
3   Colonel 147264 Patrick Andrew "Pat" Clayton DSO, MBE, FRGS, FRCS, FGS, was born in Croydon in April 1896, the son of Francis and Katherine Clayton. Educated at University College School, London, and London University, he served in the RA in Greece and Turkey from 1915 until 1920, reaching the rank of Captain. He then became a member of the Desert Survey department in Egypt, and between 1920 and 1938 he explored and mapped vast tracts of unmapped desert. He and the explorer Ralph Bagnold collaborated extensively during this period, and Clayton is the model for the character Madox in the novel and film *The English Patient*, which partly deals with desert exploration of precisely this period. In 1927 he married Ethel Williamson Wyatt; they had a son. In 1931 Clayton was awarded a gold medal by King Fuad I for *actes méritoires*; whilst mapping the area between Wadi Halfa and Uweinat (areas later fought over during the war) he encountered refugees fleeing the Italian occupation of the Kufra oasis, and conducted them to safety. for rescue of Arabs from Kufra 1931. In 1941 he would be awarded the Founders' Medal of the Royal Geographical Society for his vital mapping work.

      On the outbreak of war, Clayton was commissioned into the Intelligence Corps as a Lieutenant, but was quickly promoted and was soon a Major. He served with the fledgling Long Range Desert Group from the summer of 1940 until he was wounded and captured at Murzuk on February 1st 1941. He remained in Italian and German captivity until the end of the war, retiring from the army as an Honorary Colonel in 1953. He had been awarded a DSO, MBE and a mention in dispatches for his vital work. He wrote various works on the Western Desert and on silica glass, and died in March 1962.

4   Mander, *op.cit.*
4a   Desmond Young, *All the Best Years* (Harper & Brothers, 1961).
5   Detailed in Hargest's superb memoir *Farewell, Campo 12*, written before he was killed in action in Normandy in 1944. Hargest was an outstanding soldier, as evidenced by his decorations – CBE, DSO**, MC – though his conduct of the failed defence of Maleme airfield in Crete in 1941 has come in for much recent criticism.
6   National Archives WO224/112.
7   Young, *op.cit.*
8   Pumphrey was a Wykehamist (C, 1922-1927), like Donny. Born in May 1908 to Charles and Iris Pumphrey, he left Winchester for New College, Oxford, where he took a degree in Literae Humaniores (Classics) in 1930. He became a mining engineer for the Ashington Coal Company and joined the Territorial Army in 1931. When war broke out, he saw action as a Captain in Greece and Crete, from both of which he successfully escaped; as a Major, he was captured in Libya later in 1941. When the Veano inmates scattered, he made a successful run to Switzerland, where he remained for some time attached to the Berne embassy. He returned to Britain in 1944 and served in North-West Europe until the end of the war. AS a Lieutenant-Colonel, he went on to serve with the Rhine Coal Control before returning to the now-nationalized coal industry in 1947. He was appointed OBE and awarded the Territorial Decoration, and died in 1992.
9   Young, *op.cit.*

Chapter Twelve: Release

1   For an admirable modern overview of this cruel period of Italy's history, readers are recommended to consult *Italy's Sorrow* by James Holland.
2   Mander, *op.cit.*
3   Tower, private papers, published on-line at *http://nigelquest.blogspot.com*. Major-General 71007 Philip Thomas Tower CB, DSO, MBE, was the only son of Vice-Admiral Sir Thomas Tower, and was born in Dunbartonshire in March 1917. Educated at Harrow and RMA Woolwich, he was commissioned into the Royal Artillery in 1937. He joined 25 Field Regiment in India, where he served until the outbreak of war. According to his obituary in the *Daily Telegraph*, he described India as *a dream world... The shooting was excellent, there was polo and pig-sticking and, as Adjutant, his office had the only telephone in the regiment.* On the outbreak of war his unit was sent to North Africa, where he saw action at Sidi Barrani and in Eritrea and Abyssinia – including being on the receiving end of the last cavalry charge in modern warfare. His service was rewarded with an MBE. He was then attached to the staff of 4th Indian Division but re-joined his regiment in the desert as a Major commanding a battery of 25-pounders. In May 1942, like Mackenzie, he led a 'Jock Column' in an attempt to slow the enemy advance. In June 1942 at Tobruk he fought his battery to its last round before being captured; his tenacious defence was recognized by the award of a DSO. Two months after his release from Veano he and Nigel Beaumont-Thomas crossed the Allied lines in the south, though Tower was wounded in the chest by a land-mine in doing so. When he returned to England, he married at once; however, he and his wife – the artist Elizabeth Sneyd-Kynnersley – never had children.

     When Tower recovered from his wounds, he joined the airborne forces, receiving parachute training and being appointed Brigade Major RA with 1st Airborne Division. He dropped at Arnhem in September 1944 and helped to control the gunners there until being forced to flee across the Rhine to safety. His next task was as commander of 1st Air Landing Regiment RA in the liberation of Norway in 1945.

     Tower's post-war career was not quite so eventful. He attended Staff College and was an instructor at RMA Sandhurst; he commanded 'J' (Sidi Rezegh) Battery RHA in the Middle East in 1954 and 3RHA from 1957; he also served on the staff in Washington DC. Whilst still a Lieutenant-Colonel, he attended the Imperial Defence College in 1961, an honour usually reserved for Brigadiers. High command followed: OC 51 Infantry Brigade Group and 12 Infantry Brigade Group in Germany, after which he was promoted to Major-General as Director of Public Relations for the army (1965 to 1967). In May 1967 he was appointed GOC Middle East Land Forces, with responsibility for completing the withdrawal of British troops from Aden. There he very publicly fell out with the commander of 1st Battalion, Argyll & Sutherland Highlanders, over operations in 'The Crater', and his reputation never recovered, though he was appointed CB and mentioned in dispatches. He was afterwards posted to be Commandant of RMA Sandhurst, and retired in 1972.

According to his obituary in the *Times*, Tower was *an experienced and intelligent soldier but his flamboyant manner led mundane contemporaries to underestimate his competence. Tall and elegant, his witticisms – often at someone's expense – and sudden bursts of anger left those around him seldom at ease in his presence; yet he could be thoughtful and considerate when anyone particularly caught his eye, or if he thought they had been wronged.*

Tower had many interests: he had been Captain of Fencing at Woolwich, and took up polo after the war (3RHA won the army cup in 1960 and 1961); he was also a keen sailor, rider and shooter. The *Daily Telegraph* recorded that *after he listed gardening as another interest in Who's Who, he said that his wife had ticked him off because his role was limited to mowing the lawn; in the next edition, this activity was down-graded to 'under-gardening'.* He was Colonel Commandant of the Royal Regiment of Artillery (1970 to 1980), administrator of the National Trust's Blickling Hall in Norfolk (1973 to 1982), and county commissioner for the Norfolk St John Ambulance Brigade (1975 to 1978). Tower died on December 8th 2006, at the age of eighty-nine.

4 National Archives WO224/112.
5 Tower, private papers.
6 *ibid.*
7 Mander, *op.cit.* Lieutenant-Colonel 1830 Sydney Charles Fane De Salis DSO had been captured at Sidi Rezegh on November 22nd 1941, when his battalion (1KRRC) was over-run. The *Annals of the King's Royal Rifle Corps* describe him as follows: *he was a Rifleman of the old-fashioned sort, with a gentleman's concept of duty. Seeing himself as trustee of the reputation of a fine battalion, he was an exacting taskmaster, who would not accept second-best from officers joining as reinforcements. No exception could be taken to this, for the example came from the top, and, disregarding his own fatigue, he regularly covered one hundred miles a day across rough terrain to visit his companies in other columns... Lieutenant-Colonel De Salis's DSO had been awarded at the end of the first year of unstinting leadership of the 1st, but his work was crowned by the Battalion's brilliant feat of arms in the Sidi Rezegh attack, and it was typical of his instinct, when no reserve was left to him, to go forward with the attack, centrally placed to obtain fire support. The same instinct made him refuse to leave his men when the laurels of their achievements were turned to bitter ashes by the invulnerable Panzer division attack.*
8 Gordon Lett, *Rossano* (Hodder & Stoughton, 1955).
9 *ibid.*
10 Lieutenant-Colonel 3601 Henry Charles Lowry-Corry MC, Royal Artillery, was an Etonian and was already fifty-six years old (he was born in February 1887). Lowry-Corry had been wounded in the First World War, in which he won his MC. He eventually left Rossano along an escape route run by 'A' Force. Knighted in 1954 for political and public services in Suffolk, he went on to be vice Lord Lieutenant of Suffolk (1957-1965), and died in December 1973, aged eighty-six.
11 Lowry-Corry, IWM 7547 98/5/2.
12 Among them were a Major Oliver with three companions and a party led by Lieutenant-Colonel Lavender of the Indian Army (probably Lieutenant-Colonel 11546 Sydney Salter Lavender DSO*, 16th Punjab Regiment). It is not known whether these parties were from Veano or from other camps.
13 *Annals of the King's Royal Rifle Corps.*
14 Tower, private papers. The other five members of his party were Nigel Beaumont-Thomas; Andy Howard; "Peter" Miller; Keith Swettenham; and Driver McEntagert.
15 Beaumont-Thomas rests in grave 17.A.11 of the Oosterbeek War Cemetery.
16 Lieutenant-Colonel John Francis "Peter" Miller, born in March 1912, was educated at St George's College, Weybridge, and RMC Sandhurst, from which he was commissioned into the RTC in 1932. His obituary in the *Times* states that *he earned the nickname "Pete" or "Peter" because his squadron commander had called him "Piston Pete" when a piston in his tank failed during an exercise.* From 1935 until 1941 he was attached to the Transjordan Frontier Force, but in that year returned to take over a squadron of 6RTR in the Western Desert. He was captured at Sidi Rezegh and remained in captivity until the armistice. Having walked south for six hundred miles he was betrayed to the Germans and re-captured, remaining in captivity until May 1945. He was then re-united with his wife, Barbara Cooke, whom he had married in 1939. They had two sons and two daughters, though their elder son was killed in a motor-racing accident in 2000. After the war Miller continued to serve in the army, and in 1972 invented one of the most important instruments in the bomb-disposal officer's inventory, the "Wheelbarrow", a remotely-controlled device for the investigation and defusing of terrorist bombs. This saved countless lives in Northern Ireland, and by the end of 'The Troubles' some four hundred

of the devices had been destroyed in explosions – each time saving the life of a bomb-disposal officer who would otherwise have been there instead. Miller made no money from his invention, which has been widely copied around the world. He died in September 2006 at the age of ninety-four.

17 Major 58195 James Murray Marshall was the son of Major-General Francis James Marshall CB, CMG, DSO, and Alice Maud Marshall. From Inverness, he was a member of 1st Battalion, Seaforth Highlanders, who had been attached to 2nd Camerons. He died – according to the Commonwealth War Graves Commission – on March 1st 1944, aged thirty-two, and rests in grave XII.C.7 of the Moro River Canadian War Cemetery, near Ortona on the Adriatic coast.

Major 70744 James Frederick Syme, of 3rd Field Regiment, Royal Artillery, was the son of James Frederick Syme and Emily Syme of New Milton in Hampshire. According to the Commonwealth War Graves Commission, he died on January 1st-2nd 1944, aged thirty-two; he is buried in grave V.E.2 of the Sangro River War Cemetery.

Clearly the dates of the deaths of these two officers as given by the CWGC are inconsistent; it is more likely that they both died in January 1944.

18 They included "Gussie" Tatham and Keith Hillas.
19 Evans was awarded the MBE in March 1945.
20 Ramsay – 16th Earl of Dalhousie KT, GCVO, GBE, MC, DL – was elected MP for Forfarshire in 1945 and served as such until his succession as 16th Earl in 1950. In 1957 he became Governor-General of Rhodesia and Nyasaland, and served until 1963. He died in 1999.
21 Kedgley had been born in Auckland on April 28th 1911, and had worked in Wellington as a schoolmaster before the war. After his escape, he returned to active service with 25th New Zealand Infantry Battalion in Italy.
22 Gore and Major Newman (OC 614 Army Ordnance Depot RAOC) were court-martialled for stealing weapons and selling them not just to Jews but also to Arabs.
23 An account of their journey can be found in IWM 1989 92/15/1.
24 Lieutenant-Colonel 11109 William Edgar Bush DSO, MC, was awarded the MBE at the end of the war.

Lieutenant-Colonel 107838 Loris Clyde Cooper later went on to command a battalion of the Sherwood Foresters in North-West Europe and was awarded the DSO in 1945.

Lieutenant-Colonel 14022 Dudley Stewart Norman DSO was later mentioned in dispatches.

Lieutenant-Colonel 33558 Charles Reginald Reynalds was later to be mentioned in dispatches and awarded the Territorial Army Efficiency Medal for his service.

Major 52585 Anthony Henry George "Tony" Dobson, Royal Engineers, met a young local woman in Switzerland whom he went on to marry. He eventually became Major-General A.H.G. Dobson CB, OBE, MC, retiring from the army in November 1967.

25 Pareti, citation in Blundell Violet file, National Archives HS6/830. Translation from Italian original by author and Gabrielle Hullis.
26 Several members of Donny's battalion who had been captured at Tobruk now returned to Allied lines. Among them were: two from PG21 at Chieti – Captains 63631 Ronald George Borradaile MC and Alan G. Cameron MC (MI9 evasion reports 1556 and 1528); two from PG78 at Sulmona – Captain Norman L. MacLucas and Private Thomas W. Prentice (MI9 evasion reports 1596 and 3318 1818); and Private J.R. Findlay (MI9 2775). Borradaile was awarded the MBE for his escape efforts.
27 When Whitehead reported Zanoni's conduct for prosecution after the war, he discovered that the Italians had already shot him.
28 Mander, *op.cit.*
29 Anonymous Italian document *Capitano Mak - Capitano Ganna,* provided by Mr Claudio Oltremonti of Piacenza. Translation by author.

Chapter Thirteen: Resistance

1 Anita Basini (*née* Cavozzi), *pers.comm.* to Gregg, November 2007.
2 Natale Grassi, quoted in Finzi, *Emilio Canzi: an Anarchist Partisan in Italy & Spain.*
3 Londei, quoted in Finzi, *op.cit.*
4 Gregg, 1944 report for SOE, J/CIRC/78, in Blundell Violet file, National Archives HS6/830.
5 Giovanni Agnelli, quoted in Finzi, *op.cit.*
6 Alberto Grassi, quoted in Finzi, *op.cit.*
7 Giovanni Agnelli, quoted in Finzi, *op.cit.*
8 Albino Grassi, quoted in Finzi, *op.cit.*
9 *ibid.*

10 Primo Agnelli, quoted in Finzi, *op.cit.*
11 Anonymous Italian document *Capitano Mak - Capitano Ganna*, provided by Mr Claudio Oltremonti of Piacenza. Translation by author.
12 The officer in charge of of No.1 Special Force HQ at Monopoli was Lieutenant-Colonel R.T. Hewitt, whilst the overall commander of No.1 Special Force was Commander Gerard A. "Gerry" Holdsworth DSO.
13 See Lett, *Rossano*.
14 Gregg, 1944 report for SOE, J/CIRC/78, in Blundell Violet file, National Archives HS6/830.
15 Maria Luisa Sandys, *pers.comm.* to Gregg, 2008.

Chapter Fourteen: Liberation

1 Giovanni Agnelli, quoted in Finzi, *Emilio Canzi: an Anarchist Partisan in Italy & Spain*.
2 Alberto Grassi, quoted in Finzi, *op.cit.*
3 Londei, quoted in Finzi, *op.cit.*
4 Alberto Grassi, quoted in Finzi, *op.cit.*
5 Gregg, 1944 report for SOE, J/CIRC/78, in Blundell Violet file, National Archives HS6/830.
6 *ibid.*
7 *ibid.*
8 *ibid.*
9 *ibid.*
10 *ibid.*
11 *ibid.*
12 *ibid.*
13 *ibid.*
14 Macintosh wrote an excellent memoir of SOE operations in Italy *(From Cloak to Dagger)* which is well worth reading, even though it does not mention the Val Nure partisans.
15 Gregg, 1944 report for SOE, J/CIRC/78, in Blundell Violet file, National Archives HS6/830.
16 *ibid.*
17 Londei, quoted in Finzi, *op.cit.*
18 Gregg, 1944 report for SOE, J/CIRC/78, in Blundell Violet file, National Archives HS6/830.
19 "Paolo" was actually Alberto Araldi, formerly a *Brigadiere* (Sergeant) in the *Carabinieri*. In February 1945 he was betrayed to the Fascists by a spy whom he had trusted as a friend. He was shot against the wall of the cemetery in Piacenza, and was posthumously awarded the Italian Gold Medal for Valour.
20 Gregg, 1944 report for SOE, J/CIRC/78, in Blundell Violet file, National Archives HS6/830.
21 *ibid.*
22 *ibid.*
23 Hastings, *The Drums of Memory*.
24 Gregg, 1944 report for SOE, J/CIRC/78, in Blundell Violet file, National Archives HS6/830.
25 *ibid.*
26 *ibid.*
27 *ibid.*
28 *ibid.*
29 *ibid.*
30 Alberto Grassi, quoted in Finzi, *op.cit.*
31 Gregg, 1944 report for SOE, J/CIRC/78, in Blundell Violet file, National Archives HS6/830.
32 *ibid.*
33 *ibid.*
34 *ibid.*
35 Kesselring, *Memoirs of Field Marshal Kesselring*.
36 Kesselring, quoted in Macintosh, *From Cloak to Dagger*.
37 Gregg, 1944 report for SOE, J/CIRC/78, in Blundell Violet file, National Archives HS6/830.
38 162nd (Turkistan) Infantry Division had been recruited from prisoners-of-war taken on the Russian Front and refugees from the Caucasus and other areas to the east. Formed on May 21st 1943, it drew its men from several existing units: the *Armenische, Azerbajdzansche, Georgische, Nordkaukasische, Turkestanische* and *Wolgatatarische* Legions. The personnel underwent training at Neuhammer (modern Świętoszów, in western Poland) before being sent to Italy. From May 21st 1944 until the end of the war they were commanded by *Generalleutnant* Ralph von Heygendorff. As an infantry division,

the unit comprised two infantry regiments (each made up of three battalions), an artillery regiment, and support troops. Prisoners from the division before the end of the war were shipped back to the Soviet Union immediately, and when the Division surrendered near Padua in May 1945, its personnel were also sent back to Russia, where they received sentences of twenty years hard labour in the notorious *gulags*.

Chapter Fifteen: Ponte

1 Letter from Roberto Castignola ("Lupo") to Mayor of Bettola, July 1st 1957, *Notes on the partisan career of the late Captain Mak, in response to your request N3209 of June 26th 1957* (Archivio INSMLI Milano, *Fondo La Rosa Antonino, busto 5, fascicolo 18, sottofascicolo 9*). Translation by author and Gabrielle Hullis.
2 Canzi, letter in Blundell Violet file, National Archives HS6/830. Translation by author and Gabrielle Hullis.
3 Letter from Emilio Canzi to Fausto Cossu, October 2nd 1944 (Archivio INSMLI Milano, *Fondo La Rosa Antonino, busto 1, fascicolo 2*). Translation by author and Gabrielle Hullis.
4 *ibid.*, typed *addendum*.
5 Letter from Emilio Canzi to Fausto Cossu, October 4th 1944 (Archivio INSMLI Milano, *Fondo La Rosa Antonino, busto 1, fascicolo 2*). Translation by author and Gabrielle Hullis.
6 Letter from Political Commissar (Candiani) and Commander 4 Brigade ("Virgilio") to HQ *Giustizia e Libertà* Division, October 7th 1944 (Archivio INSMLI Milano, *Fondo La Rosa Antonino, busto 1, fascicolo 2*). Translation by author and Gabrielle Hullis.
7 Ermanno Mariani, *The Ballad of Mac and the Iron Monster.* Translation by author and Gabrielle Hullis, with assistance from Sara Marani of Piacenza.
8 Gregg, 1944 report for SOE, J/CIRC/78, in Blundell Violet file, National Archives HS6/830.
9 Letter from Political Commissar (Savio) and Commander *Comando Unico* (Ezio Franchi, i.e. Emilio Canzi) to HQs 2nd *Giustizia e Libertà* Division, 38th *Garibaldi* Assault Brigade, 60th *Garibaldi* Assault Brigade, 61st *Garibaldi* Assault Brigade, October 9th 1944 (Archivio INSMLI Milano, *Fondo La Rosa Antonino, busto 1, fascicolo 2*). Translation by author and Gabrielle Hullis.
10 Letter from Roberto Castignola ("Lupo") to Mayor of Bettola, July 1st 1957, *Notes on the partisan career of the late Captain Mak, in response to your request N3209 of June 26th 1957* (Archivio INSMLI Milano, *Fondo La Rosa Antonino, busto 5, fascicolo 18, sottofascicolo 9*). Translation by author and Gabrielle Hullis.
11 Anonymous poem entitled *Il Capitano Mak* (Archivio INSMLI Milano, *Fondo La Rosa Antonino, busto 5, fascicolo 18, sottofascicolo 9*). Translation by author and Gabrielle Hullis.

Chapter Sixteen: Farewell Val Nure

1 Quoted in SOE Operation Instruction J/CIRC/62, in National Archives WO204/7296.
2 Gregg, 1944 report for SOE, J/CIRC/78, in Blundell Violet file, National Archives HS6/830.
3 *ibid.*
4 *ibid.*
5 Lett, report in Blundell Violet file, National Archives HS6/830.
6 Gregg, 1944 report for SOE, J/CIRC/78, in Blundell Violet file, National Archives HS6/830.
7 Anonymous document *Capitano Mak - Capitano Ganna* provided by Mr Claudio Oltremonti of Piacenza. Transation by author and Gabrielle Hullis.
8 Vermouth comprised Lieutenant V. Lockwood (a Royal Artilleryman, who was also a former prisoner-of-war), an Italian Lieutenant called Giovanni, Sergeant B. Fick of the South African army, and a radio-operator named Grassi.
9 Gregg, 1944 report for SOE, J/CIRC/78, in Blundell Violet file, National Archives HS6/830.
10 Quoted in Hill, *I Wanted Wings: A Tail Gunner's Story.*
11 *ibid.*
12 Willis, letter dated July 10th 1945, from Rt.2 - Box 40, Mesa, Arizona, USA. Gregg collection.
13 Gallegos, J/Circ/63, dated November 25th 1944, in Blundell Violet file, National Archives HS6/830.
14 National Archives WO204/7296.
15 Lett, report in Blundell Violet file, National Archives HS6/830.
16 *ibid.*
17 Blundell Violet file, National Archives HS6/830.
18 Gregg, 1944 report for SOE, J/CIRC/78, in Blundell Violet file, National Archives HS6/830.

19	*ibid.*
20	*ibid.*
21	SOE Operation Instruction J/CIRC/62, in National Archives WO204/7296.
22	*ibid.*
23	SOE memorandum J/2148, dated November 25th 1944, in National Archives WO204/7296.
24	Gregg, 1944 report for SOE, J/CIRC/78, in Blundell Violet file, National Archives HS6/830.
25	The Lysander had taken off from Fano, with Flying Officer 150263 John Francis Anthony "Jack" Rayns RAFVR at the controls, and an escort of six Mustangs from 3 Squadron RAAF. However, it was spotted by American P-51s which were escorting B-17s returning from a bombing raid. One P-51 peeled off, almost collided with an RAAF Mustang, and shot down the Lysander, killing Rayns and the incoming radio-operator. Rayns was the son of Alfred Horace Rayns and Johanna Rayns, of Loughborough, Leicestershire. He was twenty-one years old when he was shot down, and now lies in grave I.B.3 of the Udine War Cemetery, Italy.
26	Beukes' citation for the award of a Military Medal in the National Archives (WO373/64) makes remarkable reading, though there is no record in the London Gazette of an MM having actually been awarded. *26606 OWII Beukes, Johann Hendrik Adriaan. Imperial Light Horse, 3 Brigade, 2nd South African Division, UDF.* *Although BEukes and two other South Africn sergeants broke through the GErman lines after the fall of Tobruk, they were captured on 25 June 42 when almost at Sidi Omar.* *At the end of September 42 Beukes participated in a tunnel scheme at Benghazi camp. He and nineteen others walked for six days before they were caught as they rested in an Arab's tent.* *When the Italian armistice was announced in September 43, Beukes was at Chiavari (Camp 52). entrained for Germany on 12 Sep 43, he escaped through a ventilator whilst the train was passing through a tunnel. With four others who had escaped in the same manner Beukes went to the nearest town, Genoa. Friendly Italians helped them to board a train for Rome, but to avoid recapture when their identity was discovered they had to jump off the train just before it reached Chiavari. One of the party failed to get away but the others reached the hills. Here Beukes joined the first partisan band that was formed in the district and his service has been praised by a British officer in the following terms:* *"While fighting with the partisans he was twice wounded. Source was told by many Italians who have been in engagements with beukes about many of his exploits, which, they said, included entering Genoa in June 44 with six others and killing thirty German SS officers in a hotel where a conference was taking place. On one occasion Beukes was wounded in the groin in a revolver duel with a German, whom he killed. On another, he had the misfortune to fall down a 200-foot cliff while on patrol. While recovering from this injury he came over to source's area, where he was made commander of a detachment of seventy partisans."* *At the end of November 44, three months after his first appointment as a partisan officer, Beukes was guided to American troops near Serevezza.*
27	Jean Kinloch-Smith, Gregg collection.
28	Memo J/M/588, dated January 4th 1945, in Blundell Violet file, National Archives HS6/830.
29	Letter from IS9 (CMF) to Lieutenant-Colonel Hewitt, No.1 Special Force, reference 1217/87, dated December 12th 1944, in Gregg SOE personnel file, National Archives HS9/618/3.
30	Pareti, citation in Blundell Violet file, National Archives HS6/830. Translation by author and Gabrielle Hullis.
31	Readers will, it is hoped, excuse the author for a short excursus on Rosa Lewis. Born on September 26th 1867 in Essex, the fifth of nine children, Lewis left at the age of twelve to enter domestic service. By 1887 she was a skilled cook in the French style (apparently Escoffier, who trained her, called her "the Queen of Cooks"). She was frequently called in by the rich – Lady Randolph Churchill, the Asquiths, the Saviles – to cater for special occasions. When Edward VII dined at Sheen House and was impressed enough to ask to meet the cook, he was so taken with her cooking and beauty (she was a blue-eyed blonde) that from then on hostesses always employed her to cook when entertaining him. In 1902 she bought the Cavendish Hotel (possibly with the financial assistance of Edward VII), in which the wealthy of England and America liked to stay; favoured guests included Lord Kitchener, the Duke of Windsor, Ellen Terry, George Bernard Shaw, Isadora Duncan, John Singer Sargent and Augustus John – both the artists painted her portrait. Lewis adopted a policy of over-charging the wealthy guests and not charging those she liked, especially officers in the armed forces. The Cavendish gained a reputation for wild parties, and Lewis' own reputation as Edward VII's mistress added to her notoriety, as did her antiquated manner of dress and willingness to procure an agreeable girl for any young officer who she thought needed one. As she said, "All luxuries are overused, but sexual immorality is sometimes the least dangerous."

Stories of her abound: she is alleged to have chased Winston Churchill, aged ten, from her kitchen with the words "Hop it, copper-knob"; she claimed that she had been forced into marriage in 1893 but had flung the ring at her new husband as they left the church; Kaiser Wilhelm II admired her cooking so much that he presented her with a portrait of himself, which during the First World War she hung in the gentlemen's lavatory; she had her own estranged husband declared bankrupt; and she was sacked from the staff of White's club in London when she refused to sleep with a member whom she described as "an amorous old woodcock in tights".

Evelyn Waugh liked her and admired her beauty even when she was old: he said that she was warm-hearted, comic and totally original woman. Others have described her life from 1918 until her death in 1952 as a grandiose and majestic decline. She was still going strong in the Second World War, and the fighter-pilot Richard Hillary wrote of her in *The Last Enemy* as follows: *One night when we were in town we walked around to see Rosa Lewis at the Cavendish Hotel. Suddenly caught by a stroke, she had been rushed to the London Clinic, where she refused to allow any of the nurses to touch her. After a week she saw the bill and immediately got up and left. When we arrived, there she was, seventy-six years old, shrieking with laughter and waving a glass of champagne, apparently none the worse. She grabbed me by the arm and peered into my face. "God, aren't you dead yet either, young Hillary? Come here and I'll tell you something. Don't you ever die. In the last two weeks I've been right up to the gates of 'eaven and 'ell and they're both bloody!" A few weeks later a heavy bomb landed right on the Cavendish, but Rosa emerged triumphant, pulling bits of glass out of her hair and trumpeting with rage. Whatever else may go in this war, we shall still have Rosa Lewis and the Albert Memorial at the end.*

She did indeed last until the end, dying in her sleep on November 8th 1952, aged eighty-five, and being laid to rest in Putney Vale Cemetery.

32   Letter to MS Branch HQ SO(M), reference CR/89/22A, dated December 23rd 1944, in Gregg SOE personnel file, National Archives HS9/618/3.
33   Gunner banked with Glynn Mills, Kirkland House, Whitehall, now part of the Royal Bank of Scotand.
34   Macintosh, Gregg collection.

Chapter Seventeen: Victory

1   Gregg, 1944 report for SOE, J/CIRC/78, in Blundell Violet file, National Archives HS6/830.
2   *ibid.*
3   *ibid.*
4   *ibid.*
5   Natale Grassi, quoted in Finzi, *Emilio Canzi: an Anarchist Partisan in Italy & Spain.*
6   Elvira Fugazza, quoted in Finzi, *op.cit.*
7   Hastings, *The Drums of Memory.*
8   Piacenza ANPI Archives. Molinari had been born in Bettola.
9   Don Giuseppe had been born in Piacenza on July 4th 1910, and had served as the priest of the village of Obolo in the Val d'Arda. He had been arrested as early as 1942 for anti-Fascist activity, but had been released at the Armistice.
10   Hastings, *op.cit.*
11   *ibid.*
12   *ibid.*
13   *ibid.*
14   Piacenza ANPI Archives.
15   Natale Grassi, quoted in Finzi, *op.cit.*
16   Alberto Grassi, quoted in Finzi, *op.cit.*
17   *Supplement to the London Gazette,* September 20th 1945.
18   National Archives WO373/64.
19   *Ministry of Defence (Army). Captain Tresham D. Gregg, of the 61st "Garibaldi" Brigade, having participated in the armed struggle against the Germans and the Fascists, is authorized to wear the honorific emblem instituted by the patriotic Volunteers for Freedom. By military decree, May 3rd 1945, no.350, Rome, September 30th 1945.*

Chapter Eighteen: Remembrance

1   *The Times,* February 5th 1945.
2   Gervase Yates, *pers.comm.* to author, 2008.

3   Brian Mackenzie, *pers.comm.* to author, 2008.
4   Dated March 19th 1945.
5   *Historical Records of the Cameron Highlanders.*
6   Letter from Roberto Castignola ("Lupo") to Mayor of Bettola, July 1st 1957, *Notes on the partisan career of the late Captain Mak, in response to your request N3209 of June 26th 1957* (Archivio INSMLI Milano, *Fondo La Rosa Antonino, busto* 5, *fascicolo* 18, *sottofascicolo* 9). Translation by author and Gabrielle Hullis.
7   Memorandum 6/G/71, dated December 10th 1952, in National Archives HS9/963/8.
8   Brian Mackenzie, *pers.comm.* to author, 2008.
9   Kit Yates, *pers.comm.* to author, 2008.
10 Brian Mackenzie, *pers.comm.* to author, 2008.
11 *ibid.*
12 *ibid.*
13 Castignola, *op. cit.*
14 *Libertà,* November 18th 1969.
15 Wright, *http://nigelquest.blogspot.com/.*
16 George Patrick O'Neill Pearson was born on February 28th 1911 and died on December 6th 1982.
17 Roger Lytollis, *Serial Wartime Escapee Visits his Darkest Tunnel,* November 4th 2005.
18 Marriott, *The Cumbrian Capitano,* in *Saga Magazine,* November 2007.
19 Anita Basini *(née* Cavozzi), *pers.comm.* to Gregg, November 2007.
20 Maria Luisa Sandys, *pers.comm.* to Gregg, 2008.
21 Gregg, quoted in *The Cumberland News,* November 4th 2005.
22 *Wykehamist War Service Record and Roll of Honour.*

Printed in Great Britain
by Amazon